Handbook of
English Crafts
and Craftsmen

by

JUNE R. LEWIS, FRSA

Foreword by
James Noel White,
Vice-President (Europe) World Crafts Council

ROBERT HALE · LONDON

ISBN 0 7091 6743 1

Robert Hale Limited
Clerkenwell House
Clerkenwell Green
London, EC1

Photoset, printed and bound
in Great Britain by
REDWOOD BURN LIMITED
Trowbridge & Esher

Handbook of
English Crafts
and Craftsmen

By the same author

COTSWOLD VILLAGES

Contents

Illustrations

PICTURE CREDITS

Ron Butterfield, Sheffield, 8; Bradley Inkle-Looms, Sussex, 9; Lullingstone Silk Farm, Herts., 17, 18; Gloucestershire and Avon Life, The Whitethorn Press, 21; Alan Winstanley, 24; Richard Quinnell Ltd, Surrey, 25; Barcham Green & Co., Kent, 26; Honoria D. Marsh, 30; Bernard M. York, 31; Dartington Hall Trust, 32; Abbey Studios, Wootton-Under-Edge, 39; Anglia Television, 40; Bryant Fedden, 41; *Westmorland Gazette*, 45; C. E. Stuart King, 46; Eric A. Homewood, 47; Pettit's Rural Industries, 48, 51. All other photographs were taken by the author.

Foreword

It is one of the paradoxes of our time that there has been a widespread revival in the practice and appreciation of crafts, despite the intense industrialization which during the last two decades has penetrated deeper into the structure of our society. This is happening throughout North America, Australia and Europe, where Britain seems to be in the forefront of practical support for the crafts. In Britain finance comes mainly from the government since responsibility for the crafts was transferred to the Minister for the Arts as part of an official policy to improve the quality of life and to extend involvement in the arts into the regions to as many people as possible.

The injection of financial help into the crafts has not only opened up a more realistic career for young craftsmen and given them opportunities to gain more practical workshop experience, it has also stimulated the interest of museums, galleries and shops, publishers and writers. An awareness of the contribution which living craftsmen make to our society is now widespread. At a time when we have been moving through the deepest economic recession for more than a generation, there is what has been called a boom in the crafts. More and more people are conscious that the crafts are part of our cultural heritage, although museums are only now beginning to ensure the continuity of their collections by buying the work of contemporary artist-craftsmen. So it is most timely that a handbook for the crafts should be available to give essential information to craftsmen about sources of finance, technical developments and markets, to collectors, museums and gallery directors and the buying public who wish to keep in touch with the craft movement in Britain. Miss Lewis has compiled a helpful work of reference to which she has added details of her own personal selection of craftsmen in whom she is interested. I hope that the extensive information which she has collected will add further impetus to the encouragement of the crafts and their enjoyment by the public who can now readily acquire for their own homes such a wide variety of crafts made in so many parts of the country today.

JAMES NOEL WHITE
Vice-President (Europe) World Crafts Council

19 September 1977

Acknowledgments

I gratefully acknowledge the invaluable help accorded to me by all who tirelessly answered my many questions in compiling this survey of the crafts in England.

I particularly appreciate the generosity of:
HRH Princess Anne,
The Rt Hon. Viscount Eccles,
Professor Lord Queensberry, and the Royal Society of Arts for allowing me to quote from their various Addresses;
The World Crafts Council,
British Crafts Centre,
Regional Arts Associations, and the vast number of other official bodies, county and community councils, craft centres and societies for furnishing me with their policies and constitutions.

Special thanks to:
Crafts Advisory Committee,
Federation of British Crafts Societies and COSIRA for their extreme courtesy and constantly encouraging assistance;
the various councils for allowing me early sight of planning proposals;
Mr James Noel White for writing the foreword;
Peter Reason for the care he has taken in printing my photographs;
my patient publishers,
and lastly, but most important, to the thousands of craftsmen who have given me insight to their fascinating and worthwhile work, allowing me access to their records and welcoming me to their ateliers, studios, workshops, back-bedrooms and converted glory-holes where they manage to carry on the marvellous English craft tradition – thank you.
J.L.

To the craftsmen of England,
about whom
this book is written

Introduction

Acknowledging the mother of useful arts to be necessity, experiment extended the staple crafts and specialization developed when diverse skills were pooled for the common weal. Self-sufficiency bred independence, and it was these two factors which knitted closer the communities into which the ancient British tribes formed – the roots from which the village evolved, still upheld as the perfect microcosm of the English way of life. The village was the natural home of the craftsman; the town the merchant's forum.

Today, the line is less definitive: there was a considerable drift from country to town in the aftermath of the Napoleonic Wars; the traditional village crafts which survived the migration became absorbed into Victorian industries, and the advent of the motor brought the materials to the worker.

Defiant, almost, of the changing world around him, the craftsman of England has not only survived the changes wrought on the village, but has actually emerged as one of a cohesive craft fraternity for whom (according to the manifestos) the world at large and the country in particular are anxious to get him recognized and rewarded. I have read many millions of words proclaiming why this should be so; but I have also been in contact with many hundreds of craftsmen to discover how practical these policies are.

It is true that there is a great deal of nostalgic thought about the traditional craftsman in particular: a quaint Dickensian character, the memory of whom is fondly cherished along with the halcyon days of harvest homes and sticky sugar mice.

Many ideas are conceived about the craftsman's role in the community, which are coloured by one kind of prejudice or another: be it admiration or envy.

There is a popular misconception that the only rival to the craftsman is the machine, but there is an indirect relationship developing between the crafts and industry which may be complementary albeit complex. Equal adversaries are the makers of antiques and pseudo-antiques and those with the conviction that nothing of merit has been made since William Morris gave tangible form to his philosophy that "we will make no more for profit, but for use, for happiness, for life".

To glorify the past at the expense of the present is to take the whole essence of craftwork out of context. The visual arts, and therefore crafts, are as eloquent as speech when communicating ideas. The schism between art and craft is artificial, it is true to say that not all artists are craftsmen, but a craftsman is artist, artificer and artisan; master of his own skills, yet forever an apprentice to his own ideals.

There are those who contend that craftwork is an anachronism in an industrialized society; others maintain that it is as an antidote to it.

It is not, however, my intention to explore the theories, but to pursue the facts. I have seen how craft becomes art in the hands of a master, how craftsmanship becomes an integral part of the complete design process, how the conceptual becomes factual, experiment is divorced from gimmickry, values distinct from prices, and development unrelated to growth. Craftsmanship enjoys an enviable prestige and recognition of the craftsman's contribution to our cultural heritage has prompted support and promotion through public funds. There is new interest in all aspects of craftwork. Human dignity is again being restored to the maker; beauty and utility are happily married; sophistication can be simplicity.

Craftsmanship is a continuous tradition, but the modern craftsman is not tied to a locality; he is to be found in the city suburbs as well as by the village green; he builds on the knowledge of his past masters but uses the materials available today; above all, he is an individual.

I would not presume to have found the answers to the problems which are inevitable in an automated 'instant' world. What works for one is an impossibility for another, but I do hope that there is some value in this book to those craftsmen who are fascinated by what goes on in the workshops of their peers.

Equally so, I trust it will dispel some of the mystique which many mistake for the mystery of the craft itself, and that the craftsmen themselves come through in their own right as neither eccentrics or outdated idealists falling between a faded Art-Deco image or earthy simple souls, for they are neither. Theirs is the articulate statement of an artistic expression which embodies all that English craftwork stands for.

1

Craftsmen of the world

For only when the crafts flourish from local roots, growing out of local history and traditions, shall we know for certain that the final divorce between beauty and utility will never take place. Instead this great pair of human values must again join forces to the enormous benefit of mankind everywhere: north, south, east and west. This is a vision of beauty for the sake of living; of art for the sake of life. A vision worth our best endeavours.

Excerpt from Keynote Address
to WCC Tenth Anniversary
Conference by The Rt Hon
Viscount Eccles

The main aim of the World Crafts Council is to gain international support for the integration of the crafts, as part of a cultural heritage, into a technological age. Founded in 1964 by Aileen Osborn Webb, primarily to enhance the cause of peace in the world through the emergence of a world family of craftsmen, the WCC has fulfilled its objectives by uniting the peoples of the earth in a common cause: that of promoting evocatively termed craftwork.

Craftwork is a term which conveys different meanings to different people: even craftsmen themselves disagree on its definitions, and yet it is something which is recognized instantly and appreciated universally.

Acclamation may be in many tongues, but whether in Queen's English or Pitjantjatjara it is understood; language, creed or culture are but incidental artificial barriers which the arts do not recognize. From Australia to Iceland craftsmen unite in a common purpose aided by WCC. Opportunities have developed for the exchange of craftsmen among countries for the purposes of study, teaching and technical training, and jointly exhibiting their work.

The WCC, not tied to any political party, is associated with UNESCO in a consultative capacity to promote the interests of craftsmen throughout the world, and is the only international organization devoted entirely to this purpose.

Philosophical platitudes are easily written, but the WCC does not offer utopianism: it has a constructive role with a progressive programme spearheaded by erudite and able committees, proudly presenting their country's incredible wealth of talent, assuring a continuity of its cultural heritage, but never complacent enough to ignore the realities of the craftsman's position in the industrialized societies of a technological age. The craftsman's creativity, ability and versatility have been proved; king of his craft he may be, but he is ever bondman to that capricious master – economy. The Secretary General declared that the aim of WCC for the immediate future is to help "as many practising craftsmen throughout the world as we can to enhance the quality of their lives, increase their financial rewards, improve their standards of work and establish their places in their own communities".

CRAFTSMEN OF ENGLAND

It is an encouraging fact that the story of the crafts in Britain in the last few years is one of development and of success: some British craftsmen are producing work of an excellence equal to that of any in the world.

Lord Donaldson, Arts Minister

In his confidence of the role which craftsmen play in the cultural and physical environment, the Arts Minister said: "we believe the crafts are a true form of art and deserve assistance in the same way as art in general terms". A view which endorsed the statement of intent declared by his predecessor, Lord Eccles, when he instigated the setting up of a new institution for the crafts, parallel to the Arts Council's support of the fine arts.

Resolute, despite the warning that craftsmen were notoriously belligerent and suspicious individuals, their morale so battered by years of neglect, that they would never trust a central body to perform services for all of them, Lord Eccles replied to the pessimists that, provided such an organization "were given a reasonable amount of money and the staff was well-chosen, it would be accepted". And it was.

The resultant Crafts Advisory Committee was inaugurated in 1971. The committee members serve at the invitation of the Minister for the Arts and comprise practising craftsmen and those with specialist knowledge of the crafts. It administers the government grant which comes from the Department of Education and Science for England and Wales (Scotland administers its own through the JCC). Its services are comprehensive: considerable financial help is offered to individual craftsmen and co-operative activities; exhibitions are held regularly, a new inception is the craftsmen's tours; a national lending collection of the crafts is purchased, often through commissions; free advisory services include an index of craftsmen in the form of an illustrated guide, a slide library for educational purposes, and a wide-ranging service gives information on courses, shops and galleries, supplies of materials and equipment, museums and publications specializing in craftwork. A non-selective register of craftsmen is also maintained.

Conferences and seminars enable those in the different craft disciplines to make contact with each other, thereby providing a forum for communication, but the greatest number of people are reached by means of its excellent magazine *Crafts* which, according to its editorial staff, has aroused reaction "ranging from hysterical rapture to ferocious hostility". That it stimulates reaction at all must be an achievement in this magazine-saturated society. Artistically produced, it gives prestige presentation to the contemporary crafts yet fulfils its practical function by letting the irascible, often embarrassingly forthright, sometimes downright impudent individual heap contumely onto the government, onto public taste, or onto a fellow craftsman's efforts or opinions by way of its correspondence columns, thus modifying the technical treatises and serious reviews. Invaluable to the craft fraternity must be the notices of exhibitions and advertisements. *Crafts* is a specialist publication unrelated to general magazines of the 'how-to-do-it' type.

The relationship of the CAC to the British Crafts Centre is not often clear to craftsmen. The direct involvement of the CAC is limited to representation on the BCC Council of Management, whilst it remains deeply committed to the development of the BCC. The BCC's major function is to promote the work of British craftsmen and provide information about it. It receives grant aid from the CAC as a non-profitmaking body financed by the subscriptions of its members and by commissions on craftsmen's work sold at its two retail outlets – in Covent Garden and at the Victoria and Albert Museum. Promotion is channelled through the national media and regional associations; information disseminated through seminars and exhibitions; education brought about by means of a comprehensive service to schools, colleges and universities; and international co-operation is sought throughout the old and new worlds by representation on the World Crafts Council.

Aiming at the rationalization of existing craft organizations, the Federation of British Craft Societies was constituted in 1970 to avoid duplication of services and intent. The federation is made up of all its member societies and speaks with one voice as a total craft profession (p. 23).

The inherent difficulties which beset the small independent business unit are magnified in the case of the craftsman. For him the burden of legislation, with its avalanche of forms, crippling taxes, multitude of regulations concerning his workshop, VAT with its interminable statutory instruments, and all the harassment of bureaucracy, is a vicious vortex in which he is constantly struggling to get on with practising his craft.

The steady decline in the small business unit since the last war prompted the first comprehensive study, official or otherwise, of the small firms sector of the United Kingdom, the definition of "small firms" being "an employment force of not more than 200". The resultant Bolton Committee, set up by the Board of Trade, revealed that whereas in 1935 small firms engaged in manufacturing represented 38 per cent of the total employment in establishments, in 1968 the figure had dropped to 22 per cent. By definition, the craftsman will be represented in this figure.

The Bolton Report described the small firms as the "seed bed" of new ideas, vital to the prosperity of the nation. All its fifty-six proposals recommending government action, mainly involving changes in existing industrial/fiscal policies, legislation on safety, price control, VAT, and – amongst other things – export services, have been considered, and of these, forty-six have been acted upon wholly or in part.

The two significant implementations were the establishment of a Small Firms Division within the Department of Industry, to ensure that small firms were not inadvertently disadvantaged by legislation or government action; and the setting up of advisory bureaux on a regional basis as a free information service to small firms.

The Small Firms Division holds a watching brief over the progress and problems of the small firm sector by means of reports received from the ten Small Firms Information Centres (SFICs) throughout England, Scotland and Wales.

Since becoming operational in July 1973, the centres deal with something like 1,100 enquiries a week and, with data banks on the services and facilities offered by some 7,000 national and local organizations, they cover a comprehensive field. A breakdown of the type of enquiries being handled – although neither the division nor SFICs maintain specific statistics about crafts, as distinct from other types of small firms – illustrates the scope of problems: management 40·4 per cent; finance and financial control 10 per cent; technical 4·6 per cent; help needed in government regulations, policies or from state agencies 32·3 per cent; local government 2·2 per cent; sources of supply 10·5 per cent.

Around 30·7 per cent arise through small firms involved in manufacturing; 47·8 per cent from service industries; and 21·5 per cent from individuals wishing to start businesses.

Without betraying confidence or indicating the bias of the SFIC, it is fair to redress the imbalance which craftsmen feel exists between their position and that of the "small industrial firm", with whom they are classified. There is more than sympathetic consideration afforded the one-man show, and, where circumstances permit, rather more is done for them than is supposed. Through their close association with COSIRA and other craft bodies they are certainly not divorced from the craft workers' sector.

COUNCIL FOR SMALL INDUSTRIES IN RURAL AREAS (COSIRA)

... We consider that support for the crafts is justifiable on the same social and cultural grounds as is the excellent service to rural industry provided by COSIRA.   *Extract from the Bolton Report 1971*

COSIRA was set up by the Development Commission in 1968 to bring together into one organization the Rural Industries Bureau (founded in 1921), Rural Industries Loan Fund Ltd (founded in 1940) and the Rural Industries Committees, with their organizers, working at county level. Financed by the Development Commission, it is charged with the tasks of providing advice and loans to help small manufacturing and servicing industries in rural areas to become more prosperous, and helping to stem the exodus from the countryside by providing more employment, whilst maintaining the ethos of a rural community. Its definitive terms are; "small industries are those normally employing not more than twenty skilled people and rural areas include country towns of up to 10,000 inhabitants".

"To collect and diffuse information" is one of the terms in the Trust Deed, realized in COSIRA's multitudinous activities which, in general, assists the small firm to become fully aware of its own value. In detail, this can mean advice on design and production, from letterheads to a completely new house style ranging from trade-marks to a showroom; sales promotion, from display boards to export catalogues, from help with exhibitions to inclusion in the *Country Workshops Guide*. Technical help given by COSIRA ranges from its own extensive library facilities to instructional books, and from special training courses to detailed work studies of processing problems.

Particularly in craftwork, which is labour intensive, the improvement in terms of actual productivity often lies in a number of small savings rather than in a drastic change in working methods, although these can often be determined by a close appraisal from an outside body. One example is where COSIRA devised, after making a number of experiments, a reliable and quick method of making leather eye-pieces for horse-blinkers. Whereas the time taken to produce a cup of leather suitable for cutting in half to make the two eye-pieces had formerly been a twelve-hour overnight period, the new method took a mere ten minutes.

Nor is the intercourse of ideas confined to this country; facilities have been afforded, for instance, for wrought-ironworkers to exchange ideas on design and production methods with their opposite numbers on the Continent. But very much on their own doorstep is one of the major difficulties facing craftsmen today – that of finding premises suitable for their needs. COSIRA has been instrumental in getting planning permission for craft workshops where it has been previously refused (p. 7).

As a government-financed organization, COSIRA is precluded from any form of political action on behalf of the small man, so seeks to help him by bringing to the attention of the Small Firms Division any cases where government decisions are particularly detrimental to the small firm, and also by keeping abreast of new legislation in order to advise small firms how best to operate within the existing law.

It is interesting to note that the countries which head the industrial progress field are also those which have set up powerful government departments to promote the interests of privately-owned businesses. The philosophy of this is that virtually all new ideas and basic inventions are conceived by individuals, and these individuals usually set up on their own account to exploit and develop their ideas. For the last decade the SBA (p. 24) has been advocating protection against political pressures and weighted competition from the monopolistic giant organizations. It is estimated that nearly ten million workers are now employed in small independent businesses. The SBA has a current membership of 1,000 and is relatively small compared with its European counterparts with whom it keeps in close touch.

It is inevitable that there is some overlap in the work of COSIRA and CAC because of their common interests and close affiliation, but there is little in their services, for CAC offers grants whilst COSIRA does not; CAC specializes in assisting the designer-craftsman, whereas COSIRA, by its terms of constitution, is much wider ranging. During a six-month period CAC dealt with 3,800 enquiries specifically on crafts from both craftsmen and the public, and this included *Index* consultations. Enquiries to COSIRA's head office over a three-month period totalled 403, of which ninety were on careers and vocational subjects, and forty-three on suppliers. This indication of the extent to which the general advisory services of COSIRA are utilized does not take into account the specialized queries which are dealt with on a regional basis. Currently there are some 9,174 small firms, with a total of 58,579 employees, being serviced by COSIRA. Of these, the crafts sector accounts for 2,465 firms, employing some 13,215 people, and although in most respects the difficulties may be symptomatic of prevailing economic or social conditions, there are problems peculiar to each county.

Each region has its own COSIRA committee, for counties have different policies; it is true of England as a whole that the people, as well as the topography, are vastly different between regions – as one organizer so nicely put it "one almost needs a passport to go from one county to another". So one does find a more sympathetic attitude to the craftsman in one area than in another. Sometimes the COSIRA organizer has been responsible for setting up a guild, whereas another – although none have appeared inimical to crafts – has laid more stress on the light engineering type of small industry and frowned a little on the nostalgic desire to tenaciously retain the traditional. Because of its close countrywide links with the rural community councils, COSIRA has its finger very much on the regional pulse.

BRITISH CRAFTS CENTRE, 43 Earlham Street, London WC2H 9LD. Tel: 01–836 6993
Membership is not restricted to practising craftsmen but is open to all who are interested in promoting the creativity and skills of contemporary craftwork. Constantly varied displays of exhibits selected by a committee for sale at Covent Garden and the Victoria and Albert Museum.

COUNCIL FOR SMALL INDUSTRIES IN RURAL AREAS (COSIRA), Queen's House, Fish Row, Salisbury, Wilts. Tel: (0722) 24411
Chief Executive, Secretariat, Press and Information, Exhibitions
The council's technical and business management advisory services are extensive and cover a wide range of subjects. Courses comprise practical exercises, lectures and demonstrations arranged for varying levels from apprentices to mastermen. Textbooks and information. List available on request. Loans for industry and tourism.

(COSIRA) P.O. Box 717, 35 Camp Road, Wimbledon Common SW19 4UP. Tel: 01–997 6761
Chief Advisory and Chief Business Management Officers, Technical staff, Workshops, Publications, Director Credit Services and Loans
Small industries are defined as those normally employing not more than twenty skilled people, and rural areas up to populace of 10,000. The service does not extend to agriculture, horticulture or the retail trades.
A preliminary talk, without obligation, can be arranged through the area organizers who having assessed the problem will advise the standard rate of charge for the work involved should the client wish to proceed.

BRITISH COUNCIL, 10 Spring Gardens, London SW1A 2BN. Tel: 01–930 8466
The council exists to promote wider knowledge of the UK and English language abroad. Enquiries regarding craft exhibitions and potential contacts should be addressed to Fine Arts Department, 87–99 Park Street, London W1Y 2NJ. Tel: 01–408 1200.

CRAFTS ADVISORY COMMITTEE, 12 Waterloo Place, London SW1Y 4AU. Tel: 01–839 1917
Founded to promote British craftwork, CAC receives a government grant by which it gives considerable financial aid to craftsmen by way of grants, loans and bursaries. Non-selective registers and a highly selective index are kept. Regular exhibitions and extensive advisory service. *Crafts*, a bi-monthly magazine, is published by CAC, available from: Circulation Manager, *Crafts*, 28 Haymarket, London SW1Y 4SU.

DESIGN COUNCIL, The Design Centre, 28 Haymarket, London SW1Y 4SU. Tel: 01–839 8000
Index, monthly publication, occasional small craft exhibitions.

WORLD CRAFTS COUNCIL, 43 Earlham Street, London WC2. Tel: 01–240 2145
A non-governmental organization founded to promote the interests of

craftsmen throughout the world, maintaining a unique information re-
source on them and their work. WCC depends upon its members for the
support of its activities including international General Assemblies.

SMALL FIRMS INFORMATION CENTRES
(Each Centre has a 24-hour answering service)

NORTHERN REGION: 22 Newgate Shopping Centre, Newcastle upon
Tyne NE1 5RH. Tel: Newcastle 25353

NORTH-WESTERN REGION: Peter House, Oxford Street, Manchester M1
5AN. Tel: 061–832 5282

YORKSHIRE AND HUMBERSIDE REGION: 5 Royal Exchange House, City
Square, Leeds LS1 5PQ. Tel: Leeds 445151

EAST MIDLANDS REGION: 48–50 Maid Marian Way, Nottingham NG1
6GF. Tel: Nottingham 49791

WEST MIDLANDS REGION: 53 Stephenson Street, Birmingham B2 4DH.
Tel: 021–643 3344

EASTERN REGION: 35 Wellington Street, Luton LU1 2SB. Tel: Luton
29215

LONDON AND SOUTH EASTERN REGION: 65 Buckingham Palace Road,
London SW1W 0QX. Tel: 01–828 2384

SOUTH-WESTERN REGION: Colston Centre, Colston Avenue, Bristol BS1
4UB. Tel: Bristol 294546

COSIRA REGIONAL OFFICES
BEDFORDSHIRE AND HERTFORDSHIRE: COSIRA, Agriculture House, 57 Golding-
ton Road, Bedford. Tel: Bedford 0234 51401

CAMBRIDGESHIRE: COSIRA, Cambridgeshire House, 7 Hills Road, Cambridge
CB2 1NL. Tel: Cambridge 0223 54505

CHESHIRE, SHROPSHIRE AND STAFFORDSHIRE: COSIRA, 11b High Street, Market
Drayton, Shropshire. Tel: Market Drayton 2721

CORNWALL: COSIRA, 14 St Mary's Street, Truro. Tel: Truro 0872 3531

CUMBRIA: COSIRA, 6 West Walls, Carlisle CA3 8UG. Tel: Carlisle 0228 25159
and Agriculture House, Appleby Road, Kendal. Tel: 0539 22556

DERBYSHIRE: COSIRA, 43 Kedleston Road, Derby DE3 1FB. Tel: Derby 0332
47454

DEVON: COSIRA, County Hall, Exeter 4QD. Tel: Exeter 0392 77977 Ext. 702
and 704

DORSET: Wessex Area Office, COSIRA, Lloyds Bank Chambers, High Street,
Gillingham, Dorset. Tel: Gillingham 07476 2423

DURHAM: COSIRA, Morton Road, Darlington. Tel: 0325 69425/6

ESSEX: COSIRA, 103 High Street, Wivenhoe, Colchester. Tel: 020 622 4688

GLOUCESTERSHIRE AND NORTH AVON: COSIRA, 24 Belle Vue Terrace, Malvern, Worcs. Tel: 068 45–64506

HAMPSHIRE: Central Southern Area Office, COSIRA, Northgate Place, Staple Gardens, Winchester. Tel: 0962 5747

HEREFORDSHIRE: COSIRA, 24 Belle Vue Terrace, Malvern, Worcs. WR14 4PZ. Tel: 068 45–64506

HERTFORDSHIRE: see BEDFORDSHIRE

KENT: COSIRA, Oakwood House, Oakwood Road, Maidstone. Tel: Maidstone 0622 65222

LANCASHIRE: COSIRA, 15 Victoria Road, Fulwood, Preston PR2 4PS. Tel: 0772 717461

LEICESTERSHIRE: COSIRA, Box 6 Chancel House, East Street, Bingham, Nottinghamshire. Tel: 0949 39222

LINCOLNSHIRE AND SOUTH HUMBERSIDE: COSIRA, 35 Orchard Street, Lincoln. Tel: 0522 29931 Exts. 304/5 and Westgate House, Westgate, Sleaford, Lincs. Tel: 0529 302724

NORFOLK: COSIRA, 14 Tombland, Norwich NR3 1HF. Tel: 0603 24498

NORTHAMPTONSHIRE: COSIRA, 9 Cheyne Walk, Northampton NN1 5PY. Tel: Northampton 0604 39160

NORTHUMBERLAND: COSIRA, 24 The Grove, Gosforth, Newcastle-upon-Tyne NE3 1NE. Tel: Gosforth 0632 855381

NOTTINGHAMSHIRE: COSIRA, Box 6 Chancel House, East Street, Bingham. Tel: 0949 39222/3

OXFORDSHIRE, BERKSHIRE AND BUCKINGHAMSHIRE: Central Southern Area Office, COSIRA, The Maltings, St John's Road, Wallingford. Tel: 0491 35523

SOMERSET AND SOUTH AVON: Wessex Area Office, COSIRA, Lloyds Bank Chambers, High Street, Gillingham, Dorset. Tel: Gillingham 07476 2423

SUFFOLK: COSIRA, 103 High Street, Wivenhoe, Colchester, Essex. Tel: 020 622 4688

SURREY: COSIRA, 2 Jenner Road, Guildford. Tel: Guildford 0483 66072

SUSSEX: COSIRA, Sussex House, 212 High Street, Lewes. Tel: Lewes 07916 3422

WARWICKSHIRE: COSIRA, Midland Bank Chambers, 126 The Parade, Leamington Spa. Tel: Leamington Spa 0926 26615

WILTSHIRE: Wessex Area Office, COSIRA, Lloyds Bank Chambers, High Street, Gillingham, Dorset. Tel: Gillingham 07476 2423

WORCESTERSHIRE: COSIRA, 24 Belle Vue Terrace, Malvern, Worcs. WR14 4PZ.
Tel: 068 45 64506

YORKSHIRE AND NORTH HUMBERSIDE: COSIRA, The Lodge, 21 Font Street,
Acomb, York YO2 3BW. Tel: 0904 793228

2

Regional Arts Associations

... The arts are in growth, and our world reputation is supported by the
talent and energy of our people in all parts of the country. ...

Hugh Jenkins, Minister for the Arts, 1975
(Extract of Statement – Arts with the People)

The post-war system of arts patronage in this country was originally
London-based, but in the national system which has been developing in
the last quarter of the century the aim increasingly has been to get a
fairer distribution between London and the regions. This has been
achieved by the setting up of regional arts associations, which are independent organizations co-ordinating and promoting the arts, in partnership with local authorities, from whom their main financial support
comes, together with grants from the Arts Council of Great Britain and
the Crafts Advisory Committee. Aid also comes from various other
sources ranging from the national media to local clubs.

The extent to which the Crafts Advisory Committee has
strengthened the role of these associations can be gauged by the fact
that something like 75 per cent of its total grant now goes to the regions.

Many of the associations' schemes have a common principle from
which they meet the particular arts' needs of their region. All provide
an expert advisory service to any organization or individual who calls
upon it; most employ specialist officers for each of the main art forms,
although here the indeterminate line between arts and crafts has
become indiscernible in the field of visual arts as crafts activities increase in both scope and content.

South West Arts was the first of the regional arts associations to be
formed, in 1956. One of its major projects has been the Beaford Centre,
an arts centre serving a 1,000 square miles area of rural Devon. It also
supports the Dove Centre. But the first to link the arts and crafts with
our heritage was Lincolnshire, which has always had a strong regional
identity of its own. The pattern for partnership with local authorities,
which has been adopted by all the regional arts associations, was set by
Northern Arts.

The extent to which crafts are promoted and supported varies from
region to region, but is a question very much to the fore with most of the
associations. Working parties have been formulating plans by which
crafts can be adequately catered for. The appointment of a full-time
crafts officer is the ideal, but this has not been a viable proposition in

many cases and a compromise has been reached whereby the visual arts officer has equal responsibility for the crafts. A number have launched pilot schemes offering fellowships as a realistic means of financial support; others have taken the initiative in setting up marketing facilities through exhibitions, and where sheer physical size strains the artistic stimulus, the association's policy is to act as a catalyst, rather than a direct promoter, by supporting local associations.

EAST MIDLANDS ARTS ASSOCIATION, Director: Robert Smith, 1 Frederick Street, Loughborough, Leics. LE11 3BH. Tel: Loughborough 67136/7
    Area: Derbyshire, Leicestershire, Northamptonshire, Nottinghamshire, and Milton Keynes district (Bucks.)
    Serving a population of 3,500,000, the association publishes an arts magazine, a bi-monthly tabloid, a monthly calendar of events and a reference catalogue. *Arts Post* streamlines existing arts mailing lists and is available free to the public and to arts organizations.
    Recent events included a crafts exhibition which was circulated to out-of-town centres, the opening of an arts and leisure centre at Newark, and the acquisition of a building in Nottingham as a centre for visual arts, to be run by the Midland Gallery.

EASTERN ARTS ASSOCIATION, Director: Christopher Rye, 30 Station Road, Cambridge CB1 2JH. Tel: Cambridge 67707
    Area: Bedfordshire, Cambridgeshire, Essex, Hertfordshire, Norfolk and Suffolk.
    Serving a wide area with a scattered rural population of 4,400,000, Eastern Arts has given financial support to crafts exhibitions and sponsored a weavers' exhibition which circulated round galleries in the region.
    Its objects include the development of projects to fill gaps or needs in provision for the arts. Information and advisory services are available. An artists' register is maintained, and a monthly broadsheet *Eastword* is published, giving free publicity to all events.

GREATER LONDON ARTS ASSOCIATION, Director: Harry West, 23/31 Tavistock Place, London WC1H 9SG. Tel: 01–387 9541
    Area: City of London and the thirty-two London boroughs.
    A number of bodies for supporting the arts exist in London, serving a population of 7,353,000, but the GLAA was designed to create a comprehensive regional policy for the arts throughout Greater London. It aims to act as a catalyst to the development of the arts, and also initiates its own projects. A monthly newsletter, *Greater London Arts,* is published.

LINCOLNSHIRE AND SOUTH HUMBERSIDE ARTS, Director: Clive Fox, Beaumont Lodge, Beaumont Fee, Lincoln LN1 1UN. Tel: 0522 33555
    Area: the counties of Humberside south of the Humber and Lincolnshire.
    This was the first regional arts association to link the arts and crafts with our heritage, with crafts as one of its special strengths. The association promotes exhibitions, opened a regional crafts centre as a focus for crafts activities

with a full-time crafts officer, and was the first to offer fellowships for artist-craftsmen. Because of the special characteristics of the region, the population of 821,000 being spread over a large geographical area, the association is predominantly concerned with the direct promotion of events and projects, using local voluntary assistance. A bi-monthly arts magazine is published.

MERSEYSIDE ARTS ASSOCIATION, Director: Peter Bevan, 6 Bluecoat Chambers, School Lane, Liverpool 1. Tel: 051–709 0855

Area: most of the Merseyside metropolitan county area – Knowsley, Liverpool, Sefton, Wirral; Ellesmere Port and Halton districts in Cheshire, and the district of West Lancashire.

A major part of the association's income is spent on grant aid to organizations and individuals, and applications for financial support for craft projects are assessed on their individual merits. A guide to applicants, called *Financial Assistance*, is available. The population served is 1,700,000. A group poster scheme, with 400 sites on Merseyrail available to arts promoters, is run by the association, which publicizes events through a mailing list, *Artspost*; it also publishes a monthly arts magazine, *Arts Alive Merseyside*.

NORTH WEST ARTS, Director: Raphael Gouley, 52 King Street, Manchester M2 4LY. Tel: 061–832 2937

Area: Greater Manchester metropolitan county, most of Cheshire and Lancashire; St Helen's metropolitan district of Merseyside, and the High Peak district of Derbyshire.

Population served: 5,000,000. About a quarter of the NWA's income is spent in supporting the development of the mid-Pennine and other area and local arts associations in the belief that these can more effectively evaluate local needs, leaving the NWA to concentrate on regional issues. Individual creative artists are encouraged to work in particular communities and works are commissioned or bought from them. The NWA Centre, with exhibition area, was opened in Manchester in 1973 as a regional arts information centre, the first of its kind.

Among the association's publications are reports on arts centres in Greater Manchester, a computerized mailing service, and a reference handbook on the arts in the North-west.

NORTHERN ARTS, Visual Arts Officer: Peter Davies, 31 New Bridge Street, Newcastle upon Tyne NE1 8JY. Tel: (0632) 610446

Area: Metropolitan county of Tyne and Wear, counties of Cleveland, Cumbria, Durham and Northumberland, serving a total population of 3,268,000.

Craft exhibitions are already financed by the council but a new policy on crafts is being currently structured. Projected plans include a regional craft centre with exhibition space, craft shop, bookshop and library, information centre and meeting room, and indices of craftsmen and retail outlets. Workshops, exhibition service, direct grants to craftsmen for specific projects, and fellowships are under consideration. Publications include a monthly newspaper.

SOUTH-EAST ARTS ASSOCIATION, Director: Peter Carpenter, 58 London Road, Southborough, Tunbridge Wells, Kent. TN4 0PR. Tel: 0892 38743
    Area: East Sussex, Kent and Surrey.
    Population served: 3,027,164. The policy towards crafts is under review. Monthly publication, *Orbit*, is distributed to members and free to the general public from bookstalls and newsagents.

SOUTH-WEST ARTS, Director: Ian Watson, 23 Southernhay East, Exeter, Devon. Tel: Exeter 70338
    Area: Avon, Cornwall, Devon, Gloucestershire, Somerset, and most of Dorset.
    The region has a scattered population of 3,400,000, so most societies tend to be somewhat small. Craft guilds and centres such as Dove Centre, and overseas, the Bristol Arts Project — an arts marketing scheme, have received grants from the association, which fosters the integration of craftsmen in the community. Bi-monthly magazine.

SOUTHERN ARTS ASSOCIATION, Director: Bernard Jacobson, South Side Offices, Law Courts, Winchester, Hants. SO23 9DQ. Tel: 0962 69422
    Area: Berkshire, Hampshire, Isle of Wight, Oxfordshire, West Sussex, Wiltshire, and the districts of Bournemouth, Christchurch and Poole in Dorset.
    The population of 4,130,400 is well served by predominantly music festivals where literature and visual arts are often important fringe events. Occasionally gives grants towards craft exhibitions.

WEST MIDLANDS ARTS ASSOCIATION, Director: John Murphy, Lloyds Bank Chambers, Market Street, Stafford ST16 2AP. Tel: 0785 2788/2022
    Area: West Midlands metropolitan county, Herefordshire, Worcestershire, Salop, Staffordshire and Warwickshire.
    Out of the total population of 5,160,000, more than half lives in the West Midlands metropolitan county, but the association is very alive to the needs of the rural communities. The visual arts officer has equal responsibilities for the crafts and is closely associated with the Birmingham marketing project. The policy of the association is for more direct promotion and development of the arts in the region. Craft fellowships have been established.

YORKSHIRE ARTS ASSOCIATION, Director: Michael Dawson, Glyde House, Glydegate, Bradford, West Yorks BD5 0BQ. Tel: 0274 23051
    Area: Metropolitan counties of South and West Yorkshire, and the counties of Humberside north of the Humber and North Yorkshire.
    A large region, with a population of 4,686,360, rich and varied in its range of activities. The possibility of a crafts officer appointment is under consideration. A design unit has been set up, its services and advice being available to outside bodies as well as to its own arts magazine.

3

Guilds and Associated Associations

... and especially to determine the Guild's role as the world rapidly
changes. Are we to be a 'learned society', a spearhead, a rallying point, a
talking shop, a gathering of friends – yes, that certainly; or an anchor in
present turmoils? And if we are an anchor, do the people who need it know
it is there?

Extract from The Master's Foreword
(David Peace, 1973)
The Art Workers Guild 90th Annual Report

Guilds were originally religious and social fraternities, later becoming
trade associations fixing wages and high standards of craftsmanship.
The pastoral care of their members then became as much their concern
as their professional integrity, making them the forerunners of the
friendly societies promoting members' welfare. Many guilds were well-
endowed; their great wealth giving them influence, so that from the
time of Edward III they were able to advance money to the kings of
England.

Medieval craftsmen wore distinctive clothing according to their
trades – hence the term *livery company*. Nowadays only the senior members are entitled to the livery, which they wear on ceremonial occasions,
or to a vote at the election of Lord Mayor and Sheriffs. There are eighty-
four livery companies, the oldest being the weavers whose foundation
dates back to 1184, the liverymen of the craft guilds totalling some
16,000.

The extent to which the companies have control over their trade has
diminished over the years, but many are still active in maintaining standards; the goldsmiths still test our coinage, and hall-mark articles of
gold and silver. Where modern science has transformed certain traditional industries the guilds have embraced the changes; so horners
are now interested in plastics, and the fan-makers in air-conditioning
and refrigeration.

Despite their associations with specific crafts, there are few livery
companies today which are actively concerned with the individual
craftsman. They maintain an interest in the trade, but usually they
become liverymen only because of family tradition, and thus we have
the case of the Worshipful Company of Wheelwrights where, in a
diminishing craft, none of the members are wheelwrights. Similarly,
about 98 per cent of the Worshipful Company of Basket-makers are not

connected with the trade. The principles, upon whose ancient foundation the guilds were inaugurated, do not change, but the companies still have a special interest in education, and some provide almshouses for the aged.

Apart from the livery companies, with their civil privileges and responsibilities, there is a bewildering array of guilds, associations, societies and councils, all furthering the cause of craftwork in general. These are not competitive and, in varying degrees, adhere to the idealism of the medieval guild by creating a spirit of community under their auspices, in their concern for the individual craftsmen.

There is no actual official difference between a guild, a society and an association, though they operate in slightly different ways; so the pedant may well look askance at a group, operating under the name of *guild*, which raises its funds by jumble sales, whereas an association might well be financed from fellowship fees. There are degrees of sophistication in the administrative structure too, but whether the members meet in an historic hall or a village schoolroom; and whether they are presided over by a resplendently robed Master and Council or a pullover-and-jeans-clad potter; is really irrelevant.

Many of the guilds and connected associations have national and even international status; all inject interest in craftwork and keep alive the germ of creativity.

It is perhaps interesting at this point to look briefly at the development of some of the eminent societies. There emerges a sense of continuity, a measure of evolution, in the arts and crafts movement inspired by William Morris, John Ruskin and Philip Webb, which resulted in the founding of the Art Workers Guild in 1884 on impulses which were said to have been as much moral and philosophical as aesthetic.

William Morris, famous for the formation of the 'Anti-Scrape' Society for the protection of ancient buildings, was much impressed with Ruskin's central thesis on freeing men from machine's bondage, which argued that the splendour of medieval craftsmanship was derived from the status of the workman himself. Morris's influence on the design and arts of his time is too well-known to need repetition here, suffice it to say that his predilection for the hand-made revived traditional or dying crafts. Superficially, his era and ours may seem unrelated, but in a world in which the capacity for producing rubbish increases, his insistence on quality and attention to detail have a continuing validity. His ideas and achievements are still a source of inspiration to creative design students today, and have now become a major part of the syllabus for both certificate and degree students at Loughborough College.

Pride in Morris's achievement does not stem purely from patriotism, for there is evidence that interest in his artistic ideals is world-wide; it is particularly strong in Italy, where his arts and crafts movement has been related to industrial design. The William Morris Society perpetuates his aims by reinforcing links with some of the major associations: SPAB (of course), SIAD and the Art Workers Guild.

The strength of a guild is not dependent on its size, but the quality of its membership. The Art Workers Guild, for instance, shuns publicity, preferring to limit its numbers so as to allow the members to know each other. It sets much store by frank and confidential exchanges of view, and has profound influence both in England and abroad.

The Society of Designer-Craftsmen, with a membership of some 520, represents the interests of the largest group of professional independent craftsmen in Britain today. This grew out of the Arts and Crafts Exhibition Society, founded by William Morris in 1888 as a direct offshoot of the Art Workers Guild, and became known by its present title when it absorbed the Cambridge society of that name in 1961. The society operates through a number of secretariats to maintain professional standards of workmanship to further the enrichment of the domestic and civic environment. Its professional liaison service is engaged in developing radical new techniques of collaboration between designer-craftsmen and architects, and maintains a register of designers, offering comprehensive information plus slide and print loans. There are moves to establish points of contact with the SIAD.

Through its lecture panel the society is effective through organizations like the WI, TWG, and local groups throughout the country. Its present influence is strongest in art colleges; affecting course structures and student goals, and offering assessment for licentiateship to students at the end of a course in art and design as a stimulus to preparing for future professional practice. Practical help is available in various forms during the period leading to full membership. Currently, some twenty-five colleges participate.

The British Institute of Industrial Art, a forerunner of the present Design Council, was set up by the government during the First World War and lasted until 1933. The Council was then composed mainly of guildsmen of the Art Workers Guild. The same era saw the formation of the Design and Industries Association, pioneered by designer-craftsmen in order to fulfil the need for clearer understanding between manufacturer and designer.

Far from being inactive during the difficult years of war, many guilds accelerated action to assist craftsmen. Twenty-seven societies, representing every branch of the visual arts, spoke with a united voice at the inauguration of the Central Institute of Art and Design in November 1940, fighting for their recognition in national life.

A great deal of constructive work – such as surveying craft workshops in which to train the disabled, contacting all craftsmen in workshops all over the country, and studying their needs and procuring raw materials

– was undertaken by the Red Rose Guild of Designer Craftsmen, sustaining the spirit of its foundation in 1921 by the talented and resolute Margaret Pilkington. For over fifty years the guild has demonstrated its adaptability to the changing needs of the times, and its interminable driving force to keep alive the interest in quality craftwork.

Some associations, by dint of their early foundation, through royal patronage or grant aids, are stronger and recognized nationally, but a closer look at their constitution will determine whether their policy and the artist's purpose are compatible.

The craft movement, although firmly rooted since the foundation of the independent societies, was, paradoxically, in danger of fragmenting, for there were too many voices clamouring to win attention to the craftsman's role in our modern society. It was due to a motion of the National Federation of Women's Institutes that a resolution was passed in 1970, pressing the government to recognize the importance of the crafts. This move was endorsed by the chairman of the SDC, and the Federation of British Craft Societies was inaugurated to speak with one voice for its members.

The federation, on the initiative of the SDC, the Art Workers' Guild, the Red Rose Guild and some dozen other established craft bodies, quickly formulated a constitution and submitted two successive memoranda to the Minister of Arts, the Rt Hon. Viscount Eccles, who appointed the Crafts Advisory Committee in 1971 to distribute and administer the government grant. This Committee provided the federation with the services of an administrative assistant and asked it to undertake a complicated allocation of funds to craft bodies. The perspicacity and prudence with which this was effected established confidence in the federation's future. The Crafts Advisory Committee's annual grant gave it the financial help to establish an independent central office and secretariat.

All member societies derive benefit from this central secretariat, mainly through the federation's newsletter which, amongst other things, publicizes exhibitions and current information on such things as administration and co-ordination of crafts projects.

Each member society is still administered by its own council and is therefore completely autonomous, retaining its own identity. But it is also an integral component of the federation, under whose aegis members are assured that no longer can any public authority justify arbitrary action towards the crafts because of the vague uncertainty of the craftsmen's feeling. The founding of the federation, in terms of its importance to the arts and crafts movement, has been juxtaposed with that of the Royal Society of Arts and the Art Workers Guild.

The membership of the federation is growing yearly as the idea of unity without uniformity takes root. Currently there are thirty-seven craft member societies and sixteen associates, therefore well over

10,000 individual craftsmen are represented through this single body.

(Where there is a guild specifically related to an individual crafts-man's métier it is indexed in the relevant chapter.)

Regional associations tend to cater for a variety of crafts, identifying with specific areas and limiting their membership on a geographical basis. National organizations range from those, like the independent ASB, whose aims are to protect all small businesses from all govern-mental pressures, to the AU, which has political allegiances.

Government departmental organizations (dealt with elsewhere) are not all strictly independent of each other. All are working for a common cause and I have found that COSIRA, for instance, has been respon-sible for setting up guilds in different areas. Likewise, county guilds have received financial help from CAC or RAA.

Generalization tends to be misleading, and repetition of each associ-ation's constitution too arbitrary. I have therefore summarized the salient points which have emerged from my survey. *The general aims,* practised in varying degrees, appear to be:

1 to promote and protect the interests and status of craftsmen,
2 to create a focus of craft activity in an area,
3 to join craftsmen in the bonds of friendship and goodwill,
4 to create mutual aid rather than competition among members,
5 to establish and maintain high standards of design and workman-ship to the advantage of the craftsman and the prestige of the county (or craft field),
6 to provide a forum for the exchange of ideas and information,
7 to form into a constituted body which would have powers to nego-tiate and raise funds,
8 to create both a sense of community within the guild and a sense of concern for the individual through the organization of social and cultural activities for its members,
9 to provide a shop window of the best of the craftwork by means of exhibitions,
10 to act as a clearing-house through which the public can be put in direct contact with any craftsman whose specialist service is required.

The advantages appear to be:
1 an accepted seal of quality is automatically assumed for the crafts-man is known to be a member of a guild whose standards are acknowledged as exacting,
2 sharing advertising and exhibition costs with other members and often deriving free publicity under the auspices of the guild's activi-ties,
3 marketing influence of the guild often reflects advantageously on the

individual's sales,
4 display facilities are often available as a regular feature of leading
   agricultural shows (such as the one the Guild of Herefordshire
   Craftsmen have each year at the Three Counties Show).

It is perhaps surprising, therefore, that despite all these advantages,
many craftsmen do not belong to any guild or association. Their
reasons seem to fall broadly in the following categories:

1 County guilds, in general, tend to be too parochial, too selective, lay
   too much stress on the social side, often devoting more time to arranging the annual dinner than to staging the exhibition.
2 Preparing special pieces for exhibition purposes is too time-
   consuming and of negligible value (this has been dealt with in more
   depth under marketing p. 43).
3 They must keep an eye on the future if they are to carry on. Too often
   they settle into a comfortable routine of demonstrations, lectures,
   outings and exhibitions. This can mean that they appear to stagnate
   and attract very little new blood, with a membership of advancing
   age making little or no impact on the community.

Few associations have been without their critics, especially in their
formative years. As an objective measure, therefore, uncoloured by
problems of a local nature, it might be helpful to look at aspects of some
of the most successful associations, in an endeavour to find that elusive
balance between aspiration and reality; bearing in mind, of course, that
there are, and always will be, differences in the capabilities of the individuals who constitute any corporate body, and the degree of group
liveliness rests, primarily, on the impact of one on another.
   Some guilds help in a positive way by sharing out commissioned
work.
   Many have eminent personalities as patrons and derive reflected
publicity through them.
   Open-days, workshop sessions and seminars reinforce the value of
annual exhibitions and give the public a chance to see the craftsman at
work in his shirt-sleeves. In this way the degree of skill can be appreciated, something which rarely comes through in the art-orientated
atmosphere of an exhibition.
   Some guilds make a point of publicizing the fact that their members
work on commissions and, having invited enquiries, recommend individual craftsmen to the enquirer.
   Others circulate college education and specialized groups of members who are able and willing to give occasional lectures or demonstrations.
   Many have permanent local display areas for their members' work,

in hotel foyers and the like, if they have no guild centre.

Some (like Suffolk) buy a selection of members' work to form a permanent collection of contemporary craftwork.

One of the most important aspects seems to be a newsletter circulated regularly to members in order to keep in touch with current news. Sussex and Surrey, for instance, produce very efficient and informative newsletters. Committee meetings' minutes, reports, and all manner of useful information, including details of available workshop space, exchange and mart columns and snippets on suppliers, all make for really valuable bulletins.

Guilds have their problems too, of course. As with so many societies, inflation poses a major problem for the future. Services, even when carried out by voluntary labour, run expensive, and people tend to drop their support of what, in less difficult times, they would consider a worthwhile cause. All the more important, therefore, is the role, albeit a kind of financial crutch, which associate members can play. All too often, however, their help is never called upon, so they very reasonably lose interest where they can not be actively involved and associated with the craftsmen they support.

In opposition to the craftsmen's criticisms are those which the guilds may level at odd members, who often do nothing in return for the body as a whole, looking upon their subscription as a right to take advantage of the facilities of exhibitions by using them as a retailing outlet only; deriding public taste or their colleagues' marketing prowess when their own way-out creations fail to sell.

Some have no meeting place and therefore rely on the annual exhibition to gather together.

There is nothing to stop members belonging to more than one guild in order to exhibit on a wider basis.

The question of attracting younger blood into the guilds, if they are not to be forgotten and discredited, is one which exercised the minds of such august bodies as the Art Workers Guild some three years ago. But in that particular case, and in the current figures from other eminent societies, there has been an increase of guild membership amongst younger craftsmen. Many—in particular the Clerkenwell Green Association – are acutely aware of the need to introduce young people to the craft field, and actively participate in educational projects.

One very important aspect emerges which, without accusing guilds of being isolated and precious entities, can be easily overlooked, and that is that close association with county councils can be beneficial in providing centres (refer to centres p. 64). Interest is often shown in guilds by those who are not members. As an important part of the nation's social history the proceedings and history of a guild can be deposited, and carefully conserved, at the county records offices. Also, the Victoria and Albert Museum welcomes reports and exhibition catalogues.

Finally, of course, there is the sobering thought that guilds are what the members make them. So, for those who have criticisms to make of their committee, it is advisable to stand up and speak up. You may easily find yourself co-opted on it if your criticisms are constructive, and thus given the chance to make it successful. This seems to draw attention to the craftsman's importance in this automated age.

GUILDS AND ASSOCIATIONS

NATIONAL

AMALGAMATED INSTITUTE OF ANTIQUARIAN CRAFTS, Bluecoat Chambers, School Lane, Liverpool L1 3BX. Tel: 051–709 5297
  Recently situated at Bluecoat Chambers: many society members; meetings and discussions.

ART WORKERS GUILD, Sec. Richard Murry, 6 Queen Square, London WC1N 3AR. Tel: 01837 3474
  The guild was founded in 1884 on the inspiration of William Morris (Master in 1892), John Ruskin and Philip Webb. The initial aim to bring together architects and other artists and craftsmen for a better knowledge and understanding of one another's skills is extended to advance education in all the visual arts and crafts, by means of lectures, meetings, demonstrations, discussions and other methods; and to foster and maintain high standards of design and craftsmanship in any way which may be beneficial to the community. The guild is recognized as an educational charity. It supports the work of many councils concerned with the conservation of our national heritage, and is actively involved with the national crafts organization. Membership is open to artists, craftsmen and others engaged in design or the practice of the visual arts who achieve the professional standards of the guild. Honorary members are those who have rendered eminent services to the arts. There is a limited number of associate members.

ARTISTS' GENERAL BENEVOLENT INSTITUTION, Sec. Miss D. P. Laidman, Burlington House, Piccadilly, London W1V 0DJ. Tel: 01–734 1193
  Founded in 1814, the institution gives financial assistance to distressed bona fide professional artists and craftsmen and their dependants. It is a voluntary organization and relies entirely on bequests and donations. Applications from established artists are considered solely on their own merits, they do not have to be subscribers to the funds to be eligible for assistance. The Artists' Orphan Fund was established in 1871, as a separate fund under the aegis of the AGBI, to support and educate orphan children of artists.

THE ARTISTS' LEAGUE OF GREAT BRITAIN, R.W.S. Galleries, 26 Conduit Street, London W1R 9TA. Tel: 01–629 8300
  Founded in 1909 as the former Imperial Arts League, membership is open to artists and craftsmen resident in Britain and the Commonwealth countries. Every branch of artistic activity is covered by the combined experience of the

Council. The League gives legal advice and, subject to the approval of the Council, conducts legal action when necessary; arranges insurance through Lloyds, at favourable rates; advises on agreements, contracts, copyright, reproduction rights and royalties; it also assists in debt recovery and advises on the credibility of firms and individuals.

ARTISTS' UNION, 125–129 Shaftesbury Avenue, London WC2H 8AD
Formed in 1972, to establish the artist's right to work in his own medium as a labour force, the union is at a formative stage but aims at affiliating to the T.U.C. to promote and protect the economic and cultural interests of the members and artists – serving a broad range of artists in all visual media. Craftsmen are eligible for membership.

ASSOCIATION OF BRITISH CRAFTSMEN, Sec: S. D. Richardson, Quartet, Noyes Avenue, Laxfield, Woodbridge, Suffolk 1P13 8EB. Tel: Ubbeston 486
Promotes the sale of British craftwork in Canada and America on a limited scale, and mediates in student vacation training. Any artist or craftsman is invited to apply in respect of taking students, but, as a guideline, the association will only recommend to visitors (mainly American and Canadian, although the project is now attracting enquiries from craft bodies of other countries) those who:
1 have had some teaching experience, but discourages those who are merely Art/Craft teachers wishing to earn pin money during a vacation;
2 apart from sound basic training, have had some years' experience at practising their craft so that their work is distinctive and stimulating to students;
3 have adequate facilities.

BLAKENEY GUILD OF MANY CRAFTS, Clerk: Cdr. H. Day, 11 New Street, Holt, Norfolk
Formed in 1951 as a direct outcome of the Blakeney Festival Exhibition, more than twenty different crafts are represented by the hundred regular exhibitors at the annual exhibition at Blakeney at the end of July, and sale at Norwich in late November. Full craft membership, subject to the court's criteria, and associate membership is open to residents anywhere in the British Isles.

FEDERATION OF BRITISH CRAFT SOCIETIES, 6 Queen Square, WC1N 3AR. Tel: 01–278 2214
Individual craftsmen are not eligible for membership, but are represented by their own guild to whom membership is offered as either:
craft societies in which at least one-third of the members are practising craftsmen; or
associate groups working for or interested in the crafts movement.
    The objectives are to promote and protect the well-being of the craft movement by representing the member societies and negotiating on their behalf. By exploring selling techniques, promotion, stimulating patronage, and extending appreciation of the crafts, the federation aims to raise the status of the craftsman's profession.

MIDLAND GROUP GALLERY, Director: Sylvia Cooper, The Wool Shop, 32–4 Carlton Street, Nottingham

The Midland Group has been in existence since 1943 and is well known to those who are concerned and involved in the contemporary visual arts, the appreciation and development of which is the aim and purpose of the constitution. Full or practising members are elected by other full members of the general committee on evidence of work, and may be resident anywhere in the country. The group has never been a self-exhibiting society; only one or two exhibitions a year, out of an average of eleven, are solely of members' work.

A craft shop and gallery, with information available on crafts in general, provide an important outlet for both local and national craftsmen. There are also plans for workshops to be built.

WILLIAM MORRIS SOCIETY, Kelmscott House, 26 Upper Mall, Hammersmith, London W6

The purpose of the Society and Kelmscott Fellowship is to make the life, work and ideas of Morris better known through talks, meetings, exhibitions and visits. It encourages the re-publication of his works and the continued manufacture of his textile and wallpaper designs. Membership, on subscription, is open to all who support its aims.

NATIONAL FEDERATION OF SELF-EMPLOYED, Sec: J. Waters, 32 St Anne's Road West, St Anne's-on-Sea, Lancs. FY8 1NY

With 509 branches throughout the United Kingdom, the organization issues policy reports and gives an advisory service to its members. Group membership is at present under consideration. Quote FBCS membership when writing.

PRINT COLLECTORS' CLUB, Royal Society of Painter-Etchers and Engravers, 26–27 Conduit Street, New Bond Street, W1R 9TA Tel: 01–493 5436

The club was founded in 1921 to enable those interested in etching and engraving to meet others of kindred tastes and to take part in its activities. Meetings, illustrated lectures, symposiums and practical demonstrations are held regularly, and a commissioned work, with a limited edition, is available as numbered proofs to members.

RED ROSE GUILD OF DESIGNER CRAFTSMEN, Hon. Treasurer: Dr H. M. Spittle, Donkey Cross, 9 Knutsford Road, Wilmslow, Cheshire. Tel: 09964 22150

Since the guild was formed in 1921 it has been raised to national status by eminent exhibitors. Nationwide membership: full craft, associate and lay.

SBA: THE ASSOCIATION OF INDEPENDENT BUSINESSES, Europe House, World Trade Centre, London E1 9AA. Tel: 01–481 8669

The aims of the association are that skill, talent and enterprise will be rewarded; thrift will be encouraged; and individual liberty will be preserved. Its wider aim is to protect independent businesses from exploitation by large public companies or nationalized corporations, and from restrictive bureaucratic interference. The SBA is not committed to any political party and is solely concerned with protecting the interests of the self-employed and all small businesses, as well as providing services regarding raising capital, importing and exporting procedures and international contacts.

SOCIETY OF DESIGNER-CRAFTSMEN, 6 Queen Square, London WC1N 3AR. Tel: 01–278 2214

The society, existing to uphold and strengthen the professional status of designer-craftsmen in this country through exhibitions, information, conferences, liaison with other organizations, awards and internal newsletters, has a specific concern for the independent craftsman operating on a full-time basis. The Standing Committee on Professional Practice issues a schedule of codes and advice prepared to meet the specific needs of craftsmen. Exhibitions are organized in various places to present a comprehensive range of activity of exceptionally high standard, to illustrate special aspects of design and to provide efficient selling outlets. Full craft membership is awarded to professional craftsmen whose work is assessed on quality, suitability for purpose, and shows evidence of an ability to recognize and tackle complex problems which may be technical, environmental, economic or artistic in nature. Licentiateship can be applied for by student members of at least six months standing and entitles the member to submit work for exhibitions. Fellowships are elected at full council meetings; associate membership is open to anyone interested in the objects and aims of the society. The letters MSD-C, LSD-C, and FSD-C are professional titles.

COUNTY

Beds. and Herts.

BEDFORDSHIRE AND HERTFORDSHIRE GUILD FOR CRAFTSMEN, Hon. Sec: Mrs Jean Younger, 8 Brackendale Grove, Harpenden, Herts. Tel: 058 27 61235

Formed in 1974 with the object of representing craftsmen; prospective craftsmen are especially encouraged. Among the facilities offered are legal advice, centralized buying, marketing, and exhibitions.

Berkshire

THE BERKSHIRE CRAFT CENTRE ASSOCIATION, The Old Brewery, Denmark Street, Wokingham. Tel: 0734 782039

An association which offers tuition in a variety of crafts. Funds are raised by local events and tuition paid by a membership and low tuition fee.

CLERKENWELL GREEN ASSOCIATION FOR CRAFTSMEN, Sec: M. Costain, 27 Old Street, London EC1. Tel: 01–253 4143

The initial aim of the association was to maintain, improve and provide small workshops in the new conservation area of Clerkenwell. Its Craft Advisory Bureau provides an advisory service, giving information on all matters related to crafts, skills and services in the London Borough of Islington. It is an administrative centre, and a focal point of craftsmen and their work.

Cornwall

THE CORNWALL CRAFTS ASSOCIATION, Hon. Sec: Joan M. Lee, The Chevin, Seaton, Torpoint PL11 3JQ. Tel: Downderry (05035) 239

An association formed in 1973 of those interested in the future of the crafts in Cornwall. Membership is open to all practising craftsmen or supporters of the crafts who live or work in Cornwall. But the committee, under the chairmanship of Wyndham Goodden, OBE, former Professor at the Royal College of Art, does practise stringent selection criteria when work is submitted for exhibition. Principal events are annual week-end and one-day seminars, with distinguished speakers from the crafts world; exhibitions; and a social events programme. Progressive projects include proposals for the establishment, in south-west Cornwall, of a residential crafts centre with workshops and a permanent exhibition gallery.

Cumbria

GUILD OF LAKELAND CRAFTSMEN, Sec: Mrs J. Williams, Low Holme, Kentmere, Kendal. Tel: Staveley 505

The guild was founded in 1951 and exhibits annually in Windermere. It covers the six (old) northern counties and membership is classified as full craft, associate craft, and lay.

Devon

THE DEVON GUILD OF CRAFTSMEN, Sec: Mrs F. S. Kline, Parkway Mill, Chudleigh, Newton Abbot TQ13 0JL. Tel: Chudleigh 853121

The guild was formed in 1955 as a composite body covering a wide variety of craftwork in the South-West. Full members are elected after submitting a selection of their work to the council, who appraise it in accordance with their criteria on design and workmanship. An annual exhibition is held of selected pieces of full members. Membership as an associate is open to any interested person. A Devon Guild week-end is held at Dartington Hall each spring.

Dorset

DORSET COUNTY ARTS AND CRAFTS ASSOCIATION, Sec: John Rome, Lydlinch Studio, Lydlinch, Sturminster Newton. Tel: Sturminster Newton 72375

Formed at the beginning of this century, "to revive and promote the study of the old handicrafts which once flourished in England", by a nucleus of craftsmen who are now well established, their annual exhibition has become one of the largest of its kind in the country.

Essex

ESSEX HANDICRAFTS ASSOCIATION, Hon. Sec: Mrs Shearcroft, White Cottage, Boyton Cross, Roxwell, Chelmsford CM1 4LS. Tel: Roxwell 648

An association open to all who are interested in craftwork. No rules governing membership. The aims are to encourage and promote a variety of crafts particularly in the schools and among the disabled, to which end classes are organized culminating in an exhibition each spring. Upwards of a thousand entries are made annually.

Gloucestershire

THE CRAFTSMEN OF GLOUCESTERSHIRE, Hon. Sec: Mrs Marjorie Smith, 66 Prestbury Road, Cheltenham GL52 2DA. Tel: Cheltenham 52782
An association formed in 1968, of full-time self-employed craftsmen with individual workshops. Its principal exhibition is held every July at the Tithe Barn, Southam, near Cheltenham.

GUILD OF GLOUCESTERSHIRE CRAFTSMEN, Hon. Treasurer: G. I. W. Brotherton, Hambutts Barn, Edge Lane, Painswick. Tel: Painswick 813559
Founded in 1933, the guild's roots go back to the ideals and genius of Ernest Gimson and the brothers Ernest and Sidney Barnsley. Membership, confined to craftsmen in Gloucestershire who derive at least part of their living by making and selling their work, is selective. The standards of the guild are high and adequate workshop facilities are essential. Membership denotes mastership of the craft. Associates usually serve for two years before final election to full membership status. Patrons are welcome as friends of the guild. An annual exhibition is held during the first three weeks of August at Painswick.

Herefordshire

GUILD OF HEREFORDSHIRE CRAFTSMEN, Clerk: Mr R. S. Hesbrook, Cosira, 24 Belle Vue Terrace, Malvern. Tel: Malvern 64506
Founded in 1953, the guild extends the general aims to include the sharing between craftsmen of commissions for the restoration of churches and other historical buildings, and providing publicity for the work of traditional craftsmen who earn their living by their craft. Membership is granted to those craftsmen whose craft, which represents their main support, reaches the standard set by the court of the guild.

SOCIETY OF CRAFTSMEN, Old Kemble Galleries, 29 Church Street, Hereford HR1 2LR Tel: Hereford 66049. Hon. Sec: Mrs C. Bulmer, Little Breinton, Hereford. Tel: 2022
A non-profit-making organization founded in 1961, the society is run by a voluntary committee to market members' work at the Old Kemble Galleries and the society's other showcases at three hotels, in addition to various exhibitions. Craft members submit samples of their work for approval and acceptance by the committee, which comprises practising craftsmen. The wares are displayed on sale or return at commission, to cover the running costs of the gallery. The Cellar Gallery can also be rented for one-man exhibitions. Membership is open to craft and lay members.

Herts

WELWYN CRAFTWORKERS GUILD, Hon. Sec: Miss P. Antink, 2 Castle Road, Fleetville, St Albans. Tel: St Albans 58435
The guild was first founded in 1945 and has up-dated its aims and purposes

to fulfil a role in modern society by exploring the possibilities of providing a craft centre for young people as a youth craft club, as well as adhering to the more conventional constitution of its original formation. Craft membership of the guild is granted to members whose work is judged to be of a consistently high standard. Associate membership is also offered to lay craftsmen or those who are simply interested in craft generally.

Isle of Man

THE ISLE OF MAN CRAFT ASSOCIATION, Sec: Mrs J. Gunnell, White Cottage, Main Road, Ballabeg, Arbory. Tel: Castletown 2607
A very energetic group of craftworkers whose range embodies: pottery, needlecraft, rushwork, dried and pressed flowers, woodware, crochet and knitwear, jewellery, sculpture, lapidary, copper and pewter work, spinning, weaving and gimping, soft toys, pebble designs, candles, shell designs, embedding, tweeds and mohair, and Manx dolls. Retailed mainly through the association's own shop in Douglas.

Kent

HAWKHURST GUILD OF ARTS AND CRAFTS, Hon. Sec: Mrs P. Davis, 12 Mercers, Hawkhurst. Tel: 058 05 3346
A guild which, according to the secretary, is "mainly for amateurs and enthusiasts", although the constitution states the same aims and rules of management which apply to most other guilds. Membership is subject to the approval of an elected committee.

Lincolnshire

GUILD OF LINCOLNSHIRE CRAFTSMEN, Sec: Mrs Sibyl Burgess, Jews Court, Steep Hill, Lincoln. Tel: 0522 33555
Membership is open only to practising craftsmen. The guild has its headquarters at the only craft centre in the county, and the only one of its kind in the country. Work from local craftsmen is displayed and sold in the two exhibition galleries.

Norfolk

NORFOLK CONTEMPORARY CRAFTS COMMITTEE, Hon. Sec: Peter Lane, The White House, Keswick Road, Cringleford, Norwich. Tel: 0603 55002
Set up initially with a CAC grant, launching several events to promote the artist-craftsman in East Anglia, there is now a permanent display of selected contemporary craftwork in Norwich Castle Museum, to which may be added work from a wider area than the immediate region, as necessary, to enable the highest quality work available to be exhibited. A crafts shop, on similar lines to the one at the Victoria and Albert Museum, is also run by the museum. Exhibitions and conferences are held, and an illustrated register of local craftsmen is produced. Future plans include the possible establishment of a crafts study centre in Norwich.

GREAT YARMOUTH GUILD OF ARTISTS AND CRAFTSMEN, Hon. Sec: Miss D. Hazel, The Hazels, Runham, Near Filby, Great Yarmouth. Tel: Fleggburgh 221

A guild which extends membership to full artist and craft members, associates, groups as affiliated associates, and juniors. Providing facilities for study and practice is one of the ways in which potential talent is nurtured.

NORFOLK RURAL CRAFTSMEN'S GUILD, Hon. Sec: Mrs M. Chapman, The Charters, Fleggburgh, Great Yarmouth

The guild was formed in 1951 to promote interest and to maintain a high standard in the rural crafts of Norfolk. Membership is restricted to craftsmen within the county who conform to the guild's standards. Associate membership is open to those who are interested in the guild's ideals.

North-west

MID-PENNINE ASSOCIATION FOR THE ARTS, 28 Back Street, James Street, Burnley, Lancs. Tel: 0282 29513

Supported by North West Arts Association to aid the artist through exhibitions. Two galleries are run by the association. The policy towards fellowship schemes is under consideration.

Somerset

THE SOMERSET GUILD OF CRAFTSMEN, Hon. Organizing Sec: R. D. F. Wild, Guild Hall, St Margarets, Hamilton Road, Taunton

The guild, founded in 1933, is governed by a Master and Court of Assistants. Craft membership is obtained by submission of work to the court for selection and is not confined to persons resident in the county of Somerset. Associate membership is also open to any interested person. The beautiful Guild Hall, the guild's headquarters where meetings are held, was built by the Abbot of Glastonbury in the reign of Henry VIII on the site of a twelfth-century lazar house. Guild exhibitions are held at least once a year, and venues have included the Bishop's Palace, Wells. Members' work is to be seen at the Bath and West Show and numerous examples can be found in their Guild Church of St Thomas of Canterbury at Pylle, near Shepton Mallet, as well as at the Guild Hall at Taunton.

Suffolk

SUFFOLK CRAFT SOCIETY, Sec: Mrs R. Jacob, Padley Water, Chillesford, Woodbridge. Tel: Orford 523

Formed in 1971 by craftsmen living and working in Suffolk, the society stages an annual exhibition at The Maltings, and has held joint exhibitions with the Norfolk Contemporary Craft Committee. Lectures and seminars are among the activities which help to realize the society's aims of educating the public about its members and their work. Members are elected after recommendation by the committee. Membership as a Friend of the Society is open to anyone interested in furthering its ideals, which include a permanent collection of members' work.

Surrey

SURREY CRAFTS ASSOCIATION, Public Relations Officer: J. C. Hollinghurst, Bureau of Industrial Liaison, University of Surrey, Guildford GU2 5XH. Tel: Guildford 71281 ext. 500

The association was inaugurated in 1975, and among its aims is the publication of a directory of its member craftworkers as a practical means of linking producers and customers. Membership is open to all who are interested in the crafts and wish to support the objects of the association. Meetings are arranged in the four quarters of the county as well as in the central area. Talks and discussions are planned on numerous aspects of the craftworkers' situation and include such vital matters as administration and management for small businesses.

Sussex

DITCHLING HANDWORKERS GUILD, Hon. Sec: Mrs E. M. Warman, Underhill Cottage, Westmeston, Hassocks, Sussex BN6 8XG. Tel: Hassocks 3505

Formed with the aim of encouraging interest in the practice of arts and crafts, the guild includes painters in its membership as well as craftsmen. An annual exhibition is held during the first two weeks of September, and has become widely known for its high standards.

GUILD OF SUSSEX CRAFTSMEN, Hon. Sec: Gordon Lawrie, 30 High Street, Steyning. Tel: Steyning 814056

Full membership of the guild, which was formed in 1970, is confined to residents of Sussex whose major source of income is derived from their craftwork, which is subjected to inspection by a panel to decide whether or not it has reached the prevailing standard set by the guild. Four or five exhibitions of members' work are staged each year. Associate membership is open to those generally interested in the crafts.

EAST SUSSEX GUILD OF CRAFTWORKERS, Hon. Sec: Miss D. Wilding, 6a Rotherfield Avenue, Bexhill-on-Sea, East Sussex TN40 1SY. Tel: Bexhill 216445

The guild was first formed in 1931 and, apart from the war years, has held an annual exhibition of its members' work which covers some thirty different crafts. Membership is open to all who are interested in handcrafts.

RYE SOCIETY OF ARTISTS, Hon. Sec: Mrs Joan Southan, 2 Roberts Row, Whitbread Lane, Beckley, Rye, Sussex TN31 6TY

Primarily founded in 1952 to bring together artists and craftsmen, the society holds lectures and a Summer exhibition.

THE WEST OF ENGLAND ASSOCIATION OF CRAFTSMEN, Hon. Sec: Mrs E. Collett, Townsend Farm, Littleton Drew, Chippenham, Wilts. Tel: Castle Combe 782441

Inaugurated in 1974, the association was formed as a result of several years' successful craft markets, held by some seventy craftsmen in the area. In addition to the arbitrary aims of the association, there is a plan to establish a permanent craft centre. Membership as craftsmen, associate or honorary, as defined by the council of the association, is open to residents in the west of England.

Worcestershire

THE WORCESTERSHIRE GUILD OF ARTIST-CRAFTSMEN, Hon. Director: Mrs M. E. Mundy, 16 Northwick Road, Evesham. Tel: Evesham 4584

The guild has been established for some twenty-three years and offers membership of three types: full craft, for proven professionally engaged craftsmen whose standards satisfy the selected committee; associate; and lay, which is not restricted to the confines of the county.

Yorkshire

GUILD OF YORKSHIRE CRAFTSMEN, Sec: Mrs J. Roberts, 29 Warner Avenue, Pogmoor, Barnsley. Tel: 0226 5166

Membership is reserved for practising craftsmen, but patrons are welcome, receiving notification of guild activities and invited to meetings and social gatherings. One of the policies of the guild is to direct the customer to the craftsman's workshop rather than involve itself in high pressure advertising.

4

Craftsmen's Common Problems

Despite the geniality generated by crafts and the promotion they receive, there are universal difficulties which create practical problems. Resolute he may be, but the craftsman has, by dint of his circumstance and indeed, his very definition, to compete in an advanced industrial society as a manufacturer and businessman. He will admit to being neither but, appellations apart, he has to sell what he makes, and is therefore subjected to the pressures of prevailing economic policies. Commerce makes no concession to the craftsman.

Particular difficulties related to different crafts disciplines are given in the sections devoted to the individual crafts. The general problems common to all are:

1 finding suitable premises in which to work, and having found them, getting planning permission to set up a workshop;
2 costing work to make craftwork economically viable;
3 marketing.

PREMISES·

> Pride in skill and achievement is an estimable trait, and everything possible should be done to provide rural craftsmen with full opportunities to ply their trades.
>
> *Extract from Report of the Committee on*
> *Land Utilization in Rural Areas,*
> *1942 (The Scott Report)*

That was thirty-five years ago. And yet the opportunities for craftsmen to ply their trades today are restricted even more, particularly in the rural areas. The very real concerns for local employment and continuity of time-honoured crafts appear to conflict although, in theory at least, the latter should solve the problem of the former. It is not a problem confined to the rural craftsman however, for his counterpart may be as easily found plying his craft within the city's wall as on the periphery of a farmstead.

Nothing more than a generalization could be given if a systematic survey of each county were not undertaken, for regional conditions are largely governed by geographical features. Therefore to put the problem in perspective local factors have to be briefly considered.

The problem of acquiring suitable premises is the one on which both the SFICs and COSIRA have formed working parties, as it appears to be general throughout the country. A survey was undertaken by SFIC (Cardiff) of the twenty-five development corporations in the UK, since the Development Commissioner's 33rd Report, published in 1974, made particular reference to the need for restoring the economic balance of the rural communities. This put forward a strong case for making a deliberate effort to introduce and maintain small industries and crafts for whom enormous openings, both national and local, are envisaged as incomes and standards rise.

Although some of the emergent points must remain confidential, it is evident that among the types of firm assisted by the Development Commission is the traditional village industry. Describing the vagaries of the employment situation, the report indicated, by evidence revealed in a similar survey undertaken in Scotland, that the small firm might be better placed to weather the storm than are the larger companies with their complex organization.

The report intimated, however, that whereas most planning authorities are prepared to set aside land for industrial development in the suburbs, they seldom extended this to the villages. Their tight planning control there, in the interest of physical amenity, often makes it impossible for a craftsman even to erect a workshop in his own garden. COSIRA, whose efforts in this field have been progressive, realistic and beneficial, tackles the problem locally through its County/Area Committees. Progress can be made through the establishment of a close relationship with planning authorities; through influencing local opinion on the need for adequate diversity of employment on the spot if a village is to be a living entity; and by laying great stress on the importance of the views of small industries committees being heard at the consultative stage of all plans for development being prepared by county planning authorities.

Coincident with the need for the identification of workshop premises was the extensive local authority reorganization: this has resulted, in some cases, in no comparable figures or records being available.

Northumberland, endeavouring to ward off the effects of rural depopulation, held one of the first of the Department of Employment's Training Opportunity Schemes in the county. This was a course in blacksmith's work and farriery operated under COSIRA instruction. Six saddlery and harness shops report full employment, with a recruitment programme launched to attract more people to the trade. Craft education, however, is also flourishing in the schools, due to the strong influence wielded by the past and present members of the Institute of Craft Education. Together with the Arts Federation of Tyne and Wear, the institute keeps the arts, in its widest sense, alive in the region (p. 79).

The Northern Arts Council was set up in 1961, but its role regarding crafts does not appear to have been very active until a working party was formed in 1975 to look closely at the craft area. This was a separate committee of the visual arts panel, with an independent craft budget.

The working party decided that craft should be firmly structured in the region before a craft officer was appointed, thereby devoting all its budget to those facilities which seemed necessary after a survey was made of craftsmen's needs. The establishment of a regional craft centre or two small quality pilot centres was regarded as an item of major significance, but the venue has yet to be decided. The majority of craftsmen are in Cumbria, but although tourist centres have certain advantages, the conurbations of Tyne and Wear or Cleveland are equal possibilities. Close attention is also being paid to the needs of young craftsmen and to the regional crafts in danger of extinction. The two local crafts of stick-dressing and pipe-making have an enthusiastic following in LEA evening classes but hardly constitute a local industry. Cumbria, since reorganization the second largest county in England, has an active crafts industry, and proposals to set up a regional craft centre have been made.

Yorkshire, also affected by the re-shuffling of local government, lost its three ridings, and contacts with former county and district councils were broken. North Yorkshire, the largest county in England, embraces a variety of crafts within its 3,000 square miles, but has scarcely a dozen saddlers to cope with something like forty-two riding schools and stables, and eight racecourses. Throughout Yorkshire, in its entirety, there are about two hundred small rural craft workshops ranging from a single ropemaker to the Mouseman's furniture concern.

Most work on marketable end-products, mainly to order. Insular and isolated, the Yorkshire craftsman tends to shun publicity and expansion. Obviously, trends and conditions vary widely in such a large region, but new planning departments contacted so far show a less rigid attitude on the siting of industry in villages, and COSIRA gave help to a number of firms which appealed successfully against planning permission refusals. Rural communities have benefited from carefully selected craft industries, where employment has been created not only in the immediate vicinity, but also further afield, by the use of out-workers.

Lancashire's boundaries have also buckled, so assessing its current craft situation is done with some reservation. Being mainly an industrialized county, it has problems of continuity in traditional crafts. Despite there being willow-beds in the western area, only three basketmakers appear to be working and have to compete with a large number of imported articles. There is a demand for more saddlers as the horse population increases but few are attracted away from the higher factory wage. A new generation of potters, many from universities, is springing up, replacing the older body of farriers, saddlers and basket-workers. In the Cheshire, Shropshire (Salop) and Staffordshire areas, farriery apprenticeship applications exceed the number of vacancies.

The Merseyside Arts Association supports the early eighteenth-century Blue Coat Hospital, acquired in 1927 by an enthusiastic arts group who formed the Bluecoat Society of Arts (p. 75), a charitable trust, who planned to administer the building as a centre for the arts.

Derbyshire, in an effort to stem depopulation, now permits a limited number of small firms to operate in the rural areas, having previously insisted on industrial sites.

Redevelopment in Nottinghamshire towns has caused widespread demolition, with the result that a fair number of firms have been seeking premises in surrounding villages. Suitable small sites are at a premium, the new industrial estates offer plot sizes far in excess of requirements, and established rural firms experience some difficulty in getting planning permission for extensions. There being no craft guilds, associations or centres, the majority of rural craftsmen do all they can to publicize each other's work, often selling for each other too. Very few are to be found in the county's tourist area. There are many willow-holts in the Trent Valley, but only one basket-maker now working.

The geographical structure imposed by reorganization on Lincolnshire and Humberside resulted in a total population of about 1,350,000. A great interest in craftwork in the county has been engendered by the policy of the Lincolnshire and South Humberside Arts, an independent regional arts association. Assistance from CAC has made possible the first full-time crafts officer employed by a regional arts association in Britain: Sibyl Burgess has wide responsibilities, which include running the crafts centre.

Several craft markets have sprung up in market towns and attract the support of the local authorities. There has been a marked growth in craft industries, maybe related to the increased tourism in the area, particularly in the pottery field; but geographical Lincolnshire has a strong regional identity of its own, and therefore many of its activities are well-established. The form of arts service to be provided in North Humberside has yet to be determined.

The North-West was subjected to an incredible transformation in Victorian times: Scunthorpe evolved from an agricultural district of five small villages into a municipality of some 70,000, due to the exploitation of the vast ironstone beds, believed to be the most extensive in Europe. Changing with the demands, some trades underwent an unbelievable metamorphosis. The most startling is the small concern originally established in 1845 to produce hand-made hats from rabbit skins, progressing through the re-cycling business to incorporation within the largest scrap metal producers in western Europe. It now efficiently converts scrap into the raw materials needed by the steelworks – a far cry from its original rural trade!

The demand for new workshops has been particularly high in Leices-tershire, but as it is a heavily industrialized area these are unlikely to be the craft type. Basketry once proliferated but has now virtually died out. Boutiques, rather than centres, tend to compete in the imported market. Saddlery is much in demand in the racing centres, but much leatherwork appears to be manufactured primarily in the Walsall area.

Northamptonshire, too, is a fairly 'horsey' area and apprentices are attracted to farriery, saddlery and wrought-ironwork, crafts stemming from the established blacksmith's trade. There appears to be no specific regional craft but a great variety are practised, ranging from boat-building to producing hand-made footwear. Rural life, on the whole, appears to be well established, but just how restrictive this situation can be was illustrated by a rural council refusing to renew planning per-missions for a crafts centre: in this case a single storey 30 foot by 20 foot building, a former tack-shed. Objections were mainly put forward in an attempt to "stop development in rural areas", but the building had not been altered, except for a notice on the door. The whole village objected to the objection. At least a quarter of the village people were involved in supplying the centre with craftwork, the only outlet for their artistic talents. The centre is still open, and of value to the community.

Although Cambridgeshire is a fast-expanding county in both agri-culture and industry, industry is barred from Cambridge itself and is segregated into zones close to large villages. A campaign has been quietly waged to establish the need to encourage small industries in the country areas.

The Royal Norfolk Show is often the stage début for most of the county's craftsmen. Many firms who began by exhibiting on COSIRA's stands have progressed to take space individually in the main part of the showground. A local furniture-makers' association is being formed. This is one of the crafts which thrives, along with sad-dlery and good quality wrought-ironwork, and potters continue to proliferate. The virtual cessation of herring fishing has affected the basketry trade, for quarter-cran baskets are no longer needed in their former quantities.

East Anglia is faced with the conflicting issues of retaining its rural aspect whilst developing in the industrial field, mainly through the GLC-sponsored estates. Traditional rural crafts continue to attract ap-prentices and COSIRA is closely involved with projected plans for sup-port for a craft society scheme.

The eastern counties, by and large, are affected by their proximity to London. It has been virtually impossible to obtain permission to build or expand workshops outside approved industrial estates in Essex, but COSIRA has done a great deal of work in exploring the possibilities of increased opportunities for the small firms north of the River Crouch. Bedfordshire and Hertfordshire are benefiting from a change in policy wrought by newly-formed councils who have their own ideas for their district, and a council-owned water-mill has been converted to a working crafts centre. A crafts guild has also been successfully launched.

Surrey's serious planning difficulties are inevitable, but there is now a greater understanding of the needs of small rural firms. Brick-making, due to clay deposits; and underwood industries, due to the chestnut coppice, grown in the county and drawn from Kent, accounted for a once thriving rural crafts sector. The arts-crafts now tend to outweigh the more traditional ones but about three hundred people appear to be engaged in craftwork of some kind, ranging from walking-sticks to straw targets, and from musical instruments to hand-made roofing-tiles.

Hand-made bricks may seem an anachronism in today's society, but more and more architects are asking for them for use in many parts of the country. One Hampshire firm was producing something like $2\frac{1}{2}$ million in 1972; but in Sussex, where it was one of the oldest traditional industries using local clay deposits, the number of companies fully operational dwindled to about 7 in 1970, compared with 104 at the turn of the century. It is a trade which is subjected to the general national expansion or recession, so the marked increase in demand for the special hand-made bricks and tiles may alter the situation yet again. Sussex is famous for the manufacture of the trug, but its effect as a regional occupation is, of course, minimal (p. 135). Traditional craft industries are sympathetically considered, for a great deal of interest in them is generated at county council level, although no formal policy or support has yet been formulated. The establishment of a craft centre is being actively pursued. A very explicit paper outlining the need for country workshops has been produced by COSIRA, for village industry in general tends to be discouraged due to increasing pressure on the space available and the need for preservation of its rural character. To direct a conservation argument indiscriminately against village industry in general can, however, jeopardize the future of the smaller close-knit communities.

Persistent lobbying of Kent planning authorities to persuade them to rethink their policies on craft workshop applications in rural areas seems likely to gain exemption for small firms from the hitherto rigidly applied Use Classes Order. Local craft exhibitions have been increasingly used on the marketing side, and the Kent Professional Potters Association has been formed.

The M4 and M40 developments further aggravated the problems of obtaining rural workshops in the Oxfordshire, Berkshire and Buckinghamshire region; whereas Warwickshire, predominantly dependent on the motor industry, offers a reasonable chance to the small craft-type industry, while the larger manufacturing concerns find difficulty in procuring the necessary larger space.

As the motorways link cities and countryside, the undesirable prospect of rural communities degenerating into dormitory villages becomes a real threat. Change is inevitable with progress, but the current pace of change has never been paralleled in the whole history of the western world. This has coloured the attitudes of the planners in those areas particularly vulnerable to urban encroachment.

Whilst the now extinct county of Herefordshire was giving cause for concern because of its progressive depopulation, the neighbouring county of Gloucestershire – the large part of which is a designated "area of outstanding natural beauty" – has been the subject of careful scrutiny by prospecting industrialists and keen conservationists. Close liaison between pertinent organizations establishes the priorities and removes the prejudices.

A consultative report drawn up by the area committee of COSIRA, who with over half a century's experience of the problems confronting the very small firm and craftsmen is well qualified to speak on their behalf, challenges the present planning policy, whereby all "industry" is bracketed together, irrespective of size or scope. Sensitive to the dangers that can arise from indiscriminate re-structuring, *The Case for Small Firms in Rural Areas* underlines the social and economic reasons for keeping the villages as "places where work was done", and sees other alternatives as a departure from their historical role.

Gloucestershire County Council has no specific policy of establishing craft industries, but considers all planning applications on their merits, taking into account all other general planning requirements and standards, environmental and aesthetic factors and availability of public services. The extent to which noise and dust will be created from the loading and delivery of materials is considered, in an effort to ensure that the establishment of a workshop will not be of detriment to adjacent owners and occupiers.

Accepting that by definition many craft uses fall within the "light industrial use" classification, it is obvious that precautions should be undertaken. Relating the planning permission to a specific applicant overcomes the problem caused by the single, silent silversmith moving to other premises, and a rather more unneighbourly, noisy, dusty "light industrial user" becoming established under the original consent. Personalized and temporary consents – the latter being useful because they can be extinguished within a relatively short period – are safeguards over the craftsmen changing their scale of operations or product, which could create environmental problems.

Wessex and Hampshire are generally responsive to the craft-type industries and have their own regional societies and exhibitions. A Wessex Inward Trade Mission, organized in collaboration with the British Overseas Trade Board, is a progressive project. Remnants of Dorset's strong craft tradition are still manifested, although on a reduced scale, through such diverse fields as hand-made bricks and net-making (p. 159). Allied to this, derived from the extensive growth of flax and hemp from medieval times, was a strong sail-making industry which is now dead. Broadly speaking, there is sympathy towards industry in villages, although the "contain industry in industrial estates" attitude still persists in certain areas. The rural council shares its building with the craft guild, and works closely with it and COSIRA. Somerset is willow land (p. 125), but glove-making was also once a local industry. Pottery, here as elsewhere, has evolved through the tourist trade. Pottery became an indigenous business early on in Devon, established because of clay deposits. Lace is traditionally associated with Honiton, and a shop in the town sells the pieces, embodied in brooches, which are geared to the souvenir market. The rural skills are kept going in this predominantly agricultural county, whereas the newly developed arts-crafts are stimulated by the holiday trade.

Tourism is one of the key industries of Cornwall, the major part of which is still designated as a development area. Taking a general view, one could hazard a fairly safe guess that the county contains more people engaged in the arts and crafts than any other region and is internationally famous in this field. The county council, as planning authority, has always tried to encourage the establishment and security of those engaged in craftwork, seeing them in true context of traditional village occupations whilst stabilizing the rural population. Even within a county, however, different policies prevail according to immediate local circumstances, so different districts have to determine their own priorities.

A large area of the Penwith District is designated as an "area of outstanding natural beauty", which restricts the indiscriminate growth of workshops, particularly as vehicular access is very limited. The urban areas, particularly St Ives and Penzance, have well-established craft markets and workshops successfully catering for both the tourist trade and the very keen local craft fraternity. Applications for conversion of old property for such use generally receive favourable consideration.

The Borough of Restormel has a general presumption against any development in the countryside unless special justification is offered, and would expect such establishments to be set up in the towns and larger villages.

Kerrier's general policy is to encourage the setting up of crafts concerns, particularly if it will introduce 'industry' on an accepted scale into villages, thereby providing local employment and retaining economically active people, creating a more virile village community.

Caradon say they have no specific policy; each application is decided on its merits in the light of general development policies. This line is also followed by Carrick, although they show favourable consideration to craft industries in locations where other manufacturing processes would be frowned upon. As an illustration of their tendency to encourage the individual crafts worker, they have granted studio potteries, and in one case a weaving concern to establish small hand-looms in the homes of the participants, with a central dispersal point in the village.

North Cornwall affords sympathetic consideration to genuine craft applications but is faced with two special problems: the demand for workshops in rural areas lacking public transport, with the difficulty in ensuring employment of local people; and distinguishing between country crafts and small industrial ventures, which often mushroom out of all proportion from their original set-up into producing nicknacks.

In holiday regions specifically, but also in Cornwall in general, there is the constant compromise between encouraging craftwork, thereby creating employment and supporting local industry, and restricting the production of gimmicky goods. Many set out full of good intentions to devote their talents to the crafts, but eventually diversify because of the insatiable tourist trade, and develop into primarily a retailing outlet for Cornish piskies made in Hong Kong and fancy goods from far-off places, thus defeating the original object. It is little wonder that such applications are viewed with caution.

Definition seems to be the crux of the whole problem. A discussion paper presented to the County Planning Officers' Society dealt in depth with the extent to which the designer-craftsman was affected by the present regulations. Choice of words has obviously played a more prominent part in the whole structure of planning permission than any other factor. Particularly open to misinterpretation are the terms: *industry, rural industry, development,* and *light industrial users.* The society were of the view that sympathetic consideration should be given to the particular position of the craftsman (a term which can also be counted on to start an academic argument), whilst stressing that the back-up information was important when applying for formal planning permission. In many cases applicants had done themselves a disservice by not being specific as to their proposed activities.

The Society of Designer-Craftsmen, aware of the problems which beset craftsmen, particularly the younger ones who have yet to establish themselves, has taken the initiative to influence planning authorities in favour of craft workshops. It has already made moves to support the Camden Lock Tenants Association, and is researching further into the property market, for the aforementioned considerations are basically concerned with the integration of craft industries in the village structure, whereas the towns and cities have their own specialized problems.

A pioneer in the complex organization which is primarily concerned with developing workshops in the conservation area of Clerkenwell, a parish of London, is Michael Murray, director of the

Clerkenwell Green Association for craftsmen (p. 76), a concept with far-reaching influence.

HELP – PROMOTIONAL AND FINANCIAL

We rarely deal with village crafts, the main emphasis is on large companies or projects with considerable success in the exporting field.

BBC – Made in Britain

So, having got his workshop, the small craftsman has to compete with the successful craftsman to get promotion of his product. It is a problem on which the Society of Designer-Craftsmen is actively engaged. The society publishes literature on the subject and seeks to establish contacts as widely as possible, but it is a volunteer organization and the pioneering needs to be greatly increased to show practical returns in the form of new attitudes towards the idea of bringing teams of craftsmen in on the ground floor of major environmental projects. A crafts promotion bureau, encouraging exports, placing work, giving slides and information to potential buyers, galleries and retail outlets is an aim of the society.

The relationship between craftwork and industry is referred to elsewhere (see especially p. 282), but it is an issue not exclusive to the English situation; other industrialized countries recognize that an industry needs to sustain and develop the art and craft forms on which it is based and to which it owes its very being.

The Design Council maintains an illustrated record of good industrial design and also holds occasional craft exhibitions. CAC has an Index of Craftsmen, a highly selective collection of colour slides and information on British artist-craftsmen's work; of the 349 craftsmen currently indexed, 105 are ceramic artists.

COSIRA offers publicity to craftsmen in rural areas by way of entry into their *Guide to Country Workshops*. The regional officers are usually able to direct enquiries to a suitable craftsman whose work is known to them. Guild secretaries also introduce potential customers to members' work.

Although the Victoria and Albert Museum had claimed to having "no specific policy with regard to the promotion or encouragement of craftwork, having been founded very largely in connection with developments in industrial design", apart from including "much craft-produced material in its collections to represent influential and important movements within the decorative arts generally", it is the first major museum to house a shop specially devoted to selling original craftwork, under the aegis of the British Crafts Centre. The impact of this historic move reverberated throughout the craft world with its record-breaking exhibition when 'the makers' demonstrated their contemporary crafts before the public.

The Victoria and Albert Museum staff have also been among the museum experts who have given valuable instruction to the members of NADFAS, an organization dedicated to the enjoyment and custody of the visual arts, on such matters as restoration. Exhibitions, demonstrations and displays, although different in form, have the same promotional aim but, as CAC puts it, they only exist while someone is looking at them and can be compared to theatrical performances, where clearly defined artistic principles have to be followed in order to attract and affect their audience.

Apart from the international intercourse promoted by WCC – its first world crafts exhibition attracting some 750,000 visitors – overseas contacts are often established through the British Council which organizes British exhibitions touring abroad as part of its aim of developing closer cultural relations between countries.

Nearer home, however, there is a great deal of free publicity and promotional aid available, if it is sought. Anything that takes the ideas out of the workshop and presents them in a tangible form to potential customers must be worth considering.

The National Federation of Women's Institutes is well known for its interest in the crafts. Local branches find their own speakers and demonstrators, and thus the skill of the craftsman is taken to village halls in the remotest corners of the country. And those who dismiss these efforts as parochial pastimes should remember the national craft exhibition held in 1975, appropriately entitled "Tomorrow's Heirlooms". Moreover, it was at the 1970 annual general meeting of the National Federation of Women's Institutes that a resolution was passed pressing the government to treat the crafts on a par with the arts. This resulted in the development of the Crafts Advisory Committee.

A few leaflets may not come amiss in the local hotels; the manager may especially welcome them if visitors are allowed in the workshop, for they like to know that guests have interesting places to visit in the locality. A sketch map is essential on these leaflets. A brief list of notable past commissions, if they can be viewed in public buildings, gives potential customers a chance to appraise the work without embarrassment.

Regional magazines, arts associations, and the British Touring Authority publish calendars of events in which notices of exhibitions are inserted free of charge. The craftsman should befriend the press and keep a cuttings-file for potential customers and impressionable journalists. He should keep a record of outstanding projects, letters, photographs, exhibitions, lectures, demonstrations and any press articles. This not only presents his work in a business-like way but also serves as his professional curriculum vitae when he is applying for membership of societies such as SDC. It also assists him in presenting his case logically and coherently to bodies such as CAC or COSIRA, if he is seeking financial aid.

Business management, within which costing, advertising and marketing is embodied, is a major aspect of COSIRA's services. The problem of quantifying time, materials and profitability seems almost insoluble to a vast number of craftsmen.

The single-handed craftsman's output capacity is naturally limited to what he can produce with his own two hands, so the self-sufficient life which is considered synonymous with craftwork is often forced upon him; smallholding husbandry cutting the household expenses. Part-time teaching is also the lifeline to solvency for the majority of self-employed craftsmen. Increased output means employing workers with the attendant worries of providing regular wages, insurance, rules and regulations, and increased paper work.

Workshop training grants are available through CAC. This is a major innovation, for in this way financial help is offered to the individual craftsman. Together with loans, they form an important part of CAC's services towards the newly-qualified craftsman getting himself established in the early years, and the established craftsman wishing to take on an apprentice. Loans on a short-term basis are also available to those wishing to modify or enlarge their workshops, and there is a further flexible scheme to any approved one-off specialized project, although up to now the response to the latter has not revealed the imaginative kind of proposal originally envisaged.

By far the most dramatic scheme was the launching in 1974 of a number of bursaries each year to established craftsmen, to release them from the pressures of their workshop and give them time to research, experiment, pursue a specific project and generally re-appraise their work. The newest grant scheme to be introduced is specifically for research study and special training for short periods.

Awards are made from a number of sources: the Royal Society of Arts give bursaries to selected designer-craftsmen; and in recognition of the revival of skilled handicraft the *Sunday Telegraph Magazine*, in association with John Player & Sons, instituted annual British Crafts Awards in 1977, organized through the main national crafts bodies. Some regional arts associations award fellowships; Lincolnshire was the first to do this, and, with practical help from CAC, provided a cottage and workshop. The bursary is for a specified period of time, usually two years, and the recipients are then encouraged to stay in the area, thereby developing a community of practising craftsmen in the region.

MARKETING

I would defend to the death the right of a craftsman to sell his work from his own front door and not be bothered with shops or galleries. If he can do this and make the living he wants, then jolly good luck to him. Otherwise, I feel he may be best advised to leave the selling of his work to shops and galleries whose sole function this is, who are *unsubsidized* and risking their own money and therefore have the greatest incentive to sell, and who are, after all, specialists in this, just as the craftsman is a specialist in making the work in the first place.

Peter Dingley

When Peter Dingley opened his shop and gallery, over a decade ago, for the express purpose of selling things made by hand by individual artist-craftsmen, it was about the only place of its kind in the country. In the very heart of England – Stratford-upon-Avon – thousands of visitors searched aimlessly for something made in Britain; now, if they are selective enough, they can buy British hand-made craft goods all over the country. The craft shop is a product of the seventies. But marketing is still a major problem. I asked the craftsmen why.

A lot of so called craft shops, yes, but a great number of them are staffed by people whose idea of craft stops at crochet egg-cosies, fancy canework from the Far East or downright gimmicky nonsense.

In most cases trade buyers mark up by 100 per cent; when we sell through a wholesaler the resultant double mark-up makes the product prohibitively expensive, except possibly in Texas!

The London stores are not interested unless you sell your craftwork dirt cheap. Many put on a 300 per cent mark-up saying their overheads are much higher than those of country towns, this puts your work in the luxury class, but does not relate to what the maker receives.

One large London store made an appointment for me to see the buyer. I was kept waiting for two hours to be told that he had all the dolls he wanted now from the Far East.

What has happened to all that "buy British" and "back Britain" fuss? I came out of a large store with my craftwork, which had been rejected by the buyer in favour of cheap imported ware, and overheard an American complaining that she had found nothing hand-made in Britain. Even the Welsh dolls and Cornish pixies, she said, had "made in Hong Kong" stamped on them.

The only overseas sale I could have made was for a Japanese firm who wanted a thousand "identical" toys: an impossibility for my one pair of hands!

Many retailers are in fact supported by the craftsman: by operating on the iniquitous basis of sale or return they live on the goodwill of the primary producer – a situation which could never happen in a commercial-industrial set-up.

Sometimes one finds ones work is classed "too good" for the average high street shop but not 'irregular' enough for the craft label where, shown with, say, silverwork, it looks 'primitive'.

We can't compete with sophisticated and high-powered advertising, selling so much today, which in turn produces a buying public unable to think for itself.

And so on. Shop-keepers, for their part, often complain that good quality work is hard to find and that the craftsman tends to push his own ideas irrespective of what the public want.

There is no doubt that making and selling are irreconcilable factors in the minds of many craftsmen. Those with their own small showroom attached to their workshop are the exception, of course, and have the advantages of direct contact with their customers, thereby assessing at first hand what sells and what does not. Profits are higher, and payment is immediate, so more money is available to buy raw materials.

On the other hand, however, the craftsman either has to employ someone to mind the shop, or else devote some of his precious working time to do so himself. There is also the dubious advantage of the potential customer being able to watch some of the processes. This ought to lead to increased appreciation of the skill involved, but in reality it often turns into a free demonstration and a condensed lecture, and therefore a loss of continuity of production. The problem of apportioning time between production and marketing is a serious one.

Exhibitions are either regarded as a lifeline by the craftsman, who derives both pleasure and benefit from meeting other craftsmen, exchanging ideas, evaluating his own work in comparison with others, and making personal contact with the public; or they are abhorred for their affected image, their expense in staging, and the unproductive hours policing the exhibits to make sure that the pieces on which money and effort have been spent to attract an apathetic audience are not stolen.

Yet many feel the craftsman's place is in the local market-place, and this is where his work is increasingly to be found. Hundreds of market-stalls have conducted business under the WI banner for over half a century. The jam-and-pickle image is rapidly becoming a thing of the past as more area organizers and 'share-holders' (who, under the unique co-operative system, do not have to be WI members) seek out the work of local craftsmen to sell. With some 350 stalls scattered in the market-places of England and Wales, and an annual turnover of around £1,500,000, the modern market-place could become as important as the medieval one was.

Regular craft-markets are a phenomenon of the last couple of years. It would be impossible to list them all; some are held as seasonal events on village greens, others as monthly or even weekly features in town halls, disused chapels and church rooms. Specialized exhibitions run by the guilds tend to attract specialists; trade fairs attract serious buyers of potential prototypes for commercial exploitation; and agricultural shows attract the family group bent on a day out – the impulse purchaser. It is of little use, therefore, to exhibit a pricey wall-hanging or expensive way-out jewellery.

It is hard to assess the value of exhibiting. Direct-sales figures are sometimes low, but customers often turn up with an out-dated catalogue seeking the craftsman years after the exhibition took place. An exhibitor's value as a means of introducing new designs is inestimable, for many customers would otherwise just seek a copy of something they had seen elsewhere – and all craftsmen welcome challenging commissions.

Official help is often rejected by the craftsman who, as a very independent individual, does not like to be too organized and sees help as just so much more paperwork. But it is finding which market suits him best which is often the problem facing the craftsman, for he sees the marketing systems available to him as fragmented: CAC as too arts-orientated, selective and exclusive; London-based centres as too London-biased; regional guilds as too parochial; arts centres too bent on entertainment; and COSIRA stigmatized by the word *industry*.

Nevertheless, many do appreciate the work done on their behalf on the problems of marketing their work; most would welcome a national retailing organization, similar to the excellent Highland Home Industries scheme run for Scottish craftwork.

MARKETS (in brief)

The Association of British Craftsmen was initially formed to promote the sale of craftsmen's work, mostly working in wood, in Canada and America. This is still done to a limited extent.

Exhibitions are regularly staged by CAC, BCC, WCC, regional arts associations, guilds and associations, and museums. Another avenue worth further exploration is the facility offered by the Museums Association for travelling exhibitions. Eight area councils have been set up to organize these in provincial museums.

Agricultural shows are a perfect forum for craftsmen's work, especially the traditional rural trades. Surprisingly, the National Farmers' Union has no official capacity in arranging for exhibitions and demonstrations of this kind, but gives willing support to COSIRA, whose area officer will be aware of big national shows staged in his region. Demonstrations are often welcomed.

Some hotels and theatres afford facilities for small displays of local craftwork.

Building societies seem, generally, to welcome changing displays of craftwork in their usually spacious windows.

Libraries are also more receptive to staging small displays, especially if related to the locality.

Most towns hold craft-markets of some kind – contact the district council.
WI stall space – contact the local secretary.

PUBLICATIONS

COSIRA: *Marketing, Export Made Easy,* and offers services on general management.

COSIRA: *Guide to Country Workshops in Britain* is an annual book listing craftsmen who welcome visitors to their workshops and retail shops dealing in crafts.

CAC: *Crafts* magazine advertises galleries, craft shops and exhibitions.

Craft Shops and Galleries (reference list 6) lists in geographical order (currently) 232 retail outlets with a note of type of crafts sold.

Index of Craftsmen, colour slides and biographical information on craftsmen selected by a committee nominated by the British Crafts Centre. The Index can be consulted by appointment with the Librarian (Tel: 01–839 8000). 10 a.m. to 5 p.m. Monday to Saturday.

Register of Craftsmen, non-selective register. Craftsmen wishing to be included write for appropriate forms.

5

Charities

There are currently some 110,000 registered charitable organizations, but it would be impossible to attempt, in this volume, to make a comprehensive survey of the importance of craftwork within these organizations. Many charities are engaged in craftwork, but do not train craftsmen themselves, unless the training benefits a section of society accepted as a charitable class, such as the disabled.

Conversely, some craft groups have formed themselves into charitable companies within the very broad confines of what constitutes a charity. The concepts of relief, advancement and benefit to the community are open to interpretation, and to keep abreast of changing social conditions the charity commissioners have a certain amount of flexibility. Craft associations register as charities to safeguard their financial position so that they can further the promotion and expansion of associate ventures. The Clerkenwell Green Association (p. 76) and True Dovetail Ltd (Dove Centre p. 77) are two examples of craft ateliers established for the purposes of setting up workshops for craftsmen and giving information and craft education to the public. According to a ruling by the House of Lords in 1891, income tax relief is given to all charities alike, not only to those working for the relief of the poor, and this, together with exemption from certain other taxes and rates, ensures some financial security.

Very few of the charities for the disabled could make handicrafts a commercially viable proposition, but the therapeutic value of this activity is immense. Many disabled, such as those in the Cheshire Foundation Homes, suffer from severe progressive diseases, so it can take a long time to make one article, and the goods produced never reaches a market wider than relatives, friends and visitors to the homes. Moreover, the nature of the craftwork produced in these homes invariably depends on the teachers available and the capabilities of the residents.

Sheltered employment for the disabled was pioneered in the late eighteenth century: health and welfare the aims; charity the means. Since those days when the disabled were initially taken out of the realms of the Poor Law, they have been brought within the acknowledged and defined responsibilities of central and local government. During the Boer War the Lord Roberts' workshops were established, followed by rehabilitation departments in orthopaedic hospitals.

The concept of sheltered employment was first crystallized in the

Tomlinson Report of 1943, which rejected as "wholly out of date" the notion that "resettlement of the disabled must be a matter of philanthropy and good will". Furthermore, it advocated that the workshops should produce "articles required for war or other public purposes, and not fancy or semi-luxury articles dependent for their sale on the charitable public". The recommendations were embodied in the Disabled Persons (Employment) Act of 1944, and were thoroughly reviewed by the Piercy Committee, recommendations of its report (1956) being implemented in the Disabled Persons (Employment) Act of 1958. The most significant of these was that the trades should be on industrial lines rather than therapeutic or recreational ones, and sheltered employment was to be under the auspices of the Department of Employment.

Sheltered employment was developed by the Department of Employment in the 1960s. In 1957 there were 10,706 workers (in 1973 the number was 13,442) who were engaged in twenty-three traditional crafts, ranging from basket-making to weaving, and twenty-six new trades ranging from assembly-work to concrete-moulding. About 1,000 workers were engaged in schemes in which they worked at home.

An inter-departmental committee of the Department of Employment was set up to look at the whole aspect of sheltered employment, and in its consultative report published in 1973 it appeared that there was a demand for craft goods in the southern part of England, but this kind of employment was uneconomic in terms of output and earnings elsewhere. Moreover, the scarcity of instructors aggravated the problem of training workers in traditional crafts. The committee acknowledged the fact that craft trades required a different attitude and a new sales image. For example, the demand for chairs to be re-seated in cane is increasing; if the work was re-named 'antique restoration' it could command a higher rate.

There are numerous voluntary organizations providing residential accommodation and employment (all are in direct touch with the Department of Employment on such questions as further development and equipment) and specializing in different fields of disablement.

Whilst the Spastics Society has never accepted that sheltered employment is an ideal alternative to the provision of opportunities for the handicapped to work in open industries alongside the able-bodied, it accepts that very heavily handicapped spastics will always have to work in sheltered conditions where demands of speed and production are not as taxing as in normal industry. There are currently some 1,360 spastics at work in twenty-seven workshops throughout England. Most of the centres are involved in sub-contract work of a light engineering nature, assembling or packing, but a few concentrate on handcrafts and six include basketwork in their wide range.

A limited number of severely handicapped spastics are trained for certain types of craftwork which can be carried out in their own homes and marketed through the society.

Sales enquiries to Homework Manager, Canongate Works, Perth Road, Wood Green, London N22. Tel: 01–888 5652

General enquiries to The Work Centre Liaison Officer, The Spastics Society, 12 Park Crescent, London W1N 4EQ. Tel: 01–636 5020

The Royal National Institute for the Blind operates a Home Industries scheme based on an establishment in Reigate, Surrey, whereby small workshops are set up for blind people who for various reasons wish to operate at home. The institute supplies the raw materials and markets the products (for blind workers in basketry see p. 128).

Notable developments include the founding of the Queen Elizabeth Foundation (p. 303) and St Loyes College, embodying significant new ideas, with training determined by the needs of the labour market. Dorincourt illustrates how successfully a sheltered workshop can take its place in the specialist craft industries. Some of the disabled residents are trained to become skilled craftsmen; designing, hand-painting, glazing and firing ceramic tiles, which find a variety of markets through private customers, cathedrals, shops, architects and builders. Searchlight workshops also exist to provide a home and an opportunity to work for men too severely physically handicapped to live without considerable help. Of the fifty-six disabled people currently at Searchlight there are thirty-five working on traditional crafts (see p. 135). Since the statutory duty of local authorities to provide employment for the disabled has been exercised under the general guidance of the Secretary of State for Employment, facilities for craftwork in particular have increased. Local conditions are an important influence, of course, and organization may vary from county to county. Gloucestershire was probably the first county to appoint a sales organizer for the craftwork done by the blind and physically handicapped. This is a county council appointment under the aegis of the social services. Over the past fifteen years six centres have come into operation within the county, and are attended by some 120 disabled people; a further 220 work in their own homes. The emphasis is on therapeutic value rather than the formation of a work force; nevertheless, there are sufficient goods produced under this homeworkers' scheme, to warrant a shop for their retail. The sales organizer also arranges exhibitions of their work at agricultural and county shows. The income goes back to the craftworkers concerned, after the cost of the materials, supplied by the service, is deducted. Very few are self-employed craftsmen, but it does supplement their income and affords some dignity and pride to the craftworkers concerned.

Age Concern of Brighton started a craft centre in 1974, whereby senior citizens could be actively engaged in a variety of handcrafts which are sold for the benefit of general funds. The scheme is successful, but could be extended to give more elderly people the opportunity of doing creative work in congenial company if transport could be found to get the housebound to the centre. Enquiries to the Organizing Secretary, Age Concern, 57 Ditchling Road, Brighton, Sussex. Tel: Brighton 683275.

Outside the official organizations there are individuals like Mrs Ida Collis who, when she became disabled, could no longer sit at an easel, and so adapted her artistic talent to a different medium. She stitches pictures now instead of painting them; and most effectively. She feels renewed independence could be offered to other disabled people who are of an artistic nature, and is anxious to explore the possibility of working together to exhibit and market their work (*see* Collis p. 173).

Charitable associations embrace various communities, of course. The Kingsway Community, associated with the West London Mission, is registered as a charitable housing association and has successfully incorporated the making of wooden puzzles into its activities (p. 339).

There are also many trust organizations for special education which feature craftwork as an all-important part of the curriculum. Peredur is one of the many centres throughout the world where an attempt is being made to put into practice the ideas of the scientist and philosopher, Rudolf Steiner. Pottery from clay dug on the premises, and fleece from the farm, plant-dyed and woven in the weaving workshop, are the two principal crafts practised and sold at this training-centre which is mainly for maladjusted school-leavers.

PEREDUR FARM AND CRAFT CENTRE, East Grinstead, Sussex. Tel: East Grinstead 23226

The Pestalozzi Children's Village Trust at Sedlescombe in Sussex caters for children from emergent and developing nations who have suitable character aspects and proven ability. Crafts such as pottery and weaving are taught, and the products sold to the general public through the village souvenir shop or from stalls on open day. This underlines the fact that reviving or maintaining the practice of craftwork is as important to the development of countries as is training in agriculture and technology.

HANDCRAFTS ADVISORY ASSOCIATION FOR THE DISABLED, c/o Greater London Association for the Disabled, 183 Queensway, London W2

Formed in 1960, when the need for a national training scheme for handcraft teachers to the disabled was recognized by the Carnegie Trust. The association's main objective is to establish a recognized system of professional status for disabled craft workers, as distinct from the occupational therapist's remedial function. A number of residential and day courses are organized, with regular competitions and exhibitions of work produced. A journal is published twice a year with articles and instructions on work suitable for the disabled, and advice is given about helpful books, materials and methods of work.

The dining-room of Dove Centre, furnished with the work of the crafts tutors

Hurdle-maker Alec Twinning

Cotswold wheelwright Dennis Tugwell with the American-style racing-buggy which he designed and built from a faded sketch

English oak seasoning in Robert Thompson's workyard, beside
the stone cottages of Kilburn where the 'mouseman' lived

A former 'mouseman' apprentice, Wilfred Hutchinson now has
his own craft workshop, trading under the sign of the squirrel

Furniture designer-craftsman, Tim Green, with one of his spinning-wheels

(*right*) Crucifix carved by Ron Butterfield, installed in the Church of St Catherine, Houghton-on-the-Hill, Leics.

(*below*) Table model inkle-loom made by Eric Bradley, finished with bees-wax from his own bees

Black Mould, the world's finest willow, towers some 8 feet
against the Somerset skyline

Gilbert Musgrave selects a 'wad' of willow from which
fishermen's hampers will be woven

(*above*) Geoff Payne demonstrates rush-weaving to the Mayor of Cheltenham after the opening of the Craftsmen of Gloucestershire annual exhibition at Southam

(*right*) Angela Witt demonstrates the art of making a corn-dolly at an agricultural show

(*left*). Tapestry-weaver
Theo Moorman

(*below*). Irene, Countess of Effingham spins
the fleece for her exclusively-designed hand-
woven cloth.

6

Craft Centres, Workshops and Courses

To make a significant and hitherto neglected contribution to the healthy re-
generation of city centres . . . this group's self-reliance and ability to adapt
time-honoured skills continues to be the life-blood of the city. These are the
people who are most at risk – despite the fact that a number of Concorde's
components needed the special skills of Clerkenwell craftsmen.

Extract of report of Urban Small Space Ltd

The first major project launched by Urban Small Space Ltd, a non-
profit distributing trust, was designed to fulfil the aims of the Clerkenwell Green Association (p. 25).

The development of self-financing, low-rental workshops from existing industrial property in the city centre was scheduled for Clerkenwell
Close. Within an ambitious project, incorporating two five-storey
blocks with ancillary area, the aim of Clerkenwell Green Association,
supported by CAC, GLAA and the London Borough of Islington, was
to provide 5,000 square feet as craftsmen's studios. A sound balance of
skills was planned within the available space. The range extends from
fine metalwork, stained glass and tapestry to handprinting and clock-
making. Workshops, music, film and rehearsal studios, with projected
plans for exhibition space, library, storage bays, administration and recreation areas are part of the integral plan for the one block. On an
underlease from Urban Small Space, the second building block will be
administered by SPACE, an Arts Council-sponsored body which provides studios for artists at moderate cost (*see also* p. 379). The project is
supported by a nucleus of eminent craft organizations, official authorities, influential institutes and prominent personalities.

The development of urban workshop co-operatives in this country
was pioneered by Michael Murray, a silversmith who established the
Craft Atelier in 1965, at 27 Old Street, EC1, and founded the Clerkenwell Green Association for craftsmen.

Workshop space in Cornwell House is included in the Clerkenwell
Close project. As one of the project directors, as well as being Director
of the Crafts Advisory Bureau which is closely associated with the
scheme, Mr Murray has a distinguished career to back up his ideals as
a practical craftsman. His co-director is Michael Franks, a town plan-
ner and architect with particular knowledge of central London planning and development. Together they have achieved the objective of

rehabilitating craftsmen and this provides a practical example which encourages those with similar aims in other parishes.

Enclaves of craftsmen have settled in the City since ancient privileges and free customs were claimed by those who produced their wares within the walls. But the exemptions and rights of Magna Carta are now of curiosity value only, and craftsmen throughout the realm are all subject to the same laws. The over-riding influence which determines where his craft is to be practised is often the temperament of the crafts-man himself: city life is a stimulant to one, an anathema to another. Some argue that location is of no account, and yet there are undoubt-edly some areas of the country which seem more conducive to craftwork than others. The setting up of craft centres would appear to be the an-swer, for this brings like-minded people together to practise their skills in a creative community. There are, however, as many variants of that essential principle as there are centres.

For instance, within the whole concept of conservation the para-mount importance of skilled craftsmen is being realized in quite excit-ing ventures. The tragic decay of many ancient buildings, too costly to maintain but too valuable historically and architecturally to lose, is directly attributable to changing needs. By finding new and economi-cally workable uses, such buildings can be saved; not as azoic museum pieces, but as practical centres where essential skills are practised; not simply for arts sake but to provide a continuing service which preserves a valuable heritage.

The Historic Buildings Council for England does not keep an index of craftsmen as such, but its architects have knowledge of the craftsmen operating in the particular area of England where they are responsible for the repair of grant-aided buildings. The whole subject of the future of craftsmen is one that is uppermost in the minds of bodies such as the Civic Trust, which, for European Architectural Heritage Year, is cur-rently organizing a working group to investigate the shortage of craft skills in the building industry.

The increasing shortage of skilled masons, together with concern for our historic buildings, led to the formation of the Orton Trust in 1968. The disused church at Orton was taken over from the Church auth-orities and has become a national stone centre (p. 78) to which stu-dents have been drawn from private firms, cathedral workshops and from the Ancient Monuments section of the Department of the En-vironment.

New uses are being found for old buildings as the conservation move-ment gains momentum; its full significance making an impact on the environment. The realization of the term conservation – conserve, with service – is taking shape by an alliance of these ancient properties with today's craftsmen. At Samlesbury the attractive old hall is both a centre for the Lancashire branch of CPRE and cultural forum for the public whilst retaining the atmosphere of a large family house. It does not, at present, fall into the category of a centre as defined in my introduction, but has certainly gained something of a reputation for craft exhibitions over the past few years. The Samlesbury Hall Trust is committed to the maintenance and restoration of the hall, but there are no immediate plans to extend its excellent facilities to make it a working centre for craftsmen, so it would properly be classified as a marketing outlet.

Martin Griffiths is working through the whole concept of practical restoration by rescuing Penrhos Court, determining that the knowledge and craftsmanship acquired in the process should become the basis of a continuing service. His aim is to set up a centre where all the practical problems of looking after ancient buildings can be taken care of, and in doing so offers full-time employment for half a dozen men living locally, with perhaps a further two dozen on holiday courses. Future plans are to embrace education in history and architecture. Penrhos is certainly a fine example of an early cruck house which has been added to since the thirteenth century. The whole complex, built around a central cobbled area and duckpond, is to be restored. Already much work has been done and the workshops for traditional building crafts are well on the way to completion (p. 74). Projected plans are also afoot for crafts of the building industry to be set up at the Avoncroft Museum of Buildings (p. 381), but details are not yet finalized so mentioning it here may be a little premature.

The approach of the National Trust to some extent has to be more impersonal in that much work of restoration of buildings is delegated to architects who themselves engage craftsmen. The limitations appear to be in the number of craftsmen skilled in dealing with certain fields. Restorers of furniture and pictures are more readily available but there are few craftsmen specializing in the repair of, say, chandeliers, or the cleaning of ormolu.

Craft centres are sometimes the ideal answer for utilizing large buildings, like St Edmunds, Salisbury – at present an embryonic scheme. Redundant churches lend themselves perfectly to such use and an admirable illustration is the old Rowland Hill Tabernacle at Wotton-under-Edge in Gloucestershire, now a showhouse for the replica Roman Pavement of Woodchester (p. 291).

A thirteenth-century church in Chichester, where the poet William Collins is laid to rest, is scheduled to become a centre of arts. A company, registered as a charity, has been formed; a Board of Trustees appointed; and a working committee established.

Up and down the country there are similar projects proposed. Plans are being prepared for a rural handicrafts centre to be set up in a watermill at Bromham in Bedfordshire, but first of all it has to be restored. Similarly, there are plans for a working crafts exhibition centre for Somerset. These are the direct results of collaboration between county guilds and county councils.

Regional craft centres would certainly fulfil some very real needs by providing a cultural centre for arts, by preserving traditional crafts of the locality, and by housing working craftsmen in low-rent workshops. These would be economically viable, and would have enormous educational potential.

Education in the arts and crafts is the aim of a great many individual ventures, for this means fostering a better understanding between the artist-craftsman and the public. Distribution of information alone is not enough; participation must also be involved to achieve complete understanding. Creative education within a production unit is an ideal rarely achieved without a great deal of careful administration.

An enterprise which has fulfilled its initial objectives is the Dove Centre, which attracted a fair amount of speculation when it set up as a single studio in 1970. It was born almost by accident, out of local interest, for so many people knocked on Anthony Horrocks's door asking for advice on craftwork and begging use of the studio facilities that a move to larger premises was made and courses were organized.

Armed with an early brochure, which was punctuated with poetry and philosophy, I sought out the remote farmstead deep in rural Somerset, in the region where King Arthur's legendary Avalon is said to be. A slip-splashed potter talked to me of the organization. It was a Sunday afternoon, he was still working, fixing handles on practical-shaped mugs. Anthony Horrocks, founder member of Dove, was at the new gallery in Street setting up an exhibition.

In six years Dove has grown from that single studio to six studio workshops, a gallery, a common-room and a playgroup. There are now only two families in residence, and the emphasis has shifted from the initial 'community' idea to that of a craft centre where craftsmen are self-employed, paying a monthly workshop rent and a percentage of sales revenue. Some outside help is engaged for teaching and a proportion of the teaching fee is paid to the centre. It is a co-operative of craftsmen, administered and run by the members. The property is owned by a charitable trust and this provides the roof under which Dove can operate.

Students aged 7 to 70 go to Dove for all sorts of reasons. Something like seventy children use the workshops every Saturday, and ten mentally handicapped people receive creative therapy there every week. There are about 200 enrolments for the weekly craft courses and the playgroup is authorized by Somerset County Council. Dove also operates an informal advisory service in response to enquiries, mostly concerning marketing, from people in the UK and overseas, and its employees act as consultants for similar centres. Altogether, some 3,000 people a year are helped by Dove in one way or another. "We are not so heady now," said Paul Stubbs, "much more realistic."

I was tempted to ask about the significance of the siting of the centre. It stands on the Dove, a figure mapped out on the earth in ancient times as part of the legendary Glastonbury Zodiac.

Judicious siting is obviously a tremendous asset. Aiming to attract canal-cruising tourists, the Foxton Crafts Centre on the Grand Union Canal is a new venture interested in promoting glass, pottery and tapestry. But attractive sites are bound to attract the competitive attention of other planners.

Plans are afoot to develop the canal-side site of the Camden Town crafts community into an office-cum-entertainment complex. Rents have already trebled but the craftsmen beaver on with dedicated total commitment: banjos get re-strung, furniture takes on form, silver a shape, sculpture is sculpted, the saddler stitches on steadily, and six jewellers work together under the trade name of the 'Five Jewellers'.

One of the big problems of a craft community is that of finding housing within easy reach of the workshops. The provision of both living and studio accommodation was recognized as particularly important, in this age of spiralling property values, by the Digswell Arts Trust, an educational charity, part of whose aim was to combat the difficulties met by creative artists in an industrialized society.

On the outskirts of Welwyn Garden City a Regency building and its surrounding cottages house a community of, on average, sixteen artists and craftsmen with their families. Assisting young craftworkers at a formative time in their careers is combined with a social aim of integrating the arts in a larger community, and, more pertinently in this case, in a new town. Assisting in social and educative work is one of the conditions of tenancy at Digswell House. The craftworkers stay for an average of four years and pay a contribution towards the running of the trust.

Not exclusively a craft fraternity, though the craft element is quite strong, Digswell's aim is to build a vibrant community where there will be an interchange of ideas and skills. Several distinguished artists and craftsmen have benefited from living at Digswell.

Crafts working groups, as opposed to groups working at a crafts centre, tend to border on the industrial by virtue of size. Whilst not detracting from the initial intent of producing original designs to a high standard of workmanship, the organization may be of a totally different character from that to which the individual artist is accustomed. Administration by management consultants obviously has economically sound bias, often, however, such interest in the crafts is purely academic and pedantic, computed to subjective data and quantitative values; an alien tongue to a craftsman's comprehension. Without doubt the successful co-operatives are those which are run by those who have the unique blend of the artist's temperament and the businessman's acumen.

The problem of the correct relationship of the individual to a group hinges on his understanding his part in and of it. The concept of community practice is not new; the ancient guilds were followed by other professions – the barristers at the Inns of Court, medical groups and, commercial voluntary trading organizations. But its potential is only just being explored and realized by the crafts fraternity. Under the wider implications of general national policy, the idea of the small group's individuality, protected by big company support, excited the eminent architects, David Rock and John Townsend. The resultant Dryden Street Experiment, to use the *Guardian*'s term, proved that this idea was a practicable one.

Some thirty-four firms, which makes a total of 120 workers, practise their diverse skills under one roof. Retaining their absolute independence, they share the overheads and communal facilities, maintaining that the latter are cheaper and better than those they could supply themselves. The experiment in 1972 of the working community at Covent Garden has now become firmly established and a more ambitious venture has been started at Chiswick, one of the old villages of west London.

Under a lease held on a former wallpaper factory until March 2003, Barley Mow Workspace Ltd, has provided a total area of some 33,000 square feet, divided into design studios, workshops, office hotel, conference-rooms and showroom for about 250 people. Workspace is rented in multiples of 100 square feet, an arrangement which allows for expansion or contraction according to immediate needs without the upheaval of moving or sub-letting.

Changing conditions can be met, such as the furniture designer who initially rented space for a small studio, later extending into a workshop area and even further into showroom space under the flexibility of the scheme, and the jewellery-designers who share space and specialist equipment, to the interior designer who recognizes that close liaison with architects and dependence upon allied skills and professions can extend to valid constructive comments over his shoulder and the availability of Rock Townsend's crockery!

David Rock, reflecting on the scheme, which has been in practice for over three years now, outlines the problems of communal risk-taking, and the need for a clearer definition between formal voting and discussion, and between firm leadership and democratic confusion.

Expansion of similar experiments would appear to point to a possible new structure in social planning and with parallel schemes underline the wider implications between the mutual support group concept and many far-reaching urban problems, not the least consideration being the urgent need to retain the small business group as a vital germ for individual creativity.

Closely allied to the social or educative aspect of craft centres in general, are those set up to fulfil a variety of needs, where craftsmen share their skills with others, and have a simple appreciation of life. These shun publicity and only the serious enquirer should encroach upon their valuable time for details of their programmes, which are usually for short-term courses as opposed to the rented accommodation of a workshop centre.

Many base their craftwork on religious and social ethics. The Guild-house at Stanton, and Blackberry Hill, both in the Cotswolds, offer companionship and facilities for the practising of rural crafts. In her cottage living-room Mary Osborn once taught village children to spin the tufts of fleece they found in the hedgerows. The Guildhouse stands today in solid Cotswold stone as testimony to the skills of contemporary craftsmen, and as the realization of her resolute idealism. As a regis-tered charity, dependent on donations for its future security, it has materialized into what Miss Osborn hoped for, a permanent centre for a more creative way of living.

Local groups use it regularly and residential courses are arranged during the summer months. It is hoped to eventually integrate the two.

Blackberry Hill also lays stress on simplicity and self-help, but whereas the Guildhouse is interdenominational, the Liengaard family at Blackberry Hill are Quakers and find that most people who partici-pate in their activities are those who appreciate periods of silence, in the belief that stillness is a creative thing out of which ideas are born.

Unfortunately, such communities do attract the curious. Any vestige of publicity brings yet another flock of unscheduled visitors to their doors, rarely contributing anything and causing a constant inter-ruption to the work. This is not a new problem: fifty years ago Eric Gill, who had been involved with Jacob Epstein and Augustus John in an abortive scheme to found "a new religion", discovered that Ditchling Common, where the famous and initially controversial Guild of St Joseph and St Dominic was founded, was too accessible to too many people, and so he took to the Welsh hills.

The idea of "a religious order of artists" was wrapped in medieval mystery and naturally attracted much speculation when it was founded deep in the heart of the English countryside. The old order has now gone, but the guild is still an enclave of artist-craftsmen, actively main-taining the tried and true tradition, working on an individual basis on commissions, and avoiding publicity.

Taena, another Christian group nestled in the lee of the hill upon which the great Benedictine abbey at Prinknash is built, has dwindled from a small community to a mere couple of craftsmen. Across the val-ley, Peter and Joy Evans are about the only craftsmen at Whiteway Col-ony, which was founded in the 1890s on Tolstoyian principles – the settlers burning the title deeds on first obtaining possession. The craft skills in this case were inspired by the desire for total self-sufficiency.

It is beyond the scope of this study to examine the reasons for one community's success and another's failure: economic, political, national and local conditions colour the individual characteristics of the corporate whole; prejudices and opinions all bear heavily on the final relationships one with another. Anthony Horrocks, of the Dove Centre, believes that it is usually the people who think and read most about communes who are the worst suited to living in communes.

Communalism, a term which is over-laden with obscure and suspect tones, often does not help the intended project, so recognizing the type of person who will fit in best to a community project exercises the powers of perspicacity of even the most experienced co-ordinator.

The problems involved in revitalizing a whole village by creating a craft centre in which rural crafts are practised, thereby creating employment in the traditional manner and re-populating the place so that the local school and clubs can be kept alive, are multiplied.

Waxing sentimental over a way of life known to our ancestors wanes a little when we consider the practicalities, so when the present owner of the Lockinge estate found the character of the twin villages of Ardington and Lockinge changing, he decided to do something about it. The experience of COSIRA was invaluable in the delicate business of selecting the newcomers. That craftsmen are drawn to the village community idea is shown by the fact that well over sixty people were interviewed for five vacancies. The project has been materializing over three years: a rush-weaver, potters, upholsterer, and furniture-maker have already established themselves and ply their skills in the old dairy, water-mill and barns. Currently, some 2,000 square feet of farm buildings, a working forge and a farrier's shop await the right type of craftsmen.

Integration into the community is of paramount importance in an area steeped in local tradition. This is a point soon recognized by a recently formed crafts centre at Stow-on-the-Wold. When ten artists and craftsmen moved in to a forty-four-room Victorian mansion, the village people raised a few eyebrows. The local Press ended its report on the impending midsummer open-day by remarking that the members "will be washing their denims for the occasion" – a puerile postscript and hardly conducive to attracting conservative Cotsallers to the centre, in which I found quiet and seriously ordered creative activity. But I am confident that the craftsmen will make their own impact on the area and inquisitive intrigue will turn to interest. The ultimate aim of the more ambitious members is the closer co-operation between the craftsmen. An enterprise envisaged by Sue Rangeley, a vivacious embroiderer, is that of some one designing clothes based on someone else's textile prints. The co-ordination of crafts is an obvious possibility in such centres, where there is privacy in the studios and living accommodation but communal meeting and exchange is possible.

Fosseway House is an extension of Michael Haynes' foundation centre called 401½, situated in south-west London, and has been achieved through his benefaction and business acumen. The atelier at 401½, a converted warehouse where some thirty young designers are working on a diversity of crafts, has become established in a mere four years and is now sought out by interior decorators and architects for the talent it houses. The occasional exotic request has also found its way to these young craftsmen, such as a commission for hand-woven bed-covers (one double and nine single) for the Sultan of Oman and his nine wives – an example of how a crafts collective can cope with an order which might be beyond the physical output of a sole craftsworker. Another successful designer at 401½ has built up her knitwear business to the extent that she can employ some forty people, working at their homes, to meet the demand from London boutiques and an expanding export market.

Design Brokers is another successful consortium of designer-craftsmen. Anthony Torrens, experienced in the field of design and conversant with the problems experienced through lack of communication, acts as a kind of catalyst, introducing the client to the craftsman.

Balancing artistry with commercial viability is the spring-board upon which so many art and design students tread precariously on completing their training. Often they rush back to the safety of teaching, and train others in the skills they long to perfect themselves, or they plunge headlong in a commercially suicidal whirlpool of capital outlay and the whole vortex of the self-employed. It was as a result of meeting so many disillusioned young people who had never been taught to make themselves commercially viable that Jocelyn Mitchell introduced the quite revolutionary idea of including a practical commercial course in her recently opened crafts centre in Hampshire. I was certainly impressed with the immediate success it achieved within two weeks of its opening. A two-hundred-year-old granary has been converted into studio workshops, rented out at a low rate to craftsmen, and students from Southampton College of Art go there for practical pottery training. The college supplied the equipment but the students buy their own clay and learn to sell their pots. Making the students stand on their own feet – artistic training never before showed them how to make a living – it is a project which is attracting the attention of more art colleges, and is a pilot scheme which seems to be steering the course long sought for the crafts world.

The *Financial Times* recognized the dilemma of the contemporary craftsman: "the small business has its special problems and one of them is accommodation. Another is lack of capital, and a third very often, the absence of administration experience".

Craft centres set out, in principle, to solve these problems, but no one has yet perfected the plan for the ideal centre; each, by virtue of its autonomous administration, offers its own terms to craftsmen. There is certainly no simple solution applicable to all situations. Ecological ideals and the good intentions of landlords who own empty buildings and hope that craftsmen will sustain them, rarely weather well. A working knowledge of their needs can only be appreciated by craftsmen themselves and, as the Crafts Advisory Committee say, it seems that the most successful group workshops spring from a grass roots movement among the craftsmen themselves.

The main points of such arrangements which have emerged from studying the ones listed here are:

Advantages
1 Workshop facilities are at low rental: a boon to craftsmen with little or no capital to get started, or where planning permission is not available for setting up a workshop.
2 The craftsman is working in close contact with others who share a common aim, yet retaining his independence.
3 Advertising fees and retailing resources can be shared.
4 The craftsman remains self-employed.
5 There is some incentive to make a go of it, the success of the venture depending on his own efforts.
6 He becomes part of a nucleus at a crafts centre rather than struggling blindly on alone.
7 The public often visit a centre to browse around, which brings in chance customers, whereas they would hesitate to encroach on a single craftsman's domain.
8 The specialist skills of one craftsman may be useful to another, as at Parndon Mill where period furniture built by one craftsman is upholstered by another, thereby completing the production in one centre. This leads to an integration of crafts, greater efficiency and increased productivity.
9 A group can often afford to pay for the administrative services which would be beyond the financial means of the individual. An accountant and a secretary at least can relieve craftsmen of the paperwork and the intermittent interruptions of telephone calls.
10 Centres often receive unsolicited publicity through the mass media, thereby reducing advertising costs.
11 Some centres have expensive equipment, such as a kiln, which is available to members, which would normally put the single craftsman in the red for years if he had to make the initial outlay himself.
12 The economies of scale which have dominated the scene for the last quarter-century can be pruned and applied to the individual within the communal enterprise. Pooling resources means that the facilities of large firms are afforded to the small ones which can still retain their independence.
13 Individual units of a craft trade often fall victim of development

pressures, whereas the united force of a craft community, especially if linked to local teaching and social activities, is regarded as an integral part of the fundamental amenities of the area, and therefore of public interest.

14 By a healthy resurgence of craftwork and associated cultural activity many villages, redundant warehouses and otherwise uneconomic buildings can be given a breath of new life in traditional manner.

The administrators obviously have established criteria by which they assess whether a craftsman is suitable to become a member of the centre, these may be:

1 the variety of the total crafts represented;
2 the rarity or range of the craftsman's métier;
3 those with educational commitments will look for teaching ability;
4 those attracting the public will look for conversant facilities;
5 a high degree of professional integrity is essential as the whole organization is represented through the individual.

Few centres could claim that they have no problems. Apart from obvious ones, such as a clash of personalities, there needs to be a constant review of their situations: craft centres are not places for comfortable complacency. The difficulties are mainly:

1 The constant struggle to keep the centres self-supporting in the face of rising rates, loan repayments and running costs.
2 Centres sometimes have to fight for their continued existence against redevelopment plans, such as Camden Lock *v.* Centre Point.
3 Finding suitable living accommodation in the area at reasonable purchase price or reasonable rent.
4 Sophisticated secretarial and marketing services, which are included in some rents, may be a superfluous and expensive luxury for some craftsmen.
5 Where space is rented on area it could work against a 'maker' who would require infinitely more workroom and display space than, say, a designer.
6 There is a world of difference between renting workspace on a site, and a community of craftsmen: the latter calls for a greater degree of personality congruence. A high turnover of members can affect the stability of a group, and lose the confidence of its supporters.
7 When committed to an educational bias, members have to be willing to sacrifice some of their free time and, to some extent, their individuality, to the common weal.

8 The proportion of time taken up by course instruction to actual production time has to be carefully calculated if the craftsman is not to
divert from his original intent and turn teacher.

9 When sited in a very rural or out-of-the-way area the most successful centres seem to offer other attractions in various forms: Dove has
its courses, Camden Lock its narrow boat, Bickleigh Mill its birds,
and Clevedon its countryside museum. Publicity leaflets, with a
sketch map on how to find the centre, are essential if potential visitors are to know of the existence of the centre.

10 Although the centres are reliant on customers, these can cause constant interruption to the concentration of the craftsman. Some form
of observation gallery, like the one which runs alongside the pottery
at Prinknash, allows visitors to watch work in progress without
breathing down the craftsmen's necks and taking up valuable
space.

CRAFT CENTRES

Avon

CLEVEDON CRAFT CENTRE, Mrs P. Huxtable, Newhouse Farm, Moor Lane,
Clevedon BS21 6TD. Tel: Clevedon 2867
Traditional and modern crafts are currently practised in six studio workshops at this picturesque farm, originally part of the historic Clevedon Court
Estate. Old farm implements and craftsmen's tools, exhibition area, craft
shop and small licensed restaurant open every day. Free admission, ample
parking space.

Cambridge

CAMBRIDGE ARTS AND LEISURE ASSOCIATION, 27 Warkworth Street. Tel: 0223
57359
Projected new centre off Newmarket Road, to include workshops.

Cornwall

SLOOP CRAFT MARKET, St Ives. Tel: St Ives 6051
Opened in June 1969, as a co-operative venture between the owners and the
craftsmen, the market currently accommodates twelve craftsmen in single
or double workshop units. Traditional local materials were used in the development of what was once the old St Ives fish cellar in order to create an
open market where the public may buy direct from the craftsmen and watch
many of the things being made. The Pudding Bag Restaurant, with views
over the harbour and bay, provides a buffet service to visitors.
The basic condition of tenancy is that the craftsmen make the goods sold
there or do specialist work on prepared materials. Inquiries regarding the
availability of stalls should be made to the Chairman of the Committee at
the Craft Market or to the owners, Percy Williams & Sons, Falmouth Road,
Redruth. Stall space is sometimes also available in Barbican Craft Workshops, Penzance Harbour.

The market is open at Easter, then from Whitsuntide till September, although some craftsmen work there all the year round.

Devon

BICKLEIGH MILL CRAFT CENTRE, Bickleigh, nr Tiverton EX16 8RG. Tel: Bickleigh 419 (413 – Craftsmen)

Opened in 1973, the centre is housed in a restored water-mill set in the lovely natural scenery of the West Country. It is an association of craftsmen who work in self-contained log cabins of locally-hewn larch wood, with the old water-wheel driving the machinery.

The aims are to show the meaning of craftsmanship, with particular emphasis on the more local and rarer types, and to create opportunities for young craftsmen to enable them to become established with the very minimum of their own capital outlay. The craftsman pays no rental for either his equipment (which is often provided free by the centre) or his workshop. He pays his own running costs (electricity and materials) and remains self-employed, with the advantage of retailing his work through the centre's craft gallery which usually purchases the goods from him in the same way as any other retailer would. Usually between fifteen to forty members are at the centre working on a variety of crafts. The criteria by which they are accepted into the association are based on the standard of their work, their demonstrative and conversant ability (the centre being held in high regard for its educational influence), and the rarity of the crafts.

Visitors may see the indoor aviary, the craft gallery, the observation beehives, attractive tea-rooms, and waterfowl and peacocks in the grounds. There is no admittance to the craft cabins, but demonstrations and educational tours can be arranged.

THE DARTINGTON HALL TRUST, Totnes TQ9 6JE. Tel: Totnes (0803) 862271

Dartington Hall, the largest and most important medieval house in the west of England, is the centre in which various enterprises have taken root to fulfil the trustees' aims of securing employment and restoring economic vitality to this part of the country. The integration of cultural, educative and artistic activities give a depth of personal development within the working community which, although not exclusively a crafts concern, is deeply sympathetic to the crafts. This is shown by the plans to establish workshops within the craft centre, which embraces a craft museum, shop and pottery training studio, and was established with the assistance of CAC.

Courses: details of adult education (day and evening classes) from the warden, Shinners Bridge Centre, Dartington, Totnes.

Essex

ESSEX CRAFT CENTRE, R. and M. Bloom, Maltings Farm, Great Oakley. Tel: 025 588 821

Rented workshop space, non-residential, for craftsmen who are also required to teach at the residential courses. Retailing and general administration undertaken by the proprietors on a commission basis. Exhibition area.

PARNDON MILL, Director: Jim Dobson, off Elizabeth Way, Harlow. Tel: 0279
20982

> Jim Dobson and his wife have converted an old flour-mill to provide rented
> studio space for artists and craftsmen. There is a very active design con-
> sultancy, co-operation and interchange of ideas between craftsmen, essen-
> tial to the kind of commissions in which they specialize, undertaken for
> architects, corporations and interior designers. There is an exhibition gal-
> lery, with a Friends of the Gallery scheme which includes advice on all
> aspects of the visual arts.

Gloucestershire

FOSSEWAY CRAFTS WORKSHOPS, Fosseway House, High Street, Stow-on-the-
Wold

> Some dozen studio workshops, with residential accommodation above
> them. The tenant craftsmen make the day-to-day decisions and meet once a
> month with the director, Michael Haynes of $401\frac{1}{2}$ (p. 76).

WEATHERALL WORKSHOPS, Coleford GL16 8QB. Tel: Coleford (05943) 2102

> Weatherall is well established in the field of decorative art through the work
> of Lillian Delevoryas, whose international reputation has lifted needlecraft
> into the arts-craft class. Workspace is sometimes available for co-ordinated
> crafts to be carried out. Currently these include tapestry needlepoint (both
> designs and finished product), a design service for trammed and printed
> needlepoint canvas kits, appliqué for furnishings and fashion, painted
> murals, ceramic tiles, wood-turning and simple wooden furniture. There is
> also a gallery.

Hampshire

WILLOWPOOL, Jocelyn Mitchell, Lockhams Road, Curdridge SO3 2BG. Tel:
Botley 2403

> Permanent, separately metered, workshop sites let on small rent to crafts-
> men. No commission extracted from sales. Art gallery and craft shop on
> site.

Herefordshire

PENRHOS COURT, Director: Martin Griffiths, Lyonshall, Kington. Tel: Kington 720

> A building-preservation group based in the historically and architecturally
> important court. Workshops on site for timber-frame building and repairs,
> stone-building and stone-tiling, lead-glazing and glass-making are accom-
> modated within an ancient barn where craftsmen are trained to provide the
> specialist skills for the proper repair of old buildings in general. Already an
> eighteenth-century stone barn has been converted into a restaurant, which
> was selected for commendation by the British Tourist Association.

Hertfordshire

DIGSWELL ARTS TRUST, Administrator: Bill Parkinson, Gordon Maynard Gallery, 22 Parkway, Welwyn Garden City. Tel: 01–96 21506

Founded in 1957 as a community of resident artists and craftsmen, the trust aims at the social involvement of its fellows by running a programme of cultural activities: exhibitions, educational visits, lectures, and tuition to which the public is invited. There is a mixture of disciplines within the community but no restrictive social, political or artistic dogma. Fellows are allowed to take on commissioned work, both private and industrial, and to go out to talk and demonstrate.

Leicestershire

CARTER DESIGN GROUP Ltd, John Carter, Maximum Space Studios, Foxton, Market Harborough. Tel: East Langton 441/2
Workshop space is sometimes available at this crafts centre on the Grand Union Canal.

Liverpool

BLUECOAT SOCIETY OF ARTS, Administrator: Celia Van Mullem, Bluecoat Chambers, School Lane L1 3BX. Tel: 051–709 5297
A centre for the arts and various cultural societies. Rented studio accommodation for individual craftsmen, artists and musicians. The societies are autonomous and information about their activities can be obtained from their honorary secretaries. Enquiries regarding the concert hall, reception-hall, music-room, annexe, studios, and practice- and teaching-rooms to the administrator.

London

BARLEY MOW WORKSPACE, Barley Mow Passage, Chiswick W4 4PH. Tel: 01–994 6477
Workshops, studios and showrooms for about thirty craftsmen and designers.

BATTERSEA COMMUNITY ARTS CENTRE
(see Puppets p. 333) Some workshop space.

CAMDEN LOCK, Commercial Place, London NW1 8AF
An association of tenant craftsmen who run their cottage industries in waterside workshops, open to the public as a Saturday market. Cobbled squares and colourful canopies add atmosphere to this picturesque canal-side location, a unique artisan centre where one can find a whole range of craftsmen, artists and photographers. There are stalls selling bric-à-brac and old fairground machinery, together with a cafe and *patisserie*, and *Jenny Wren* – a narrow boat which travels backwards and forwards between the Lock and Little Venice at weekends from April to October, and on week-days during school holidays.

CHIPPENHAM HILL ARTS GROUP, Director: John Midgeley, 192–8 Villiers Road, NW2. Tel: 01–459 5289
Working studios run as a co-operative. Retailing is through the individual studios.

CLERKENWELL GREEN ASSOCIATION, 27 Old Street, EC1. Tel: 01–253 3693
 The association was established for charitable purposes only, the principal object is "to promote any charitable purpose which will encourage the exercise and maintain the standards of crafts both ancient and modern, preserve and improve craftsmanship and foster, promote and increase the interest of the public therein". Its work over the past five years in providing workshop space is reaching fruition through the Clerkenwell Close project (*see* p. 61).

DESIGN BROKERS (Holdings) Ltd, 90 Lots Road, SW10. Tel: 01–352 7454
 The Designers Trust Foundation was formed in February 1974. Creative workshops, converted from banana warehouses, are rented to craftsmen and artists. Membership is open to groups or single craftsmen throughout the country who, like the tenant artists, can utilize the facilities of conference-room, exhibition-hall, studios, and the marketing-service based in Chelsea. As a designers' consortium the foundation can provide an overall service, taking ideas from their conception through to the production of the finished article.
 By creating a pool of creative potential the design services available range from pottery and textiles to fashion and advertising photography, conference, exhibition and stage design. Companies can affiliate to DTF if they would like closer contact with the designers and their work. Enquiries to A. A. Torrens.

51½, Director: Fianne Bastick, 51½ Stroud Green Road, Finsbury Park, N4. Tel: 01–263 1482
 Occasional small workshop space available for rent.

5 DRYDEN STREET, Covent Garden, London WC2. Tel: 01–240 2430
 Some thirty studio-workshops rented by designers and craftsmen.

401½, Director: Michael Haynes, 401½ Wandsworth Road, London SW8. Tel: 01–622 7262
Workshop space for about thirty designer-craftsmen, many of whom are ex-Royal College of Art. Architects and decorators have already made use of the wide range of talent gathered under the roof of this crafts collective.

ROTHERHITHE WORKSHOPS, Hope Sufferance Wharf, St Marychurch Street, SE16
Craft workshops, Beshara Design Centre and store of timber. Enquiries to Clerkenwell Green Association (See above).

Norfolk

THE COUNTRY AND COTTAGE CRAFTS PROJECT, 'Risings', Wroxham Road, Coltishall NR12 7DW. Tel: 549 (060–543)
 Launched in 1972, to promote the work and interests of talented craftsmen of the region and to provide a wide range of high-quality traditional handcrafts, this is a non-profit-making centre which has future plans for on-site workshops. The products of over fifty craftsmen are displayed in attractive,

unpretentious showrooms. The only financial contribution the members (the associated craftsmen) make is a percentage of sales to meet operating costs and overheads. They pay no rental or subscription fees, and avail themselves of the showrooms, office and all facilities.

Oxford

OXFORD AREA ARTS COUNCIL, 40 George Street. Tel: 0865 722648
Conversion of old fire-station into workshops, some occasionally available for rent.

Somerset

DOVE CENTRE, Butleigh, Glastonbury. Tel: Baltonsboro 682, also at Crispin Hall, Street. Tel: Street 5172
An arts and crafts centre organized on a co-operative basis by a group of professional craftsmen and administered by True Dovetail Ltd, a registered charity. The members are self-employed and devote usually one day a week to teaching in a number of courses run at the centre. The educational policy is to incorporate practical experience with a minimum of theory so that students are involved in practical activities from the start.

The facilities open to non-residential students are: short courses and holiday courses in a variety of crafts; Saturday morning young people's workshop; creative playgroup; tours and talks; and use of public workshop rented on an hourly basis.

Additional workshops at Crispin Hall in Street, where a gallery houses permanent exhibitions of both local and national importance.

TUITION COURSES

Because programmes of courses change from year to year it is advisable to send a SAE for a current prospectus.

Berkshire

SOUTH HILL PARK TRUST LTD, South Hill Park, Bracknell. Tel: 0344 27272
Arts, crafts and leisure centre based in a Victorian mansion set in fifteen acres of ground. Craft courses.

Buckinghamshire

THE REYNTIENS TRUST LTD, Burleigfield House, Loudwater. Tel: 0494 25068
Specialist courses on stained glass. Summer and weekend courses from painting to pottery.

Cumbria

THE BREWERY, 122a Highgate, Kendal. Tel: 0539 25133
Arts and some crafts.

Derbyshire

ALFRETON HALL, Alfreton. Tel: 077 383 2201
Corn-dolly-weaving to copper-tooling.

Devon

BEAFORD CENTRE, Beaford, Winkleigh. Tel: 080 53 202
    The centre is sponsored by the Dartington Hall Trust and arranges events
    throughout North Devon. Arranges craft exhibitions and tuition courses in
    various crafts.

DEVON CENTRE FOR FURTHER EDUCATION, The Warden, Dartington Hall,
Devon Centre. Tel: Totnes 862267
    Residential courses for the general public under the auspices of Devon
    County Council.

Gloucestershire

BLACKBERRY HILL, Keld and Anja Liengaard, Blackberry Hill, Horsley, Nailsworth, Stroud. Tel: Nailsworth (045 383) 3652
    Craft weekends ranging from basketry to patchwork, spinning to building
    craft. Vegetarian meals are provided. Up to four weeks residential course for
    learning a specific craft or skill is also offered. Some craftwork on sale and
    commissions taken (*see* p. 67).

Kent

THE HARRIS CENTRE, The Director, Hawkhurst, TN18 4AP. Tel: 05 805 3315
    Established for the encouragement of design and craftsmanship in weaving,
    spinning and for instruction in other craft skills the centre, in a fine six-
    teenth-century house, runs non-residential summer schools on a regular
    basis, conducted by distinguished craftsmen. A limited amount of studio
    workshop space, equipped with looms and basic furniture, is available on
    rent. Other crafts, excluding pottery, also catered for. Information and
    lecture services.

London

LONDON COLLEGE OF FURNITURE, 41–47 Commercial Road, London E1. Tel:
01–247 1953
    Courses in the design and manufacture of play equipment and creative
    studies in toy-making.

Northants

THE ORTON TRUST, Stoa House, Brigstock, Kettering. Tel: Brigstock 253
    This is the national stone centre. Courses include basic and advanced set-
    ting out, introduction to gilding, advanced gilding, lettering and headstone
    design, walling, monumental carving, restoration carving, restoration, and
    geology for stonemasons. Seminars for architects.

Suffolk

CLOCK HOUSE, P. Heriz-Smith, Clock House, Bruisyard, Saxmundham. Tel:
072 878 512
    Small groups, varied courses.

Sussex

WEST DEAN COLLEGE, The Principal, West Dean, Chichester PO18 0QZ. Tel: Singleton 301

Offering the most comprehensive range of short courses in England, the college caters for over a hundred different crafts to be taught to students of post-school age. Amateurs, semi-professionals and craft teachers are offered weekend, five or seven days length courses; closed courses can be arranged for clubs and societies. Three programmes of courses are published each year and are obtainable from the registrar.

Tyne and Wear

THE INSTITUTE OF CRAFT EDUCATION (Northumberland, Tyne and Wear Branch), Hon. Sec: D. Gibbs, 32 Beachcroft Avenue, Tynemouth, NE30 3SN. Tel: North Shield 76019

This branch holds regular Saturday morning meetings every month, along with craft demonstrations.

WHITLEY BAY AREA ARTS FEDERATION, Sec: Jean Scott, Whitley Bay Area Library, Park Road, Whitley Bay NE26 1EJ

Contact the secretary for details. The federation is endeavouring to keep arts and crafts, in the broadest sense, alive in Tyne and Wear.

Worcestershire

THE STANTON GUILDHOUSE TRUST, Mary Osborn, The Guildhouse, Stanton, nr Broadway WR12 7NE

Local groups are held regularly, together with some residential courses for spinning, dyeing, weaving, woodwork, pottery, puppetry; wrought-iron and stonework are planned. Craft skills are practised, not on any commercial bias, but along with other arts and music as a contribution to a more creative way of living, including conservation on all fronts. (*see* p. 67).

York

ST JOHN'S COLLEGE, Lord Mayor's Walk. Tel: 0904 56771

Summer school offers a wide range of crafts from lapidary to bobbin lace-making, musical instrument-making to paper-making.

County education offices compile lists of local courses; the standard may vary between classes and most authorities are governed by total enrolments for a subject before the class can start.

Most counties have an adult education centre or college (see p. 380 for directory of addresses) and evening-classes are held in a great number of schools throughout the country. The Inner London Education Authority publish an annual directory of evening classes, called *Floodlight*, which is usually on sale at booksellers in August.

Courses are also offered on a variety of subjects by University extra-mural departments and the Workers' Educational Association.

Arts centres often have craft-orientated courses and workshops sessions: it is therefore worth contacting the Regional Arts Association (p. 12–14).

SUMMER SCHOOLS, SHORT COURSES AND CRAFT HOLIDAYS

Cornwall

Mrs Wake, St Minver Lodge, Wadebridge. Send SAE for craft holiday brochure.

Devon

SHINNERS BRIDGE CRAFTS AND CULTURAL CENTRE, Dartington, nr Totnes. Hobby holiday courses – printing, pottery, spinning and weaving.

Hereford

HEREFORDSHIRE COLLEGE OF ARTS, Director: Gwyn Vaughan Williams, Folley Lane, HR1 1LT. Usually last two weeks of July. Most craft subjects.

Hertfordshire

YHA-ADVENTURE HOLIDAYS, Trevelyan House, St Albans, AL1 2DY. Week-long courses studying rural crafts.

Lancashire

COLLEGE OF CRAFT EDUCATION, prospectus from Ian Anderson, 18 Hallmoor Close, Aughton, Ormskirk.

Sussex

G. W. SALMON, The Old Rectory, Fittleworth, RH20 1HU. Leisure courses, April–September. Various crafts.

Yorkshire

ROBERT ELLWOOD, Elmfield, Bromley Road, Bingley. Craft holidays.

PUBLICATIONS OF COURSES

Activity Holidays in England (currently 60p. plus 20p. postage) includes some craft activities, published by English Tourist Board, 4 Grosvenor Gardens, London SW1W 0DU

Residential Short Courses (currently 35p. plus 9p. postage) (England and Wales), and *Year Book of Adult Education* (currently £1) a directory of organizations providing adult education here and in some countries overseas, published by National Institute of Adult Education, 35 Queen Anne Street, London W1 Tel: 01–637 4241

Vacation Courses Abroad (currently 35p.) published by the Central Bureau for Educational Visits and Exchanges, 43 Dorset Street, London W1 Tel: 01 486 5101

7

Wood

Whole villages once drew their livelihood from the woodlands; hardly another craftsman could start his work without the products which the woodmen made available. The thatcher turned to them for his spars; the charcoal-worker and attendant industries of pottery, iron and glass needed them to supply their fuel, the toolmaker his ash handles, the carpenter his wood. The mighty Tudors launched the noble naval tradition through the stout-hearted English oak. Trees were turned into trestles and wheels, carts and casks, spindles and shafts, buckets and barriers. No other single medium has proved so utterly versatile as wood.

Nowhere else in Europe has the process of deforestation by grazing or burning, by clearing for agriculture, timber and fuel supplies, been so drastic as in Britain. Little natural forest remained by the fifteenth century, when an Act was passed by Edward IV in an attempt to protect the woodlands, but it was not until the crown lands were disposed of to the wealthy landowners that any management of woodlands was undertaken.

During the seventeenth century the landowners formed high forest plantations, which were to be extended in the more prosperous century which followed. The development of silviculture in Britain has, therefore, been based on planned and planted coppices and woodland, rather than the natural evolution of ancient forestry.

Present British forestry policy dates back to 1919, when the Forestry Commission was founded, primarily to build up a strategic reserve of standing timber to make good the depletion which occurred during the First World War due to reduced imports. Currently, approximately one twelfth of Britain's land area is afforested – some 716,000 hectares of productive woodlands, of which 476,000 are in private ownership. The production of timber is still the commission's prime objective, it harvests its own timber and trees are sold standing to timber-merchants either by tender or auction.

Altogether some 3·6 million cubic metres of timber are harvested in Britain in a year, supplemented by 604,000 cubic metres of imported woods. The breakdown of the home production is, roughly, two-thirds softwoods and one-third hardwoods. The private sector, whose interests are represented by the Timber Growers' Association, is responsible for about a third of the softwoods and almost all of the hardwoods.

Most craftsmen working in wood buy their materials from timber merchants, though some have contact with local estates and select their timber standing.

WOODLANDS AND COPPICE CRAFTS

My chief tools are a fromard – for splitting the poles – a drawknife and a mortice knife.

Frank Wicks, hurdle-maker.

The last of a long line of Hullavington hurdle-makers, Frank Wicks uses the tools of his forefathers, all locally made by the village black-smith. Over the past twenty-five years his range of work has embraced all kinds of coppice crafts from thatching spars to rustic furniture, but as the only hurdler where there were once five, he finds enough work to keep him busy making sheep- and pig-hurdles for farms and markets, for although there are some half-dozen hazel-wattle hurdlers in the willow-growing area of Wessex there is a substantial decline in bar hurdle-makers. The greatest market is for racing hurdles and Frank supplies most of the well-known racecourses in the country.

Hurdlers are cleavers of wood, not sawyers, this is why copses provide the right size for their use and why hurdlers worked in the woods in the days when they selected, cut and converted what was suitable for their needs. Ash is the natural choice with its hardening properties.

"I was given best for turning, [Alec Twinning reminisces] then I've been at it since I was 11 and threatened with a hammer if I didn't get it right – you had to do as was said, then. I showed some big estate fellow once how to split a pole with a fromard, gave me half a crown, he did. Easiest half a crown I'd ever earned in my life. He was back in no time – no, you can't teach what it takes a lifetime to learn: most I ever got from a pole was twenty-seven spars – that's fair to middling I reckon."

Such was the extent of woodland industries that the management of coppices was the first consideration under the "Act for the preservation of woods", passed by Henry VIII in 1543 with the sole object of securing small-sized material for hurdle-making, fencing, firewood and charcoal, and bark for tanning leather. A rotational system of cutting was followed to ensure an annual supply.

Escalating prices of land have caused some noticeable reversion of coppice woods to agricultural use, a situation accelerated by the new capital gains tax which meant more woods falling to the axe. This has been very obvious in Essex where one firm has had to change its source of supply three times in the last six years. The picture is as gloomy in Suffolk where the future of woodlands is also in jeopardy. Four men are primarily engaged in making riven ash-hurdles at the Barrow Hurdle

Factory which has been in operation for the best part of this century, but they see it as a dying trade and train no apprentices to take over when the present craftsmen retire. They accept the dwindling demand for riven sheep-hurdles as part of changing agricultural practice, but the increased call for broaches, liggers, pegs stack and house spits from thatchers all over the country seems to emphasize the fact that there is increasing difficulty in obtaining coppice hazel in other parts of the country. In Wiltshire, however, coppice industry is being revived at the forestry and natural history centre, a woodland park of some 120 acres.

A truly rural industry is Whelnetham Woodwork, whose proximity to a protected medieval coppice means they have less problems in getting raw materials than similar enterprises. Producing the kind of hand-tools which were once made in most agricultural localities, they are probably one of few surviving craft concerns to do so today, and their orders come from far and wide. Some are obviously intended more for decoration than use, but Ron Hack is not entirely unhappy about this, for he will not lower the standards to turn the traditional tools into folksy art, and sees it as a survival line rather than 'preserving' the factory with such fascinating hand-built machinery as is used – powered by an ancient diesel which also generates the factory's only electricity. Some thirty workers were employed when the factory started in 1912, today there are three – including Ron who is also manager and typist. He does not fear the fierce competition of mass-produced hayrakes for their quality and durability cannot compare with those with cleft teeth, inserted by hand and hand-pointed. Once a localized agricultural market, the 'beetles' (large wooden mallets shod with heat-shrunk hoops), hayrakes and scythe 'snaths' (handles), have become specialized implements used by river boards, golf-courses, parks and public gardens.

The rustic besom, too, holds its own in this plastic-bristled age. Picking leaves off lawns in the way no other broom can without damage to the grass, its construction has remained the same since its Saxon inception. Gypsies once made a reasonable living from the heather brooms they assembled off the Hampshire heath commons, but have left their rustic pursuits in favour of more lucrative scrap dealings. The ancient craft is still carried on by A. West, who has been making them for well over fifty years, following a long family tradition. He does not have to resort to hawking them as his forefathers did, his customers come to him: and even royal gardens are swept with the birch and heather besoms. It looks deceptively simple, the drawing of withy bands out of clefts and binding the bundle of birch and heather on the 'brooming horse', but it is an art acquired after much practice. Nor are the bundles gathered and bound on the spot: the birch has to be cut, bundled up and stacked so that the pile will not collapse during seasoning. Hazel is favoured for handles, and, traditionally, willow or skinned bramble for the binding, the latter being of more tensile strength than wire.

The most progressive of the underwood industries seems to be the chestnut fencing section, where some $3\frac{1}{4}$ million yards of fencing are produced in a year, but fencing is obviously easier to measure than the production of rustic furniture generally.

Garden furniture of deceptively simple construction, bereft of intricate jointing and ornamentation, lifts coppice craft from rusticity to artistry when made as the Far Forest Works make theirs. Most of the oak saplings are locally grown and hand-peeled with an old-fashioned peeler, and heather from nearby Wyre Forest is used for thatching bird-tables.

Woodland and coppice crafts are, to a great extent, more anonymous than any other. Their purpose is purely functional and their form determined by their material. Our countryside can only be the poorer for their passing, for the men who work these woods are not purposefully setting out to appease their artistic temperament but simply to illustrate how man can work in harmony with nature.

TRUG-MAKING

The traditional way has never changed, we've never found anything better
Thomas Smith (Herstmonceux) Ltd

The materials of the Sussex trug determine its inclusion in the 'wood section', rather than in basketry. It was over a hundred years ago that Thomas Smith set willow-boards in sweet chestnut frames to make a boat-shaped basket. The success of the design inspired him to show it at the Hyde Park Exhibition of 1851, where it was so admired by Queen Victoria that she ordered a number of them to be specially made. It was a proud but tired Thomas Smith who personally delivered the order to Buckingham Palace – for he walked every step of the sixty-mile journey! From such auspicious beginnings the Sussex trug has become known all over the country. Thomas Smith's descendants still carry out the craft, using the templates he made and bending the hand-cut wood over steam from a pine-fired stove.

WALKING-STICK-MAKING

In stick-dressing we are aware of the fact that we have to make do with what nature has provided
Norman Tulip

Nature rarely provides the perfectly-shaped stick – excluding, of course, the workaday thumbstick or stave. No longer the fashionable asset it once was, the walking-stick still has its place, even in this motorized age, although there are only two walking-stick manufacturing firms in the whole of Britain: one is one of the underwood industries of Surrey, the other in the Cotswolds where at the turn of the century, with others in the area, more sticks were produced in the Stroud valley than the rest of the world put together.

Few sticks are 'grown' (artificially cultivated into a curved handle), in fact Chalford Stick Company, whose work is under special contract, say their three-year-old sweet chestnut saplings are anything but straight when they are cut; one end will be too thin and the other end too thick. They are then selected for length and strength before being boiled, peeled and washed to remove their sticky sap coating. They are straightened by hand through a 'horse', a leather strapped plank.

The crook is shaped, as of old, by immersion in hot, damp sawdust – a similar method to the steaming of ships' timbers, and assumes its permanent bend through its natural moisture being dried in. Enthusiastic scrubbing, which also used to be with damp sawdust, removes all whiskery residue and the crook end is trimmed to shape. The nose is put on the curved end, and the stick cut to one of four lengths. Four different weights and thicknesses and twelve variations make up the range. Various finishing processes are carried out and the stick tested for feel before it is fitted with a foot rubber. No fewer than fifteen operations are performed on one stick before it is fit for the health service.

On the other hand, shepherds' crooks, the speciality of Mr Blake, are cut out of a block. His walking-sticks are cut from local woods during the winter months when the sap is down, and seasoned for a year before he works on them. Mr Blake applies no process of steaming to his sticks and shapes them according to their natural growth, a craft skill which he has demonstrated on television and one which has brought orders from all over the world.

November is the month when Northumberland stick-dressers go forth in search of hazel blocks and shanks, selecting the shoots from which they will carve their distinctive decorative sticks. A stick-cutting expedition often leads them out of their own county in search of suitable material, for fishermen cut the saplings for making their crab-pots, and rabbit-catchers cut them for their snare pins. Between them therefore, they take the best stick-dressing material at an early stage in the growth of the shoot.

In the old days, stick-dressing was practised in the remote hills of the Border country by many people, but there were only two Northumbrians in the whole of the British Isles practising it after the last war. It was raised to an art form by Ned Henderson and the late George Snaith who, despite their close friendship, competed against each other for over thirty years. The secrets of the craft were once jealously guarded and inherited with the family fortune. Eventually, as the stick-dressers grew older and realized that their craft was in danger of dying with them, they passed on some of their knowledge.

Norman Tulip is an expert stick-dresser. His collection of about eighty exquisitely carved sticks represents about 20,000 hours' work. He acknowledges his apprenticeship to the late George Snaith and the initiative of the local education authority which has played a major part in reviving the craft by having it taught over the last decade within its evening-class programmes.

There is little fear of the Northumbrian dressed stick becoming mass-produced like the 'Empire made' Cornish pixie, however, for if anyone can persuade the hundred or so stick-dressers to part with their work they will have succeeded where others have failed, for this is a truly local craft practised by Northumbrians for the sheer love of it.

COOPERAGE

> Coopering is dying. In the commercial world, only certain stages of the craft
> are still practised.
>
> *Death of a Craft (Crafts)*

This comment introduced Fiona Adamczewski's article on the situation at Hall and Ryan, one of the last two cooperagers still operating in the London area, an area which supported some 3,000 coopers thirty years ago, whereas today there are an estimated 200.

The cause of this craft's decline is the increasing use of metal casks which the majority of larger breweries are already using for beer, although the wine and spirits trade still uses wooden casks because wines and spirits mature better in wood.

Cooperage can best be described as engineering in wood, each stave acting as a keystone in the construction of the cask, supported by other staves as a base; and in more than 2,000 years of scientific progress the double-arch construction of the wooden cask has not been improved upon.

Wooden casks are referred to in the First Book of Kings, and were used in ancient Greece. Cooperage reached a high standard in Roman Britain and as a craft guild dates back to at least 1307. A century later it was strong enough to require the passing of an Act of Parliament restraining anybody but authorized coopers from making casks.

One of the oldest of London's livery companies, being constituted in 1502, the Coopers Guild received a new charter in 1662, under which it still acts. Some of the ceremonies of the medieval guilds have been maintained to the present day, including the 'trussing' of a new cooper inside the cask which he has completed without the assistance of the journeyman cooper or machines. Apprenticeship now lasts four years, and is indentured under a legal agreement binding the employers to provide facilities for the boy to be taught the craft.

The first record of brewers employing coopers to make and repair casks is an Act of 1531. Today, Buckley's of Cheshire are the only remaining independent brewery coopers of any substance in the whole of the United Kingdom, and they too, aware of the diminishing use of the traditional oak cask, fashion a range of bar furniture on the principles of cooperage.

WHEELWRIGHTING AND CARRIAGE BUILDING

It is when one comes to 'offer them up' (putting one thing with the other) that a wheelwright tests his craftsmanship which Gimson so admired, for he has to be skilled in so many materials and so many crafts.

Dennis Tugwell

"There is a wheelwright in nearly every village", wrote Richard Jefferies in the 1870s. There are about fifty in the whole of England in the 1970s.

Wheelwrighting is a truly rural craft; the wheelwright a truly village craftsman. He, along with the blacksmith and the thatcher, served a social purpose by working for his neighbours, the farmer and the local squire. Now the structure of the village, its agriculture and mode of transport, has changed, and with this change comes the inevitable risk of losing yet another craftsman indigenous to his locality, for there were great variations between vehicles of different counties, the design and detail having evolved from the topography and agrarian needs of their native areas. But the basic principles of construction and choice of timber were followed by each craftsman as he made the wheels. Elm, quickly disappearing from the English timber scene, is invariably chosen for the nave; oak for the spokes; and ash for the felloes. The wheels are assembled in a steaming and sizzling orderly bustle as the iron tyre is put on hot, doused with water to prevent fire and shrunk into place, and the wheels are bound within metal rims.

The demand on the wheelwright's skill has waxed and waned. Supreme in the heyday of coach travel, he became almost superfluous after the Industrial Revolution, but was brought back for honourable service during the crucial years of the Second World War, when it became essential to maintain existing farm vehicles, although he almost faced redundancy soon afterwards.

As a craft, wheelwrighting gained early recognition. The Worshipful Company of Wheelwrights, set up by Royal Charter in 1670 for the benefit of practising wheelwrights, originally supervised the workmanship of its members and records show that fines were imposed for substandard work. No wheelwright was allowed to ply his trade within the City of London if he was not a member of the company. Today, there are no practising wheelwrights who are members of the company. As with some other livery companies of diminishing crafts, its aims are to maintain the standards of the City and support charitable work. Membership, restricted by charter to 300, is dependent on obtaining the Freedom of the Company and then the Freedom of the City.

So, what of these remaining wheelwright shops registered for England? Are they assigned to becoming a tourist attraction as working museum pieces? Not a bit of it. Wagon- and cart-bodies, old seed-drills, wheelbarrows, sack-lifters, threshing-machines – all find their way to the wheelwright's shop, and often he is called out to repair or renew the heavy beams of the old farm barns. It has not been unknown for him to have also been, or still be, the village undertaker.

It is perhaps this ready adaptability and, more importantly, the extensive working knowledge of the different qualities and uses of timbers, that has ensured the survival of the wheelwright. No longer dictated to by the fluctuating prosperity of agriculture, his kind is to be found in communities where ability to work in wood has overcome the problems of a changing technological age.

Prognostications on the future of the wooden wheel were made after the invention of the pneumatic tyre, although experience has shown that iron-tyred wooden wheels are superior to rubber in most rural areas; but the height of a cart and the strain of the load often leads to conflicting interests between the farmworker and horse. Matching strength of design to stress in use is the delicate balance which the wheelwright has to maintain.

Turning roughly-hewn wood into a slender-spoked wheel starts with cleaving the oak for the spokes, this reveals any fault in the timber which is not shown in sawing. The nave, or hub, is mortised to hold the tenoned ends of the spokes, and the felloes form the wooden rim. The spokes are set at such an angle to give a dished effect, relating to the angle at which the axle is set; a flat wheel would never withstand the rigours of constant use.

Calculating points to horizontals and projections to angles in order to achieve the right 'hang' of the wheel is but a part of the skill, for the metal strip for the tyre is measured by a combination of algebra and intuition. The circumference is carefully measured, but only experience teaches a craftsman to allow for the extra length needed for 'shutting', so that the metal rim binds the wooden wheel exactly.

"The larger the wheel the better it rolls" is a maxim proven by the racing buggy which Dennis Tugwell built, based on a brief sketch in an old encyclopaedia. The design holds the record of being the fastest drawn by a pair of horses, and was based on Studebaker's Modern American Buggy, one of his famous horse-drawn carriages from which Studebaker progressed to design cars.

The buggy, made of mahogany with ash panelling, with its head-board painted black according to tradition, attracted the attention of Prince Philip who was competing in the driving championships at Cirencester Park.

It is in the horse-drawn carriages of yesteryear that the upsurge of interest is shown. Farm-carts and wagons still come to the wheelwright's shop for repair, and often are almost completely rebuilt, but the numbers reflect the marked decrease in the number of horses used in agriculture. A century ago England and Wales used 830,000 horses, excluding mares kept for breeding; ten years ago that number dropped to 19,000; today, including mares kept for breeding, there are a mere 5,000 used for agricultural purposes, out of a total horse population of 164,000.

The British Driving Society, of which Prince Philip is Patron, has some 2,000 members, and since its inception in 1957 has stimulated interest in the hitherto dying craft of carriage-building. Many of the society's members carry out work on their own vehicles, varying from painting and upholstering to actual body-building and ironwork. There are also some fourteen carriage museums in this country, many of which rely upon the wheelwright's extensive skills for repairs and renovations.

Not all true wheelwrights are carriage-builders of course, but many are. Likewise, some craftsmen who are not termed wheelwrights do build horse-drawn vehicles. An example of the latter is Pilgrims of Blandford who build anything from two-wheeled gigs for ponies to four-wheeled brewers drays for a team of heavy Percherons, but they do not undertake refurbishing of old vehicles.

Renovation means big business from American clients. No fewer than thirty-two carriages, ranging from a large circus-wagon to a stage-coach, were recently assigned for complete renovation to Eric Home-wood of North Devon by an American millionaire industrialist.

Mr Homewood has restored the carriages in the National Trust collection on the Arlington Court estate, and draws upon his intimate knowledge of them to reproduce scale models of the four outstanding ones for collectors and museums.

By far and away the largest builders of showing standard horse-drawn carriages in Europe is Harewood Carriage Co. Ltd of Devon. Over a hundred vehicles of different types are produced each year. The whole range of crafts associated with carriage-building: wheelwright-ing, shaft-making, body-building, under-carriage- and spring-making, coach-trimming, painting and varnishing, is carried out at Holsworthy. The oak and ash is home-grown and air-dried.

The aesthetic values and traditional craftsmanship which earned the nineteenth-century English carriage industry a world-wide reputation for excellence are certainly still maintained today.

TURNERY

> Many women are craftworkers – not so many turners, although there are several; it was a field in which I felt a woman's ideas might bear fruit.
>
> *Margaret Bellamy*

Literally fruit – for Margaret Bellamy produces the sort of decorative fruits that were made in the eighteenth century: pears and apples in yew, oak, steamed beech and plane, and figs in cherry. Like many turners, she is also a carver, and combines the skills in such items as her oak spinning-chairs.

It may be that the opposing facets of the two skills are practised for the sheer mastery of their different approaches, turning basically being an application of tools to rotating wood; whereas carving is completely hand-controlled, the depth of a cut being the result of direct pressure of tool to timbers.

The turner's products are collectively termed *treen*, which embraces domestic and tableware made of wood. The humble bowls and platters which were ousted from the cottages in favour of china are being restored with dignity but, like other craftsmen, the wood-turner is having to fight for his existence against the cheap, varnished woodware imported from the East. Discriminating customers will look beyond the gay packaging however, and will gladly pay a realistic price for the hand-turned article which shows the craftsman's knowledge of which woods are suited to culinary use. Sycamore, for instance, having neither taste nor smell, is a popular choice, but the craft world is full of enterprising designers, such as Robin and Mary Ellis, who have exploded the myth that pine can never be successfully turned. The fact that it can, and to tremendous effect, is proved by their superb tableware. No longer shackled by its weight, wood is so finely turned that only the satin knots and swirling grain indicate that it *is* wood. Its potential has been developed a step further by the addition of a permanently sealed surface, so that the Ellis's pine tableware can be washed up; a fiery curry on the platter or mulled wine in the goblet has no sad effect on the wood whatsoever. A. Moore, the Peldon woodturner, specializes in seventeenth-century goblets treated for use so that, like the first Elizabethans, we can enjoy the pleasure of drinking wine from wood.

Another craftsman to confound the pedants is Peter Spear of Sussex, not so much by his use of elm and yew for tableware as by the way in which he evolved his business without any formal training. It is the kind of success story which every writer loves. A farmer for whom falling pig prices dealt a drastic blow to an agricultural venture, Peter Spear fashioned his first bowls on an old lathe which he had haggled for £1 from a blacksmith who had used it for turning cartwheel hubs. By the light of a paraffin lamp he got the treadle to work whilst waiting for his sows to farrow. Inspired by that indefinable instinct which drives such men to explore a skill for which they have never received even one lesson, Peter Spear is among the best of his kind today – a member of county guilds and the Society of Designer-Craftsmen, with a full order-book from customers across the world. An enviable position one might wish on any one of a dozen craftsmen, but few would merit it more, for indeed, it was and is hard-earned. Countless cold nights after long farming days were spent in that cart-shed perfecting his skills, with only the working of the treadle to keep him from freezing; nor did he presume to wrest a living from his craftwork until he had sought the advice of the then Rural Industries Bureau. Even now he is still his own traveller, delivery boy, sawyer, carter and turner, working a thirteen-hour day in his wood-dust-covered workshop at the end of a farm lane.

Wood for hand-turning has, of necessity, to be of top quality, and the finishing often takes as long or longer than the actual turning; this, in turn, is reflected in the final cost. But many of the designs can be exploited for a mass-market, having been cheapened by the use of inferior materials and by automatic turning. There is also a marked difference between a skilled turner, a craftsman in his own right, who can copy to perfection; and one who can design and create as well, for a design for turning has to be done by the turner on the lathe which perhaps accounts for the relatively slow development in turnery. Many craftsmen deplore the attitude to turnery in schools, for lumping it under the general term *woodwork* hardly gives it the craft status to which it is entitled. Few cabinet-makers proper are turners, or *vice versa*, although turning is often an integral part of the craft of furniture-making, so turners, such as T. Godley of Cirencester, are invaluable to furniture-restorers. Most turners specialize in, say, tableware, whereas others, like A. Rogers of Chesham, extend the craft to twisted banister-rails and clock-case parts – Joseph Byrne of Liverpool takes that to its ultimate conclusion by making the clock movements as well.

The ordinary lathe probably developed from the principles of the potter's wheel and can be traced back some 3,500 years to the Greek woodworkers. Its history was researched by Robert S. Woodbury and issued by the Society of Ornamental Turners for the *History of Technology*, Ohia, but never put on general sale. The best known treatise on the subject is Holtzpaffel's *Turning and Mechanical Manipulation*. The finest practical example of a lathe is the pole-lathe; portable, and of simple construction, it fulfilled the requirements of the chair-bodger who worked where his materials were to hand – in the plantation. Basic, home-made, and functional, it was designed by those who would operate it.

Equipment
During the last decade much emphasis has been laid upon the influence which craftsmen could have upon industrial design. This seemingly

obvious point is demonstrated by the fact that the most successful equipment for craftsmen is designed by craftsmen who are specialists in that particular field.

One of the few designers of hand-weaving equipment now operating in the British Isles is Victor Edwards, whose Harris looms are considered to be the best of their kind anywhere in the world. The tremendous increase in the demand for both weaving and spinning equipment keeps about a dozen craftsmen working full-time to supply Colleges of Technology and Art with hand-looms for designing purposes, and larger Dobby and Jacquard looms for more advanced diploma work. They also supply rehabilitation centres, hospitals, and individual weavers. It is not surprising that Harris looms have a world-wide market, for Victor Edwards is an eminent weaver whose lectures take him all over the country, and his courses at Hawkhurst Craft Centre are fully subscribed.

Eliza Leadbeater is another household name in the weaving world. Her comprehensive equipment business was begun because of her own desperation at inadequate supplies, and the unattractive alternative of bulk-buying or importing. Her husband's interest in turnery developed during his research work as a physicist and Eliza, with feminine wisdom, directed him to her collection of textile tools which were in need of repair.

Another husband and wife team specialize in making an improved version of a very early inkle-loom. Having made the looms by hand in their Sussex garage, and finished them with bees-wax from their own bees, the only publicity they had was the interest shown in the mini-loom worked by an old lady on a bus travelling from Littlehampton to Brighton. Bradley inkle-looms now go as far afield as Australia and Botswana. A charming couple, Eric and Lavinia look upon their customers as friends rather than clients; they say they are constantly amazed at what can be achieved on their inkles!

Tailoring equipment to the craftsmen's individual needs is not confined to any one field. Len Huxley of Oxfordshire concentrates the skills of his specialist joiners to build potters' wheels designed by potter Bill Read, knowing that the timber body and control pedal is suited to the natural materials with which a potter works. The potter's wheel is a craftsman-like piece of furniture, aesthetically pleasing and functionally precise.

ORNAMENTAL TURNING

It would take more than a lifetime to acquire all the capabilities of an Ornamental Turning lathe.

W. A. Bourne

The potential of the lathe for ornamental turning was being explored at the time of Leonardo da Vinci and was developed by other Europeans until Holtzpaffel started to make it a commercial proposition at the end of the eighteenth century. By furthering the development of the milling machine it could be said that he contributed to the Industrial Revolution, yet ornamental turning never became a successful commercial venture.

The mechanical manipulation of the devices appealed not only to engineers; Peter the Great and royalty in France and Sweden were known to have both owned and used ornamental turning lathes. It became the traditional hobby of the well-to-do until the internal combustion engine ousted it out of favour and the artisan and enthusiast took over. As an art-craft it virtually died out between the two world wars. The formation of the Society of Ornamental Turners fanned the dying embers of interest into life and is entirely responsible for reviving the utilization and preservation of existing lathes, but the paucity of machinery and worthwhile materials now imposes limitations. Craftsmen are resolute beings, however, and the capabilities of the modern lathe are being explored for use in ornamental turning, and the results are encouraging. Materials present a different problem: ivory, the prime choice, is both scarce and expensive; blackwood is almost unobtainable; and perspex is limited in range.

The society has the co-operation of the Worshipful Company of Turners, the Science Museum and Birmingham Museum, the two museums having ornamental-turning machinery and work on view. But of the society's 230 members – 180 in the United Kingdom, the rest overseas – there is probably only one professional ornamental turner left. Although most will sell their work they insist on an amateur status, which is belied in most instances by the quality of their work.

BOBBIN-MAKING

Each community of lace-makers has its own kind of bobbin, but English workers in the East Midlands favour the double-necked, produced in an almost endless variety of turnings.

R. W. J. Norton

A different kind of turning is needed for making bobbins for lace-makers. A wide range of woods is used: the pink cherry, white and pink beech, grey holly, yellow box, brown and black rosewood, green greenheart, purpleheart, tan muhuhu and grey-brown olive, adding colour to the lace-maker's pillow. Mr Norton introduces variety to the smooth, single-necked bobbin necessary for the making of Honiton lace by combining different woods in the same bobbin, by incised decoration and, sometimes, inscriptions of names and dates to commemorate family occasions or public events, thus following in the tradition of lace-bobbin-makers of yesteryear.

The upsurge of interest in lace-making over the last decade brought a sudden demand for bobbins. There are plastic forms available but the discerning lace-maker rejects them as totally unsuitable, their weight is rarely right and their finish invariably wrong, sharp edges in the castings breaking the fine threads. Antique dealers quickly exploited the situation and their shops fairly bristled with bobbins – at a premium. I have traced two lace-bobbin-makers from whom a dozen beautifully turned bobbins can be bought cheaper than can one of dubious origin with artificial woodworm decoration; both developed their business initially to supply local demand. Both work to full capacity and receive orders from all over Britain. Neither has needed to advertise, orders coming by way of personal recommendation. Something like a thousand a year find their way from Mr Brown's workshop, and Mr Norton reports that the most active lace-making areas are Devon, Leicestershire, East Midlands and Yorkshire.

Close-grained woods are becoming increasingly difficult to obtain so Mr Norton uses ramin for most of his work, reserving the rarer timbers for reproducing the fascinating bobbin types: 'Mother and Babe', 'Cow and Calf', 'Tigers', and 'Gingles', so popular with the early lace-makers, given as tokens of affection like the Welsh love-spoons.

WOOD-CARVING

Visiting the church and talking to the parents of the young man to whom a hanging rood was to be carved as a memorial helped me to get some feeling into the face of Christ.

Ron Butterfield, SCC

Creating a tangible object from an abstract idea is a facility expected and accepted of craftsmen in general, but of the sculptor in particular. Ron Butterfield, whose work is to be seen in churches throughout the country, was asked to carve the face of a monk which appeared in his client's recurring dream. "How was I to see into her dream?" he quite reasonably questioned. He could not, of course. But he set to work and still wonders what profound powers guided his chisel into the wood for when he had finished the lady exclaimed, "that's him". And the dream ceased!

Like so many labour-intensive crafts, that of the wood-carver's can never be among the commercially viable, and even those whose range extends across the whole range of sculptural design, from carving a wafer-box to re-designing an entire church interior, say they would not subject an apprentice to the vagaries of the career although many are happy to make others aware of our heritage by teaching at adult centres.

Ashley Iles, who produces hand-forged tools in the traditional way, reports a continuous increase in the practice of wood-carving since the war. A skilled carver may use up to 150 chisels or gouges of varying forms and sizes and it is because of this immense complement of hand-tools that industry cannot cope, or would find it uneconomic to cope, with intricate work on carved pieces. It is, therefore, to the craftsmen that the special jobs go, and an artist's sensitivity is thus expressed through an artisan's skill.

Carvers like Roy Pitcher of Olveston often adapt implements and tools alien to a wood-carver's work-bench. The need to roughen a background to give more relief to the carving means making special punches, one of which he uses to imprint his trade-mark, an ant, on his work. A cooper's gimlet and a shipwright's hammer are amongst a motley collection of tools lying in the shavings. In the tradition of wood-carvers he draws on nature for his subjects: brambles and acorns, oak leaves and squirrels, bulrushes and owls emerge from the oak which he stores so zealously.

The Church, as of old, is still the biggest patron of the sculptor.

Lettering, lifted to an art form by Eric Gill, also accounts for a fair amount of the carver's work. Conversely, those crafts derived from art forms such as the wood engravings, which were the main form of nineteenth-century book illustration, are practised by very few today, making such exquisite works as those of Joan Hassall the more valuable, and she adds her own distinguished contribution to a noble tradition.

FURNITURE-MAKING

Things men have made with wakened hands,
and put soft life into, are awake,
with transferred touch and go on glowing for long years.
For this reason, some old things are lovely,
warm still with the life of forgotten men
who made them . . .

All possible should be done to widen understanding of the implications of this poem.

Edward Barnsley, C.B.E.

Few designer-craftsmen can be better qualified than Edward Barnsley to assess the value of craftsmen's work. A venerable veteran whose workshop experience spans over half a century, Edward Barnsley's intense interest in his craft might be more properly termed dedication, for he is acutely aware of the present-day problems facing craftsmen, yet fully endorses that craftsmen can make a particular contribution to the country's industry. Subscribing to the sentiments of the poem heading this section, devoid of sentimentality, he marries the merits of mechanization to the principles of handcrafts to achieve excellence of technical qualities and efficiency without compromising the individuality of the design, which is not *adapted* to machine production.

The question of powered tools in a crafts workshop is one which excites academic argument. One craftsman (a weaver) commented that commercially-printed labels promoting hand-made goods renders the whole concept of craftwork suspect, so the arguments can range from the sublime to the ridiculous. The issue is a particularly difficult one for furniture-makers, but surely the question is not so much *whether* machinery should be used at all but to what *extent* it should be employed, and this is usually decided by considering the economic viability in relation to the labour involved in the enterprise. Thus, responsibility to his employees is an additional factor which the master has to consider, for few furniture-makers have made an adequate living by producing hand-made goods since the Ruskin-Morris period; many have taken pupils or taught part-time to supplement their income.

The affinity between master and apprentice seems stronger in the furniture-making sector than in other crafts. Master craftsmen will acknowledge the skilled makers who reflect credit on their workshop, maintaining the standard they themselves have set. Edward Barnsley's foreman and manager, Herbert Upton, started as a lad in 1924; and George Taylor and Oskar Dawson have put in some seventy years' work between them; with Hugh Routh, Michael Bowen and apprentice Mark Nicholas joining the team on which he says he relies entirely to achieve the highest standards for his designs.

Total involvement results in total commitment. This is Tim Green's policy at Crowdy's of Clanfield – a small place where wood is turned into everything from buttons to doors, spinning-wheels, and complete sets of restaurant furniture – is that everyone, including the most junior apprentice, completes a job from start to finish, from selecting and machining the rough timber to the final finishing process. With larger pieces of furniture, the craftsman who made the article will often assist with delivery to the customer's home.

Pilgrims of Dorset have their pieces signed by the men who make them, their names being carved into the wood. They now have customers who come back for additional pieces specifying the craftsman for the job. Eventually whole rooms, and even houses, are completely furnished by one man's work. Each piece carries, in addition, the carved pilgrim trade-mark.

In the way of medieval masons who scored geometric codes into the stonework for which they were responsible, craftsmen working in wood have adopted their own trademarks. Originator of the woodland animals signs, particularly common in Yorkshire, was Robert Thompson, the famous 'mouseman' of Kilburn, who was carving a beam on a church roof when another carver murmured something about them being as poor as church mice, and on the spur of the moment Robert Thompson carved one. He later adopted it as his trade-mark, likening the way a mouse manages to scrape away the hardest wood with its chisel-like teeth, to the work of the craftsmen hidden away in his own workshop in the Hambleton Hills.

Robert Thompson started his career in his father's joinery and wheelwright shop, making carts and mending gates. The medieval oak-work of Ripon Cathedral fired his imagination and inspired his ambition to resurrect the spirit of ancient craftsmanship, which eventually made him world-famous. From his first commission to carve an oak cross for Ampleforth, Thompson's ecclesiastical work was to be seen in seven hundred churches up and down the country, among them Westminster Abbey and York Minster. By 1950 he had an overflowing order book and enough jobs to use a hundred tons of timber.

Since his death in 1955 the firm has been carried on by his two grandsons, Robert and John Cartwright, in the same tradition. The Kilburn community of craftsmen has risen to forty-six and will probably never rise much above that, despite pressure of work, for the noise and clamour of a big firm would be alien to the principle of "industry in quiet places" – its founder's motto. The ubiquitous mouse is still there, nestling on a chair-leg, skirting a bowl, climbing a candlestick or perched on a pew.

There is no shortage of apprentices to learn the trade of the 'mouseman'; two or three are chosen each year on recommendation of the local employment officer. Although there is no special apprenticeship scheme their first task is to learn to carve a mouse.

Apprentices acknowledge their masters too and proudly present their names as credentials – yardsticks against whom their early talents were measured, who saw and helped them to develop their potential. But whilst paying tribute to those who watched over them, tolerated their early years, and shaped their future, few purposely emulate them. Their craft skills may have been perfected under their master's eye but their designs are their own.

Wilfred Hutchinson's apprenticeship piece – a box with a mouse on its lid – stands testimony to his craft training, but he carves and planes and adzes under the sign of the squirrel, symbolic of the English oak, the material in which he works almost exclusively. His early work in the Kilburn community is perpetuated in the traditional hand-dovetailing joints, tapering pin-joints and meticulous attention to detail which has made his furniture investment pieces; but the clean line is indicative of Sheraton.

Alan Peters served his cabinet-making apprenticeship with Edward Barnsley, but is noted for modern furniture. The versatility he gained from his craft training has served him in such diverse activities as making an intricate jewel casket for presentation to H.M. the Queen, to converting a double-decker bus into a mobile showroom. He does, however, observe his master's creed of keeping his concern small enough to enable him to participate personally in it.

The ideals of great masters will always be perpetuated in some form or other by others. Ernest Gimson and the Barnsley brothers have passed into the craftlore of furniture-making for what has been termed "the Cotswold tradition". Influenced somewhat by William Morris, their delight in the beauty of wood and their rule that simplicity of construction is the basis of good design in turn took root in Broadway in the north Cotswolds where there was no tradition of cabinet-making. Some 2,000 people now sit on Gordon Russell's English oak chairs in Coventry Cathedral, and specialist contract work makes the name of Gordon Russell known in universities and churches, hotels, ships and embassies throughout the world.

An almost total rejection of that tradition appears at first glance to be present in John Makepeace's work, which has excited writers into searching for new adjectives to adequately describe his distinctive furniture designs. Institutions eagerly add his work to their collections and critics go into paroxysms of poetic praise every time he exhibits another incongruous combination of materials. Unconventional his designs may be – certainly reflective of the modern age – yet his skills and sheer craftsmanship are but a continuation of the tradition of Barnsley and Gimson in whose policies he trained as a cabinet-maker, and which he now perpetuates in his school for wood craftsmen at Parnham House in Dorset. John Makepeace has recently been appointed as consultant to the EEC and the Commonwealth Secretariat on the development of wood products in the Third World.

The title of cabinet-maker probably evolved in the early eighteenth century when new foreign woods were brought back as ballast by merchants returning from overseas expeditions. A new race of craftsmen was beginning – furniture-makers as distinct from carpenters, who previously made and fixed all the woodwork in a house, including movable furniture. The definition of a cabinet-maker seems to be a little

more difficult to determine, for his skills are called upon to make anything from a small jewellery casket to panelling a room, as well as restoring and repairing pieces which were made in an age far removed
from his own.

Commissions are usually for reproduction pieces in traditional
styles, but the imaginative faculty of some clients can usually be
matched by the ingenuity of the craftsmen. A cursory glance at their
order-books, over their shoulders and amid the wood shavings is a revelation, for there are the challenges unencountered by the machinist on
the factory floor. It seems invidious to select some from the many, but I
do so to illustrate the fact that today's craftsman is every bit as capable
of producing the same kind of work as was done by his predecessors, for
whose passing the nostalgics keep up a long and loud lament. For
obvious reasons I cannot name the craftsman who made a secret panel
to cover a safe in a chimney breast from a design drawn on the floor-
boards so that it could be cleaned off on completion of the project.

Interpretation tantamount to telepathy would often seem to be called
for on the craftsman's part, but an inherent sensitivity serves one such
as R. H. Fyson sufficiently to make a rocking-horse "to look like a horse
with a nice face"; to carve bargeboards for the main gables on the
famous Compton Wyngates House exactly as a craftsman had done in
1492; or to fashion a Regency-style sofa-table out of a partly-burnt Victorian dining-table.

Every article produced is really a speciality, and 98 per cent of the
furniture-makers whom I have contacted have reported increased
orders, attributing their full order-books to word-of-mouth recommendations, direct sales and integrity of workmanship, rather than any
formal exhibitions or advertising. Growth, that pet word of the econom-
ists, does not necessarily follow full order-books however. Most are still
one-man concerns and wish to remain so. An extreme example is a
small firm who within the last three years has grown from three men
working part-time to six men and an apprentice working full-time, to
produce furniture at the value of some £80,000 per annum, which shows
that high quality craftwork is still much in demand. The tradition of
many companies is maintained, promoted and encouraged by training
through the Learnership scheme, under the National Labour Agreement for the furniture-manufacturing trade, and by compulsory craft
day-release training at Furniture College through the City and Guilds
approved courses.

The British furniture-manufacturers federated associations and the
local Learnership Committee monitor the training of young persons in
liaison with the Furniture College and the unions, as well as group
training officers, careers officers and furniture-manufacturer representatives, in craft trades such as cabinet-making, carving, and upholstery.

The High Wycombe Furniture-manufacturers' Society makes

awards to students at the High Wycombe College of Technology (the Art School of Design and Furniture) and the John Hampden School, at the society's annual dinner. Similar awards are made by the eight other furniture associations representing the United Kingdom, as well those made by the Worshipful Company of Furniture-Makers, City and Guilds and numerous individual companies.

Enquiries to COSIRA for advice on methods of improving the standard of furniture finish – in which many craftsmen agree that there is probably more technique than in the actual making – still outweigh all other. Their assistance has been given in the polishing of such diverse items as archery bows, wooden jewellery, toys and shop-fronts.

The Craftsmen Furniture-Makers' Association decided to dissolve in 1965, after a decade of struggling to remain in existence. Many furniture-makers would welcome an association of their own, perhaps on less formal lines, and the opportunity to be in contact with their own kind. A pioneer in his field, thriving and successful, was the Thirsk Woodworkers' Discussion Group, formed some twenty-four years ago to keep its members abreast of new products, developments and legislation affecting the industry, resulting in general co-operation and the sharing of contracts.

Perhaps the future may rest on such local lines. It was not so long ago that High Wycombe chair-makers wore a miniature chair, suspended on ribbon and mounted on a rosette, as a buttonhole when supporting their local football team at away matches. And no craftsman would deny the contribution that the old chair-bodgers made to English furniture as they worked in the Buckinghamshire beech woods astride the home-made 'horse', shaping the rough wood ready for turning.

ANTIQUE FURNITURE RESTORATION

> One of the main difficulties we have to face in the field of furniture restoration is the public's suspicion of restorers, whom some regard as fakers and others have suffered at the hands of 'bodgers'.
>
> *M. G. Hay-Will (Aruncraft)*

The specialist restorer inevitably deals with a wide range of furniture. He has to have the skills of a cabinet-maker, gilder and polisher; his knowledge of timbers is encyclopaedic; and his approach to their chemistry analytical.

Recognizing the real need for specialist restorers, the (then) Rural Industries Bureau started an antique furniture restoration training scheme at the direct request of the Ministry of Works and Historic Buildings Council as far back as 1956, with the purpose of establishing a nucleus of highly skilled restorers.

The City and Guilds of London Art School has a three-year diploma course in wood and stone restoration; West Dean has professional courses of one year in antique furniture-restoration and antique-clock-restoration, both in conjunction with the British Antique Dealers Association; and other shorter courses are often offered by practising craftsmen themselves; yet there is no guild or association of furniture-restorers, although there have been attempts to form one.

Exhibitions have little relevance to their work in that specific field, but related aspects of the craft are usually useful channels through which the restorer can exhibit his work, such as the limited edition of scale miniatures of sixteenth- to eighteenth-century furniture which F. M. Howard of Aruncraft constructed in yew wood which was some 4,000 years old.

There seems to be a steady demand for the restoration work but the good quality materials, veneers, exotic timbers and suitable furnishings are difficult to get, and many craftsmen are having to turn their hand to make metal fittings, knobs and the like to get their projects finished on time.

MARQUETRY

Marquetry cannot correctly be so called unless executed by a marquetarian who has been indentured to another marquetarian who was himself indentured.

A. C. Harrison

It may be, on this premise, that there are few craftsmen who qualify for the title 'marquetarian'; however, titles apart, the number of those who practise the craft has increased sufficiently to warrant a marquetry society with a current membership of about 700. In its first five years almost 6,000 members have been recorded, drawn from many parts of the world.

Marquetry is a development of intarsia, the true inlay of wood upon wood which originated in Italy in the early thirteenth century, and was confined almost exclusively to ecclesiastical work until the Italians made more general use of inlay and marquetry in the decoration of household furniture some four centuries later.

From the early arabesques and elaborate scrolls, designs evolved into pictorial scenes – buildings, perspectives and flowers acquired naturalistic forms by the use of acid solutions, stains and scorching for rounding and shading effects.

As the craft spread across the Continent the Dutch developed their techniques and gained a world-wide reputation for the excellence of their work, furthered by the expansion of commerce, which made available to the marquetry craftsmen a wide variety of veneers. Marquetry of the most elaborate character was produced during the seventeenth and eighteenth centuries when more ornate materials were employed: tortoiseshell and copper on ebony became fashionable and several marquetarians rose to great eminence; André Boulle's name being perpetuated in the Anglicized form of *buhl*, as in *buhl work*. England followed the continental fashion for chairs enriched with inlaid designs during the reign of William and Mary, although marquetry appeared in a developed form during the late Stuart period, but generally it had but a minor influence on English designs and all but disappeared during the long French wars.

The original techniques, once guarded with great secrecy by the guilds which existed to protect the craftsmen's status by restricting the practice of marquetry to indentured marquetarians, are researched, explored and taught freely today and the craft is enjoying a great revival. Suitable materials and tools are expensive and difficult to obtain, added to which the time involved puts marquetry into the luxury class. Nevertheless, there seems to be a steady demand for high-class work, which in turn commands high prices: a mural measuring 8 feet by 2 feet was exhibited within the last few months at an asking price of £3,000.

Marquetry of every conceivable type is produced by A. C. Harrison of Bath for customers all over the world, and ranges from single pieces for the repair of antiques to panelling for ocean liners. Judith Hughes, a cabinet-maker from Devon, is a specialist in inlaying marquetry monograms in her modern furniture designs and has noticed that clients are increasingly asking for initials and dates to be put on, illustrating again that today's craft-made pieces are regarded as tomorrow's heirlooms.

SOCIETIES

CARPENTERS COMPANY, Carpenters Hall, Throgmorton Avenue, London EC2 Tel: 01 588 7001
Established in the fifteenth century, the company awards a number of scholarships for builders and architects.

HIGH WYCOMBE FURNITURE MANUFACTURERS' SOCIETY, Wycombe House, Amersham Hill, High Wycombe, Bucks. Tel: High Wycombe 23021/2
Caters for all types of furniture-manufacturers. Student awards.

INCORPORATED BRITISH INSTITUTE OF CERTIFIED CARPENTERS, Alderman House, 37 Soho Square, London W1. Tel: 01 437 6588
Founded in 1890 to maintain and advance the traditions of the craft and the status of its craftsmen. Meetings, international exchanges, awards, examinations and general assistance.

THE MARQUETRY SOCIETY, Hon. Sec: Mrs G. M. Walker, 113 Kingsway, Petts Wood, Kent BR5 1PP

Founded in 1952, the society is recognized as a leading authority on the craft of marquetry in all its branches. Advice and guidance are available from a panel of expert craftsmen. Exhibitions, competitions and group centres are arranged and a quarterly journal is published. Membership is open to anyone who aims to further their knowledge and appreciation of the craft.

THE SOCIETY OF ORNAMENTAL TURNERS, Hon. Sec: W. A. Bourne, 2 Parry Drive, Rustington, Littlehampton, Sussex BN16 2QY. Tel: 09062 5430

Membership is open to anyone interested in preserving existing ornamental lathes and keeping alive the craft.

TIMBER RESEARCH AND DEVELOPMENT ASSOCIATION, Highenden Valley, High Wycombe, Bucks. Tel: 0240 24 3091

Independent research on behalf of members: regional offices. General enquiries from the public are dealt with by the National Wood Council, Stag Place, London SW1. Tel: 01 828 5154

COPPICE CRAFTS

BARROW HURDLE FACTORY, 6 The Street, Barrow, Suffolk. Tel: Barrow 218 Head Office: 1 Aut Northgate, Bury St Edmunds, Suffolk. Tel: Bury St Edmunds 2864

A small business of four craftsmen skilled in hurdle-making and interwoven fencing. Primarily concerned with the making of sheep-, pig-, cattle-, and racing-hurdles in riven ash, any type or size of hurdle will be made to customers' specifications. Hurdles may also be hired. Thatchers' goods: spits, rods, stack-pegs, etc., available; additional types made to customers' requirements. Interwoven fencing panels, posts, gates, trellis, rustic arches and teakwood garden furniture. Sundries range from peasticks to linen props and hay drying tripods to firewood logs.

C. BEENEY, Hopes Grove Farm, Tenterden, Kent

Buys and cuts areas of chestnut underwood, mainly in East Sussex. Posts and palings made up from the wood are generally retailed through a larger manufacturer, but some local sales.

E. C. BLAKE, Higher Cleave, Wilmington, nr Honiton, Devon EX14 9SG. Tel: Wilmington 277

Hand-made walking-sticks of all types cut from local woods, all natural – no steaming. Speciality is the making of shepherds' crooks. Featured on television. Exported to many countries.

CHALFORD STICK CO., St Mary's Mills, Chalford, Stroud, Glos.

Manufacture, essentially under contract, of crafts-made walking-sticks for the National Health Service.

THE FAR FOREST WORKS (W. H. Doolittle), Far Forest, Nr Kidderminster, Worcs. Tel: Rock (Worcs.) 266203

A small family business; sole makers of the 'Forest Glade' rustic garden furniture from locally grown oak saplings. Each piece is individually fashioned in either standard (with bark left on) or *de luxe* (hand-peeled in the old-fashioned way and treated with preservative) oak. Arches, rosaries, pergolas, rosary fencing, nesting logs, garden-seats, armchairs, tables and shrub-tubs; rustic gates, summer-houses, bridges and heather-thatched bird-tables. Most of the oak and the heather come from Wyre Forest. Quotations for customer's own design or specification. Rustic timbers can also be supplied for own construction.

THE HIGH AND HAZEL WOODS WOODLAND PARK, Brokerswood, nr Westbury, Wilts. Tel: Westbury 2238

A forestry and natural history centre of some 120 acres of woodlands where a coppice industry has been revived to produce thatching-spars and rustic poles. Bean- and pea-sticks, flower-stakes, and Christmas-trees.

ALEC TWINNING, Rose Cottage, Quenington, Nr Cirencester, Glos. Tel: Coln St Aldwyns 317

Hurdle-maker whose craft has been televised and recorded.

A. WEST, West Street, Tadley, Hants.

Birch besom brooms with hazel handles made in the traditional manner for which the West family has been noted for at least three generations.

WHELNETHAM WOODWORK LTD, Station Yard, Whelnetham, Bury St Edmunds, Suffolk 1P30 0DT. Tel: Sicklesmere 300

Probably the last surviving producers of hand-made wooden hay-rakes, twitch and garden-rakes, mauls, beetles, and mallets. Scythe snaths in Suffolk, Norfolk or American styles; quotations given for Northampton and English patterns, also straight Roding Snath for steep banks, etc. Tools made by the trinity of craftsmen of this rural industry have appeared in several films and are preserved in a number of museums, including the Plymouth Plantation pilgrim village museum in Massachusetts. Camping woodware, stakes, arch timbers, birch besoms and firewood also quoted for.

F. V. WICKS, 2 Hill Hayes, Hullavington, Chippenham, Wilts.

The last of a noted family of hurdle-makers, Frank Wicks has made hurdles for race-courses at Haydock Park, Taunton, and many others as well as hurdles for riding-schools, ponies, pigs and sheep. Rustic furniture, bird-tables and thatching-spars to order.

M. D. VINCENT, Ashbourne Cottage, Ilmington, nr Shipston-on-Stour, Warks. Tel: Ilmington 232

Hurdle-maker using local willow mainly for sheep-hurdles, hedge and netting-stakes, garden-seats and children's climbing-frames.

WHEELWRIGHTS (as shown in Worshipful Company of Wheelwrights' register)

ALBERT E. BAILEY AND SON, Stumble Cottage, Kingsnorth, Ashford, Kent

JOSEPH BAILEY AND SONS, Durham Road, East Rainton, Houghton-le-Spring, Durham

G. BALL, Implement Works, North Milworth, Rugby, Warwickshire

HERBERT BELFIELD AND SON LTD, Rocks Mill, Smallbridge, Rochdale, Lancs.

R. BISHOP, Hillside, Toby Lane, Woodbury Salterton, Exeter, Devon

F. G. BRITTON, The Sawmills, Withleigh, Tiverton, Devon

W. BROWN, 'Wheelwrights', The Rocks, Burwash, Sussex

E. E. BURROUGHES, Southgate Farm, Rickinghall, Diss, Norfolk

A. G. BYSOUTH, Oakley, Park Street, Baldock, Herts.

C. E. CARRUTHERS, 92 Westway, Throckley, Newcastle, Northumberland

JAMES COCKER AND SONS, (Southport) LTD, Kew Works, Meols Cop Road, Southport, Lancs.

B. CRANWELL, Crawley End, Chrishall, Nr. Royston, Herts.

CROFORD COACHBUILDERS LTD, Dover Place, Ashford, Kent

G. DARLEY, Rosedale, 5 Hull Road, Coniston, Hull, Yorks.

ELLIS AND SON (vehicle-builders) LTD, Five Oak Green, Tonbridge, Kent

D. T. FLOWER, Brendon Bungalow, Farmborough, Bath, Avon

C. GAPP, Fairview, South Green, Dereham, Norfolk

GLOVER, WEBB & LIVERSIDGE LTD, 561 Old Kent Road, London SE1

HAREWOOD CARRIAGE CO. LTD, Dobles Lane, Holsworthy, Devon

HOAD AND SONS, Basin Street, Kingston Cross, Portsmouth, Hants.

G. H. HOPKIN, 1 Manor Cottage, Lillingstone Lovell, Buckingham

H. HORNSHAW, Dunnington, York

R. J. HOSKING, 'Penrose', Cockwells, Penzance, Cornwall

JACKS WAGON WORKS, 11 Memphis Street, Liverpool 7

J. H. D. KELLAM, Mill Lane, Waltham-on-the-Wolds, Melton Mowbray, Leics.

JAMES KELLY (Blacksmiths) LTD, Clay Lane, Oldbury, Warley, Worcs.

D. C. KEYTE, Wheelwrights Yard, Paxford, nr Chipping Campden, Glos.

R. LOCKE, Upper Brailes, nr Banbury, Oxon

A. W. LOWN, The Green, Freethorpe, Norwich, Norfolk

J. E. MATTHEWS AND SONS LTD, South Bridge, Northampton

J. & P. MOON, Horse Stone Cottage, Parr Lane, Eccleston, Chorley, Lancs.

G. A. MORRIS, 2 Brampton Byan, Bucknell, Salop, Lancs.

F. H. PARR, Butts, Buckerell, nr Honiton, Devon

R. J. PERRY, 1 South View, Queen Camel, Yeovil, Somerset

K. G. POTTER, Houghton, nr Stockbridge, Hants.

E. J. POWELL, The Folly, Wormbridge, Herefordshire

ROBERTSON BROS, 128–130 Weston Street, Bermondsey, London SE1

H. ROGERS, 1 Bay Road, Porlock, Somerset

J. ROWAN, 58 Green Leys, St Ives, Hunts.

RODNEY SALTER, Woodbeer-Perriton, Traps, Perriton, Whimple, Exeter, Devon

PERCY SISSONS AND SON, Beswick, Driffield, Yorks.

STUBBINGS AND SON, Biscombe, Stapley, Church Stanton, nr Taunton, Somerset

W. H. SUTTON AND SONS, The Old Brickyard, Oreton, Worcs.

H. TAYLOR, 51 Woodhouse Street, Leeds 6

W. H. THOMAS, Wayside Cottage, Penzance Road, Churchtown, St Buryan, nr Penzance, Cornwall

F. W. TINGLE AND SONS, 61 Warmfield Lane, Warmfield, Wakefield, Yorks.

D. TUGWELL, 3 Trewsbury Road, Coates, nr Cirencester, Glos.

T. TWEDDLE, 82 Stand Lane, Radcliffe, Manchester

J. F. WATTS, 3 Church Lane, Frampton, Dorchester, Dorset

THE WELLINGTON CARRIAGE CO. LTD, Long Lane, Telford, Salop

J. WILLISON AND SON, Watling Street, Hockliffe, Leighton Buzzard, Beds.

R. YOUNG, Chapel Bungalow, Didley, Wormbridge, Herefordshire

CARRIAGE-BUILDERS

JAMES CROMBIE, Taynton House, nr Gloucester. Tel: Newent 820284
Builder, restorer and model-maker of horse-drawn vehicles. Member of Guild of Gloucestershire Craftsmen.

HAREWOOD CARRIAGE CO. LTD, Dobles Lane, Holsworthy, Devon Tel: Holsworthy 253061
Horse-drawn carriages, showing-harness, traditional candle-illuminated carriage-lamps.

ERIC A. HOMEWOOD, Mill Farm House, Arlington, Barnstaple, Devon EX31 4LN. Tel: 027 182 306
Horse-drawn carriages, restorations, miniatures.

PILGRIMS, Old England Yard, Shillingstone, Blandford, Dorset Tel: 025886 673
Horse-drawn vehicles, wheels and parts, reproductions.

DENNIS TUGWELL (see wheelwrights)
Horse-drawn vehicles, restorations from farm-wagons to Romany caravans.

COOPERAGE

H. & J. E. BUCKLEY LTD, Tame Valley Cooperage, Park Road, Dukinfield, Cheshire SK16 5LP. Tel: 061–330 3677/8
Solid oak casks, water-butts, tubs, buckets, and bar furniture hand-made in the traditional style. Cask repairs and maintenance. Complete range of coopers' tools, equipment for brewing and distillery industries, stable and saddle-room fittings.

CRAFTSMEN IN WOOD

ARUNCRAFT (M. G. Hay-Will), Riffards, Burpham, Arundel, Sussex

BN18 9RJ. Tel: Arundel 883143
   Specialist restorers, catering for a whole range of furniture from the humble
to the exotic antique. Original and reproduction pieces are undertaken from
time to time to meet customers' special requirements.

ASTON WOODWARE (M. A. Hunt), Aston Hill, Lewknor, Oxford. Tel: Kingston
Blount 51500
   A small family business grown over the last fifty years from a wheelwright's
shop to production of individually made refectory-tables, chairs, bar furniture, garden-sheds and garden-furniture.

E. J. BAILEY, 34 Park Avenue North, Northampton.
   Woodwork of small dimensions to special order: sewing-tables, jewellery-
boxes, carved fruit-bowls, etc.

EDWARD BARNSLEY, CBE, Froxfield, Petersfield, Hampshire GU32 1BB. Tel:
Hawkley 233
   Designer-craftsman of furniture, in whose workshop Herbert Upton,
George Taylor, Oskar Dawson, Hugh Routh, Michael Bowen and appren-
tice Mark Nicholas work to the individual designs of Edward Barnsley to
produce outstanding work of fine craftsmanship. Notable commissions have
included designs for furniture for the King of Siam in the thirties, case in the
House of Lords to hold Books of Remembrance, furniture for University
College of Ghana, prayer-desk and chair for use of Archbishop of Canterbury in Nave Choir.

T. S. BARROWS AND SON, Hamlyn Lodge Cottage Industry, Welbeck, Worksop,
Notts. Tel: Worksop 85252
   A father and son partnership of cabinet-makers. Individually designed furniture hand-made in any timber and to any style. Residential short courses
are organized in antique restoration for the collector, who is afforded the
benefit of forty years' experience of these skilled craftsmen. Showroom facilities have recently been extended to embrace an art gallery where exhibitions of the work of artists and craftsmen are mounted.

E. S. G. BEAVEN, Ampney Crucis, Cirencester, Glos. Tel: Poulton 646
   Hand-made musical boxes which are miniature copies of old English chests,
including a charming reproduction of an oak cradle which rocks automatically whilst playing Brahms's Lullaby. The chests are designed as ciga-
rette boxes or velvet-lined for jewellery.

MARGARET F. BELLAMY, Thorn House, The Street, Chiddingly, Sussex. Tel:
Chiddingly 466
   Designer-craftswoman specializing in carving and wood-turning. Sculptured birds, fish, etc., mostly designed to enhance the grain of the wood.
Hand-turned trays on which initials can be carved to order. Candle-bases,
dishes, bread, and cheese-boards, book-ends and solitaire board (supplied
with 1 inch marbles). Decorative fruits as made in the eighteenth century –

pears in various woods, including yew; apples in oak, fumed oak and yew, and figs in cherry wood.

DOUGLAS BOUNDEN, Whitley Court, Upton St Leonards, Gloucester. Tel: Gloucester 66669
Cabinet-maker, wood-carver and instrument-case-maker. Member Guild of Gloucestershire Craftsmen.

BRADLEY INKLE LOOMS (E. and L. Bradley), 82 North Lane, East Preston, Sussex BN16 1HE. Tel: Rustington 70108
Husband and wife team who specialize in making table model inkle-looms with yew shuttles. Each loom is hand-made and finished with bees-wax from the Bradleys' own bees. The regular size warps up to 7-feet length, the mini-loom warps up to 2 feet. A special model with a lever attachment to make the sheds is designed for the handicapped. Niddy-noddys and looms are dismountable for overseas mailing.

A. A. BROWN, Woodside, Greenlands Lane, Prestwood, Great Missenden, Bucks HP16 9QU
Hand-turned lace-bobbins of various woods: cherry, holly, greenheart, yew, box, muhuhu, East African olive, beech, or rosewood according to availability, supplied drilled but not spangled. The finish is smooth and natural, not waxed or varnished. Special types made to customers' requirements. SAE for prices and details.

DAVID BROWNING, Waterend, Longney, Gloucester. Tel: Hardwicke 287
Furniture-maker. Member Guild of Gloucestershire Craftsmen.

J. A. N. BURRA, Dingle Hill Products, Hollybush, Ledbury, Herefordshire HR8. Tel: Bromesberrow 240
Man and wife team making spinning-wheels; willing to reproduce spinning and weaving equipment as one-off commissions, small wooden items, and high quality garden chairs in Western red cedar with brass screws and waterproof glue.

RON BUTTERFIELD, Taurus Studio, 57 Rustlings Road, Sheffield S11 7AA. Tel: (Studio) Sheffield 662352, (Home) 667674
Designer-craftsman specializing in church furnishings. Sculptor and carver of wood or stone. Ron Butterfield's work is to be seen throughout the country and abroad: crucifixes, madonnas, eagle lecterns in oak; animal and bird newel capitals on the staircase of Vesey Grange, Warwickshire, are but random examples. This eminent craftsman designs from a collection plate to complete refurnishing of churches; his stonework ranges from a dog's gravestone to a financier's coat of arms; his commissions extend from Houghton-on-the-Hill to the ancient church of East Meon. Member of the Society of Church Craftsmen; Guild of Yorkshire Craftsmen; the Society of Craftsmen, Hereford; registered by the Council for the Care of Churches.

CLOUD NINE-ONE OFF, Camden Lock, Commercial Place, London NW1 8AF

Designers and woodworkers of custom-built pieces.

CORBETT WOODWORK, (R. Corbett) Corpusty, Norwich NOR 14Y. Tel: Saxthorpe 268
Three craftsmen producing dining-room furniture. Special commissions have included an oak reredos for a church.

RICHARD CORY, Summerlands, Widemouth Bay, Bude, Cornwall EX23 OAA. Tel: Widemouth Bay 259
Artist whose craft is developing driftwood from the Cornish beaches into interesting shapes. The finished models are brought to a fine finish and polished with bees-wax. Sales are to private individuals and through exhibitions. Richard Cory is well known in the West Country as a lecturer in this field of craftwork.

COUNTY CRAFTS, (Cyril and Martin Sunley) East Cottingwith, York YO4 4TA. Tel: Melbourne 454
Father and son team of wood-turners and carvers. Hand-made domestic woodware includes carved spinning-chairs. Special line is their use of local bog oak from a Bronze Age forest. Retailed through craft shop on premises.

CROWDYS WOOD PRODUCTS LTD, (Tim and Rosalind Green), The Old Bakery, Clanfield, Oxon OX8 2SP. Tel: Clanfield 216
Individually designed wooden goods. Range: tableware, kitchenware, garden and domestic furniture from dining-tables to rocking-chairs, lamps, toys and spinning-wheels. Special requests are always considered and Tim Green is willing to make almost anything within reason from restaurant furniture to milking-stools, doors and buttons. Craft shop on premises.

EDMUND CZAJKOWSKI AND SON, 96 Tor O'Moor Road, Woodhall Spa, Lincs. LN10 6SB. Tel: Woodhall Spa 52895
Father and son furniture-designers and cabinet-makers. Each piece is individually designed and made to order only. Church furniture, including carving and gilding, to commission. Antique restoration work.

JOSEPH DAWES, The Street, Corpusty, nr Holt, Norfolk
Cabinet-maker and wood-carver whose work has been accepted in many important exhibitions. Work is to customers' special requirements only.

MARTIN J. DODGE, Southgate, Wincanton, Somerset. Tel: Wincanton 2388
Maker of fine English furniture. Large choice of pedestal tables; chairs include designs of Sheraton, Chippendale and Adam. Special exhibition pieces have included Adam marquetry commode. Antique restoration and special commissions by arrangement. Member of the Somerset Guild of Craftsmen.

ROBIN AND MARY ELLIS, Rumwood, Horseheath, Cambridge CB1 6QX. Tel: Cambridge 891729
A unique combination of design and turning producing high quality

tableware, paperweights and jewellery. By judicious selection of each piece of wood and the application of the individual skills of a group of talented craftsmen, the range of hand-made tableware extends to plates and goblets, bowls and schooners. Permanent sealing of the finely grained surface enables pieces to be washed up quite normally in hot soapy water. Commissioned pieces always considered: recent one-off designs have been special bowls, church chalices and patens, gospel lights and church candlesticks. Direct mail order, agricultural shows and craft markets. Export direct to shops (p. 91).

PETER AND JOY EVANS, Makins, Whiteway, nr Stroud, Glos. Tel: Miserden 366
Cabinet-maker and wood-carver. High quality hand-made furniture ranging from stools to cradles of individual design from carefully selected naturally seasoned woods. Domestic and decorative woodware hand-carved by Joy Evans, relating design to the natural grain of the wood.

CHRISTOPHER FAULKNER, Ashridge, Dartington, Totnes, Devon. Tel: Totnes 862861
Designer-maker of fine furniture to private commission. Exhibiting member of Devon Guild of Craftsmen, exhibited also in London.

BARRY FELDMAN, Design Brokers (Holdings) Ltd, 90 Lots Road, London SW10. Tel: 01–352–7454
Product design: Barry Feldman's work has attracted the attention of the *Sunday Times* and the architectural Press with his design for adjustable tables and chairs.

RODNEY FORSS, Ginger House, High Street, Blockley, Moreton-in-Marsh, Glos. Tel: Blockley 429
Woodcraftsman and sculptor. Member Guild of Gloucestershire Craftsmen.

E. J. FREEBORN AND SON, 2 The Shambles, York YO1 2LZ. Tel: York 23153
Craftsman in wood whose work is to be seen in York Minster and the Bishop's Chair in Tadcaster. Trained by Gordon Russell of Broadway, Mr Freeborn is a Member of The British Crafts Centre and lectures on antiques. Commissions and restoration work. Squirrel trademark.

DENNIS E. FRENCH, Rock House, Brimscombe Hill, Stroud, Glos. Tel: Brimscombe 3054
Domestic woodware-maker. Member Guild of Gloucestershire Craftsmen.

R. H. FYSON, Manor Farm, Kencot, Lechlade, Glos. Tel: Filkins 223
Cabinet-maker whose range of work embraces furniture for church, college and domestic use, architectural joinery, antique restoration, carving and gilding (see p. 100).

T. H. GODLEY, 18 Corinium Gate, Cirencester, Glos. GL7 2PX
Woodware, mainly turnery, using home-grown timber, mainly yew, walnut,

elm and sycamore, although more unusual woods are used as available. Coffee-tables and chess-sets as well as the more usual range of domestic items. Turning also undertaken for furniture restorers.

LEONARD GOFF, 52–54 Carey's Road, Paulerspury, Towcester, Northants NN12 7NX. Tel: Paulerspury 666
A craftsman who makes original and reproduction period furniture to order, but is also willing to consider the unusual commission. Recent orders have included a complete dining-suite for Australia, a set of Chippendale style mahogany dining-chairs, a carved shield for Trinity College, and a complete new body in ash for the ex-Nuvolari K3 M.G. racing-car.

GOULDINGS NAME PLAQUES (M. J. Cooper), 111 Jaywick Lane, Clacton-on-Sea, Essex. Tel: Clacton-on-Sea 22792
Husband and wife team making hand-carved, individually designed house-signs and garden-furniture to order.

M. D. GRATCH, 17 Bruce Road, Wealdstone, Harrow, Middx. Tel: 01–427 1831
Speciality lines are woodware bowls, plates, boards, etc. Custom-built kitchen units (and fittings). Re-rushing and caning of furniture.

D. GREENWOOD, The Clock House, Bidborough, Tonbridge, Kent.
Hand-made small wood and inlaid items such as chess and backgammon boards, jewel-boxes, etc. Specialist constructional restoration of antique furniture.

GUILD CRAFTS, The Old Brewery, Fontmell Magna, Shaftesbury, Dorset. Tel: Fontmell Magna 597
Hand-crafted gifts in wood. Visitors are welcome to watch work in progress in the workshops. Seconds are available in the shop on site.

DAN HAGEN, Heath Farm House, Ingham, Norwich NR12 0TR
Designer-craftsman working to commission. Everything from dining-furniture to church work.

PETER HALL WOODCRAFT, Danes Road, Staveley, nr Kendal, Cumbria LA8 9PL. Tel: Staveley 633
One-man business making traditional English furniture mainly in oak and mahogany to order. Emphasis is on craftsmanship. Exhibiting Member of the Guild of Lakeland Craftsmen.

WILLIAM HALL, The Pottery, Winchcombe, Glos. Tel: Cheltenham 603059
Furniture-maker. Member Guild of Gloucestershire Craftsmen.

CHRISTOPHER HANDLEY, The Company's Arms, Chalford, Stroud, Glos. Tel: Brimscombe 2556
Designer-craftsman of fine furniture. Member Guild of Gloucestershire Craftsmen.

HARRIS LOOMS LTD, North Grove Road, Hawkhurst, Kent TN18 4AP. Tel: 058 05 3315
Victor Edwards, member of the Society of Designer-Craftsmen, is one of the few designers of hand-weaving equipment now operating in the British Isles. Harris looms, designed by him, are considered to be among the best in the world, a claim substantiated by world-wide sales and specialist lines designed for educational and hospital use. Colleges of Technology and Art use these hand-looms for designing purposes and the larger Dobby and Jacquard looms for advanced diploma work.

LESTER HARVEY, Highbury, Upper Hayes Road, Nailsworth, Glos. Tel: Nailsworth 2838
Cabinet-maker. Member Guild of Gloucestershire Craftsmen.

HEAL FURNITURE LTD, 79 Essex Road, Islington, London N1. Tel: 01–226 9351
Furniture-manufacturers whose range falls broadly into three categories:
1 limited quantities of high quality furniture for the retail departments;
2 special contract furniture from exclusive designs for hotels, banks and private companies;
3 architectural and decorative joinery for government and public buildings, and shopfitting joinery for banks and various companies, both to Heal's own and architects' designs.

HENFIELD WOODCRAFT (Peter Spear), Harwoods Farm, West End, Henfield, Sussex. Tel: Henfield 2820
Peter Spear is a wood-turner whose range of bowls, egg-cups, platters, revolving cake-stands, miniature wine goblets and yew chalices, finished with bees-wax or olive oil, is to be found in all corners of the world. Retail is direct from his workshop. Member of Ditchling Handworkers Guild, Guild of Sussex Craftsmen, and Society of Designer-Craftsmen.

HENLEY WOODWORK (Maurice and Mary Leach) Henley, Langport, Somerset TA10 9BH. Tel: Langport 250750
Wood-turning and individual hand-made furniture.

L. H. HOLMAN, Beacon Hill Cottage, Kelvedon Hatch, nr Brentwood, Essex. Tel: Coxtie Green 72398
Wood-carver. Evening-class tutor.

THOMAS HUDSON, 35 High Street, Sharnbrook, Beds. Tel: Bedford 781423
A small country workshop where furniture is designed and made individually by hand to suit the needs of the discerning customer. Church furniture, wall-panelling, and antique furniture restored.

JUDITH E. HUGHES, Norstead, Downs Road, Tavistock, Devon PO19 9AG
Cabinet-maker. Specialist in inlaid marquetry monograms. Modern handmade furniture and fine woodwork in English and foreign timbers and veneers designed and made to order.

WILFRED HUTCHINSON (Squirrel Craft), Husthwaite, York. Tel: Coxwold 352
Designer-craftsman specializing in English oak furniture of exceptionally high quality. Each piece is hand-made and carved with a squirrel – Wilfred Hutchinson's trade-mark. Commissions have ranged from making the Bishop's Chair for Birtley Church, to completely furnishing the new chapel of Friarage Chapel, Northallerton. Hand-carved chairs, seated with cowhide, are pin-jointed in the traditional manner using hand-made tapered wooden pins; drawers of sideboards have dove-tailed joints (*see* p. 99). Awarded first prize in the Great Yorkshire Show of 1968 for his English walnut grandfather clock.

LEN HUXLEY, (Developments) 30 Pyrton Lane, Watlington, Oxon. Tel: (Office) Watlington 2545, (Workshop) Marlow 3526
Specialist joinery and wood craftsmen producing individually hand-built potters' wheels designed by potter, Bill Read. The design can be modified to suit a customer's personal requirements, either by incorporating any special feature or tailor-made to specified dimensions. Demonstrations, without obligation, are given.

CECIL JORDAN, Throstles, Haresfield Lane, Brookthorpe, Gloucester. Tel: Painswick 812052
Wood-turner. Member Guild of Gloucestershire Craftsmen.

KERMESSEE, Camden Lock, Commercial Place, London NW1 8AF
Furniture-designers and builders. Ivan Foster and Judi Keightley specialize in furnishing children's rooms with imaginative custom-built furniture.

KEY CRAFTS (Ray Key), 20 Vine Street, Evesham, Worcs.
Wood-turner producing mainly teak tableware; speciality line is an hour-glass. Commissions for specific items undertaken. Retail outlet is through the craft shop (above). Member of the Worcestershire Guild of Artist Craftsmen.

ALAN KILBY, 1 The Dingle, Knighton, Powys.
Hand-made traditional refectory tables in English ash and oak.

KILVINGTON STUDIO (K. A. Wilkinson), South Kilvington, Thirsk, Yorks. YO7 2LZ. Tel: Thirsk 22328
Individually designed furniture. Mr Wilkinson does not follow any particular style or work in any specific wood, preferring to develop each piece to customer's requirements on the basis of simplicity of design to enhance the natural grain of the hardwoods used. Contract joinery also undertaken. Showroom open daily.

ALBERT J. LAIN, Grove House, Rendham, Saxmundham, Suffolk 1P17 2AS Tel: Rendham 567
Craftsman in wood designing and producing village hall furniture – folding-tables and card-tables. Speciality is individually designed units and play equipment for children. The range is extensive: from sets of bricks (complete

with storage box), trucks and trailers, to book-cases and climbing-frames. Hand-made domestic furniture to order. Stock lines of smaller items such as dressing-table mirrors.

ANGELA LOWERY, Whitley Court, Upton St Leonards, Gloucester. Tel: Gloucester 66669
Sculptress. Member Guild of Gloucestershire Craftsmen.

JOHN MAKEPEACE, Parnham House, Beaminster, Dorset DT8 3NA. Tel: 0308 862204
Designer-craftsman who was described in 1977 by the design correspondent of *The Times* as "the greatest furniture-designer in this country". The new buildings of Keble College, Oxford are largely furnished by John Makepeace, and form but part of a long list of important commissions for public and private collections.

Inaugurated in September 1977, The Parnham Trust Ltd, a non-profit-making educational charity, offers an intensive, residential two-year course to trainee craftsmen in wood to develop craft skills and design skills, and provide experience of business management and marketing, under the direction of, and adjacent to the workshops of, John Makepeace.

From the outset students have an integrated introduction to the work, extending beyond the purely craft skills into those areas essential for running a workshop and earning a livelihood as a craftsman.

STEPHEN MARCHANT, The Pottery, Becketts Lane, Winchcombe, Glos. Tel: Cheltenham 603059
Wood craftsman. Member Guild of Gloucestershire Craftsmen.

KENNETH MARSHALL, The Workshop, Christchurch, Coleford, Glos. Tel: Coleford 3851
Furniture-maker. Member Guild of Gloucestershire Craftsmen.

JOHN R. MILLMAN, Chippings, Nailsworth Road, Avening, Tetbury, Glos. GL8 8NH. Tel: Nailsworth 2204
Wood-turner producing a wide range of domestic ware and traditional games in wood.

RODNEY P. NAYLOR, Turnpike House, 208 Devizes Road, Hilperton, nr Trowbridge, Wilts. Tel: Trowbridge 4497
Wood-carver and sculptor – traditional and modern styles. Trophies, chess-sets, etc., to order, sometimes available from stock. Antique restoration – adviser to the National Trust.

R. W. J. NORTON, 34 Larch Road, Exeter, Devon EX2 9DG. Tel: Exeter 56610
Wood-turner making pillow-lace-bobbins. An almost endless variety of turnings is achieved and prices vary accordingly. Each bobbin is supplied drilled but not spangled. Mr Norton has some fifty or more patterns available representing English and Continental forms, and is prepared to reproduce specific designs to order. Exhibited at the British Crafts Centre.

D. OFFLEY & CO., 16 Chapel Street Place, Ilkeston, Derbyshire DE7 5JY. Tel: Ilkeston 71653

A husband and wife partnership. Cabinet-maker and wood-carver, David Offley has turned his skill to many forms from sculptural woodwork to specialist restoration.

THE PELDON WOODTURNER (A. Moore) Peldon Hall Cottage, Church Road, Peldon, nr Colchester. Tel: Peldon 228

Wood-turner working to his own designs, specializing in finely turned reproductions of seventeenth-century wine goblets – treated for use. Work extends into many fields – antique restoration, boat-yards, picture-frames, builders' materials, etc. Mr Moore's commissions have included the making of replacement parts for wooden barges, and policemen's truncheons.

ALAN PETERS, Aller Studios, Kentisbeare, Cullompton, Devon. Tel: Kentisbeare 251

Designer-craftsman specializing in modern furniture and presentation pieces. Single pieces or complete room schemes are undertaken to commission among which have included furnishing a private study for clients in Kuwait, a presentation gavel for The Royal Society, the ambassador's desk and study furniture in a new embassy residence, in Pretoria, the Art Director's office in the offices of the Reader's Digest Association, and refectory furniture for Farnham Castle. Member Devon Guild of Craftsmen, Craft Centre, and fellow of the Society of Designer-Craftsmen (*see* p. 99).

PILGRIMS, Old England Yard, Shillingstone, Blandford, Dorset DT11 OSA Tel: Childe Okeford (025 886) 673

Fine hand-made solid wood furniture to order. Each order is treated individually, details are passed to one of the six craftsmen who creates the entire thing from selecting and cutting the timber, through all the processes to the final polishing, and carving a pilgrim – the firm's trade-mark – on it, and also carving his signature so that every piece can be identified with the man who made it.

The scope is as wide as customers' requirements and commissions have included a completely fitted kitchen in solid wood, furbishing of public houses and restaurant complete with oak wall-panelling, oak-boxed beams and solid wood furniture; and a prestige bedroom in a country house on the Isle of Aran which involved erecting a complete panelled wall across one end of the bedroom, with secret catches to open concealed doors in it giving access to a massive fitted wardrobe. All sales are made direct from the showrooms which are attached to the workshops.

ROY PITCHER, Olveston, Bristol. Tel: Almondsbury 3273

Wood-carver who works almost exclusively in naturally-seasoned English oak. Mr Pitcher's carvings are mainly drawn from nature: cabinet-panels carved with brambles, foot-stools bearing the imprints of animals, interlaced bulrushes on a spinning stool back and a coffee-table tastefully decorated with acorns and oak leaves, all these illustrate his attention to detail and surface texture. Commissions have ranged from making of lamp-stands and lecterns to the restoration of a gipsy caravan.

BERNARD R. PUMFREY, MSDC, FIAL, FRSA, Landsdowne, 14 Oakleigh Road, Stratford-upon-Avon, Warwick CV37 ODW. Tel: Stratford-upon-Avon 67410
Designer and craftsman in wood, specializing in individually designed furniture, and decorative and turned woodware. Qualified teacher whose departmental work in project technology has featured on BBC Blue Peter programme and ITV News. Specialist lecturer for summer schools and in-service courses; author of many papers on craft education and environmental design. Past president of the Institute and College of Craft Education.

CHRIS PRESTON, Belmont, Courtlands, Shipton-under-Wychwood, Oxon. Tel: Shipton-under-Wychwood 830575
Elm furniture a speciality: special commissions undertaken by arrangement.

ERIC J. RICE, Red Field, Chapel Hill, Aylburton, Lydney, Glos. Tel: Lydney 2636
Furniture-maker. Member Guild of Gloucestershire Craftsmen.

A. ROGERS AND SONS, 64 Higham Road, Chesham, Bucks. Tel: Chesham (02–405) 5276
A family wood-turnery concern of father and two sons, making a comprehensive range of wooden tableware. Prototype work also undertaken and reproduction of period pieces such as twisted banisters and clock-case parts.

GORDON RUSSELL LTD, Broadway, Worcs. Tel: Broadway 3345
The story of Gordon Russell furniture is essentially that of a family firm – which it remains today while employing some two hundred people. The firm has its own design team and covers the whole range of furniture-making by marrying the traditional skills of cabinet-making to the technological training of the twentieth century. This means that schools can have furniture which came from the same workshops as commissioned pieces for the Palace in Baghdad. By appointment suppliers of furniture to HM the Queen and HM Queen Elizabeth the Queen Mother.

MICHAEL SIMPSON, Windrush, East Keal, Spilsby, Lincs. Tel: Spilsby 3557
Wood-carver using mainly locally grown yew and laburnum. Specialist lines are madonnas 6 inches to 16 inches in height and small sitting birds about 4 inches long. Large abstracts suitable for home or garden undertaken on commission. Occasional lecturer at weekend courses.

EDWIN SPENCER, 36 Fore Street, Seaton, Devon.
A fully-trained craftsman who developed the potential of exotic woods and other natural materials by turning them into original costume jewellery.

BOB STENNET, Design Brokers (Holdings) Ltd, 90 Lots Road, London SW10.

Tel: 01–352 7454

Professional carpentry – exhibition design.

STOGUMBER WOODWORK (Ralph Farrer), Wayshill, Stogumber, Taunton. Tel: Stogumber 205

Modern furniture, mostly to the designs of Ralph Ferrer, which are traditional but simple in detail. Exhibiting member of Somerset Guild of Craftsmen, widely exhibited in the West Country.

ROBERT THOMPSON'S CRAFTSMEN LTD, Kilburn, York YO6 4AH. Tel: Coxwold 218

The famous 'house of the mouse' founded early this century by Robert Thompson, whose traditions are carried on by a school of craftsmen under the leadership of the mouseman's two grandchildren, Robert and John Cartwright. Domestic furniture in English oak from bureaux and bedsteads to work-boxes and plant-troughs. Ecclesiastical woodwork has been carried out in hundreds of churches up and down the country, among them Westminster Abbey and York Minster. Homes, schools and public buildings at home and overseas have been furnished from the Kilburn workshops where, whether it be on panelled walls of a library or a napkin ring, the mouse is carved as a symbol of "industry in quiet places".

EDWIN TURNER, Home Farm, Gislingham, Eye, Suffolk. Tel: Mellis 280

A small workshop under the skilled craftsman Edwin Turner, specializing in oak furniture and large wall-units and book-cases to house TV sets, hi-fi equipment and heaters.

W. UEDELHOVEN LTD, Gretton, Cheltenham, Glos. Tel: Winchcombe 602306

Wood-turning and antique restoration. Demonstrations of wood-turning are given to groups by appointment. Teas provided.

T. D. WALSHAW, Low Sadgill, Longsleddale, nr Kendal, Westmorland, Cumbria LA8 9BE. Tel: Selside 277

An extremely well-qualified engineer, whose aptitude for mechanical manipulation has derived more from the rare art of ornamental turning than the artisan usually achieves. A limited number of commissions are undertaken by Mr Walshaw, whose articles on the art have been published in *Woodworker*; he insists that he is an amateur ornamental turner. Member of Guild of Lakeland Craftsmen, and freeman of The Worshipful Company of Turners.

K. A. WATERWORTH, Orders taken at the Salon Phoenix, Moore Road, Bourton-on-the-Water, Cheltenham, Glos. Tel: Bourton-on-the-Water 20133

Hand-crafted furniture from locally grown elm.

JOHN WHITEHEAD, Linfitts Farm, 84 Denshaw Road, Delph, Oldham OL3 5EU. Tel: Saddleworth 4578

Furniture individually designed and hand-made. As well as for domestic furniture, John Whitehead undertakes commissions for garden furniture.

RALPH H. WILLIAMS, The Studio, Chapel Street, Berkhamsted, Herts.
Wood sculptor specializing in bird studies, using local woods.

WOODMANCRAFT (Stephen Newton) St Helens, Cemetery Lane, Woodmancote, nr Emsworth, Hants.
Designer-craftsman specializing in solid pine furniture. Each piece is hand-
fashioned with due regard to the wood's natural attraction. Extensive range:
refectory and gate-leg tables, pews, settles, bench-seats, Welsh dressers, and
fitted kitchen units.

YEOMAN FURNITURE (E. Mark Jolliffe), Cromer Road, Overstrand, Cromer,
Norfolk. Tel: Overstrand (026 378) 488
Husband and wife business producing hand-made furniture in English elm,
Scots pine and oak. Traditional designs. Commissions undertaken by ar-
rangement.

GEORGE UPFOLD, Coles Farmhouse, Chichester Road, Selsey, Sussex. Tel:
Selsey 3161
Reproduction and miniature furniture, speciality clock-cases.

CLOCK-CASE-MAKERS AND HOROLOGISTS

J. P. BYRNE, 164 Park Road, Formby, Liverpool. Tel: Formby 74089
Designer-craftsman specializing in clock-cases. Commissions accepted for
the design and construction of the one-off clock to customer's requirements,
covering the whole field of clock-movements, eight-day weight-driven, electric or battery or battery-pendulum movements, etc. Author of book on
clock-making for the amateur craftsman. Treen and turnery in fine woods,
architectural designs to specification and production of the 'Formcraft'
series of hand-made clocks.

F. CLARK, CMBHI, 91 Selby Road, Leeds 15. Tel: Leeds 641437
Horologist: grandfather and antique clocks, rare curios, complicated clocks
and watches renovated and reconditioned, including the making of new
parts to replace worn and missing parts.

EDMUND CZAJKOWSKI AND SON, 96 Tor O'Moor Road, Woodhall Spa, Lincs.
LN10 6SB. Tel: Woodhall Spa 52895
Clock-cases made to order. Restoration of antique pieces including antique
clock movements.

PETER HILL, The Old Toll House, Littleworth, Winchcombe, Glos. Tel:
Winchcombe 602151
Antiquarian horologist. Specialized restoration from early English to
chronometers. Clocks of any kind made to special commission. Member of
the Craftsmen of Gloucestershire.

STEPHEN NEWTON, St Helens, Cemetery Lane, Woodmancote, nr Emsworth,

Hants.
Grandfather-clock-cases.

ROBERT THOMPSON'S CRAFTSMEN LTD, Kilburn, York YO6 4AH Tel: Coxwold 218
Grandfather-clocks.

BRITISH HOROLOGICAL INSTITUTE, Upon Hall, Upton Newark, Notts. NG23 5TE. Tel: 0636 813795/6
Founded in 1858 following a public meeting of the Watch-makers of London "for the purpose of electing a committee to oppose the Introduction of Injurious Alterations into the Watch Trade". Today, the institute co-ordinates the various branches of the craft, draws them together and keeps them aware of horological developments. Technical classes, apprenticeship indenture, lectures, library, information and advisory services further its aims, and it is the recognized examining body throughout the Commonwealth for the award of diplomas in horological subjects. As part of its educational policy, the institute also conducts correspondence courses. It is the pioneer horological society of the world and one of the oldest British scientific associations with a current membership of some 3,000.

MARQUETRY

ROBERT DUNN, 42 Fleetwood Road, Dollis Hill, Willesden, NW10 Tel: Glad (452) 4753
Professional marquetarian whose skill ranges from large murals – of which the Gallaher panels based on the history of tobacco is a fine example – to specialist restoration. Noteworthy among his renovation work was the lifting and relaying of the rose design marquetry on a floor in Buckingham Palace.

H. L. HAMBLING, 37 Hanover Close, Charlbury, Oxford OX7 3TA
Marquetry, mostly to commission, mainly clients' houses on wall-plaques or boxes.

A. C. HARRISON, 50 Third Avenue, Oldfield Park, Bath, Avon
A professional marquetarian whose small family business has included commissions for marquetry for the liners *Queen Mary* and *Queen Elizabeth*, the French Blue Trains, and the coats of arms on the furniture in the Bath Pump Room. Every conceivable type of marquetry is undertaken, falling roughly into the following classifications: single pieces for antique restoration; faithfully reproduced copies of antique patterns for the makers of reproduction furniture; traditional types for makers of modern furniture; modern designs for the panelling of ocean liners and prestige offices; coats of arms and modern types for prestige souvenirs. Mr Harrison, the third generation of marquetarians in his family, has sent work all over the world.

GLADYS M. WALKER (Mrs) 113 Kingsway, Petts Wood, Kent BR5 1PP. Tel:

Orpington 23581

Marquetry tutor at adult education classes, who has herself completed several fine pieces, notably a mural depicting London 1066–1966. Sales normally through exhibitions of the Marquetry Society.

W. A. LINCOLN, 'World of Wood', Industrial Estate, Mildenhall, Suffolk. Tel: 0638 712550

President of The Marquetry Society, author of *The Art and Practice of Marquetry*, comprehensive supplies from kits for beginners to exotic veneers, plans and musical movements.

8

Rush, Cane, Willow and Woven Fibre

Rushes featured in social history since Moses was found cradled in them. As a material they have been used in building houses, constructing roads over swamps, in making hassocks and horse collars, pleating and goffering fine linen, for wrapping soft cheese, for tapers and, just as traditionally, for caulking wooden casks.

From early Anglo-Saxon times to the days of Shakespeare they were scattered on the damp, cold floors of English churches and houses, and rush-bearing ceremonies are still carried out in some parts of the country. Chaucer refers to weaving of rush in *The Canterbury Tales*, and it is in this form that the craft has survived to this day.

The English bulrush, *Scirpus lacustris*, leafless with a slender green stem, quite different from the fluffy brown-headed plant which rush-workers refer to as 'sedge', has become scarcer as river drainage improves, but efforts are being made to encourage an increase in the growing of rushes in East Anglia, where two of the larger rush industries are based.

Deben rush-weavers harvest their rushes from the local rivers, standing chest-high in water and using hooks to cut the rushes below water-level. According to tradition this is done between the hay and corn harvests, but not before the longest day. Girls follow the cutters into the river, gathering the floating rushes into bolts – a bundle of about $4\frac{1}{2}$ lb – and keep the bolts together in the water until they are collected, because cattle in the riverside meadows would soon devour them if they were left on the banks.

The demand for hand-made rushware is far in excess of what can be produced, even with imported European rush, for it is a craft ever susceptible to riverain farming trends. The effects of Holland's drainage programme have already been felt by the craftworkers. The once plentiful small Dutch rush is becoming scarce, and the thicker Spanish variety is often unsuitable for the finer degree of seating required in the restoration of antique chairs. Whilst freshwater mud grows lush reed, rush and sedge, suitable for plaited and woven articles, it is salty tidal water which produces the fibrous quality sought by the chair-workers.

Rushware has gained considerable status since the National Trust and church properties have used it to great advantage where the public can appreciate the natural colouring and texture harmonizing with the surroundings. A particularly fine length by Waveney rush-workers is in the library of Blickley Hall, and Deben rushes are to be found under the

Great Bed of Ware at the Victoria and Albert Museum. Rush matting, once the humble cottagers' carpet, is to be found in many a stately home, even St James's Palace has been supplied with it.

Rushwork was once predominantly women's work, it being regarded as somewhat menial labour rather than the respected craft it is today, and the children 'put in the corners' for their elders before or after school. It is pretty tough work on the hands and the rushes have to be stored most carefully. When harvested they have to be dried, but dampened again to make them pliable enough to work, otherwise they are brittle and break. If, on the other hand, they are stored damp, they go mouldy and rot.

Cane, as with rush, has had a revival as far as seating goes, due to an upsurge in antique restoration. Very few craftsmen work entirely in cane, for imported articles from southern Europe and Asia, where low labour costs are reflected in the retail price of the goods, offer fierce competition to those which are British-made. As an imported material, there can be no way of controlling the initial cost and centre cane in particular has become very expensive.

The idea of bamboo handles on ceramics is of Oriental origin, and it was at the request of a Japanese potter living in London that Fred Nettleship, who had made cane furniture for some thirty years, made his first cane handle. Specializing now in cane handles, his firm – Cane Craft – has built up over the last twelve years to supply potters throughout this country and a wide overseas market – without a single penny spent on advertising.

It could be that civilization is stamping out the cane of the Malayan and African jungles, or that the workers have turned to more lucrative work in industry, whatever the reason the result is again a diminishing source of raw materials. Basket-makers have ceased trying to compete with Chinese fancy basketry, but still need the cane of the Far East where the natives now demand comparable rates for harvesting it as those commanded for collecting rubber. Fish-baskets have to be made with cane as it is stronger than willow.

English basketry is indisputably the best in the world. Despite the flooding of the market with cheaper and more ornate basketware, the orientals have never quite perfected the technique of preparation and finish. Not unnaturally, an English basket-maker becomes incensed when he is approached by a firm of importers and asked to make handles for a shipment of foreign baskets bought at a knockdown price. Another irritation which basket-makers suffers is the stigma inflicted upon the craft, no doubt unwittingly, by some magistrates who sentence young offenders to, say, a Saturday afternoon detention centre "to do basket-making". This, to many craftsmen, lumps it together with sewing mail-bags and is hardly conducive to attracting apprentices to this skilled craft. Basket-making is a time-honoured craft and one of the few which has survived the vicissitudes of progressive ages, during which the method of workmanship has not changed, as shown by the study of the most ancient and unique pieces in existence, dating back to the Egyptian XIth Dynasty (2965–2778 B.C.). These are small *Shabti* baskets made of fibre. Another interesting example, discovered in Egypt by the British School of Archaeology during their excavations in the Fayum Prehistoric Settlement, was coiled basket ware used to line pits sunk in the ground, which served as caches for the storage of grain. This has been dated to the Bardarian Period (8000–1000 B.C.).

Records speak of osier-beds growing where Westminster Hall now stands. The Westminster monks, like their contemporaries, would have put the willow to good and varied use. Quicker to grow and easier to handle than timber, willow was not only woven into baskets to carry the stone for building, but was also plaited to make the scaffolding. Tangible evidence of willow having early roots in English soil was found during the excavation of the City when a relic of basket work, dated *circa* A.D. 120–150, was unearthed from the bed of the Walbrook River at the same time as, and not far distant from, the Temple of Mithras.

The discovery is of some interest, albeit but the chance thread of coincidence which draws together aspects of historical significance, for the Walbrook outfall into the Thames is immediately adjacent to the Innholders' Hall, off Dowgate, where the Worshipful Company of Basket-makers now holds its court.

The company was incorporated in 1569. One of the earliest records discovered is an entry in a brewer's company book, which appears to have been a guide to letting its hall to those companies and fraternities which did not possess halls, and is listed under the "titles of divers crafts of old accustomed and still continuing in this the ninth year of Henry V". As a city livery company it still carries with it civil privileges and responsibilities. A petition by the Court of Aldermen has now granted an increase of members to 500, whereas 150 years ago there were only 30.

The present position of the company with regard to the basketry trade is, as with many others, rather limited after over 400 years. But a definite interest is maintained as far as it is effective in Britain where the trend is for training to be for the better-class work which justifies cost. It gives help and encouragement in the continuance of the craft, and it is by no means unusual for the clerk to help would-be purchasers to find suppliers, and to help basket-makers to obtain materials. The company is particularly conscious of the need to assist the blind.

A survey into the actual state of basket-making as an industry would give the impression that it is in a very healthy state; that every basket-maker has a full order-book and the demand far exceeds the supply. In reality, the reason why basket-makers are so busy is that there are far fewer of them. One case in point is the village of Mawdesley in Lancashire, which once relied almost entirely on the basket industry for a living. There are still at least three basket-making firms in the area, but the withy-beds of west Lancashire do not yield sufficient for their needs and a great deal of material has to be imported.

The picture changes somewhat from county to county. In Nottinghamshire, where there are willow-holts in the Trent Valley, the last full-time basket-maker is already past retirement age. Basketry output based on local materials was once prolific in Leicestershire, but that county's basket-makers have "all died off" I am told, and Surrey records but one basket-maker. There are several one-man businesses scattered throughout the country, with the only sizeable concerns sited in Yorkshire, Norfolk and Somerset.

Burdekins of Ossett had seventeen basket-makers at their centenary in 1970, together with four apprentices, all of whom were treated to a week-end in Amsterdam, to celebrate the occasion, by Frank Burdekin, grandson of the firm's founder. That number has now dropped to eight, with no apprentices to justify a training scheme. Originally the trade was involved in making baskets or skeps for the local textile mills and rag-sorting warehouses. The output increased in the last war when they made many thousands of the two million panniers and willow hampers which were parachuted to resistance movements on the Continent, many were dropped by Frank Burdekin himself, who was an RAF pilot. A switch of production has been made since then, by sheer economic necessity, to extend the skills of the basket-makers to fashion a fascinating range of cane and wicker furniture.

The famous Sea Bird Brand basketware of Stanley Bird Ltd is made by some dozen basket-makers, whose skill is taxed to the full on the wide range of basketry which they are called upon to make today for all industries and all purposes. Whereas, like similar firms, they once concentrated on specific types – theirs being fish-baskets – they now have to be extremely versatile and produce all manner of basketry from one-ton cargo-baskets to a Moses cradle, from the almost extinct Yarmouth herring-swill to a willow-shape for a busby. Their osier-beds are at Burgh Castle but, again, are insufficient supply for their needs. Holland, Belgium, the Argentine, Poland and Spain used to be the main overseas suppliers, but some of these markets have now ceased.

Willow, in its widest sense, is among the earliest recorded plants of pre-Ice Age origin and appears in different varieties from the Soviet Arctic to the riverain areas of Australia, but the best willow in the world is English, grown in Somerset where, unlike Yorkshire, moors indicate marsh. It is in King Alfred's land that we find most of the south-western moors: Currymoor, Stanmoor, Northmoor, Saltmoor, Perrymoor and Sedgemoor, and the marshy conditions of these moors which produce the high quality 'withies', as they are called locally. The low-lying land, on sea-level, has flooded since time immemorial from Burnham-on-Sea. But it is these flood-waters, the muddy tidal water meeting the fresh water of the two rivers, Parret and Tone and overflowing on the light clay, which create the ideal soil for osier-beds.

Much nonsense has been broadcast about willow trees that have been cut down "being useful for basket-making". Willow from trees is used for wicker chairs; willows for cricket-bats are specially grown trees, and willows for basket-making are properly planted and culti-vated as with any harvest crop. The land has to be ploughed and cleared before planting. Much depends on the first operation which is a very professional job: sets 11 inches long, are cut from the best willows of the previous crop and carefully pushed into the soil to about $1\frac{1}{2}$ inches from the top; 14 inches apart in the ranks and 27 inches between rows. There are many varieties, each with its special name, such as Cham-pion Rod and Newkind Osier, but the premier one is Black Mould which normally grows in one season to 8 feet, although other sizes within that strain, from 3 feet upwards, are necessary for different kinds of baskets and hampers.

Frost is the enemy of the young shoots, so early growth is discour-aged. The crop is remarkable in that the actual growing period is only from the middle of May until the end of September. There are few love-lier sights than a bed of withies shimmering in summer sunlight, and such is the phenology of the Somerset willows that the leaves start dying on the last day of June, without exception.

Cutting starts in December, when the leaf is off, and is mainly done with an ordinary hook. Mechanical harvesting has gained recognition over the last decade, but is effective only on dry ground. The withies are then taken to the grower's yard and drafted into 3-, 4-, 6- and 8-feet lengths. Sorting is mainly carried out by women; the bolts are put into a sunken pit and graded for length against a measuring stick. Men tie the wads into carefully measured 2 feet 7 inch bundles: the Somerset wad is 37 inches round the butt end. It is the only known trade which receives the attention of the weights and measures inspectors; quarter-cran her-ring-baskets, a recognized measure for a quantity of fish, are also sub-jected to government scrutiny and bear an official stamp.

Osiers become white, buff or brown after preparation. White is willow stripped of its bark; buff is willow which has been boiled and stripped, resulting in a rust colour; and brown is natural willow with the bark left on, the tone varying from red/brown to green/brown, and is attractive in rustic work.

Buff willow has the advantage of being available all the year round after it is treated. The bundles are put into a tank of boiling water and kept at boiling-point for six hours, after which they simmer overnight. When they are taken from the boiler the bark is stripped off. The stripped willows are then spread on wires in the fields and carefully stored when completely dry.

White willow is willow stored in large water-filled pits until May when it becomes ripe. The skin then comes off quite easily, but it is essential to work quickly as there are barely three months before the bark toughens again and will not come off. This white willow, which is not boiled, is usually required for food and fine laundry-baskets.

Stripping the willow was such an important part of the rural calendar that a country dance of that name evolved from it, and well into this century school children were given a month's holiday for the purpose of 'stripping'. The social connotations were invariably lost to this aspect of the craft when acute labour shortage ousted the local 'brakes', which almost every house in the district had at one time, in favour of a simple but efficient bark-stripping machine.

Mechanization in the willow-growing industry for many years had been fostered under the Rural Industries Bureau in collaboration with the Long Ashton Research Station. Willow-tying equipment was introduced in 1958, along with kiln-drying to replace air-drying and, more recently, an attempt at mechanical grading. But I saw no real evidence of these innovations even supplementing this very labour-intensive crafts field.

The area under basketry willow crops in Somerset was estimated to be about 835 productive acres in 1965, a reduction of some 370 acres in six years. Some new planting has been carried out since then, but it is doubtful if the acreage will ever be sufficient to meet the demand. Somerset-grown willows attract export orders, but so far the potential has never been realized to the full, being labour-intensive it becomes commercially unviable, is hard work very often in wet conditions, and has never attracted any government assistance. Crop returns tend to be too slow for the rapid turnover demanded by modern business ventures, so the whole future of English basketry rests with such stalwarts as Gilbert Musgrave whose knowledge of the craft is encyclopaedic. These craftsmen, concerned with both the farming and fashioning of the willows, develop an affinity with their raw materials, so that returns are often unrelated to monetary values.

First-year growth produces a maiden crop, unsuitable for baskets, but ideal for weaving hurdles. Quality usually improves during the second year, but there is normally a light yield. It is not really until the fifth year that the willow-bed comes into its own, after which, if properly cared for, weeded and sprayed against pests, it can be harvested every year for thirty to forty years. The average yield is about five tons to the acre.

Willow, like rush, although grown in wet conditions, has to be dried carefully when harvested, kept dry during storage, then dampened for working. It is made supple by steaming for hurdle-weaving. Green willows (those that are freshly cut) shrink, and are therefore unsuitable for baskets, but are used for making crab- and lobster-pots in Devon and Cornwall.

The largest number of basket-makers is centred around the Bridg-water-Taunton area. But despite the full order-books, the industry fails to attract trainees.

While a small degree of mechanization may assist in the harvesting of willow, the weaving of it has defeated the cunning of the engineers, and is universally respected in the crafts world because it has resisted the invasion of the Industrial Revolution which has subjected so many other crafts to the anonymity of automation. The skill of the basket-maker remains unchallenged – and often unrewarded. Hundreds of basket-workers have been eased out of the trade by poor rates of pay which have been imposed on our countrymen, who are bedevilled by cheap imports and moulded plastic. The estimated average earnings of blind basket-makers from 1969 to 1971 varied even between insti-tutions: workers of the Royal London Society for the Blind averaged £3·10, Bristol Royal Workshops for the Blind averaged £4·25 and RNIB £2·25. Rates of pay within the same organizations also varied considerably for different occupations, but agricultural occupations for each of the three were higher – in the case of RNIB, £13 as against the basket-makers £2·25, with piano-tuners and repairers averaging £11.

No government has yet moved to protect the pay of these craftsmen, and the basket-maker is with his back to the wall.

Gilbert Musgrave has watched his number of basket-makers dwindle from a couple of hundred to a couple of dozen, and yet, not content to accept an uncertain fate, he has made some positive steps towards eli-citing recruitment. Subsidy, not sympathy, is what is needed. He has already interested COSIRA in his outlines for an official govern-ment-sponsored training scheme, akin to the already established ap-prenticeships in rural crafts.

The sentiments inscribed on official arms are rarely pragmatic, but the motto of the Worshipful Company of Basket-makers, "let us love one another", is a maxim which does perpetuate through the craft. It is a very friendly trade and one craftsman will always help another. Such an example is Bertram Jelfs whose artistry with cane and willow could have secured him prominence, but, content with sheer survival in the craft to which he devotes his entire energy, he found a different reward in teaching the techniques to the blind, to whom it has long been the traditional craft, sensitivity of touch and dexterity of the hands being the essential 'tools' of the trade.

Training for the blind was pioneered by Dr T. R. Armitage, a founder member of the British and Foreign Blind Association, now the Royal National Institute of the Blind, which was set up in 1868. He pressed for adoption in this country of the system operated in Saxony, where blind people were trained in craftwork, a scheme which specified basket-making as the most suitable, together with brush- and rope-making.

However, a homeworkers' scheme had been launched in London as early as 1854 by a blind man, W. H. Levy, who rented a cellar and formed a partnership with Elizabeth Gilbert, a blind philanthropist, for the purpose of supplying blind workers with materials and a retail outlet for the finished goods, which were brushes, mats and baskets. By 1875 there were some fifty-six workers in the scheme, which had to be supplemented by charitable funds.

The specific training scheme advocated by Dr Armitage was never adopted to any real extent by the British institutions, and it was not until 1920, under the guidance of the Ministry of Health and stimulated by Treasury grants, that it took root in Britain, with basket-making the main craft. A committee was appointed by the Secretary of State in June, 1971 "to look into existing arrangements for assisting blind homeworkers; to consult with appropriate associations of local authorities and organizations of and for the blind about any changes which may be desirable, and to report".

A consultative report from the Department of Employment showed that the normal training period for a blind basket-maker is four years, that there were insufficient training facilities, and there was little future in the craft, mainly due to the long training period.

There was a marked decrease in the number of blind people engaged in basket-making within the homeworkers scheme: 96 in 1970 as opposed to 169 in 1961. These figures have been accounted for by the fact that local authorities tend to run their own schemes, and that more opportunities are available in open industry, but a working-party report of 1961 showed no blind basket-makers in "open employment". More specifically, one of the well-established institutions, the London Association for the Blind, is phasing out basket-making as being an uneconomic occupation. There are currently about twenty blind basket-makers employed in that association, making heavy commercial baskets for the Post Office and Admiralty, and for use as containers of builders' rubbish, laundry, and theatrical costumes. These baskets are not normally sold to the public but generally made under contract. It seems wrong that charitable institutions are being forced, through sheer economics, to concentrate on purely industrial employment. As the department runs down, the remaining basket-makers will be transferred to PVC welding. Older men are retiring and the association say they are not training any new basket-makers. If the ratio of blind to sighted still applies, the total number of operative basket-workers is remarkably low. According to the Department of Employment's consultative document of 12th December 1973 there were, out of a total sheltered labour force of 2,318 blind people in blind workshops, 39 in sheltered workshops and 96 homeworkers engaged in basket-work in 1970; a total of 135 against 994 of 1961. This latter figure was estimated to be about a quarter of all the basket-workers in Great Britain. It is impossible to trace every basket-maker in England today – perhaps two hundred is a fair estimate.

In an attempt to save this crafts discipline from extinction, a new society has just been formed. Embracing chair-seating and straw-work, the association is relying on its combined strength to tackle the problem of supplies and standards. It is currently actively working on all its declared aims and encourages those interested to take a good course of instruction, such as the City and Guilds Basketry course. The possibility of establishing regional branches is dependent on its total membership.

STRAW-PLAITING

> The Corn-Dolly Cross on the screen with its accompanying mobile angels are a recent innovation and made locally. It is rumoured that during any long sermons the choir boys 'grin and bear it' by taking bets on how often all three angels point in the same direction at the same time!
>
> *Raymond Rush*

The Christian Church has absorbed many pagan customs, and in doing so eliminated the primeval superstitions attached to their practice. The corn-dolly, symbolizing the goddess of fertility, naturally took on a female form in which the spirit of life was 'captured' and woven into the last straws of harvest. Joyfully carried in ceremonial procession to her refuge from the ravages of winter, the spirit was kept in a place of honour in the farmhouse to be paraded again in style and reverence in springtime to the ploughed field, and there released to germinate the newly-sown grain. Seedtime and harvest were the all-consuming life-cycle and the fates were propitious to pagan piety.

The word *dolly* seems to be a corruption of idol, but there is no evidence that the effigy itself was worshipped in England, as was the practice in other countries, but merely symbolized the spirit of the ancient rite. The figure became more abstract in aspect as straw-weaving took on more artistic form. Special designs evolved in different localities, and it is these 'Welsh Border Fans', 'Suffolk Bells', 'Norfolk Lanterns', 'Kentish Ivy Maids', 'Devon Crosses', 'Oxford Crowns', 'Okehampton Mares', 'Staffordshire Knots', and 'Yorkshire Candle-sticks' – to name but a few – that have survived the years as favours or lucky charms, symbols of peace and prosperity, suggestive of the curious country conceits found on thatched ricks and roofs as protection against evil spirits and witchcraft.

Corn-dollies have lost their original connotations and it is because straw is an easy material to work into an art form, rather than for any other reason, that woven straw shapes are accepted quite readily as church ornaments. Raymond Rush, author and broadcaster on country life and customs, started the craft of corn-dolly-making from the improbable beginnings of one of the sermons which he is wont to give at the church which stands at the top of his garden. When a corn-dolly was used to illustrate the text, the choir was so curious about it that Mr Rush found himself giving instructions on how it was made. He now travels the nearby counties giving craft lectures – about 150 in a year – between his own seedtime and harvest, for he is still a working farmer.

Demonstrations of this particular craft are very popular as those with nimble fingers usually achieve reasonable results after a few hours' tuition, a proficiency acknowledged with reservation by professional corn-dolly-makers, many of whom maintain that amateurs often spoil the market for them. Accusations are levelled particularly at those who do it for a hobby, who earn pin money from craftwork, selling all and any of their efforts before perfecting their standards. Another aspect of this is where they sell to gift shops at lower prices than the professionals can afford to, simply because the amateurs do not have to make a living from their craftwork. The protection of standards and ethics ultimately depend on the retailer's integrity, and finally on the discerning customer. For all this, the professional straw-plaiters are amazingly helpful to those who have a genuine desire to learn the techniques, such is their aim to preserve this ancient craft which would have been extinct by now if it had not been for a handful of enthusiasts.

The advent of the combine harvester accelerated the decline of the craft, so the professionals are forced to grow their own wheat and rye if they cannot enlist the services of a 'tame' farmer. Modern strains are no use to the plaiter who needs hollow straw. Angela Witt, who not only grows her own *Elite le People* French wheat and an old variety of British red wheat with a chestnut head and creamy-coloured straw, which she uses for re-seeding, but also harvests it by hand with a hook, uses something like 150 sheafs of wheat and 40 of rye in a year.

There is a national market for traditional corn-dollies extending from agricultural shows to folk museums, who often commission a whole range of designs. The plaiters are forever exploring the potential of straw as a material and weave it with deceptive dexterity into extraordinary art forms. From the spiral of the traditional dolly, designs have become models of the utmost complexity. Elizabeth Smith spent 135 hours plaiting straw to make the model of Norwich Cathedral which can be seen in the Cathedral Shop; one illustration of how the skill of craftsmen has to be sound enough to fulfil any such commission which comes their way. Apart from moulding into models, straw is becoming a fashionable material for jewellery and mobiles; Jaquie Baker even makes chess-sets of woven straw.

There is an increasing demand for the old-fashioned straw bee-skep, but Thorne, the specialist bee-keeping firm who export to almost every country in the world, especially the oil-rich areas, say they have difficulty in finding craftsmen to make them. Compared with the intricate twisting and counting of straws in dolly-making, the craft is relatively simple – according to John Skaife, a Yorkshireman whose family has made traditional straw skeps for over a century. But he too reports an apathetic response to his offer of teaching the craft to anyone interested. It would seem, therefore, that as a functional material straw has little or no future; as a decorative art the potential is enormous.

This is borne out by the incredible success of a cottage industry which has become about the largest firm of its kind. Somerset House Wedmore Ltd was formed four years ago for the express purpose of keeping alive the ancient skill of corn-dolly-making by producing craft-made articles for the gift trade, reasonably priced; and so providing local employment. These objects have been achieved and illustrate the essential marrying of business acumen to craftsmanship, each playing its professional role.

The firm was started by a management consultant and a corn-dolly-maker, there are now some fifty homeworkers in a fifty-mile radius producing approximately 50,000 corn-dollies a year. About forty of the workers are now shareholders which adds incentive to an already satisfying job. Meetings are held and rates negotiated. Groups are trained by skilled corn-plaiters and are responsible to supervisors who constantly check on quality. The workers are encouraged to submit their own designs for approval and each dolly – whether a 'Wedmore Wheel' (the firm's own design), a 'cornucopia', 'fan', 'rattlewattle', or whatever form it takes – bears a code on its label to identify the maker. Sales are made in all parts of the country through gift and craft shops. So, if you come across the rare sight of a harvest binder, wait a while longer and you will see corn 'stooked' in the fields as in days gone by, some 5,000 sheaves in fact – just enough to keep the Somerset corn-dolly-makers going until next harvest.

SOCIETY

BASKET-MAKERS' ASSOCIATION, Sec: Mrs Joy Viall, Bierton House, Dean Way, Chalfont St Giles, Bucks. Tel: 02407 2296

A newly-formed association whose declared aims are:

1 to promote the knowledge, making, study, collection, teaching and use of basketry;
2 to set standards of teaching and quality of workmanship and to encourage original design;
3 to use its combined strength to assure supplies of materials necessary for the craft;
4 to promote classes, courses, exhibitions, discussions and lectures as required;

5 to award bursaries for further study of the craft where circumstances are appropriate. Publication: newsletter.

Membership is open to all interested in basketry and its related crafts, namely: willow, cane, coiled basketry and hedgerow basketry, rushwork, chair-seating, corn-dollies and straw-work.

CANE, WILLOW AND WOVEN FIBRE

STANLEY BIRD (Basketware) LTD, 28 Southgates Road, Great Yarmouth, Norfolk NR30 3LL. Tel: Office and Works 3392 (after office hours: Burgh Castle 8295)

A family business, established over a century, making by hand a wide range of best quality basket and caneware.Specialist makers of all types of fish-baskets, including the almost extinct Yarmouth herring swill baskets of Norfolk unpeeled willow and hazel ribs. Baskets for every conceivable use: bushel and garden-skeps, hampers; flower-troughs and osier fencing. Woven fibre and cane furniture. If there is still an item which you cannot find in this firm's exhaustive list then send them your own design and they will make specially to your requirements. Repairs also undertaken.

J. BURDEKIN, Flushdyke, Ossett, Yorks. Tel: Ossett 3103

A family business, established for a hundred years, where craftsmen specialize in cane and willow work. Indoor and garden furniture, tableware and floral art containers, full range of baskets, split cane or unpeeled willow fencing-panels.

CANE CRAFT (Fred and Trevor Nettleship), 153b High Street, Gorleston, Norfolk NR31 6RB. Tel: Great Yarmouth (0493) 67386

Father and son partnership specializing in cane handles for pottery tea-pots. Standard sizes increasing in $\frac{3}{4}$ inch widths from 3 inches to 7 inches. Non-standard handles willingly made to requirements. No minimum or maximum quantity specified. Occasional cane furniture. Exports to many countries.

FRANK CLARKE, 17 Leyland Avenue, Merridale, Wolverhampton

Basket-maker of some fifty years standing.

THE DEBEN RUSH-WEAVERS AND BASKET-MAKERS. (office, osier-beds and market garden) Reed Hall, Holbrook, nr Ipswich, Suffolk. Tel: Holbrook 327 (workrooms and shop) High Street, Debenham, Stowmarket, Suffolk. Tel: Debenham 349

Rushware plaited by hand from East Anglian rushes – place-mats made on a hand-loom. Wicker-work bottle and glass carriers, bread hoppers, furniture. Baskets for cutlery, cycles, cats, fishing, flowers, fruit, logs, linen, picnics and pigeons. Saddles and donkey-panniers, thatched bird-houses, trays. Bamboo furniture and cane cradles. Repairs to chairs can include repolishing and replacement or repair to woodwork and carving by skilled craftsmen who also repair and restore antique or modern furniture.

ARTHUR HOLMES AND SONS, 133 South Road, Bretherton, nr Preston, Lancs.
Family business, father and two sons, specializing in making pigeon trans-
porter baskets. Suppliers of pigeon training baskets to the Royal Lofts at
Kings Lynn.

BERTRAM JELFS, Goose Grout, Wraxall Road, Warmley, Bristol BS15 5DW.
Tel: Bristol 673849
Basketry of all types, essentially of English design in Somerset willow. Cane
furniture a speciality, vast range extends from wine caskets to baby cradles.
Member of the Craftsmen of Gloucestershire.

LONDON ASSOCIATION FOR THE BLIND, Pelican House, 88–92 Peckham Road,
London SE15 5LH. Tel: 01–703 6153
Skilled basket-makers in the long-established workshop of the association
produce commercial basketry by hand. The emphasis is on the heavier type
of specialized baskets. Not normally retailed direct to the public as orders
are usually under contract.

MARTIN AND PAT MULLEN, Bridgefoot, Mantle's Lane, Heytesbury, Warminster, Wilts. Tel: Sutton Veny 544
A husband and wife team whose speciality is the restoration of rush and
cane-work on antique furniture. Work also undertaken on modern furniture
as required. Contract work accepted on negotiation.

GEOFFREY MUSGRAVE AND SON, Stoke St Gregory, nr Taunton, Somerset TA3
6JE. Tel: Burrowbridge 218
Premier osier-beds of the world. Willows, hurdles, hand-made baskets and
hampers for fishing and pets, pigeons, cycles, laundry and game.

NEVILLE NEAL, School House, Stockton, nr Rugby CV23 8JE. Tel: Southam
3702
Father and son business engaged solely on the making of rush-seated chairs,
mainly to the designs of the famous Cotswold craftsman, Ernest Gimson.
Stools and traditional ladder-back dining-chairs, armchairs, children's
chairs and rocking-chairs, entirely hand-made from locally-grown ash,
seated with locally-harvested rush.

W. R. OUTHWAITE AND SON, South View, Hawes, Wensleydale, North Yorks.
Probably the last single-handed rope-maker in England, Tom Outhwaite's
craft has been televised and featured in many newspapers. The main lines
are cow-bands for tethering cattle in their stalls and halters for both cows
and horses.

GEOFF PAYNE AND MICK MARKS, (FAIRFORD RUSHWEAVERS) Back Lane, Fairford,
Glos. Tel: Fairford 712052
Rush-weaving in the traditional manner. Restoration work carefully exe-
cuted on antique furniture. Canework also undertaken. Exhibited at British
Crafts Centre. Member of the Craftsmen of Gloucestershire.

R. J. G. REED, The Truggery, Cooper's Croft, Herstmonceux, Hailsham, Sussex
BN27 1QL

Trugs of sweet chestnut frames with willow-boards.

RHONA J. ROSIER (Mrs), Old Brickfields, New Road, Guilden Morden, nr Royston, Herts. Tel: Steeple Morden 852480
Cane seating, restoration work and private commissions.

SEARCHLIGHT WORKSHOPS, Mount Pleasant, Newhaven, Sussex BN9 0NQ. Tel: Newhaven 4007
Basketry, rush and cane chair-seating by physically handicapped craftsmen. A small range of other work such as weaving, soft toys and rustic garden-furniture.

M. B. SMITH, 1 Old Malt House, Corsham, Wilts.
Basket-maker specializing mainly in pet-baskets for the wholesale trade. Other types of basketry undertaken includes laundry and log-baskets, hampers, chests and furniture.

THOMAS SMITH, (Herstmonceux) LTD, Herstmonceux, Sussex Tel: Herstmonceux 2137
The original makers of the Royal Sussex trug basket. Craftsmen still use the original templates and traditional methods to produce the now world-famous trugs for a variety of garden uses, or poker-worked as an attractive shopping basket. Bowls, on struts, are also made.

TOOCRAFT (C. HOLT-WILSON), 2 Canon Square, Melksham, Wilts. Tel: Melksham 703041
Rush-seating, stools and chairs woven to order. Speciality lines are children's rocking-chairs and settees in cord. Re-seating of antique chairs in rush or cane also undertaken.

ELSIE M. TUCKER, Hencote Cottage, Daisy Nook, Failsworth, Manchester M35 9WJ Tel: 061–681 4420
Mainly cane seat restoration.

NAOMI VOWLES, Greenwood Cottage, Bleadon, Weston-super-Mare, Avon
Canework, mainly restoration.

WAVENEY APPLE GROWERS LTD, Aldeby, Beccles, Suffolk NR34 0BL. Tel: Aldeby 345/6/7/8
Rush products entirely hand-made: carpets, bound each end with a fine binding in rush; mats, various shapes; matting, by the yard and unbound; various kinds of baskets, chair-seating. Waveney Rush carpeting is to be seen in many of the stately homes owned by the National Trust; an impressive length is in the library of Blickling Hall. Supplies are through the retail trade, names of nearest stockists will be sent to interested customers.

SHEILA J. WRIXON (Mrs), Barwick Farm, Yeovil, Somerset. Tel: Yeovil 21517
Rushcraft. Demonstrations and lectures. Member of Somerset Guild of Craftsmen.

CORN-DOLLY-MAKERS AND STRAW-PLAITERS

GWYNNETH AKINS (Miss), 33 Glod Street, Riseley, Bedford. Tel: Riseley 461
    Corn-dollies of varying sizes and patterns. Tutor at local craft centre adult
    classes. Commissioned work includes range of designs for Chester Folk-
    Museum.

S. J. BADBY, 220 New Road, Booker, High Wycombe, Bucks. Tel: High
Wycombe 34057
    Corn-dollies: lecturer and tutor.

JAQUIE BAKER, Weavers Dream, Barton St David, Somerton, Somerset. Tel:
Baltonsborough 584
    Corn-dollies: traditional from 'true lovers' knot' to 'Mother Earth'; county
    designs, minute baskets, mobiles and corn jewellery. Member of Society
    Designer-Craftsmen.

RITA CLITHEROE (Mrs), Park Bungalow, Hedenham, Bungay, Suffolk.
    Corn-dollies.

ALEC COKER, 12 Chiltern Close, Chalgrove, Oxford OX9 7RN. Tel:
Stadhampton 346
    Mr Coker is an authority on the craft of corn-dolly-making and gives lec-
    tures and demonstrations to local organizations.

CELIA GARDINER (Miss), Amadeus Cottage, Hutton Sessay, nr Thirsk, Yorks
    Corn-dollies.

M. LAMBETH (Mrs), Hind Loders House, 22 Stonebridge Lane, Fulbourn,
Cambridge CB1 5BW
    Corn-dollies, harvest emblems and traditional straw-work. Author of in-
    struction books on strawcraft, and will give free instruction and advice to the
    serious enquirer.

T. D. LISTER (Mrs), Faceby Lodge Farm, Carlton, Middlesbrough, Cleveland.
    Corn-dollies.

WINIFRED NEWTON-SEALEY, Perton Craft, Stoke Edith, Herefordshire.
    Straw-plaiter and corn-dolly-maker.

MEG PETTITT (Mrs), 2 Southgate, Lydford, Okehampton, Devon.
    Corn-dollies.

MARGARET PRATT (Miss), 33 Queen's Road, Harpenden, Herts. AL5 1QW.
Tel: Harpenden 2012
    Corn-dollies to customer's direct orders.

RAYMOND RUSH, The Golden Cross, Siddington, nr Macclesfield, Cheshire
SK11 9JP. Tel: Marton Heath 358

Corn-dollies; traditional designs sold at his farm shop. Commissions undertaken for churches, museums and special exhibitions. Lecturer and broadcaster on country crafts and customs.

JOHN SKAIFE, 51 Potter Hill, Pickering, Yorks. Tel: Pickering 72908
Straw bee-skeps as made by Mr Skaife's family for over a hundred years. John Skaife is able to cope with only a very limited amount of orders, but has expressed a willingness to teach young bee-keepers the craft if genuinely interested in what he terms a relatively simple skill.

ELIZABETH SMITH, Corn-Dolly House, Edgefield Road, Briston, Melton Constable, Norfolk NR24 2H2
Designer and maker of corn-dollies specializing in unusual designs such as 'traction engines', 'horses and carts', 'gypsy caravans', 'swans' and 'crabs'. Elizabeth Smith's work is retailed through shops of the National Trust and Sandringham, but she will also consider private commissions.

SOMERSET HOUSE WEDMORE LTD, Station Road, Cheddar, Somerset BS27 3AE. Tel: (0934) 742210
This is probably the largest firm of its kind in England to be running a cottage industry whereby corn-dollies are made by hand by local women, each trained in the craft to a high standard. The range of well-known traditional designs are frequently added to and includes straw-plaited novelties which are functional as well as decorative, such as babies' rattles and dollies filled with pot pourri or lavender. A corn-dolly kit is also produced which contains sufficient specially grown corn, and detailed instructions needed for making four different designs. Retail outlet is through craft and gift shops throughout the country.

E. H. THORNE LTD, Beehive Works, Wragby, Lincoln LN3 5LA. Tel: Wragby 555
Straw bee-skeps as available.

ANGELA WITT, Model Farm, Tytherington Road, Corton, Warminster, Wilts.
Corn-dollies, favours (*see* p. 131) and jewellery from specially grown straw. Demonstrations given at agricultural shows and craftsmen's exhibitions.

SARAH MILLMAN, 'Chippings', Nailsworth Road, Avening, Glos.
Corn-dollies and favours in traditional designs.

9

Textiles

Few materials could escape inclusion here, particularly if all the constituents of contemporary textile hangings were analysed. Wood has been woven since ancient times so basketry as a textile art is not a new concept. Cleft willow, drawn through a metal-toothed comb, became the *wass* or *wace* – wood-fibre as flexible as thread which was woven in Wiltshire until the nineteenth century. Modern technology has refined wood into even finer thread by dissolving its component cellulose fibres and spinning them as artificial silk.

Raw silk is the only natural fibre with a continuous filament or thread and can be taken almost immediately to weave fabrics, but is usually 'thrown' to twist the threads together making a stronger yarn for weaving. It is one fibre which has a natural affinity with dye and happily glows through a thousand different shades.

Of the hair fibres, wool is the most widely used – being of more prolific and regenerating growth than other animal hair. But ordinary hair must also have its place in textile crafts; even human hair has not escaped the craftsman's hand. An exquisite miniature portrait of Charles I was embroidered with the king's own hair, and the old lace-makers of Elizabeth I's day wove strands of their silver grey hair into their lace. Money for human hair figures among the expenses of the Tudor queen and *point tresse* (hair lace) was sent to Mary Queen of Scots from the mother of Darnley as a token of affection and symbol of her repudiation of the suggestion that Mary was involved in the murder of her son.

SPINNING AND WEAVING

Man wove before woman span. Stone-age man intertwined branches and reeds, brushwood and grass to make windbreaks and baskets, but his clothes were of animal skin. It was not until the Neolithic period that the art of weaving cloth was practised, since the craft of making yarn was hitherto beyond man's cunning. He who first twisted fibres together to make a continuous thread has passed into oblivion, un-named and unsung. But his simple skill has lived on, practised throughout the millennia in its most primitive state on the spindle and whorl – a stick with a weight at one end, a universal implement, as evidenced by the fact that whorls of varying sizes and designs have been unearthed from sites all over the world. It is interesting to note that linen made in ancient Egypt of hand-spun thread has proved to be much finer than that made on modern machinery; with as many as 150 threads to an inch. It is said that the sails of the Spanish Armada were also spindle-spun.

Experts assume, without substantial evidence but with some reason, that India was the birthplace of the spinning-wheel. Leonardo da Vinci exercised his inventive ingenuity and technical talent to develop spinning and winding in one operation by means of a moving flyer, but this idea was not brought into practical use until some twelve years after his death. In Johann Jürgen's design a series of hooks was inserted along the arms of the flyer, which did not move, but the spinster had to change the thread from hook to hook as the bobbin filled. It was Richard Arkwright's device for even winding, similar to Leonardo's except that the bobbin moved instead of the flyer, which achieved success and pioneered the principles upon which the modern spinning industry are based.

The Industrial Revolution had a disastrous effect on the established cottage industries of the wool trade. But to put the craft in perspective we have to look at the extent to which the wool trade in general has affected our economy, for the crafts of spinning and weaving were almost wholly concerned with woollen cloth until the beginning of the seventeenth century, when cotton was introduced, which in turn died out as a handcraft with the advent and advance of the machine. But, whereas cotton was a newcomer to the textile scene, wool is an indigenous agricultural crop, suited to our climate.

England gained a dominant hold on the wool-weaving industries of Italy and the Low Countries and held an exalted position for the excellence of her fleece from the early Middle Ages. The Normans must have been duly gratified to find such a thriving industry growing from the hillsides; sheep dominated the pastoral scene and English staplers dominated the Continental wool markets. During the fourteenth century demand increased for finished cloth instead of the raw staple: it was the age of the merchant. And of the weaver. Men became websters and the women remained spinsters. Industry settled in the homes of the artisans.

Great wealth accrued from English wool: commerce and politics of the time centred on it; ransoms were paid in it; and the medieval kings' wars financed from it. Nowhere in Europe was Cotswold wool equalled. The Cotswold sheep, direct descendants of the Roman Longwool, produced such heavy fleeces of top quality wool that the breed was protected by licence of the king in 1434, and their exportation was controlled. Records speak of the king of Portugal requesting sixty sacks of Cotswold wool to make "cloths of gold" for court ceremonial dress.

England's earliest guild was that of the Burford merchants in 1082.

Cirencester's wool market was reputed to be the first in the kingdom, and its weavers were granted a charter by Queen Mary for the "customes and constitutions of olde antiquitie out of tyme and mynde belonging to the crafte and occupacion of weavers in the towne of Cisceter". It was truly the age of the golden fleece: wealthy merchants built magnificent churches high on the hills and down in the dells, enriching the region with the finest architecture, with pious sentiments on their precious memorial brasses to ease their way through the golden gates.

Exiled Huguenots found sanctuary among the woolmen and taught them much cunning in their craft: 'narrow', 'brode' and 'huswyff's wayving' appeared on the looms. All was not entirely well, however, before the first machines were fully operational: the quaint and ineffective Burial in Wool Act was passed, inadequate measures to still an advancing tide of change which eventually swept wool into a small corner of the world market.

The 'spinning jenny' and factory system progressively replaced the hand-looms, and many village greens were ablaze as spinning-wheels were burnt by women anxious to get parish relief. Unable to compete with industry, the hand-spinners were forced by circumstance to destroy their wheels to legitimately claim they had no means by which to earn a living.

As a reminder of the significance of our wool trade, the Lord High Chancellor's seat in Parliament was a woolsack – and is still referred to as such. But all is not history. Wool is still making a valuable contribution to the country's overseas earnings with more than half the British clip exported in recent years. What is noticeable is the different geographical pattern of sheepfarming, wrought by changing agriculture. England has some 44,930 wool-producers, of which the northern region has 19,510, with Yorkshire the dominant contributor; the southern region, comprising twelve counties, has the smallest number. The weight of wool varies considerably, of course: the average clip-size from certain parts of Wales and Northern Ireland tends to be slightly lower than that of the average clip for the United Kingdom, which is currently about 950 lbs.

With very few exceptions, all wool producers in the United Kingdom with more than four adult sheep register with the British Wool Marketing Board, which was set up in 1950 to stabilize returns to farmers and achieve maximum prices for British wool by presenting it in ways which meet users' needs. The Board is responsible for virtually all the fleece wool produced here and has about forty merchants to act as its agents. The sheep farmer chooses a merchant in his area whom he wishes to handle his wool and submits an estimate of the number of sheep he expects to shear, and the date on which his wool will be ready for delivery to the warehouse. The merchant grades each producer's clip – an exacting test, for there are around 350 grades for greasy wool and a corresponding number for washed wool.

With ever-increasing competition from synthetic fibres, the Board plays an essential role in safeguarding the market for British wool. Harris Tweed, by regulation, has to be made from wool grown in Scotland and woven on hand-looms, but the spinning is carried out by firms located in Stornoway so only half the process is truly hand-made. Figures show a decline in the amounts of wool used by the Harris Tweed industry, despite the fact that Scotland is now the second largest wool-producer in the United Kingdom.

It is impossible to get exact figures which show the extent to which hand-spinning and weaving is practised in England, owing to the fact that wool merchants buy at auction sales and thereafter agencies handle the transactions. In general, all the Board's wool goes to auctions conducted by the London Wool Brokers, but some hand-spinners and weavers do approach the Board direct for fleece, and there has been a marked rise in this type of sale in recent years. Some 9,205 lbs of wool was sold last year – an increase of about 30 per cent on the previous year's sales – but much of this was sold direct to American shops to meet their growing demand.

The resurgence of spinning and weaving generally in this country has lagged considerably behind that generated by our transatlantic friends – the wheel was still being used in the USA into this century, long after it had been removed from our English firesides. Revivalists found little interest in England initially and crossed the Atlantic in pursuit of perfecting their skills where our American cousins plied the craft, reviving and developing ancient native techniques in their desire to lift a utilitarian task to the status of an arts form.

Interest has increased here, however, over the last few years, and is finding its way into the schools; many craftsmen are being inundated with requests for advice from those wishing to include the use of wheel and loom as part of a very new curriculum. People are no longer regarded as odd for filling their homes with wheels, their gardens with weeds, and harvesting their own flax.

Those craftsmen who do everything by hand to turn fleece into fabric are comparatively rare, and therefore worth seeking out. Their output is naturally limited so relatively more valuable as investment pieces. Irene, Countess of Effingham, is such a craftsman. Her work is in constant demand but so are her services as a lecturer and demonstrator.

It is somewhat of a revelation to realize that a spinner and weaver has to be a mixture of artist, artisan and 'alchemist'. Grading the wool takes experience, and the fleece is sorted into 'diamond', 'broke' and 'britch'; soft shoulder wool is separated from that of the centreback, the latter being naturally coarser because it weathers the worst of the elements. Lady Effingham lays great emphasis on careful carding, the most important ancillary skill in the preparation for spinning, whereby the staples (tufts of wool fibre) are 'teased' out into individual filaments. This process removes any foreign matter such as straw, seeds, mud and brambles which get entangled in the wool. The separate fibres are twisted into a continuous thread on the spinning-wheel by a rhythmic motion incorporating constant control over tension and thickness. Most spinners prefer to 'spin in the grease', the natural lanolin in the wool which keeps their hands soft and supple, and do not wash the wool until it has been spun. Skeined on a little frame called a niddy-noddy, the wool is tied into hanks, washed and prepared for dyeing.

The art of dyeing is ancient. William Morris searched the writings of Pliny, culling old recipes to recapture the art which had become divorced from the modern commercial process, brought about by the introduction of aniline dyes produced from coal-tar. The dyer has to have an elementary knowledge of soil chemistry in order to understand how fleece from the same breed reared in different localities will produce quite different effects, the iron content of the water plays no small part in this. In the old cottage industries it kept six spinsters busy to supply the yarn for one weaver, most weavers, therefore, have to supplement their hand-spun yarn with manufactured yarns.

Working so close to nature, care and concern for the environment is inherent in craftsmen, so conservation of the natural plants which are the integral ingredient of their dyes is always uppermost in their minds as they search out the bark and bedstraw, coltsfoot and ivy, madder and dock, ragwort and rue, nettle and weld, for the delicate hues peculiar to vegetable dyes. The slow-growing lichens are particularly effective and particularly vulnerable to wholesale destruction – a crustaceous species can take up to twenty years to produce a plant of two-inch diameter. Laws to prevent the despoliation of the countryside prohibit indiscriminate picking and plucking, and dyers carefully catalogue samples so as to avoid wasteful experiment.

Making a living from weaving (which includes spinners, of course, for mostly they weave the yarn they have spun) is hard work, but this is true of craftwork in general. Each field has its own problems, but it is interesting – and helpful to others, one hopes – to look at a few individual ventures.

Brontë Tapestries has the advantage of being situated in the now old world birthplace of the famous sisters, so there is an immediate romantic association with the Yorkshire moors, but it is also in close proximity to the centre of the textile industry. Rod Taylor's experience in industry before setting up his hand-loom weaving business must have proved useful as far as contacts are concerned, besides which he never started off with any illusions of the 'simple life'. He agrees that one must take risks and not be frightened of a maturing overdraft, and has expanded his range and outlets considerably. Not without trying every marketing channel, though, plus fourteen years of hard work. The

business is a co-ownership scheme: seven self-employed weavers working together. One sixth of all their earnings is left in the business until
such time as they have provided their share of the capital to make them
all equal partners.

Another weaver, working alone, finds it difficult to sell his work
locally simply because he *is* in the middle of a textile area where the Industrial Revolution took root, bringing distress to the hand-weavers.
"To many", he says, "weaving is a dirty word". This is reflected in the
ageing membership and paucity of new younger members in the Birmingham and District Guild of Weavers.

Most agree that weaving cloth for sale by the yard is commercially
unviable and even the top fashion-designers are reluctant to pay a realistic price for it. Hand-woven cloth made up into articles seems to be a
more successful venture for the best weavers who can then design the
cloth specifically for the type of garment. Malcolm McDougall, the
Grewelthorpe hand-weaver, has moved into the field of dress-design,
working out the design and cloth in consultation with the customers
and weaving sample pieces in front of them. Geraldine St Aubyn
Hubbard's work is already well known and includes block-printing on
silk, cotton and linen for the linings of her hand-woven garments.

Hand-woven cloth does present difficulties to the amateur dressmaker and is obviously better left in the hands of the professional who,
like Mary McNeill, will know exactly where to let in any openwork or
applied patterns for sleeve edges or yokes or panels. This knowledge
prevents wastage.

It is true also that much more publicity is given to a woven hanging
than is ever devoted to a length of cloth, and often it is the bold use of unusual materials, such as driftwood, polythene, glass and cane, which
attracts attention by showing the craftsman's ingenuity and skill in incorporating such alien bits and pieces. Whilst some will freely admit
their works are not intended for any functional purpose and see these as
an extension of their own personal interpretation of an art form through
a textiles medium, all strive to produce interesting textures.

Touring exhibitions of contemporary hangings are reasonably successful for gathering commissions, although they do not actively promote sales; in fact, buyers often have to be quite persistent in their
efforts to secure an exhibited work. Static one-man shows attract attention but not a buying public. Well-illustrated exhibition catalogues are
often used as textbooks by students all over the Commonwealth and
this has resulted in some subsidiary sales of photographs of work to
authors. Many mourn the passing of the Weaver's Workshop, seeing no
comparable publicity for British textile artists: the arty-crafty catalogue, highlighting isolated aspects out of context, serves no real
purpose for a student.

Sisal, hemp, jute and agricultural bailing twine, once inexpensive, always beautiful to work with, have become almost scarce enough to be collectors' items.

Fibres, especially those of exotic origin, cannot be employed with impunity for craftsmen have to be constantly aware of current laws. Especially affected has been goat-hair yarn, the importation of which has been prohibited under the Anthrax Protection Order 1971. The Multiple Fabric Co., of Bradford, specialize in yarns for hand-weaving, all processed entirely in Britain. Joyce Coleman claims to be the only person in the British Isles to have spun and woven mink – a beautiful fibre she says – and she is the acknowledged expert in unusual yarns. You may not be able to get cloth of musk-ox-hair, or spun dog-hair in Bond Street or in the Rue de Rivoli, but you may find them in Speen, which is scarcely a village.

Some craftsmen feel it is morally wrong to use synthetic fibres as they do not rot into their original constituents like natural yarns, and so return some nutrients to the earth. However, most prefer not to consider their craftwork in relation to its suitability for future compost! But almost all the weavers in this survey have commented on dwindling supplies; a couple even find it worthwhile to travel up to Scotland to buy a van-load of yarns to see them through a working year. Most English weavers decry the limited range of supplies available to them compared to those offered in the USA. Compassion and commiseration for fellow craftsmen have prompted weavers like Eliza Leadbeater, Evelyn Green, Mike Halsey and Lore Youngmark to market equipment as well – the latter two through the Hand-weavers Studio and Gallery, where studio facilities are offered as part of its aim of promoting hand-weaving and allied textile crafts.

Lavinia Bradley teaches inkle-weaving on the looms her husband makes, based on a design of a very early inkle-loom.

Inkle-weaving is probably of Scottish origin. The word *inkle* is Old English for a kind of linen tape or braid. The early English looms were fixed to the floor and used to make 'galluses' (garter bands and draw strings), which makes them sound very limiting, which they are not! Despite its size (28 inches × 14 inches × 2 inches) it takes a 7-feet warp length and is capable of most sophisticated work that would need six shafts on a conventional loom. Its portability and noiselessness makes it most popular, making weaving available to people who have insufficient space or resources to have large looms. There is also a model which can be operated by the handicapped. The table model is of an early North American design.

It is infinitely easier to make changes in a design as it progresses on a hand-loom, and it is for this reason that many enterprising textile-designers in industry insist on working through a pattern rather than merely designing on paper.

The dobby-loom, traditionally called the 'witch engine' by virtue of its automatic shedding device which seems endowed with some element of 'magic', is comparatively rare, with only a couple of craftsmen producing the type today. More scope for patterning is made possible by the weaver pegging his design on to the lag and playing out long repeat patterns, whilst operating the dobby by means of the treadle.

The Harris Centre has recently opened as a craft centre with the emphasis on spinning, dyeing and weaving, for this is the home of the world-famous Harris looms (*see* p. 78). It offers studio workshop facilities as well as tuition and advisory service.

Local interest, promotion and varied facilities are provided by regional guilds, who have a total membership of about 1,200 and are represented by the Association of Guilds of Weavers, Spinners and Dyers, itself a member of the Federation of British Crafts Societies. Traditionally concerned with protecting the interests of weavers, the Worshipful Company of Weavers, founded in the twelfth century, confines its activities to the provision of educational grants, principally to help post-graduates at northern universities.

The quest for new materials is unceasing. Weavers seek out boat-chandlers for the linen twine with which they sewed the sails before nylon took over, and are often forced, more by circumstance than by design, to adapt and adopt their techniques to new materials.

A tapestry-weaving course at West Dean College, established with the advice of Karen Finch of the Textile Conservation Centre, has two aims: to provide an intensive training in the basic art of tapestry-weaving for students wishing to teach or become professional tapestry-weavers, and to provide an essential introduction for anyone considering tapestry conservation as a profession.

Most textiles exhibited on international lines are woven hangings and tapestries, and are intended to cover large areas. To counterbalance the extent to which sheer size was dominating the textile world, the first International Exhibition of Miniature Textiles was held at the British Crafts Centre in 1974. With the success of two exhibitions behind them, the organizers envisage these as bi-annual events alternating and contrasting with the Lausanne Tapestry Biennale where exhibits, of a minimum size of five square metres, challenge the scale and scope of the individual weaver. But the textile artist working in miniature has perhaps the more exacting task, for the scale is not large or imposing enough to absorb any technical flaws. The results have been incredible; from Kaffe Fassett's knitted map to three-dimensional cubism. All the techniques associated with the woven, wound, pleated, plaited, hung, hooked, knitted and knotted textile forms which spread across and jut from the world's walls, have been employed in this Lilliputian landscape.

Probably no other age has given birth to so many inspired artists, and above the clamour of the young graduates anxious to get their voices heard is the distinctive statement expressed by Theo Moorman through her highly individual work. In pursuance of her ideal of progressive craftsmanship, in which she neither compromises to keep alive past traditions nor competes with the machine, she combines technical experience with an artist's inspiration to lift a utilitarian craft to an art form. Theo Moorman aims at an interpretation of an idea or form which is abstract in design and more meaningful than a faithful copy of the object of her inspiration. Her work is known half-way across the world where she travels to demonstrate the unique form of tapestry-weaving she has perfected, already accepted in the arts-crafts world as the 'Moorman technique'.

The vogue for woven wall-hangings has given weavers a freedom of technique which is denied to them in the rigid conformity necessary for cloth, where correct setting and tension are needed to prevent sagging and seating in wear. Time being the most important element in the craftsman's costing, he should make the most valuable thing he can in the available time and this means an exclusive design for the individual, be it a skirt-length or furnishings. The popular conception of a weaver is one who weaves tweed, but since tweed is a very competitive product, it is appreciated more for its aesthetic value than any other factor, moreover, it leaves very little scope for individual design and less for artistic expression. Perhaps, because of this very limitation imposed upon him, he who is content to ply his skills with no desire for national acclaim is the more worthy because, like F. Mercer, he sells to local countrywomen, deriving satisfaction from seeing them working about the farms of his lovely north Pennines in his hard-wearing tweeds. These tweeds take something like five hours for each yard woven, plus the hand-finishing, which he does in the traditional way of the old cottage weavers – using his feet!

SILK

> I am by no means the first person in England to dream of producing raw silk here.
>
> *Zoë, Lady Hart Dyke*

James I dreamt of it too, and ordered his loyal landed subjects to plant at least one mulberry tree, 10,000 of which he imported from France; but unfortunately he ordered the wrong variety and by the time the black species of mulberry had grown sufficiently to support the silkworms, everyone had forgotten the purpose for which they were planted. After his abortive attempt to develop sericulture at home, he admonished his colonists in Virginia to "apply themselves diligently and promptly to the breeding of silkworms, bestowing their labours

rather in producing this rich commodity than in the growth of that per-
nicious and offensive weed, tobacco". Apparently to little avail – Virginia tobacco is indisputably more famous than Virginia silk!

Records speak of many attempts to rear silkworms in England but
none were as resolute as Zoë, Lady Hart Dyke, whose fascination for
the subject started at the tender age of four years. An absorbing hobby,
it weathered the vagaries of childhood and the calls of motherhood to
develop into a commercial enterprise.

Sericulture is really two distinct processes, each totally dependent on
the other: the first is the farmer who rears the silkworm to provide the
cocoons and the second is the reeler who unwinds the filament of thread
to produce raw silk. Silkworm farming, despite government aid and
subsidies in other countries, is essentially the smallholder's province.
Even in Japan, whose output of silk fabrics is larger than that of all the
other eighteen silk-producing countries added together, the incredible
number of cocoons produced is the sum total of the output of a multitude of small farmers whose individual crops average less than 200 lb
each. Just what this represents in the scale of silk-farming can be calculated from their approximate figures showing the yield: 450 lb fresh
cocoons raised on an acre of fully-grown mulberry produces 66 lb raw
silk; a year's production being in the region of 21,500 metric tons, out of
a world total of 39,368. The silk reeled from a single cocoon weighs
about 0·012 ounce.

The life cycle of the silkworm is a fascinating study, and an educational service, non-profit-making and subsidized by the Silk Association, offers information to schools showing the whole process of silk
production.

The origin of the silkworm and its introduction into each silk-
producing country is shrouded in romantic mystery, with a touch of
intrigue. Traditionally, it was the Chinese Empress, Hsi Ling Shi, who
cosseted the caterpillar and reaped her due reward from the gossamer
thread it spun for her, which she wove on a loom of her own invention to
produce the richest textile in history. China, it is said, derived its name
from *Seres*, meaning 'the silk country'. Altars were set up and prayers
offered to Her Highness's gentle genius, and successive empresses
tended the worms with their own fair noble hands. Written Chinese still
expresses the name silkworm as 'heavenly insect'. For 2,000 years its
production techniques were closely guarded secrets and silk later became the most precious export. Legend has it that the first silkworms to
be introduced into Europe were smuggled in by two Persian monks on
the orders of Emperor Justinian, A.D. 552.

Whatever truth is in the legends, the rather insignificant, very ugly,
decidedly voracious little worm is an incredible technician whose
unique, age-old process produces a raw material which scientific technology has failed to surpass. A filament from 500 to 2,000 yards long

can be unwound from one cocoon, too fragile for commercial use alone, but stronger than steel wire when spun. Its unrivalled properties are distinguished from skilful and spurious substitutes by the new Silk Mark, recently adopted to identify the products of the principal firms in the British silk industry who are included in the Silk Group.

Lullingstone Silk Farm, whose travels have taken it from Surrey to Kent to Hertfordshire, has survived all the vicissitudes associated with specialist agriculture and breeding, and the traumas of requisition and damage inflicted by wartime and excavation for gravel in the grounds. The silkworms are reared and the silk is reeled at the farm. The raw silk is then sent to Messrs Sudbury Walters for processing, and for throwing and weaving, a craft which has been carried on at the mill for some 250 years, there being only two silk mill throwsters in the country.

The aspirations of James I to produce English silk have been realized by the late Lady Hart Dyke, whose silk-farm achieved a unique position – it being the only one of its kind in Europe. And it has supplied the silk for all the major royal occasions, from coronation robes to the Queen's trousseau, and more recently the investiture robe for the Prince of Wales and Princess Anne's wedding-dress.

The silkworm's place in textile history was never overlooked by Lady Hart Dyke, after the founding of her silk-farm she carried out the ancient Chinese custom of the ceremony of the Blessing of the Silkworms.

EMBROIDERY

Egyptian tombs seem to be one of the storehouses of the arts of the civilized world, and embroidery has therefore been positively classified as of very ancient origin since fragments have been found as tomb-hangings. The oldest extant piece of an embroidered garment dates back to the fourth century B.C., and probably the earliest written reference can be found in the details for embroidered hangings for the tabernacle described so vividly in the Book of Exodus.

Embroidery was introduced to England by the Saxons, accomplished needlewomen who paid great attention to the working of coloured threads. The cope and mantle of St Cuthbert, who died in A.D. 685, was wrought with gold embroidered lace, and by the tenth century the chasuble – the origin of which is to be found in the antique *penula nobilis*, which succeeded the Roman *toga* – was decorated with embroidery or orphreys. Added at first to cover the seams, the orphreys became the outstanding ornament of the chasuble, giving the shape of the Latin or *Y* cross. It was the richly embroidered orphreys of the English clergy in 1246 which led Pope Innocent IV to allude to England as "our garden of delight". *Opus Anglicanus* was consequently held in high esteem throughout Christendom.

During the fourteenth century the austerity of a cloistered life was often tempered by the bizarre deformities of nature which the nuns wrought with their needle: awesome animals winged their way across winding sheets and fearsome fantasies were caught on armorial bearings, while fanciful foliage enlivened altar cloths.

Elizabethan extravagance used the art of embroidery to enrich personal dress and stringent measures were enforced to maintain standards of excellence, including a law which required that embroidery be hallmarked, as precious metals are today, and prohibited its sale by candle-light. The Church and the Court remained the two prominent patrons.

But needlecraft fell behind the more robust crafts in succeeding reigns and prompted a Miss Hulton to write to the *Spectator* in 1700, deploring the modern girls' total disregard for the art, seeing them as "proud, idle flirts sipping their tea for a while of an afternoon in a room hung with the industry of their great-grandmothers". Apathy was obviously not solely the sin of the English needlewoman, embroidery had been dormant for over 200 years when M. Louis Grossé revived the art in the Bruges School of Embroidery. The House of Louis Grossé was founded in 1783, and when it opened in London was the first shop in Sherlock Holmes's Baker Street. For almost 200 years it has been carrying on the tradition for ecclesiastical embroidery (which includes hand-woven fabrics, orphreys, braids and fringes) under the direction of the now seventh generation of the Grossé family. Vestments, the origins of which lie in the ancient traditions of the Church, receive as much attention as any fashion garment. Just how progressive the designs are can be judged by the intense public interest generated by the exhibition mounted at Chelmsford Cathedral by the House of Grossé as the world's first ecclesiastical fashion show. A chasuble, designed by John Piper to match his tapestry, contrasted with one of hand-woven worsted, and prize-winning antique embroideries vied for attention with Patrick Reyntiens's design for the world's first PVC cope. All the items are made to original design, and are therefore completely unique, which shows the craftsmen's artistic approach and pride in their work.

Out of the Victorian decadence into which crafts had sunk William Morris pioneered a revival of the art of tapestry-weaving, which had been lost with the closing of the Mortlake Royal Tapestry works a hundred years before. Morris's name is synonymous with the tradition of English design, which he classified as being of pre-Tudor origins. But in late Victorian church architecture the dominating school was that of Bodley, Garner and Scott, which included many of the greatest craftsmen of the early twentieth century. George Bodley was the brother-in-law and first pupil of Sir Gilbert Scott, and it was he who gave Morris and Co. their first church commission. Of the two companies set up to carry out their schemes, Watts and Co. was founded, in association with Gilbert Scott the younger, to provide needlework and textiles. Some of the most famous vestments designed in the last century have been made in their workrooms, including the altar frontal given – in accordance with the tradition of newly-crowned monarchs – by Queen Elizabeth II to Westminster Abbey at her coronation. The copes for the last three coronations were also made and embroidered by Watts and Co., who consider themselves fortunate in still having the skills of first class craftsmen at their disposal. Although one of Britain's foremost church furnishers, they are not exclusively concerned with ecclesiastical work, and foremost among examples of secular embroidery is the canopy of the Speaker's Chair in the House of Commons and the heraldic banners hung in the Guildhall for the twelve senior livery companies.

Heraldic embroidery is a specialized craft, and an expert in the field is Berowald Innes who employs the two traditional stitches for his wool-on-canvas designs – *petit point* for the detail and *gros point* for the larger areas. A heraldic frieze may contain some 160,000 stitches, representing over five hundred hours' work.

A quick, easy rhythm, akin to the regularity of a spinner at her wheel, is necessary in needlepoint, especially if the tapestries are made without a frame as they are at Weatherall. Lillian Delevoryas stretches her considerable creative talents in many directions and has certainly brought art into needlework, which so many modern embroiderers have attempted but never quite achieved. Reacting against the insipid crash-and-cotton image of the 'lazy-daisy' stitching which once passed as embroidery, students have often attacked the craft out of crude contempt for traditional technique, and the results have been just as unsuccessful.

Lillian Delevoryas's paintings are reminiscent of Morris but are no slavish adherent to his style. She is American but her work could not be more English. With the endurance of a medieval monk she plys her craft with dedication; a needlepoint hanging 7 feet by 5 feet will take all of 5,000 hours of accurate, intricate stitching alone, apart from the designing, backing and finishing. In contrast to the muted tones and twining tendrils is the vibrant and vigorous vegetation which swirls and splashes in bold designs over sweeping cloaks and richly flowered bedspreads which won first prize in both the appliqué and needlepoint sections of the 1974 Art in Needlework exhibitions.

Within about five years, Weatherall Workshops has achieved its aim of providing apprenticeship training in certain crafts, initially needlework and painting. There are now two full-time apprentices and several skilled outworkers – a scheme which Lillian equates with the old guild system – with a week-end training programme. The success of the venture rests squarely on Lillian's academic artistry and her husband's administrative acumen. Integration of individual skills is the maxim from which Weatherall's reputation for developing the most exciting contribution to decorative art has grown to international level, but Lillian will not allow herself to sit back in comfortable complacency – progressive craftwork means expression of her personality in many media – through soft watercolours, textural tapestries and smooth ceramics. An increasing involvement of local craftsmen creates employment and provides the work force to produce the volume of work necessary to keep the workshops a viable proposition.

This liberation from the rigid confines of stylized needlework has become increasingly prevalent in the work produced by the students of the four colleges in England where degree courses in embroidery are offered. Manchester's diploma show in particular is a launching-pad for many exciting projects. Offering two alternative approaches to textile printing, one with a fine arts bias, and the other geared to industrial and commercial design, balances the ideals with the realities. The freedom of expression which might manifest itself in an elaborately embroidered chair or a formally structured textile pattern is a reflection of Anne Butler's influence as head of department, and the importance she attaches to liaising with the print, weaving and fashion departments; from this so many of the graduates acquire the confidence to go it alone.

Professionalism in the craft has generated from such individuals and its status has been raised by their efforts. Alison Barrell, head of the embroidery department at an adult education centre in Kent, spearheads a textile studio group of skilled students to form an exhibiting body where individual or joint commission projects can be undertaken. Academic achievement is not, surprisingly enough, the main objective of the majority who attend adult courses. Only 20 per cent of those on the embroidery and design course actually take an external qualifying examination, the rest attend for sheer personal improvement, learning to design for themselves rather than relying on commercial patterns.

Education in this sense produces, not, as some cynic put it, "a breed of amateurs who take the bread and butter from the professional craftsman's mouth by dabbling in the crafts themselves", but a more discerning public who can appreciate the skill and time which goes into the work. It is this appreciation of hitherto underestimated art of needlecraft which prompted sixteen young ladies to meet in London in 1906 to form a society "to deal entirely with embroidery and with the object of keeping up a high standard of work and design", the membership to be restricted to certificated embroideresses. Today, the society – the Embroiderers' Guild – has 4,340 members in its seventeen UK branches, and some twenty-eight associated societies overseas. A recognized charity and non-profit-making organization, it arranges classes and lectures given by recognized experts. Its permanent collection is extensive and includes a Coptic fragment from the sixth century. Its library contains some thousand titles, and members are allowed to borrow pieces or slides from its 2,500 samples.

Any pre-conceived notion that embroidery meant stitching samplers would be cause enough to make it an unattractive pastime for the young, a fallacy to be scotched once and for all by the imáginative pieces entered in the inaugural exhibition of the Young Embroiderers' Society. One of the youngest exhibitors, Isabel Myerscough, worked her "Geranium Plum Tree" with a five-year-old's ingenuity; whilst her big sister, twelve-year-old Seona, demonstrated how exciting the craft can be in her beaded and sequined "Mouse in Armour".

Greater public awareness of the soft arts medium is furthered by the professional group within the guild, which was formed in 1962 to promote the highest standards of design and to encourage a fine arts approach to embroidery. There is a rigorous annual selection for membership and this has been reflected in the success of their exhibitions. Interest has grown every year but keeping membership to an administratively manageable number has imposed even more stringent criteria by which some sixty-three people work as the '62 Group'.

QUILTING, PATCHWORK AND RAG RUGS

The versatility of quilting almost defies analysis. Its baldest definition is two layers of fabric, softly padded, and kept in place by cross lines of stitching; but the ways in which this can be interpreted are innumerable. All manner of needlecraft is employed, from the traditional quilting done on a frame with soft sculptural effects, to low relief appliqué, trapunto, or patchwork.

Quilting is a decorative medium which was perfected in the north of England, where it is still practised, though more to keep the craft alive than as a means of livelihood. But as a cottage industry it survived in the northern dales until the Second World War and Mrs Florence Fletcher, an expert quilter whose work is exhibited in a number of museums including the Victoria and Albert Museum, who is also an author on the subject, recalls her childhood when many of the Durham cottagers earned some form of living as quilt-wives. 'Quilt clubs' were formed of twenty customers, each subscribing a shilling a week for twenty weeks, at the end of which each received a handsome quilt for their £1. Although not confined to one particular locality, it is the Durham quilt which is always cited as the traditional one. The bottom layer of fabric was secured to a wooden frame, and the layer of fleece spread evenly on top with the covering drawn taut and secured over the padding. The pattern, of which there were many local variations, was traced with a needle round a template. Short running-stitches, equally spaced, secured all the layers together and accentuated the pattern. Quilted clothing, as seen in the jerkin of Edward the Black Prince, was in use long before the skill was applied to bedcovering. It was not until Tudor times that bed quilts became fashionable, and English patchwork quilts can only be traced back to the sixteenth century.

That it was no parsimonious piecing together of bits and pieces but a serious aspect of needlecraft is evidenced by the existence of a scrap of bed-hanging of 'applied patchwork', reputedly worked by Mary Queen of Scots, herself a fine needlewoman. But its origins go back to the royal and noble families of ancient Egypt, where a canopy of gazelle-hide, patched in five colours, served a queen, a thousand years before Christ. Where patchwork ends and appliqué begins can only be judged on individual pieces, for one often passes for the other. The Knights Templars told of the vivid 'patchwork' they had seen on the banners of the East and it may be through them that it was introduced to England.

The need for economy, when scraps of material were so valuable that they had to be recycled, was uppermost when the pioneers went out West, taking their craft with them. It is estimated that some 75 per cent of the homes in rural America own a patchwork quilt, family heirlooms made between 1775 and 1885. A permanent gallery has now been opened in London's Sloane Avenue to display a vast collection of them.

The craft developed into a tradition in which a bride-to-be might have thirteen different patchwork quilts in her bottom drawer before she married. The designs evolved as symbols of their social history – 'slave chain', 'Indian hatchet', 'log cabin', names which evoke pioneer colonizing days.

Whereas much of the American quilt is machined, English patchwork has remained essentially a handcraft and is being lifted to, if not the fine arts proper, an honourable position as a valuable folk art. Betty Randles, a fine arts graduate and textile lecturer, now "lives and breathes patchwork", and has developed a flourishing cottage industry which employs some half a dozen needlewomen on a variety of articles. One interesting project which Betty recently undertook was the renovation of two quilts, made by the grandmother of H. G. Wells, which were stuffed with yellowing financial papers and accounts. The revival of interest in this fascinating craft prompted the Victoria and Albert Museum to hold a Victorian Sewing Bee where their embroidery expert demonstrated the technique to beginners.

The stringent economy exercised out of necessity in eighteenth-century cottages produced the ultimate in recycling of materials in the shape of rag rugs. These were basically made of strips of rag hooked through a hessian base; the hessian in this case being a closely woven potato-sack, opened up and washed. The rug was then backed with another sack. A latched rugging-hook was to be found in most homes, with the sharp point safely plugged into a cork when not in use.

The concept of weaving with rags was not exclusively a British domestic industry, the rural areas of Scandinavia were similarly occupied, combining straw and rush with their rags. The technique was exported to America with early settlers and a fine mid-eighteenth-century example in the American Museum, Bath, incorporates a bold design of a lion surrounded by birds and trees. Just where the principle of hooking rugs originated is difficult to trace, examples of differing form and materials seem to be found in most countries, I have even seen one in the home of an Ojibway Indian.

Our forefathers may well be amazed to find that two centuries later the humble rug into which went the family's well-worn dresses and jackets, with sister Dora's red flannel petticoat "to brighten the corners", has been lifted to the sphere of textile-weaving by a Royal College of Arts' graduate. The ability to turn a pile of rags into a woven rug of vibrant colour and fascinating texture is a significant step in elevating a humble cottage craft to an art form.

HORSEHAIR DRESSING

East Anglia has a long association with textiles which stretches back to the medieval wool trade, and today boasts the unique craft industry of horsehair dressing – the only one of its kind in England.

English dressed horsehair has a world reputation for superior quality and its uses are almost limitless: as drafts for brush-making; as hair for weaving horsehair cloth; in sundry trades for violin bows and plumes; and as a by-product for making curled hair to stuff furniture with. The stiffer tail hair makes household and industrial paint brushes; the tapered end is sometimes flagged so as to hold the paint, preventing it from running down the brush. Mane hair, which is softer, is used for finer brushes. The textile trade uses the longer hair in such hard-wearing materials as damask, interlinings and padding in tailoring, and South African railway-blinds. There is also a constant demand for horsehair in the toy-making industry where it becomes rabbit-whiskers and, appropriately, manes and tails for rocking-horses.

Essentially a handcraft, the skills of sorting, hackling and double-drawing the horsehair, which comes from America, Brazil, Australia, Russia and Mongolia, require nimble fingers and strong arms. Up to nine months' training is needed to master the techniques: a sharp eye and deft hand being sensitive skills denied to mechanization.

When the hair arrives in 500-lb bales it is disinfected, sorted mane from tail, black from white and grey, soaked overnight then thoroughly washed. Cleaning, untangling and straightening is done by hackling (the process of drawing the wet hair through upright steel combs, this also grades out the very short hair) the combings, which are sent to curlers for stuffing mattresses and upholstery.

When the hair has thoroughly dried on its racks it is double-drawn:

this involves assembling locks of several hundred strands of various lengths; loading the cards demands a trained hand for each clutch of hair has to be drawn separately through steel combs similar to those used for hackling. Trimmed and bound into bundles, the hair is ready for despatch to manufacturers all over the United Kingdom, America and Europe.

Arnold and Gould have been in the trade for seventy years. A family business in traditional manner, generations of the same family tend to take up the craft in much the same way as in the older rural trades. The organization closely follows the true cottage industries, for several of their many employees are outworkers who do certain stages of the processes in their own homes.

ROPE-MAKING

Fears for the future of rope-making by hand made dismal reading when Tom Outhwaite announced his retirement last year. Derbyshire's rope-making had just finished as Herbert Marrison retired; he was the last of a continuous line of craftsmen who had tramped the long rope walks for four hundred years in the yawning cavern in the Peak District.

Yorkshire's tradition of rope-making stretched over some two centuries, with traditionally simple methods, and primitively functional equipment: a 'sledge' at one end, with a hook and a head of hooks at the other – which Tom called his 'twisting machine' – with a cow's horn for incorporating certain refinements such as a 'nose loop'.

Cow-bands, woven on a hand-loom until ten years ago, still account for a big proportion of the orders, "when they fasten up cows in the shippons the bands have to be soft to avoid chafing . . . no, there's no shortage of orders, although farming methods have changed".

The local paper reported that Tom was willing to give free tuition to anyone who wanted to take on the business: there was plenty of interest, but as a trade it has to be economically viable; and the craftsman must be conversant with the materials he has to handle, as well as possessing the dexterity needed for a manipulative skill.

It was not sentimentality which brought Dr Peter Annison to Tom Outhwaite's workshop. A textile chemist and senior lecturer, whose educational background has given him knowledge of more than just the cotton, hemp and sisal used for making halters, Peter Annison is exploring the potential for expansion of the craft, hoping to create extra jobs in that pocket of the Dales, whilst retaining the traditional aspects of the craft. Meanwhile, the academic-turned-craftsman treads the same path as those generations of fibre rope-makers before him.

KNITTING, KNOTTING AND NETTING

It is thought that knitting originated in Arabia; a red sandal sock dating from A.D. 500 is in the Victoria and Albert Museum; but evidence of the craft having been practised in England does not go further back than the Middle Ages, when knitting guilds were formed. It was almost exclusively a man's craft at that time, with an apprenticeship period of six years: three served under a master craftsman and three as a journeyman knitter. Admission to the guild included the knitting of felted leggings, a woollen shirt and a patterned carpet. Silk and metal threads were used as much as spun wool and it is examples of the former that have survived, mainly, one supposes, due to the durability of the thread and the more careful preservation accorded to ecclesiastical articles.

Hosiery was generally made from woven woollen cloth until the sixteenth century, when the art of hand-knitting stockings was seen in the house of an Italian living in London. The technique was soon learned and practised, the improved fit appealing to rich and elegant Elizabethans. Hand-knitting of stockings became a professional craft and, at that time, the principal export of the Channel Islands. The stockings were costly but popular; the extravagance causing the fashionable queen some misgivings, not only for the effects on her own purse but the inevitable ruin the new industry would bring on the cloth hosiers. It is said that she even accepted the gift of hand-knitted silk stockings with reluctance and became secretive about wearing them.

Knitting sheaths, attached to the waist, were used to speed up the process of hand-knitting by securing the right-hand needle leaving the hand free to weave the wool faster over the tips of the needles. These sheaths were often of wood, or made of leather stuffed with sheep's wool, and became popular betrothal gifts, carved and ornamented, in much the same way as lace-bobbins were presented to lady-loves.

One suitor who did not find the clicking of knitting needles conducive to courtship was a clergyman from Calverton. The Rev. William Lee, although exasperated by his fiancée's preoccupation with her knitting, became fascinated by the process, and set about exploring the possibilities of making it a mechanical procedure. The result was the hand-frame, which he invented in 1589. Of incredible complexity for its era, comprising some 3,500 components, it was the first knitting device to be invented since two straight needles, often made by countryfolk from bone, came into use in the Middle Ages. Each stitch now had its own needle instead of one needle to a row of stitches, the whole was mounted on a wooden frame and the work became known as framework knitting, operated by hands and feet. Stockings, knitted flat and seamed by hand, were mainly produced on the hand-frame. Lee died in Paris a poor man, his invention never having been accorded the patronage he sought for it.

The inventor's death did not, however, see the end of the invention. His idea eventually took root and was developed on a large scale. By 1750 there were 12,000 frameworkers in Nottinghamshire, a similar number in Leicestershire and some in Derbyshire. Never an industrialized industry as such, the frames were often hired from a local master and installed in the worker's cottage, attic or large outhouse, with all the family taking part in the processes in much the same way as the weavers ran their cottage industries. There are still many buildings in the east Midlands where evidence of larger windows being inserted, to give maximum light to the workers, give some clue to their former use as a 'knitters' house'. Shepshed in Leicestershire has many former frameshops, and at Ruddington the restoration of a knitter's premises is part of a museum project.

Calverton, the inventor's village, has many fine examples of traditional knitters' cottages with their enlarged windows. Nottinghamshire, the birthplace of the hand-frame, is particularly rich in these houses, which is not surprising when one learns that there were 16,382 at work in that county alone in 1844, Lee's knitting-frame having been improved upon by then by Jedediah Strutt in 1758.

Such is the tenacity of the English craftsman that right in the centre of the area where the Luddite Riots took place early in the nineteenth century due to cheap cut-up stockings being produced on the frames to the detriment of fully-fashioned craftmade frame stockings, there is a generation of genuine hand-frame knitters who have been through a full apprenticeship, possibly the last, at work on frames some three hundred years old.

There are now only about twenty frames worked in the whole world: thirteen at Mr Hurt's place at Chilwell, all producing Shetland lace-type shawls and fine knitwear. There are still a few worked at Hucknall, but the craft has all but died out in that area. No apprenticeship scheme is now in existence, but it was operated as a seven-year period of training until the mid-sixties. About eight years ago theirs must have been the country's smallest union, with possibly the longest name: the Shawl, Fall and Antimacassar Trades Union of Hucknall and District; now disbanded due to lack of numbers.

The industry was moved to the Midlands from London in the eighteenth century, to take advantage of the cheaper labour, but the guild was initially very much a city institution for the first charter, one of but a few granted by Cromwell, applied only to London's framework knitters. Charles II granted a second charter which extended the guild's power throughout the country, protecting the standards by searching out inferior work, the "searchers" being empowered to cut this up with shears and impose fines.

The Worshipful Company of Framework Knitters had its own hall, master's coach and gilded barge, with liveried servants. Its present day role is chiefly concerned with maintaining its charities: retired hosiery workers have been accommodated in cottage homes at Oadby, the foundation stone being laid by the Lord Mayor of London; and encouragement is given to hosiery students of the City and Guilds of London Institute by the annual awarding of medals.

The craft has gone full circle: the hand-frame superseded the knitting-needle, automation ousted both; and now, in this age of technical achievement when machines are computer-controlled, creative artists are looking at yarn as though it were a new medium. Never before have so many people turned to hand-knitting. Labour is expensive once again: exclusive design at a premium.

Information on the nature and production of various fibres allied to knitting and crochet as creative crafts has been made available to schools through a unique service provided by the Knitting Council for Schools (p. 378) in the form of an illustrated lecture. Although financed by a consortium of fibre-producers and knitting-yarn-manufacturers, the lecture is non-promotional and entirely educational, illustrating the almost unlimited techniques of the crafts. An average of 5,000 schools avail themselves of the service each year.

Designers go to odd corners of the earth specially to seek inspiration and in the hands of a craftsman the permutations of pattern, texture, colours and shape produce an infinite variety of the same garment: yarn itself being almost anything that can be spun into a thread.

The fabric of a knitted garment is often more important to the young designers who are finding self-expression through knitting. One exhibition illustrated just how deeply such craftsmen are involved with their material. The texture and shape were enhanced by actually building the design into the fabric so that, as one person remarked, "when you took the garment off you'd want to hang it on the wall to look at it".

Kaffe Fassett taught himself to knit initially to interpret a whole range of visual images ranging from Byzantine mosaics to landscapes. His designs have evolved into patterns too complicated to be compatible with industrial processes, and he has concentrated mainly on designing for hand-knitting and making tapestries for the exclusive Beatrice Bellini hand-knits range.

The ultimate expression through knitting must surely have been reached at an international collection sponsored by the International Wool Secretariat, when artists produced an incredible exhibition ranging from knitted poached eggs to knitted figures of mother and baby. A digression indeed from the homely occupation of knitting of warm clothing. The clicking of goose quills as the old fishermen knitted their 'ganseys' has died out, along with many of the older traditional patterns, passed on in the same way as local folktales. Sailors have always been good knitters and some lighthouse-keepers still practise the craft today as a hobby.

Men have tied knots since time began, but it was the seafarers who developed an essential act into an intricate art. We shall never know the sailor who first twisted and tied the coils of rope at his feet in an idle hour, but knot-tying reached its peak on board ship early in the nineteenth century. Macramé, the art of decorative knotting, is enjoying a revival as a craft and, despite the time it takes, some craftsmen actually make a living from it.

Because the British are islanders, the sea has always featured in their lives and the most tenacious of their knitting patterns are those generally termed as *Aran*: a whole chronicle of stitches symbolic of sea-faring ways and representing life-lines such as cables and ropes, herring-bones and diamond shapes, emulating fishing-nets, have survived the changes of fashion.

As complex as a knitting-pattern are trawl-nets, and up in J. and W Stuart's big loft in the fishing-port of Lowestoft women still make every loop of them by hand. Averaging some 80 feet by 84 feet, the nets are made in the traditional method, hanging from rods whilst women weave the shuttles of twine back and forth at an alarming rate. The pieces are later sewn together by men. The trawler-owners often meet to discuss the general patterns for the nets, and sometimes the skippers have specially tailored ones for their individual requirements.

Where there were once eighty women making the nets, there are now only eight. As one lady who has been making them for half a century said, "you can't get the girls to go in for it. They do their training, then off to the factory to shovel peas down a chute for twice as much".

Apart from the inevitable drift to more lucrative, if less skilful, work, the craft is so closely connected with the fishing industry that it shares its vicissitudes. Running costs, owing to the substantial oil price increases, have risen dramatically, putting many trawlermen out of business completely. The stalwart fishermen are competing against those in the EEC who receive subsidies in one form or another from their respective governments, resulting in subsidized foreign fish being dumped into this country, which has a detrimental effect on prices paid for our own trawler catches. When diminishing returns and spiralling running costs keep our fishing-fleets off the seas, it reflects directly on a craft industry such as trawler-net-making.

Bridport has been the centre of British net-making since the early Middle Ages, because of its locally grown flax and hemp. There seems to be none cultivated in any quantity now, but the importance of home-grown fibres is stressed in times of national danger. Penalties were once imposed for not growing hemp, and bounties granted to encourage the cultivation of flax. Experiments were made during the wars exploring the possibilities of using nettle fibres (hemp is a close cousin of the stinging nettle).

The largest net manufacturer in the United Kingdom, Bridport

Gundry Ltd, still has its main factory in Bridport, which is an amalgamation of all but two of the pre-war net-factories. The advent of modern materials and mechanization has greatly reduced the numbers of those formerly employed as outworkers, but the Redport Net Co., set up after the last war, carries on the tradition of the old cottage industry type of work. There are currently some 100 women employed by the company in making nets by hand. Of these, about 80 are continuously involved in making billiard-pockets from cotton twine. The outworkers are trained in the necessary skills by experienced workers visiting their homes.

Like the Lowestoft ladies, the net-makers of Dorset prefer to have lower wages than the national average and the prospect of work to do, than higher wages and none to do. But loyalty to the craft to which they are trained is not enough to safeguard the future of net-making. Statutory wage increases are making nets commercially uneconomic to make, and large imports of nets produced in the Far East have started to appear on the market. Unless legislation is introduced, net-making by hand will disappear among the crafts of yesterday.

LACE

Lace has been technically defined as a network of linen made by interlacing threads continuously without carrying them twice over the same ground. Interpretations of this technique are, if anything, complicated by centuries of inventiveness.

There seems to be differing schools of thought on its precise origin: both crochet and embroidery can be considered a form of lace, or, quite simply, it may have evolved from plain darning, whereby it may be juxtaposed with weaving, although lace-makers claim a connection with spinners and share their patron saint, St Catherine.

Made in the Middle East from ancient times, the craft travelled all over Europe, reaching its zenith in Italy where its manufacture became a local industry. The Venetians were celebrated for their lace during the sixteenth and seventeenth centuries, but as a means of livelihood it had waned by 1872, when a severe winter brought great depression. The 'ancient industry' was revived through the foundation of the Burano School for lace, but only one old lady could be found who still possessed the skills of her ancestors. Within its first decade, however, there were 320 lace-makers making a humble living.

Weight for weight, lace was more valuable than gold in the eighteenth century; many and curious are the tales of smuggling across the frontier between Flanders and France, coffins were often impounded for the highly prized and highly priced lace was often stuffed around corpses in an attempt to evade the heavy excise taxes. The fashionable French enjoyed but a relatively short period of lace luxury. Louis XIV founded lace schools under the tuition of Venetian experts, but 120 years later the lace-makers became embroiled in the violence of the Revolution – the rabble making no distinction between the aristocracy and the craftsmen who made their extravagant apparel.

England acquired her lace-makers from the exodus of craftsmen fleeing an even earlier European persecution: thousands of Flemings fled from Philip II's satanic rule, among them the lace-makers who established their craft wherever they settled and inspired the saying "all the world and Little Billing village made lace". A form of bobbin lace had been introduced earlier to Bedfordshire by Catherine of Aragon. Fashion is a fickle master and the state of the industry followed the caprices of the monarchs: Elizabeth's court kept numerous nimble fingers busy – even her "tooth-drawer", "corne-cutter" and the "mouse-trappe man" figure in her household accounts for the "loope leace, green leace and copper leace" which enriched their doublets and cloaks. Charles I prohibited the importation of foreign "purles, cut works and bone laces" to protect the home industry. Cromwell's puritanical rule was a different story, of course, but at the Restoration the pillows were brought into use again and lace even appeared somewhere on footwear. Highwaymen relieved their victims of lace in preference to cash and asked to be hanged in it when caught.

Workhouse institutions exchanged the spinning-wheel for the lace-pillow in the early eighteenth century, as a more profitable occupation for the inmates, and the Society of Anti-Gallicans was founded to maintain both standard and output. Queen Victoria gave the order for her wedding dress to the Devon lace-makers as the Honiton technique was more suited for the symbolic motifs to be incorporated. It took one hundred women to make the dress at a cost of £1,000.

Lace schools were founded where boys and girls were taught the rudiments of reading, writing and lace-making in the large room of a cottage under the lynx-like eye of a strict matron. Certainly not the happiest days of a nineteenth-century childhood, as recalled by one old lady who said "when I was five, mother took me to the lace school and gave the teacher a shilling. She learnt me for an hour, smacked my head six times and rubbed my nose on the pinheads". Shoddy work was heavily penalized; diligence and skill rewarded – by allowing the young craftsmen to witness a hanging! The ultimate prize was a commemorative bobbin.

Six hangings were recorded by these bobbins, which are collectors' pieces today. Bedford, one of the centres of lace-making, had more than its share of hangings, and many pillows were hung around with criminal records – the Victorian platitudes and pious inscriptions on other bobbins modifying the levity.

Jealous of their tradition, proud of their pillows, on which as many as a thousand bobbins may hang, inscribed and spangled, from an intricate pattern, the lace-maker was always poorly paid, but as late as 1850 there were still 1,770 lace-makers in Oxfordshire. What attempts there were to provide education in the villages had to combat a long tradition of child labour. The rector of Marsh Gibbon wrote to the Bishop of Oxford complaining of the "chief difficulty being from lace-making which draws the girls away from school before they are six years of age and makes it impossible for me to have a girls' school". The 1867 Factory and Workshop Act, prohibiting employment of children under eight in handicrafts, went some way towards laying the foundations for compulsory education and reduced the number of apprentice lace-makers and consequently the meagre household income, at a time when the highest skilled worker could expect 6*d.* for a day's work of some fifteen hours. The insidious practice of the dealers buying the lace on condition that the makers bought all their materials from them – which amounted to about a third or more of the money they were paid for the lace – was pursued to its despicable limit by those who also owned shops and forced the lace-makers to be paid in truck.

There is more than a touch of romance about the lace-maker's pillow, which no reminder of a wretched past can dim; and now that it is not a viable mode of employment the study and practice of the old skills started to attract a wide audience. A lace club was started in America in 1953 on the initiative of four members of the national doll clubs who were interested in learning more about the lace on dolls' clothes. Membership has grown to 1,045 – eighty-five of whom are in England. The name of the club has kept abreast of the growth and overseas membership: originally Old Lacers, it became National Old Lacers, and then International Old Lacers in 1971.

Little enclaves of dedicated lace-makers have done all they can to preserve the skill and charm of lace-making, especially in the celebrated English centres, so credit must be given to people like Mrs Dora Mackerness, who has shared her knowledge of the making of Beds Torchon lace with WI members, and Mrs Margaret Charlett, who has started village groups and helped numerous students to master the intricate patterns.

To co-ordinate the several lace-making classes within the city and interested people who had no means of getting instruction in the craft, the Sheffield lace-makers formed a society in May 1973 which has a membership of about seventy. It is a very active working group, holding practical meetings, some of which last all day on Saturdays, when members go armed with their pillows to discuss ideas, or simply make lace.

Potential lace-makers have been lost because no one knew of them, old skills have been allowed to pass away and valuable patterns destroyed through ignorance; attempts to run courses have failed through the information not getting to the right people and suppliers of materials have been notoriously hard to trace. Instead of bemoaning these past failures, Doreen Wright took a positive step towards righting them. Resolutely rounding up all those known to be interested, at her own expense, she circulated a proposal to form a guild. The response bore out the feeling that a great many were indeed interested. The inaugural conference was held in April 1976, the Lace Guild was constituted and accepted as a member of the Federation of British Crafts Societies. Catering for those interested in lace in its broadest terms – tatting, crochet, bobbin-turners, and collectors – its current membership is around nine hundred. Undeterred by threats of education cuts, the suggestion has been made that the guild may even arrange its own classes and eventually train its own teachers. Examination boards have now included lace-making in O level and CSE syllabuses as a study craft in needlework. Obviously, a new chapter is opening in its long and turbulent history.

SPINNING AND WEAVING SOCIETIES

ASSOCIATION OF GUILDS OF WEAVERS, SPINNERS AND DYERS, (C/o Federation of British Crafts Societies) Hon. Secretary: Mrs C. M. Laycock, Five Bays, 10 Stancliffe Avenue, Marford, Wrexham, Clwyd. Tel: 097 883 2386
Publishes a quarterly journal to further the aims of the guilds which are: to encourage and maintain integrity and excellence of craftsmanship; to foster a sense of beauty of material, texture, colour and design; to provide opportunities for interchange of information, for enlarging knowledge at holiday schools, for demonstrations, lectures and library facilities; and to co-operate with other guilds with similar aims.

Regional Guilds
BERKSHIRE: Mrs J. Allaway, Hammering House, Pearson Road, Sonning, Reading
BIRMINGHAM AND DISTRICT: Mrs F. Stringfellow, 680 Evesham Road, Redditch, Worcs. Tel: Astwood Bank 2535
BUCKINGHAMSHIRE: Mrs M. Howard, 47 London Road, High Wycombe
CHESHIRE: Mrs L. Littleton, 26 Glebelands Road, Knutsford
CORNWALL: Mrs Brit Varcoe, 15 Berveth Close, Three Milestone, Truro
COVENTRY AND DISTRICT: Mrs J. Lane, 52b Warwick Place, Leamington Spa, Warwicks.
DEVON: Mrs H. Lee, 16 Whiteway Road, Kingsteignton, Newton Abbot
DORSET: Mrs E. Bath, Cornford Cottage, Holwell, nr Sherborne. Tel: Bishops Caundle 412
GLOUCESTERSHIRE: Mrs B. Martin, Victoria Villa, Cotswold Close, Brimscombe, Stroud
HALLAMSHIRE AND DISTRICT: Mrs M. Anderson, 28 Longford Road, Bradway, Sheffield S17 4LQ
HAMPSHIRE: Miss N. Goschen, 36 Shortleath Road, Farnham, Surrey

HERTFORDSHIRE, WEST: Mrs R. George, 38 Orchard Drive, Watford WD1 3DY. Tel: Watford 22660

KENT: Mrs F. Slinn, 2 Evergood Cottages, Lidwells Lane, Goudhurst

LANCASHIRE AND THE LAKES: Miss Margaret Scragg, 69 Brookhouse Road, Caton, Lancaster

LONDON AND HOME COUNTIES: Registrar: Miss Raie Barnett, 7 Ralston Street SW3. Tel: 01–352 8740

MIDLANDS: Mr B. Wardell, 20 Jacey Road, Edgbaston, Birmingham B16 0LL. Tel: 021–451 5013

NORFOLK AND SUFFOLK: Miss I. Sturgeon, 21 Cotmer Road, Oulton Broad, Lowestoft. Tel: Lowestoft 5958

OXFORD: Mrs J. Potter, 47 Park Town, Oxford OX2 6SL

SOMERSET: Mrs T. Fraser, Kibby's Staplegrove, Taunton. Tel: Taunton 3810

SUSSEX, EAST: Mrs N. Heys, 21 King's Drive, Eastbourne BN21 2NX. Tel: Eastbourne 29286

SUSSEX, WEST: Mrs J. Dixon, 25 Ormonde Way, Shoreham-by-Sea BN4 5YB

WILTSHIRE: Mr A. Haynes, Witches Wood, The Firs, Kingsdown, Chippenham

WORCESTERSHIRE: Miss V. Lockyer, 41 Howsell Road, Malvern Link

WORSTEAD: Mrs T. Morris, 25 Harvey Lane, Norwich NOR 625; St Mary's Guild, Worstead Church, Norwich

YORK AND DISTRICT: Col. H. R. Barton, 25 Grosvenor Terrace, York YO3 7AG 7AG

THE HAND-WEAVERS STUDIO AND GALLERY LTD, 29 Haroldstone Road, London E17 7AN. Tel: 01–521 2281

The gallery operates as a centre for the sale and display of hand-woven and allied textiles of all kinds. Individual tuition from fleece-sorting to cloth-finishing by arrangement; regular short courses; hire of studio equipment. Suppliers of hand-weaving materials and equipment.

THE HARRIS CENTRE (*See Courses* p. 78)

Exhibitions promoting selected, but mainly textiles, crafts. Studio workshop space available on hire. Looms and weaving accessories and comprehensive range of craft books.

THE MULTIPLE FABRIC CO. LTD, Dudley Hill, Bradford BD4 9PD. Tel: 0274 682323

Worsted spinners producing yarns for hand-weavers: British white wool, Russian and Chinese camel-hair, Eastern Europe grey hair, Texas, Cape and Turkey mohair, and South American horsehair.

EMBROIDERY

THE EMBROIDERERS' GUILD, 73 Wimpole Street, London W1M 8AX

Membership open on subscription to all interested in embroidery and its related crafts. Advisory and loan service, courses, exhibitions, competitions. Special services for schools. Publication – quarterly magazine *Embroidery*.

Young Embroiderers' Society membership is open to under-18s. Membership of local branches is open only to members of the Embroiderers' Guild – further information can be obtained from the secretaries:

Branches in England (addresses of the rest of the British Isles and overseas societies can be obtained on receipt of SAE from the guild)

BERKSHIRE: Mrs M. P. Taylor, 4 Sewell Avenue, Wokingham

COTSWOLD: Mrs M. Burt, 59 Little Herberts Road, Charlton Kings, Cheltenham, Glos.

CUMBERLAND: Miss A. M. Brown, 13 Church Street, Stanwix, Carlisle

DERBYSHIRE: Mrs D. M. Kilbourne, 34 West Drive, Mickleover, Derby DE3 5EX

DEVON: Mrs E. B. Barrett, Longridge Cottage, Abbotskerswell, Newton Abbot

EAST KENT: Mrs M. E. Johnson, Flanders House, Mersham, nr Ashford

GLOUCESTERSHIRE, HEREFORDSHIRE AND WORCESTERSHIRE: Mrs K. F. Meyer, Solbakken, Yew Tree Lane, Bewdley, Worcs.

KINGSTON: Mrs M. Best, 19 Cleveland Road, New Malden, Surrey

LEAMINGTON AND DISTRICT: Mrs H. M. Barnes, 19 Maynard Avenue, Warwick

LEICESTERSHIRE: Miss S. Seage, 8 Southleigh Grove, Market Harborough

LINCOLNSHIRE: Mrs K. Pratley, White Lodge, Main Street, Scothern, Lincoln

THE LONDON CLUB: Chairman: Mrs Ann Virgin, 3 Dawlish Mansions, 154 Gray's Inn Road, London WC1

MANCHESTER AND CHESHIRE: Mrs E. Sullivan, 12 Darley Avenue, Gatley, Cheadle SK8 4PQ

MERSEYSIDE: Miss D. Moncrieff, Flat 8, 8 Park Terrace, Bramhall Road, Waterloo, Liverpool L22 3XB

MID-WESSEX: Mrs J. V. Blackburn, 31 St Francis Road, Salisbury, Wilts.

NORTH-EAST: Miss P. S. Steel, 63 Bolbec Road, Newcastle upon Tyne NE4 9EQ

NORTHAMPTONSHIRE: Mrs M. H. Scopes, J. P., Allerton House, Isham, Kettering

NOTTINGHAM: Mrs E. V. Waite, 44 Derby Road, Eastwood, Notts.

PORTSMOUTH: Mrs J. B. Ling, 19 Inverness Road, Gosport, Hants.

PRESTON: Mrs A. Stanley, Pipers Wood, Halton Hall Gardens, Halton, Lancs.

SHEFFIELD AND DISTRICT: Mrs R. Stenton, 27 Mowson Crescent, Worrall, Sheffield S30 3AG

SOMERSET: Mrs W. Lewis, Clappers, 5 Brae Road, Winscombe

SOUTH LAKELAND AND FURNESS: Mrs E. M. Best, Hurrock Wood, Kirk Head, Kents Bank, Grange-over-Sands

SUFFOLK AND NORTH ESSEX: Mrs Radford, 12 Mill Lane, Felixstowe, Suffolk

SUSSEX: Mrs S. C. Akers, Primrose Cottage, Hartfield, Sussex

TEESSIDE: Mrs H. Barnes, 8 Farndale Drive, Hutton, Lowcross, Guisborough, Yorks.

WEST HANTS AND DORSET: Mrs W. E. V. Tuck, 10 Plecy Close, Ferndown, Wimborne, Dorset BH22 8QL

WEST MIDLAND: Mrs M. J. Pearce, 76 Wentworth Road, Harborne, Birmingham 17

WINCHESTER AND EAST HAMPSHIRE: Mrs M. Oldham, Greenhunters, Grange

Road, St Cross, Winchester, Hants.
YORKSHIRE: Mrs E. E. Jackson, 8 Aireville Drive, Shipley, Yorks. BD18 3AD
YORKSHIRE COASTAL: Mrs W. S. Hall, 7 Westbourne Road, Whitby, Yorks.

62 GROUP – THE EMBROIDERERS' GUILD. *Membership:* Beryl Chapman, 3 Orchard Drive, London SE3; *General:* Alison Barrell, 120 Rectory Lane, Leybourne, West Malling, Kent. Tel: 0732 842536
The group consists, in the main, of art-trained professionals. Membership is by rigorous annual selection where evidence of new developments in embroidery and allied art forms, creativity, individual expression and good technique are the criteria.

NEW EMBROIDERY GROUP, Mrs I. Dorrington, 137 Colney Hatch Lane, London N10. Tel: 01–883 6046
Regular meetings, demonstrations and practical sessions.

THE LADIES' WORK SOCIETY, Delabere House, New Road, Moreton-in-Marsh, Glos. Tel: Moreton-in-Marsh 50447
Established for over a century as specialist suppliers of hand-painted canvases by the Ladies' Work Society, almost all of which is to special order. Stretching, cleaning, mounting, repairing, upholstering and making up of all types of embroidery. Embroidery classes and courses are held periodically.

SILK EDUCATIONAL SERVICE, 37 Chinbrook Road, Grove Park, London SE12 9TQ. Tel: 01–875 4839
Booklets on silk-manufacturing processes, notes on dressmaking and the care of silk. Illustrated material on the life-cycle of the silkworm. Prices of publications on application.

LULLINGSTONE SILK FARM, Ayot House, Ayot St Lawrence, Herts. Tel: Stevenage 820221
A seasonal exhibition, with guided tours, is held March to September every year, and shows the production of raw silk from the silkworm egg to the reeled hank. Silk souvenirs, some of which are made at the farm, are on sale: there is also a picnic area. Special terms for school parties.

MESSRS STEPHEN WALTERS, Sudbury Silk Mills, Sudbury, Suffolk
Specialist English silk-weavers.

SPINNING AND WEAVING

DOROTHY ABLETT, Wantage House, 76 Dean Court Road, Rottingdean, Sussex, BN2 7DJ. Tel: Brighton 32530
Hand-weaver and spinner in wools, silk, linen and cotton; also works creatively in such diverse materials as acetate, polythene, driftwood, PVC, rush and cane. Range includes wall-hangings, tabards, cushions. Fellow of the Society of Designer-Craftsmen; member of the World Crafts Council and Association of Textile Arts; exhibiting member Crafts Centre of Great

Britain; member Guild of Sussex Craftsmen.

JAQUIE BAKER, MSDC, Weavers Dream, Barton St David, Somerton, Somerset.
Tel: Baltonsborough 584
Hand-weaver on traditional wooden loom. Many yarns hand-spun; Alpaca,
Dorset Horn, Jacob; others often natural dyed from hedgerow plants.
Range extends from rugs to handbags and Inkle belts, with horn buckles.
Hairpin crochet shawls.

RAIE BARNETT, The Hand-weavers Studio and Gallery Ltd, 29 Haroldstone
Road, London E17 7AN. Tel: 01–521 2281
Hand-weaver. Extensive experience with hand-weaving yarns and contacts
with the British spinning industry. Commissions accepted. Founder
member and Registrar of the London Guild of Weavers, Spinners and
Dyers. Member British Crafts Centre.

RITA BEALES (Mrs), Flax Cottage, Vicarage Street, Painswick, Glos. Tel:
Painswick 813417
Spinner and weaver. Life member Guild of Gloucestershire Craftsmen.

W. BEAR, 55 Turton Road, Bradshaw, Bolton BL2 3DX
Hand-weaver: woollen rugs, rush mats on a linen warp. Powerloom woven
tie cloths. Member of the Society of Designer-Craftsmen.

LAVINIA BRADLEY, Bradley Inkle-Looms, 82 North Lane, East Preston, Sussex
BN16 1HE
Inkle-weaving specialist, lessons by arrangement. Retailer of inkle-looms
(*see* suppliers).

BRONTË TAPESTRIES, Rose Villa, Storr Heights, Thornton, Bradford, Yorkshire
BD13 3QT. Tel: Bradford 832409
Hand-loom weavers. Fabrics and range of clothing, rugs, wall-hangings,
bedspreads. Member of Guild of Yorkshire Craftsmen, British Crafts
Centre and Society of Craftsmen. Goods selected by the Design Council.

GERALD B. CARTER, Sherra Handwoven Fabrics, Tunley, nr Cirencester, Glos.
Tel: Frampton Mansell 259
Weaver. Member Guild of Gloucestershire Craftsmen.

HELEN CAVANAGH, Corner House, Hollesley, Woodbridge, Suffolk.
Hand-weaver of fine wool for clothing.

NANCY LEE CHILD, The Hand-weavers Studio and Gallery Ltd, 29 Haroldstone
Road, London E17 7AN. Tel: 01–521 2281
Hand-weaver with wide experience of weaving–designing both in America
and England. Commissions accepted. Member American Crafts Council,
Textile Museum of Washington, London Guild of Weavers.

COX (Mrs), 49 Upper High Street, Worthing, Sussex.

Hand-weaver. Member West Sussex Guild of Weavers. Spinners and Dyers.

DAWES (Miss), 34 University Crescent, Gorleston, Great Yarmouth, Norfolk. Weaver. Member Great Yarmouth Guild of Artists and Craftsmen.

A. S. EVANS (Mrs), Shepherd's Halt, Porlock, Somerset.
Hand-weaver exclusively of her own hand-spun yarn, chiefly local fleece from Exmoor sheep. Natural dyes of local vegetable, walnut, ling, etc. Knee-rugs, scarves, cushions, etc. For many years Mrs Evans spun for the Sheep Breeders' Association at the Royal Shows and still supports all local exhibitions and the Bath and West Show.

JUDY EVANS DESIGNS, 53a Highgate, Kendal, Cumbria. Tel: Kendal 24234
Tapestry-weaver. Work displayed in gallery above. Member Lancashire and Lakes Guild of Weavers and Spinners.

SUSAN FOSTER, 1 Manor Drive, Manchester M21 2QG. Tel: 061 434 2354
Hand-weaver, specializing in cushions, hangings, rugs and lampshades.

EVELYN AND JENNIFER GREEN, Campden Weavers, 16 Lower High Street, Chipping Campden, Glos.
Hand-weavers and spinners mainly in woollen yarn, specializing in individual articles and lengths of tweed. Retailers also of spinning-wheels, yarns for hand-weaving and fancy embroidery yarns, mail orders accepted. Commissions welcomed for individual articles.

MYRIAM GILBY, 242 Prospect Road, Woodford Green, Essex 1G8 7NQ
Woven hangings, main technique is tapestry but other experimental weaves employed for textural variety. Author *Free Weaving* (Pitmans), illustrations of work in many craft publications. Two solo exhibitions, widely exhibited in group exhibitions. Member World Crafts Council, London Guild of Weavers, Weavers Workshop and National Society, British Crafts Centre, Society of Designer-Craftsmen.

PAT GREGORY, The Old Mill, Norton Saint Philip, Bath, Somerset. Tel: Faulkland 279
Hand-spinner and weaver, specializing in unusual coloured fleeces with emphasis on design. Individually designed lengths of hand woven fabric in either natural colours or vegetable-dyed, also knee-rugs and scarves. Hand-knitted sweaters, hats, etc., from hand-spun yarn. Batik painting on silk and satin. Retail outlet – Society of Craftsmen's galleries at Hereford. Commissions accepted.

GREWELTHORPE HAND-WEAVERS (Mr and Mrs M. McDougall), Falcon House, Grewelthorpe, Ripon, Yorkshire HG4 3BW. Tel: Kirkby Malzeard 209 (closed on Mondays)
Hand-weaving to customers' specific requirements, thereby creating an entirely exclusive and genuinely new design each time. This approach enables the customer to be in consultation with the weaver (Malcolm McDougall) at

any stage of the design, allowing for weaving in of borders, cuffs, collars or contrasting weaves as desired. Mr McDougall will weave sample pieces in front of the customers from which they can choose or suggest variation. Fine worsted cloth in dress- and skirt-lengths. Wall-hangings. The weaving workshop is in a quiet corner of rural Yorkshire and customers are invited to watch the hand-weaving. The adjoining crafts shop is stocked with an ever-changing selection of craftwork, basically the best in each field of over 100 craftsmen.

MIKE HALSEY, The Hand-weavers Studio and Gallery Ltd, 29 Haroldstone Road, London E17 7AN. Tel: 01–521 2281
Hand-weaver with specialist background as technician in weaving and textile-designer. Extensive experience of mounting and display for weaving exhibitions for organizations and individual craftsmen. Part-time lecturer. Co-author with Lore Youngmark of *Foundations of Weaving* (David and Charles). Commissions undertaken. Member London Guild of Weavers and British Crafts Centre.

SHEILA HARRISON, 3 Frome Road, Rode, Bath, Avon BA3 6PW
Hand-weaver: skirt-lengths, jerkins, ties, table-mats, cushions. Member Wiltshire Guild.

CHARLOTTE HEATH, Design Brokers Ltd, 90 Lots Road, London SW10
Weaver.

BEROWALD INNES, Pinkney Pound, nr Sherston, Malmesbury, Wiltshire. Tel: Sherston 373
Hand-weaver specializing in floor-rugs and wall-hangings with co-ordinated schemes for both. Stock items include bags, cushions, etc. Specialist heraldic embroiderer (wool on canvas) for commissioned work.

IRENE, COUNTESS OF EFFINGHAM, 1 Court Close, Shipton-under-Wychwood, Oxon OX7 6D7. Tel: Shipton-under-Wychwood 830537
Hand-spinner, dyer and weaver. Range includes floor-rugs, cushions, shoulder-bags, table-napkins and mats, etc. Crochet shawls from hand-spun fleece. Lengths of woollen cloth woven to order. Commissions for speciality lines by arrangement. Member Craftsmen of Gloucestershire.

JENNIFER (Miss) E. ANGOVE, Crantock, Newquay, Cornwall. Tel: Crantock 254
Hand-weaver of woollen and cotton goods: tweeds, rugs, work-bags, towels, etc. Visitors welcome from Easter to end of September to the small shop in the garden where the work of two other Cornish weavers is also on sale.

WILLIAM KING, 15 Barton Chambers, 6 Norton Street, Liverpool 3
Hand-loom weaver. Hand-tufted rugs mainly of Persian knot technique. Commissions accepted.

NORMA LANCASTER, 13 Heswall Avenue, Culcheth, nr Warrington, Cheshire
Hand-spinner and weaver. Exhibitor and demonstrator. Member Cheshire Guild of Spinners, Dyers and Hand-loom Weavers.

ELIZA LEADBEATER, Rookery Cottage, Dalefords Lane, Whitegate, Northwich, Cheshire. Tel: 0606–882879

> Hand-spinner and weaver. Natural dyes. Offers complete service to spinners and weavers (*see* suppliers).

NEIL AND ISABEL MACKAY, Polzeath, Sunnyfield Lane, Up Hatherley, Cheltenham, Glos. Tel: Cheltenham 39480.

> Weavers. Members Guild of Gloucestershire Craftsmen.

MARY MCNEILL, 32 Parkstone Avenue, Southsea, Hampshire PO4 0QZ. Tel: Portsmouth 31075

> Hand-weaving and allied crafts. Qualified dress-designer therefore able to hand-weave and make up dresses, suits, etc., accessories. Embroidery and hand-made braids. Range extends from floor-rugs, bedspreads, christening shawls and cushions to finger-woven wall-hangings. Wall-hangings purchased for museums both at home and overseas. Member of the Society of Designer-Craftsmen.

BETTY MARSHALL, Overcourt, 128 Slad Road, Stroud, Glos.

> Hand-weaving: rugs, bags, cushions, etc. Beadwork. Demonstrations, by arrangement, at home.

F. B. MERCER, Eastern Cottage, The Park, Hallbankgate, Brampton, Cumbria CA8 2PF. Tel: Hallbankgate 309

> Hand-loom weaver specializing in tweeds of various weights, mainly checks from small dog-tooth to large plaid, herringbone or diamond variations and block tapestry type patterns. The cloth is hand-finished in traditional manner. Sets of table-mats, braids and ties are also available.

THEO MOORMAN (Miss), Stonebarrow, Tibbiwell Lane, Painswick, Glos. Tel: Painswick 812035

> Tapestry-weaver. Author *Weaving as an Art* (Van Nostrand Reinhold Co. London, 1975). Member Guild of Gloucestershire Craftsmen.

GWEN AND BARBARA MULLINS (Graffham Weavers Ltd), Shuttles, Graffham, Petworth, Sussex. Tel: Graffham 260 and 348

> Hand-weavers specializing in wool, 90 per cent of which is dyed with natural materials. Range: floor- and knee-rugs, bedspreads, bags, cloth and some clothes.

MUSWELL HILL WEAVERS (WILMA J. HOLLIST), 65 Rosebery Road, London N10 2LE. Tel: 01–883 4190

> A domestic workshop of two weavers among whose interesting commissions was a set of twelve tapestry panels to be hung as double-sided shutters in three sets of four panels for the windows of the Great Hall of a 'wee' Scottish castle. Woven from hand-spun fleece from local sheep and dyed from plants of the area they were finished by waulking in the fashion of Scottish tweed. Having studied closely the techniques of dyeing, the weavers have recently

developed 'The Russell Dye System (Wool)', a kit designed to make dyeing easier and more accurate for hand-spinners, weavers and embroiderers.

MARY NIVEN (Mrs), 2 Woodstock Road South, St Albans, Herts. Tel: St Albans 67158
Hand-weaving, spinning and natural dyes. Commissions accepted for hand-woven lengths of cloth, long pile rugs hand-spun with natural dyes to special design. Mrs Niven will also hand-spin odd pound-lots of yarn (for knitting etc.) to special order and undertake speciality lines to match furnishings; some specialized batikwork. Lecturer and demonstrator to schools and groups. Member Hertfordshire Guild of Weavers.

EILEEN QUINLAN, Camden Lock, Commercial Place, London NW1 8AF
Spinning and weaving.

JESSICA ROWLEY (Mrs), 4 Hungerford Road, Chippenham, Wilts. SN15 1QW. Tel: Chippenham 3020
Hand-weaver of own hand-spun wools – natural coloured knee-rugs and shawls, also colourful ties woven in Yorkshire-spun (manufactured) worsted wools. Occasional teaching.

GERALDINE ST AUBYN HUBBARD, Stable Cottage, Watergate, West Marden, Chichester, Sussex. Tel: Compton 434
Hand-weaver principally concerned with design, quality and drape of cloth and colour, using both natural and synthetic dyes. Designs and weaves cloth for clothing and furnishings in wool, silk, linen and cotton. Block-printing on silk, cotton and linen.

SPEEN WEAVERS AND SPINNERS (Mrs), J. O. COLEMAN, Speen, Aylesbury, Bucks. Tel: Hampden Row 303
Hand-spinner and weaver specializing in unusual fibres, textures and designs. A wide range of linens, woollen materials, rugs, blankets, tapestries and wall-hangings. Specialist silkwork, and French inlay in various yarns.

SUSAN SPOONER, Trehu, Pulla Cross, Chacewater, Truro, Cornwall
Hand-weaver of tapestries. Coat-designs incorporating tapestry landscapes and other clothing to commission.

COLIN SQUIRE, Sheldon Cottage, The Bottoms, Epney, Saul, Gloucester GL2 7LN. Tel: Saul 639
Designer-weaver of rugs, hangings and textile constructions. Exhibiting member of British Crafts Centre, and Association of Guilds of Spinners, Weavers and Dyers, and on occasion with Group 5.

ARJA STEELE, 11A Eastern Villas Road, Southsea, Hants. PO4 0SU. Tel: Portsmouth 33761
Designer-weaver currently engaged in study and weaving of smooth-surfaced rugs, which sometimes develop into tapestries and hangings, in direct contrast to the designing and weaving of rya rugs for which she

received many important commissions. Mrs Steele works continuously on commissions for rugs, tapestries, shawls, dress and upholstery fabrics.

ANN SUTTON, Parnham House, Beaminster, Dorset DT8 3NA. Tel: 0308 862204
Textile-designer and weaver whose work has been widely exhibited. Member of the Society of Industrial Artists, and member of the management committee of the British Crafts Centre. An experienced lecturer and teacher, Ann Sutton is one of the tutors at the courses held at Parnham House. Co-author with Pat Holtom of *Tablet Weaving* (Batsford).

MARY J. TOULSON, 1 Wrenshall Cottage, Stanton Road, Walshall Le Willows, Bury St Edmunds, Suffolk
Woven rugs and wall-hangings. Considering the possibility of organizing short (week-end or week) courses.

MESSRS STEPHEN WALTERS, Sudbury Silk Mills, Sudbury, Suffolk
Silk-weavers.

WHITE HORSE SPINNERS AND WEAVERS (MR AND MRS C. G. CHARLES), Beech Bank, Bratton, Westbury, Wilts. Tel: Bratton 382
Hand-spun knitting wool and knitted garments, hand-woven and vegetable-dyed rugs, stoles and tweeds. Tie-dyed pure silk scarves. Pot-pourri made from old English recipes.

JOAN WILLIAMSON (Mrs), 120 West Street, Bridgwater, Somerset
Hand-spinner of natural colour fleece which is woven on a hand-loom into cloth and rugs. Other yarns woven to meet commissions. Member Somerset Guild of Craftsmen.

LORE YOUNGMARK, The Hand-weavers Studio and Gallery Ltd, 29 Haroldstone Road, London E17 7AN. Tel: 01–521 2281
Hand-weaver and textile-designer. Tutor in adult education institutes. Co-author with Mike Halsey of *Foundations of Weaving* (David and Charles). Joint organizer of Chelsea Fair. Member London Guild of Weavers and British Craft Centre.

OTHER TEXTILE CRAFTS INCLUDING EMBROIDERY

MARGRET ALLDRIDGE, Camden Lock, Commercial Place, London NW1 8AF
Batikwork.

HELEN ATTEWELL, The Crafts Centre, Wadenhoe, nr Oundle, Peterborough. Tel: Clopton (08015) 620
Patchwork specialist, retailing through the Craft Centre which she runs. Recent orders have included an evening-skirt in patchwork using the client's material of sentimental value.

ALISON BARRELL, 75 London Road, Maidstone, Kent. Tel: Maidstone 675281
Embroiderer artist. Exclusive 3D panels and commissions. Member Society
of Designer-Craftsmen, 62 Group, exhibiting Member Textile studio.

BELINDA, Design Brokers Ltd, 90 Lots Road, London SW10
Textiles

HUGH AND SOPHIE BLACKWELL, The Maltings, Upper Up, South Cerney, Glos.
Tel: South Cerney 370
Fabric-printers. Member of Guild of Gloucestershire Craftsmen.

E. BOURNER (Mrs), 19 Brookside, South Mimms, Potters Bar, Herts.
Bedcovers in traditional hexagon patterns with toning valence frill.

ANNE BUTLER, 10 Belfield Road, Didsbury, Manchester 20. Tel: 061–445 7021
Embroidered panels: ecclesiastical commissions. Quilts, etc. Principal lecturer in charge of the BA (Hons) course in Embroidery at Manchester Polytechnic. Lecture-demonstration tour USA 1974. Author of several books
and publications on embroidery.

IDA COLLIS (Mrs), Flat 1, Berrylands, 199 Milton Road, Cambridge.
Embroidered pictures using the delicate silk on satin technique which is traditionally a Chinese art, rarely practised by Western craftsmen.

ROSINA DERRICK, Beautiful Pea Green Boat, Atlanta Cottage, Swells Hill,
Brimscombe, Stroud, Glos. Tel: Amberley 3348
Designer and dressmaker of exclusive clothes, all sizes and types.

GWEN EDWARDS, Cobblestones, Coverack Bridges, Helston, Cornwall TR13
0LY. Tel: Helston 4341
Creative textiles, incorporating hand and machine embroidery, collage and
macramé. Lecturer in embroidery and design. Exhibitions included W.I.
Heirlooms. Some enamelling.

EQUITY PRINTERS (David Humby), Camden Lock, Commercial Place, London
NW1 8AF. Tel: 01–267 4901
Silkscreen printing on fabric.

JANE AND ALAN FORD, Bree Cottage Crafts, Selsey Hill, Stroud, Glos. Tel:
Stroud 6540
Batik.

PAULINE GODDING, 62 The Oval, Gloucester
Fabric-printing, dyeing, batikwork.

LOUIS GROSSÉ Ltd, 36 Manchester Street, London W1M 5PE. Tel: 01–486 9802
Ecclesiastical vestments and church embroidery. Commissions have extended from making all the vestments for Coventry Cathedral to the original
and exclusive Grossé Shapes, designed by artist John Piper; a set of copes for

St Paul's Cathedral, to the world's first PVC cope designed by Patrick Reyntiens. The exquisite hand-embroidery, appliqué and artistic interpretation of the subject on the fabric has been widely exhibited both in this country and overseas, and have featured in articles and radio programmes. Official suppliers of embroidery requisites and fabrics to Art Schools and Colleges. Recommended by the Embroiderers' Guild.

HARINGTON CARPETS (Robin and Jane Dwyer), Frox Field Green, Petersfield, Hampshire GU32 1DQ. Tel: Petersfield 3998
Hand-tufted rugs, carpets and wall-hangings in pure new wool. Recent commissions include a wall-hanging for a church in Sydney, and a hopscotch play carpet for the children of Great Ormond Street Hospital. Their speciality is sculptured effects created from piles of differing heights. Export to many parts of the world, and retailed through leading stores in this country.

ROSEMARY HARRIS, Wheelwrights Cottage, Shilton, Oxon.
Smocking.

STUART HOBBS, Woodmancote, Cirencester, Glos. Tel: North Cerney 212
Tailor: Member of Guild of Gloucestershire Craftsmen.

R. HUGHES (Mrs), Pentre Farm, Bredwardine, Hereford
Rugs.

BEROWALD INNES, Pinkney Pound, nr Sherston, Malmesbury, Wilts.
Heraldic Embroidery and woven rugs.

ROY AND PAULINE LILL, The Sloop Craft Market, St Ives, Cornwall
Embroidered pictures, painted day badges.

MAGGIE B. (Mrs S. Tyrrell), 4 Harts Way, Everton, Lymington, Hampshire. Tel: Milford-on-Sea 3968
Fabric collagist, exhibits locally and annual one-man exhibition, retail outlet through the Craft Centre, Yaldhurst, Lymington.

GUIDO MARCHINI, Peter Dingley, 16 Meer Street, Stratford-upon-Avon CV37 6QB. Tel: (0789) 5001
Hand-painted silk squares, completely individual designs with hand-rolled edges.

TERESA NOBLE, Design Brokers Ltd, 90 Lots Road, London SW10
Designs and makes appliqué dresses.

JILL PARKER-JARVIS, Lane Cottage, Watledge, Nailsworth, Glos.
Patchwork.

PATCHES, Daylesford, Wellington Square, Cheltenham, Glos. Tel: 0242 55640
Machine-stitched patchwork. Hand-stitched patchwork in traditional design in consultation with customer.

ANN PRUDHOE, Berwun Drive, Marchwel, Wrexham (also at 6 Aintree Lane, Liverpool 10)
Nail and thread pictures in unusual designs to commission.

JANET RAWLINS PARFITT, 5 Moseley Wood Way, Cookridge, Leeds LS16 7HN
Commissions have included collages for leading industrial organizations.

D. REYNOLDS (Mrs), 53 Church Street, Wells-next-the-Sea, Norfolk. Tel: Wells-next-the-Sea 498
Patchwork, mainly bedspreads and cushions to commission. Lecturer and demonstrator for Norfolk Education Committee, Hotel 'teach-ins', and annually in Switzerland and Austria. Mrs Reynolds 'signs' each bedspread with an embroidered Michaelmas Daisy (her Christian name) together with the date. Member of Guild of Many Crafts.

JULIA ROBERTS, Coscote Manor, Didcot, Berks. OX11 0NP. Tel: Didcot 3266
Creative designer in patchwork, appliqué and fabric pictures, using machine technique which she developed, subsequently published by the Embroiderers' Guild (1972). Individually designed furnishings from curtains to cosies. Where light penetration would entirely preclude the use of traditional patchwork, for example, in lampshades, openwork or semi-sheer screens or dividers, the technique used overcomes this and allows for greater flexibility in the design so that jig-saws, shells, leaves, hearts and interlocking circles can be incorporated as well as the traditional geometric shapes.

PATRICIA ROBINSON, Little Compton, Whiteway, Stroud, Glos. Tel: Miserden 553
Fabric-printer. Member of Guild of Gloucestershire Craftsmen.

MARGARET SEED, 9 Fore Street, Ide, Exeter, Devon. Tel: Exeter 72999
Specializing in goldwork embroidery, ecclesiastical vestments, pictures, panels and small embroidered boxes, developing own designs while adhering to the traditional techniques to which she was apprenticed. Member of Embroiderers' Guild and Devon Guild of Craftsmen.

KATHARINE SKILLEN (Mrs), 10 Silver Street, Tetbury, Glos. GL8 8DH. Tel: Tetbury 52488
Batikwork.

KATHERINE SNELLING, 8 Chatham Row, Bath, Avon
Traditional smocks. Embroidery, appliqué and original dress-designs.

THE STABLE STUDIO, Mrs B. Randles, Aston, nr Stevenage, Herts. Tel: Shephall 271
Patchwork, hand-weaving and various cottage crafts.

MISS EVE STUART, Thimble Cottage, Lower Littleworth, Amberley, Glos. Tel: Amberley 3593
Embroiderer. Life member Guild of Gloucestershire Craftsmen.

SUNFLOWER WORKSHOP, 34 Bonneville Gardens, London SW4. Tel: 01–673 6087
Hand-printed gifts: from aprons to stationery, and wrappings.

DIANE SUTHERLAND, Sloop Craft Market, St Ives, Cornwall
"Dolittles", hand-made individual clothes for adults and children.

WENDY TODD, Bedlam Barn, Old Church Lane, Pateley Bridge, nr Harrogate, Yorks. Tel: Pateley Bridge 472
Hand-printed fabrics designed and fashioned: dress- and furnishing-lengths, table-linen and linen greeting-cards.

TUMERIC LTD, (Jane Wake, Suzanne Defour, Sanna Wake Walker) Design Brokers Ltd, 90 Lots Road, London SW10
Soft-furnishing products.

DINAH TUTTON, Sundene, The Nursery, Kings Stanley, Stonehouse, Glos.
Smocking, embroidery, crochet, collage.

WATTS & CO. LTD, 7 Tufton Street, Westminster, London SW1P 3QB. Tel: 01–222 7169
Renowned since 1868 for embroidery and needlework for both ecclesiastical and secular use. Metal and woodwork, sculpture and typography. Hand-printed wallpapers still made from the original carved pearwood blocks comprise one of the most complete collections of late Victorian wallpapers still in production.

WEATHERALL WORKSHOPS, Coleford, Glos. GL16 8QB. Tel: 05943 2102
Needlepoint tapestries, both designs and fully produced ones, appliqué wall-hangings, design-kits for furnishing and clothing, design facilities for decorative work of all kinds, under the direction of Lillian Delevoryas. Other crafts include woodware and ceramics, aiming at providing a complete service with co-ordination of different craft disciplines.

JANICE WILLIAMS (Mrs C. Squire), Sheldon Cottage, The Bottoms, Epney, Saul, Gloucester GL2 7LN. Tel: Saul 639
Embroidery covering a wide range of techniques from goldwork to canvas, hooked canvas rugs using nylon strips and polystyrene. Exhibiting member of British Crafts Centre, Embroiderers' Guild, the Association of Weavers, Spinners and Dyers and occasionally with Group 5.

JULIA WILLS, Bedcroft, Pitchcombe, Stroud, Glos.
Original batik hangings, cushions, scarves, etc.

MARY YOULES (Mrs), Hillside Cottage, Windsoredge, Nailsworth, Glos.
Embroiderer. Member Guild of Gloucestershire Craftsmen.
(see also Weavers, especially for rugs and hangings)

ROPE-MAKER

W. R. OUTHWAITE & SON (proprietor: P. Annison). Town Foot, Hawes, North Yorks. Tel: (Home) Bainbridge 349
Traditional fibre rope and halters.

DRESSED HORSEHAIR

ARNOLD & GOULD LTD, Glemsford, Sudbury, Suffolk CO10 7QA. Tel: 0787 280243
Hand-dressed horsehair for brush-manufacturing industries, upholstery and textile trades.

KNITTING, CROCHET AND MACRAMÉ

HELEN DELLER, 56 High Street, Malmesbury, Wilts.
Crochet. Bedspreads to any size, shawls and clothing.

PAT GREGORY, The Old Mill, Norton Saint Philip, Bath, Avon. Tel: Faulkland 279
Knitting from hand-spun wool.

PATRICIA M. HOBBS, 5 Vicarage Close, Holme, Peterborough. Tel: Ramsey Hunts 830135
Crochet in cottons and wool.

IRENE, Countess of Effingham, 1 Court Close, Shipton-under-Wychwood, Oxon. Tel: (0993) 830537
Crochet shawls from hand-spun wool.

SAPPHO (Linda Townsend) Design Brokers Ltd, 90 Lots Road, London SW10
Knitter

SUSSEX SHAWLS, 4 St Malo Court, Ferring, Sussex
Hand-crocheted shawls in wool and mohair. SAE for price list and details.

JANET THOMAS, School Farm, Nancetuke, Redruth, Cornwall
Crochet to special order.

H. WILLETT, 21 Bendlowers Road, Great Bardfield, Braintree, Essex CM7 4RR
Macramé: bags, belts, wall-hangings. Occasional lectures and demonstrations.
(*see also* Spinners and Weavers)

PEMBROKE SQUARES, 8 Pembroke Square, London W8 6PA. Tel: 01–937 4974
Exquisite hand-crocheted bedspreads based on original designs in tapestry wool.

HAND-FRAME KNITTING

G. H. HURT & SON, 65 High Road, Chilwell, Nottingham NG9 4AJ. Tel: Nottingham 254080

Very fine lace knitted shawls, scarves, stoles, bed-jackets and jumpers made on hand-frames, some 300 years old, by genuine hand-frame knitters.

MARY MORRELL, 27 Birkdale Road, Harthum, Stockton, Cleveland TS18 5LZ. Tel: 0642 583394

Hand-frame knitter. Woollen clothing to commission ranging from specialized items for clubs and expeditions to individual designs for deformed persons. Specialized restoration work in embroidery and lace-mounting. Textile Folk Craft Consultant.

NET-MAKERS

REDPORT NET CO. LTD, Asker Works, 94–96 East Street, Bridport, Dorset DT6 3LL. Tel: Bridport (0308) 22592

A true cottage industry which concentrates on the production of billiard pockets, completely hand-made by outworkers in their own homes. Worldwide market of billiard table-net makers and repairers. Angling-nets, made up in a wide range, are sold mainly to fishing-tackle wholesalers for retailing. Specialists in hand-braided nets who can supply an almost endless choice of keep-nets to suit customers' requirements.

J. & W. STUART LTD, Star Buildings, Beach Road, Lowestoft NR32 1EA. Tel: Lowestoft 5326

Net and twine, cotton spinners and doublers. Traditional trawl-nets completely hand-made.

LACE

MARGARET CHARLETT (Mrs), 83 Bicester Road, Kidlington, Oxon. Tel: Kidlington 3200

Lace-maker. Widely exhibited. Tuition to groups and individuals by arrangement. Mrs Charlett demonstrates her craft and gives talks by arrangement. Instruction booklet available on lace for beginners, Price 50p. plus 9 inch × 6 inch SAE.

M. HUCKLE (Mrs), 'Castle Hill', Buckland Newton, Dorchester, Dorset. Tel: Buckland Newton 370

Lace-maker.

ISOBEL KENNETT (Mrs), 34 Rise Park Gardens, Eastbourne, Sussex

Laces are the specialist lines, but also undertakes crochet, tatted, knitted and macramé laces. Bobbin lace patterns include Beds Maltese, Italian, French and Spanish designs, but Mrs Kennett also designs exclusive pieces when necessary. Honiton sprigs are mainly mounted in pictures, paperweights, brooches, pendants and key-rings. Hand-woven linen table-mats with matching lace border, also linen handkerchiefs. Private tuition by arrangement.

NINA LOVESEY (Mrs), 16 Wood Row Drive, Wokingham, Berks.
   Lace-maker and craft co-ordinator at Southill Park.

ELSIE LUXTON (Mrs), 5 Trees Court, Topsham, Exeter. Tel: Topsham 4989
   Honiton lace. Tutor at W.I. annual residential course at Exmouth, and at
   various colleges including West Dean, Chichester; King Alfred's, Winchester; Bedford and Stafford. Mrs Luxton is the only tutor to go out of Devon to
   teach Honiton lace-making. Widely exhibited and can count several members of the Royal Family among her clients.

DORA MACKERNESS (Mrs), 12 Sandy Lane, Heath Road, Leighton Buzzard,
Beds.
   Lace-maker of traditional patterns.

M. A. WATTS (Mrs), Ashdean, Swindon Road, Malmesbury, Wilts. Tel:
Malmesbury 3565
   Lace-maker.

Lace societies

INTERNATIONAL OLD LACERS, Mrs J. H. Wareham, P.O. Box 346, Ludlow, Mass
01056 USA
   Principal purpose is to promote interest in fine lace; to study it to learn the
   arts of making and using it.

THE LACE GUILD, Mrs Doreen Wright, Charlecote, Harewood Road, Chalfont
St Giles, Bucks. Tel: Little Chalfont 2444
   Membership is open to all those interested in lace-making, including collectors, bobbin-makers. Registration fee and yearly subscription. Publishes its
   own magazine.

THE SHEFFIELD LACE-MAKERS, Hon. Sec: Mrs D. A. Bird, 31 Parker's Road,
Broomhill, Sheffield S10 1BN. Tel: 0742 661408
   Membership is open to all who make or study bobbin lace. Meetings and
   lace-making sessions.

10

Leather

Most of the old leather trades were located at the termini of the drovers'
roads when the medieval custom of slaughtering beasts before winter,
and large-scale markets, concentrated the cattle into centres where an
adequate water supply enabled manufacturers using the by-products
to be established. These localities have often given their name to the
goods made there.

As a natural material, leather cannot be surpassed and its superiority
is the more evident when it is compared with imitations. Changes in
agricultural methods have resulted in hides being less fibrous and more
gelatinous than they used to be when cattle were allowed to grow older
and their skins became more weathered. One problem now is to make
tough leather from tender hides.

To foster the tradition of craftsmanship in the leather trades, the
Cordwainers Technical College was founded ninety years ago by interested City livery companies, the City and Guilds of London Institute
and various employers. All aspects of the leather-goods trade which
have need for special craft skills are covered in the various courses and
some of the staff have unique experience in working on solid foundation
work, but by and large the demand for knowledge of this kind is too
small to allow the college to run viable courses, and this skill is in
danger of being lost forever. Keeping alive its name, specialist cordwainers are also catered for. Although mass production of footwear
means that traditional craftsmanship has been lost, orthopaedic and
bespoke footwear requires very special hand skills.

FELLMONGERY

The dressing of skins with the hair on is a very special and unusual trade
today. During the 'twenties there was a small dressing-yard with craftsmen
in nearly every village – that decade saw most of them close and now the tan-
yards handle anything around 100,000 hides a week. Our old tools will not
be understood after my generation has gone.

Walter Chapman

Much of the skill of using the old tools starts with the sharpening of
them. For some sixty years, Walter has plied his craft in traditional
manner, never conceding to the influences and pressures of big business
– other than modifying some of the processes so that his work can be
continued satisfactorily after his retirement.

Tanning the hides with alum for the whipthong-makers of the Midlands, and for saddlers to cut into laces for sewing harness, he developed a knacker business in the seventeenth-century corn-mill; dressing skins with the hair on from calf, deer, fox, badger and goat, and making calf vellum for drums and tympani. The war wrought changes in the whipthong and saddlery trades, drums were gradually covered with plastic; the safari hunters took cover and aimed their sights at more aggressive adversaries. Since then demand for dressed sheepskins has increased, but Walter, helped by his son, is still able to cope with the lion-, leopard- or sealskins which find their way to him for the crafts skills which either the big firms do not employ or are too commercially biased to undertake.

Sheepskins are perhaps the only ones which are processed and manufactured within the same company. John Wood of Somerset processes raw sheepskins, mainly from the west of England, and will undertake the dressing of unusual animal skins for individual customers. The hand-stitched articles are made on a cottage industry basis, employing about eighty outworkers, all of whom are previously trained in their rather specialized technique in the firm's workshops. The City of London Hide and Skin Co., based in Devon, are also sheepskin tanners and manufacturers.

Much purely manual work is involved in the fellmongering industry in the processes prior to and during the separation of the wool from the pelt and sorting into grades. A figure of some 36,000 has been published as the total of tanners and leather-dressers in England and Wales, but there are, in fact, very few tanners still in operation.

Curriers, like Henry Gilling & Co., buy their leather tanned, re-tan it and dress to their own requirements – or to those of their most exacting customer. Theirs is a very old established business, operating on the original site since 1815 and one of the most modern currier works in the country supplying leather for the shoe trade, but mainly for the bridle-and harness-makers.

Hand-staining and currying makes it possible for each pair of buts to be treated individually in a selective manner so as to ensure that the leather is dressed throughout the fibres, which is not the case with the now more common drum method. Hides produced in such a way are necessarily expensive, but justifiably so, as testified by those craftsmen who insist on them. Saddlers have been the only group in this survey who have reported satisfactory and adequate supplies for their craft, paying tribute to the tanners and curriers who "know what we want".

SADDLERY

Complete subjugation of the horse as servant of man was not achieved until the saddle, stirrup and bit were developed to give absolute control of rider over horse. The initial improvement upon the *shabrack*, used in Assyria from the ninth century B.C., was a stuffed pad, attached by a girth; modifications of which appeared by *c.* 380 B.C., with elements of the ridge at the back and front as the first concession to protection of the rider. The precarious perches which served the early horsemen had gradually evolved into some semblance of the saddle we know today by the time of the Norman Conquest, judging by the pictorial evidence stitched into the Bayeux Tapestry. By then the Romans' disregard or ignorance of the necessity for distributing the weight each side of the horse's spine was rectified. The earliest surviving example of how this was achieved is the saddle tree of Henry V, which can be seen in Westminster Abbey, where it has remained since his funeral in 1422.

If the early horseman's position was precarious, his female contemporary's was literally perilous if she did not ride astride as medieval women did. There was very little improvement made on what amounted to a cushion secured by a girth-strap, on which Roman matrons sat, facing sideways with their feet dangling, until the crutch was introduced, reputedly by the notorious Catherine de Medici, a notable horsewoman. The side-saddle is only rarely used today, and the quaint pillion, one supposes, never.

By the seventeenth century English saddlery was considered the best in Europe, and in 1740 had set the pattern from which modern riding-saddles evolved. The English hunting-saddle has received many minor modifications since the 1800s, the most revolutionary being its final divorce from the *shabrack*.

The saddlery trade, under the auspices of the Retail Leather Goods and Saddlery Association, and in conjunction with the Board of Trade and COSIRA, mounted its first specialized exhibition at the 48th DLG Ausstellung in Hanover in the mid-sixties, with the object of promoting British saddlery and equipment. The result more than justified the effort but highlighted the shortage of skilled master saddlers. Government help was given through COSIRA, who played a major part in the introduction of the National Joint Saddlery Apprenticeship Scheme. The first course for apprentices started in September 1964 at the Cordwainers' Technical College, with ten entrants. A nine months' full-time introductory course is offered, covering bridle, saddle and harness work. It is not unknown for girls to take up this craft.

The latest figures show that there are some 288 small saddlery firms, representing a total of 700–800 people, and prove that this is one of the few truly rural crafts to have maintained its original intent. The Worshipful Company of Saddlers, one of the oldest City livery companies, is practically unique in having associations with an unchanged craft.

COSIRA provides the secretariat for the Society of Master Saddlers, which has its roots in an association formed in 1898. Aware of the problems which beset an old craft in a new world, it is forward-looking and modern in its approach, working with the Cordwainers' College and apprenticeship council to ensure that apprentices are recruited, and holding a watching brief on indentures.

Great pride and skill have gone into making equipage for horses, and the carters of old lavished as much care and 'elbow grease' on the black harness of the draught horses as grooms did on the tan leather saddlery in their stables, but the little group of 'working-harness- and collar-makers' is in danger of extinction. There is a tremendous and successful effort being made by the Southern Counties Heavy Horse Association (which has a nation-wide membership) in promoting interest in the lovely old working horses; and, fortunately, there is a dedicated handful of craftsmen at the Old Almshouse Saddlery who are sufficiently interested to teach themselves the almost lost art of making harness for farm horses and even goats.

COSIRA has now included harness-making in its schedule of courses in general saddlery for those who have been out of touch with this type of work. The council's technical staff has recently published a text-book on saddle-making step-by-step. If not the first of its kind in the English language, it is certainly the most up-to-date.

Although the saddlery trade is under great pressure to mechanize and mass-produce its goods as a result of fierce competition from low-cost imports, saddlers are confident that it will remain essentially a craft trade because of the demand by a wealthy clientele for individually made articles – and the discerning customer will always go to the saddler whom he trusts.

Safety of the rider, concern for the horse, integrity of workmanship and quality of materials are the criteria upon which the saddler's reputation is founded. As illustrated in other crafts, the best equipment is made by those who have a working knowledge of its use. Osier Saddlery, interested especially in equipment for showing in hand, have produced bridles and headcollars for use on their own ponies and when attending horse shows will carry out repairs on the spot, so they have first-hand knowledge of where the stresses and strains occur. Using the best materials for the purpose means hide entirely hand-stained and curried, hand-stitched with well-waxed thread which, in the case of stirrup leathers, is also hand-made for maximum strength and durability.

Some measure of how English saddlery is still held in high esteem can be gauged by the order placed with a Surrey saddler to make the harness for the coronation of the Shah of Persia. Using sixty hides, dyed to a deep shade of peacock blue and embellished with gold and bronze decoration, the export order was worth some £20,000. Special orders rarely reach such heights, however, nor do they attract publicity, but are usually for the difficult jobs which defy the limitations and economies which mass-production methods have imposed upon its operators and accountants. But many a saddler can produce a letter of thanks from somewhere among the bags and bridles, crops and cords, bales of wool, slivers of hide, tangles of twine, needles and nips and bees-wax and the whole earthy, leathery-smelling 'orderly confusion' in which he works, which testifies to his craftsmanship. Such a letter is one of those old-fashioned courtesies which eminent persons have maintained, and improves the lot of a lone saddler like dear old George Elliott, who practises his craft in a cosy, cramped cottage. "Saddler, etc." states the board above the tiny window – it is the "etc." for which he used *his* needle in the depressed years, to embrace the "fancy stuff" – bags and dog collars and the like, and sandals by the score went all over the world during the war years. Well into his eighties, George still gets orders from all over the country; mainly for saddlery, now that the equestrian field is well populated once more; and occasionally for the "special little job", like a set of laced leather boots for a dog!

An elephant's boot is an even more unusual order, but Hayes of Cirencester fitted an elephant up with a lovely leather boot braced with heavy steel irons for its sprained ankle. They were well experienced in modifying saddles with special metal clamps and cups to hold the artificial legs of riders so that they may take an active part in the field, this part of England being the territory of a big hunt, and the internationally famed polo ground.

The intense interest and personal involvement of our Royal Family in equestrian events in general, and Princess Anne's patronage of the Riding for the Disabled Association in particular, have focused much attention on the role of the horse in leisure and competitive pursuits, and on the craft of saddlery.

It was a justifiably proud Mr Crofts who shuffled the Press photographs around on his leather-strewn bench to show me Princess Anne receiving the saddle he had designed and made for the disabled as the year's President of the Society of Master Saddlers. I was happy to share vicariously in his pleasure as he recalled the Princess's delight. Having looked after Captain Mark's horse before he went to Lambourn, A. W. Crofts had a personal interest in designing a saddle, on behalf of Wicks Saddlery, for the royal wedding present – calling the design the Badminton Mark I. Despite his forty-odd years at saddlery, Mr Crofts said it took some hundred templates before the saddle was what he termed "just right". Just one interlude in the life of a saddler in the midst of the racing stables of Lambourn, where the horses outnumber the population, and the jockeys are known as 'Knights of the Pigskin'.

LEATHER IN FASHION

Today, the leather industry is going on show and from what I have seen of it, it is a very fine shop-window indeed. Obviously the leather industry is in a very healthy state and it is particularly encouraging to see such diversity and such an enormous increase in the fashion department. Indeed, all of you gentlemen are preaching to the converted as far as I am concerned.

HRH Princess Anne
(extract of opening speech at Leather Expo '74)

Animals' skins preceded woven cloth as a form of clothing, when primitive man draped himself in crudely-cured hides out of necessity. Local industries developed around the dense deer-forests and cattle-markets. Glove-making was practised as a cottage industry in the villages sheltering under the mighty Wychwood Forest, and acquired no small degree of importance. Over the last few years, leathers, in their vast variety, have become increasingly fashionable again and few materials have attracted more imitations. The humble sheepskin of yesterday's hill shepherd is a luxury coat of today's city executive, or a prestige piece of furnishing as a rug, a chair-drape or a car-seat-cover.

Susceptible, always, to the vagaries of fashion, the value of leather as a material has been acknowledged over the centuries: the Roman legions tramped across their vast empire in it, and Henry VIII used Russian buff urus hides for military purposes; real buff leather would turn the edge of a sword and, being pistol-proof, was in great demand during the Civil Wars.

The British Leather Federation is an umbrella for various organizations in the leather trade. One of those is the Leather Institute, whose main lines of promotion are the leather products of the manufacturing industries, but it does not engage in any specific promotional activity to sell products of individual craftsmen. Encouragement is given to young designers through the institute's annual competitions, in which cash prizes are awarded to leatherwear-design students. It also provides funds for a bursary at the Royal College of Art for student designers in leather goods, and contributes to a glove-design competition organized by the Glove Guild of Great Britain.

Leather accessories find their salvation by marrying durability with timeless design and demanding, therefore, the degree of craftsmanship afforded to other aspects of leatherwork.

Hand-carved decoration is deceptively simple: a pattern is traced on the leather, the outline is cut with a sharp tool and is bevelled by being hammered down one side of the cut, which in turn raises the pattern, giving it an embossed effect, but, as B. P. Burrows says, "there is quite a knack in it". He learned the technique in Canada; the Hawkworths of York learned theirs in Spain.

John Williams trained as a painter but works mainly in leather. His boldly patterned belts have excited the fashion world, appearing in glossy magazines and the national Press. But he still admits there are many marketing difficulties and goes as far as to say that anyone practising crafts in a society attuned to industrial processes is inevitably put in a very artificial position. However valid that comment may be, there is certainly nothing artificial about his leatherwork, for which he uses both bookbinding and saddlery tools. Hand-stitched, patterned, dyed, and polished with the mixture of lanolin, cedar oil and bees-wax which the British Museum uses on its books, each beautiful belt takes two full days to complete. He admits that he would not want to make just belts forever, his range is therefore not limited, nor even defined, for he has recently undertaken commissions for painted furniture.

COBBLED BOOTS

A cobbler, by definition, is a mender of shoes; by connotation, he is an able and skilled shoemaker – a cordwainer. It is a title to be found in the old tales – a figure of fiction and fable, but by any name he existed in every village – shoeing those who could afford to be shod. Those who could not bound their feet in rags or went barefoot.

It was mass-production methods which made shoes available to all on a scale and at a price incompatible with the labour intensity of hand-made footwear.

The brothers Crispin and Crispinin, shoe snobs of the third century, gave their saintly patronage to the craft which is of great antiquity. Throughout its long history, leather has been the natural choice for footwear. Being slightly porous, leather soles acquire a hard-wearing crust from particles of grit.

At the turn of the century Britain was invaded by imported footwear from America. Cheaper, ready-made shoes brought variety and competition into the trade as other countries mechanized their production and entered the world market. Few bespoke boot-makers survived. Those that have survived eluded the conglomerates by resolutely sticking to traditional methods and, in the main, classical styles. It is the typical British shoe which attracts the export orders, so no attempt has been made to emulate Continental styles.

Compromising between the pressures inflicted by big business and the quality craftsmanship upon which they founded their company over a century ago, Church & Co. have shown remarkable tenacity by streamlining their production without cutting corners. Their English shoes still depend on a high degree of manual dexterity and, as of old, use a number of skilled home-workers for special handwork.

Trickers, of even earlier foundation, is a small firm specializing in hand-made shoes and sandals, with an output of about 800 pairs a week. Their heavy 'tramping' shoe, with a half-inch leather sole, has been made to the same pattern on the same last for over fifty years and is still one of their best selling models.

They report an increased demand, showing that the extra care which handwork involves is appreciated and will be paid for. They also still make shoes for individuals from lasts made on the premises of their retail outlets.

Exclusiveness is at a premium today, but that it exists at all is a valuable asset to English craftsmanship.

Booting the nobility and the famous is the prerogative of the few who make bespoke footwear. It is one of the specialist crafts which, surprisingly, still lends itself to the cottage industry set-up. A number of outworkers, scattered across the country from Cornwall to Scotland, do specialist handwork for Lobb of St James's, the royal boot-maker.

Many of their craftsmen work at home, thereby following an old tradition. One boot-maker worked for the firm for sixty years without ever setting foot on the premises after his initial engagement. Each home-worker has his own kit of tools and can arrange his working week around his interests – or the weather. For those who work at the well-worn benches there is the steady flow of the noble and famous to add interest to the day, for the kings and princes of royal houses, stage, and screen, sit in comfortable old chairs close to the work-benches and discuss their business. But they are all considered equal as customers. Lobb's reputation for excellence has been acknowledged by the highest awards in terms of gold medals and royal appointments; they achieved this reputation because of the attention they pay to detail at every stage, their old-world courtesy to all customers, and the quality of their products. About six principal craftsmen, each of whom would have served a minimum of three years' apprenticeship, understand all the aspects in the construction of a boot or shoe, and form the nucleus of the firm.

The *fitter* interprets not only the measurements of the foot but also its physical features; no knobbly bone or bumpy bunion, hammer toe or fallen arch escapes his detection, even if his fingers cannot actually feel the foot he has to measure, a well-fitted, worn shoe will convey all in its creases and shape. Upon the practised eye and experience of the fitter the success of subsequent operations depends. Oscar Asche, obviously appreciated this point by giving his Chu Chin Chow cobbler these lines:

> And as I cobble with needle and thread
> I judge the world by the way they tread,
> Toes turned out and toes turned in,
> Heels worn thick and soles worn thin,
> There's food for thought in a sandal skin.

The *last-maker* chops and carves hornbeam, beech or maple into a beautifully sculptured model of the customer's foot. E. Buchholz, who has worked in the trade for almost half a century and can carry out all the processes involved in making a shoe, likes working in beech; he says it can be worked either way and does not split. To watch him guillotine a rough block with an enormous blade is to see a marvel in manual dexterity; to watch him slicing slithers off so that it assumes shape whilst he is talking to you is a hair-raising experience, but fears for the safety of his fingers are unfounded, for he proves that he "can judge without looking". Interpreting the fitter's patterns and notes, the last-maker cuts and rasps and sandpapers the block into an exact replica of the foot which is to be shod. Even the ugliest foot in the flesh looks an elegant sculpture as a Lobb's last.

The *clicker*, earning his name from the clicking sound of leather being cut, selects the skin or hide for the purpose of the shoe and the build of the customer, who will have chosen the type of leather: Russian calf, brown calf, antelope or doe, willow calf, patent, Scotch grain, crup or kid, crocodile, lizard, ostrich, morocco or seal, python, kangaroo, elephant or whaleskin; tanned according to the type. Rare skins are kept in a safe. Soles are traditional: tanned by the bark of English oak. Good clicking ensures that correctly selected leather will be used to best advantage. The simplest style has no less than eight pieces of leather in the upper alone. Paper patterns of the pieces of leather which are to form the uppers are made with the aid of the last.

The *closer* cuts the pieces to the final shape and stitches them together, incorporating all necessary lining, stiffeners and tongue by moulding them over the last. The upper takes on its correct shape and proportions and the lasting distinction of the hand-made shoe is dependent on good closing.

Completing the assembling of the shoe is the *maker* who 'lasts' the upper round the wooden last, every part drawn taut and secured with minute rivets, then stitched by hand with interlaced stitches. The mellowed, dampened inner-sole is moulded to the bottom of the last and stitched to the uppers with a *welt*, a thin strip of leather running round the shoe. Strands of hemp or flax, the number depending on the type of shoe, are well waxed to make a thread. The favoured 'needle' is a pig's bristle spliced on to the thread. The length of each stitch, set in a channel around the welt, is governed by the weight of the sole and upper. Only the correct number of stitches to the inch give maximum strength, more or less would weaken the shoe. The waxed thread sets firmly in the leather and the stitches are hidden. After the channel covering is replaced, the sole, in a moist condition is then stitched to the welt, and the heel built up with 'tingles'. These rivets are the only nails in the shoe. It is interesting that the founder, John Lobb, raised his capital on the success of a hollow heel in which gold dust could be hidden; which, of course, cornered an important market of Australian prospectors.

It is still often some time before the customer receives his hand-made shoes, however. Even the Queen has to wait until they have passed at least two close inspections by the craftsmen-directors, who are often to be seen at the bench attired in the traditional long aprons, working at the craft to which they have all been apprenticed, minding their business as no one else can. Diplomatically, the boot-makers agree that they number the world's most eminent personages among their many customers, but a guardsman's tall duty boots receive the same attention as do the riding-boots for Prince Charles. It is the library of lasts which is fascinating. Each last is numbered and named, and stored on long wooden shelves stacked from floor to ceiling – a veritable '*Who's Who*' of 'feet'.

Trees are made by Lobb's own tree-maker in a Dickensian workshop in Soho, but the polishing is done at St James's. Not only spit and polish, literally, but brush and cloth, bone and bare fingers bring the leather up to perfection, keeping at least one employee constantly engaged.

The advantages of bespoke footwear over the factory-made counterpart are self-evident. What it really boils down to is the difference between fitting a foot into a shoe and fitting a shoe around a foot. Plus the materials, and the craftsmanship. But, one must concede to the power of mechanization, which has made ready-to-wear shoes available to us, even if (to quote an old Cotsaller) "we have "to wear them a week before we can get them on!""

BOOKBINDING

It is interesting to observe that the three main problems presented to a bookbinder today are those that confronted the medieval craftsman. The first is still how to hold together the leaves of a book; the second, how to protect those leaves; and the third, how to decorate or otherwise identify the protective cover.

Ivor Robinson

The art of the bookbinder is still relatively little-known considering the antiquity of the craft. Some historians date the development of the book from *c.* A.D. 200; others from as early as *c.* B.C. 200. The craft has succumbed to a highly mechanized form in this century; often the only hand application being that of moving the books from one machine to another. Although more craft-orientated, the remaining commercial hand-binderies are generally conservative in their undertakings, and are safe, non-exploratory and non-creative in type.

The craft bookbinder, of necessity, works almost entirely alone or within small intimate groups, undertaking every aspect of the work:

advanced craft bookbinding involves something like forty distinct and different manual operations, between which drying periods must occur before the next stage can be proceded with.

A very small minority concentrates entirely on the design aspect of bookbinding, undertaking neither repairwork nor teaching, either to organized classes or apprentices, thus creating an arty-crafty affected image which is not true of the majority. In fact, few can afford to turn down the renovation which makes up the bulk of their orders. Salvaging ancient scrolls, fitting together the pieces, strengthening spines, washing and sizing paper are but a few of the tasks to which a bookbinder may turn his talents.

Conservation is the over-riding factor which exacts the skill and artistic creativity of the bookbinder. James Brockman, under whose direction the Eddington Bindery has established a prominent place in the bookbinding world, acknowledges the medieval monks' mastery and understanding of the techniques essential for durability. He has developed the revival of oak boards and metalwork and uses these as successfully on modern bindings as on ancient manuscripts. In bookbinding, the knowledge of the chemical properties of paper is as important as the actual craftwork. Acidity causes the fibres to break down and treatment may involve washing (which can be done with hand-made paper), sizeing (often with animal-based gelatine), and deacidification. Badly damaged books are completely dismantled and each page separately treated with hand-made paper, grafted in where necessary, before being assembled again and resewn on a frame; cords are then laced in. Headbands are sewn on, adding strength to the vulnerable spots and showing the weakness of glued-on tabs which break down the spine. Everyone follows through all the processes so the five-year apprenticeship is meaningful. Even the tools used for the design on a William Morris volume were cut at the bindery.

Industrial and commercial binderies have strong trade union affiliation; the master bookbinders have no independent organization of their own but are embodied within the powerful British Printing Industries Federation; the craft bookbinders founded their own guild in 1955 to act mainly as an exhibition society.

Re-organized and re-named in 1968, the Designer-Bookbinders is one of the three most important bookbinding societies in the world. It justly claims to be the main custodian of the craft in this country today, its strength vindicative of the extraordinary excellence of its professional members – a mere twenty in the whole of the country – it gained three medals in the 1971 Prix Paul Bonet, the first international bookbinding competition, in which fourteen countries participated. In their individual works the twenty members have elevated the craft to an art form, whereby the bindings are designed with special reference to the thematic contents of the book, rather than as arbitary decorative covers. Nevertheless, they have not lost sight of the fact that three-quarters of the work is between the covers, and it is this study of the structure of the book as a whole, rather than just producing an attractive wrapping, that particular members were able to play such a prominent role in the vast book rescue operations in the wake of the disastrous flooding of Florence in 1966. This spearheaded the significant contributions to the subsequent restoration procedures through the establishment and staffing of the book restoration laboratory in Florence.

This was a dramatic rescue operation to which the world's attention was drawn, but invaluable work is going on in quiet corners all over England, saving works of inestimable value from the ravages of the centuries and ignorant handling. The metamorphosis which a mangled mess of manuscript undergoes, to emerge as a beautifully bound book under the skilled hand and eye of Alan Winstanley, is simply incredible.

In a building behind the British Museum, dedicated craftsmen patiently beaver away on what amounts to about a hundred years' work on book conservation. Since 1760, the museum has employed bookbinders to look after its vast collection, and HMSO took on the job in 1927. About 150 employees produce some 16,000 cloth and buckram bindings, and about 4,000 first-class leather bindings a year, but it is the upkeep of some 9 million books, ranged around 100 miles of shelves, which keeps nine binders constantly busy on furbishing. A colossal piece of restoration work was that of the Klencke Atlas – 6 feet 3 inches × 3 feet 6 inches. A super large skin, measuring 46 square feet, was used in the re-binding.

Individual bookbinders handle most exacting and exciting assignments too, but the volume is of necessity very limited. Most have a personal production of only six bindings a year, and report long waiting-lists; it sometimes takes up to three years for completion of a commission. Ivor Robinson produced a modest estimate analysing the time which could be involved in one typical exhibition binding as: designing time 20 hours, forwarding (binding) 40 hours, finishing (gold tooling) 50 hours, making a lined book box 10 hours. But as much as 300 hours may be spent on gold tooling alone. It is evident that making bindings for general craft exhibitions is too expensive, both in outlay and time, to be justified by a chance commission. Mostly, it is through the specialized exhibitions of the society that work is forthcoming, but orders do also come through the dealers in antiquarian and fine books. An important venture was undertaken by a small firm two years ago when thirty-nine bindings were commissioned as examples of 'British Bookbindings Today', the title of the exhibition from which the whole collection was bought by the Lilly Library of America. Only the lavishly illustrated catalogue remains in England, an important record of both the art of the modern bookbinder and a reminder that patronage of the craft does still exist.

Luxurious and prestigeous, the craft of bookbinding appears to be conspicuously absent from the programmes of the eminent craft examination boards. The syllabuses seem to be against producing an intelligent and original approach to the making of books, with virtually no encouragement of hand-binding as such, perhaps considering it of little social validity, being the prerogative of the wealthy bibliophile. Yet it has both cultural and therapeutic value. Everywhere there is an increasing demand to work the craft; classes are over-subscribed and tutors are difficult to get.

There are a few, in common with craftsmen in other fields, who thwart the efforts of amateurs – supposedly for the potential threat they constitute to either the prestige of the craft or their own livelihood, both of which are invalid arguments in this case owing to the exclusiveness of the métier. Others, aware of the complementary role which craft enthusiasts play, help and encourage them. Students of the late Eric Burdett, determined to keep alive the skills their eminent master taught them, formed their own guild, relying on each others experience and the professional lectures which Frank Brown gives them, and never purport other than an amateur status.

Bookbinding, therefore, is in a peculiar position today, for despite the increasing demand to learn the craft there seems very little support in the way of training facilities in schools of art; what there is, is usually limited to conservation of old worn books, rather than the creation of new and original bindings.

Philip Smith has built upon the wide knowledge of the leading bookbinders with whom he trained, to emerge as a unique and profound influence on twentieth-century bookbinding. Experimenting with new and evocative finishes has resulted in his pioneering a revolutionary approach to the craft. He has been responsible for important innovations in the structure of books, mainly reinforcements and other aids to durability, such as the concept of the book wall, with its endless decorative possibilities. His present work makes use of inlays and onlays of a patent material, 'maril', comprising specially prepared fragments of multicoloured waste leathers, deriving its name from *ma*rbled *i*nlaid *l*eather. The complexity of his particular media means anything from 150 to 600 hours on each creative binding. Creator of special appliances and gadgets for improved efficiency, such as the single-post multi-purpose sewing-frame, Philip Smith is developing an electric spokeshave for paring leather, and his recent CAC bursary will allow him to reappraise and develop his work. He firmly advocates the exploration of new materials for use in book structure, and believes the future development of original hand-binding must stem from formal training in art and design.

To quote Ivor Robinson again: "the ability to strike the subtle and delicate balance between the book as literature, the book as typography, and the book as material for binding, requires a special form of scholarship".

PARCHMENT, PAPER AND PENMANSHIP

It is recorded that ancient Persians wrote on skins, and reference is made to the belief that "in a remote period many centuries before the time of Eumenes" Ionians wrote on goat- and sheepskins. The origin of writing on skins is rather obscure but, officially, the invention of parchment is credited to the Egyptians, *c.* 1300 B.C.

It is not surprising that records are difficult to trace as it was common practice up to Tudor times to re-use parchment. How many accounts of historical importance, or fine poems, were pared off older manuscripts to make way for a lesser works will never be known. To quote an old French writer,

> some parchments have been restored three or four times and have successively received the verses of Virgil, the controversies of the Arians, the decrees against the books of Aristotle and, finally, the books of Aristotle themselves. Parchment is like an easy man, who is always of the same opinion as the last speaker.

Authors in the eleventh century often had to prepare their own parchments. Hildebert, Archbishop of Tours, in a sermon on the Book of Life says:

> do you know what a writer does? He first cleanses his parchment from the grease, and takes off the principal part of the dirt, then he entirely rubs off the hair and fibres with pumice-stone: if he did not do so, the letters written upon it would not be good, nor would they last long. He then rules lines that the writing may be straight. All these things you ought to do, if you wish to possess the book I have been displaying to you.

PAPER-MAKING BY HAND

> An American customer who saw paper made by hand, said "I used to wonder why your paper was so uneven and no two sheets alike, but now I wonder how you manage to make any good sheets at all with so much handling". Well, that just depends on the people who handle it.
>
> *J. Barcham Green*

In comparison with the preparation of parchment as described by

Hildebert, paper-making by hand is a far more esoteric craft involving a great number of different processes and much time. In its heyday a paper-mill would engage the labour of the whole of a small village. Allowing for the maturing periods between operations, it still takes about three months to make good hand-made paper.

Paper-mills once punctuated the river valleys where the water was particularly clear – an important factor in the manufacture. A river which runs against the sun is said to have special qualities; the northward-flowing Isbourne in the Cotswolds certainly has some peculiar properties, including a total absence of iron. Today, production at Postlip, which has a long history of paper-making is mainly concentrated on absorbent papers and filter-papers.

Established in Somerset for something like four centuries again due to the purity of the water, making paper by hand has also died out in that county. The Inveresk Paper Company concentrate mainly on producing security, technical and mould-made paper, having produced very little hand-made paper since their move from Wookey Hole – where examples of the craft are preserved as museum exhibits.

The number of mills producing hand-made paper in commercial operation had fallen significantly in the last 180 years, but there is now a marked increase in interest in it, which has produced amateur paper-makers, particularly in the United States but also in this country although to a lesser extent. The demand encouraged Simon Barcham Green, whose family has been engaged in paper-making since the end of the seventeenth century, to form a new company, which ensured continued operation of the mill in Kent.

Although there are technical procedures to be strictly followed, there is in paper-making, as with most other traditional crafts, the question of feeling what is right, so that a true craftsman will recognize and approve a good sheet of paper with a good weight. But only by actually making sheets of paper by hand can the whole process be learned.

Woven rags were the basic raw material of paper-making for many years, but their merits were often overstated and there were very many technical disadvantages in using them. Absolutely clean and pure cotton linters, the purest form of cellulose available, together with other textile fibres, are used nowadays.

Quite distinct from the harder, shiny and impersonal mould-made type is the top quality hand-made paper. The highest degree of permanence is ensured by the type of materials used; the character and texture result from the way it is made and the quality of the hand-felts, which are especially designed to suit the individual needs of the paper-maker. The making of hand-felts is a very specialized craft of spinning, weaving and fulling the woollen cloth which interleaves the sheets of damp paper. The weave of the felt is determined by the grain required on the surface of the paper.

The making of paper starts with the fibre being beaten to a pulp, which is then strained through a knotter into the vat. The water is heated by direct steam, size is added to the pulp, which is agitated by a paddle in the base of the vat, called a 'hog'.

The vatman is traditionally the key craftsman in the process and in the past was very much a father-figure who arranged apprenticeships and wages. His is perhaps the job with the least variety but he has the 'feel', acquired through skilful application and experience, which makes him master of his craft. He slips into a rhythm of dip, draw, shake, pause, slide, lift – movements which make or mar the paper: changing the shake as the wave crosses the deckle (the specially constructed outer frame of the mould) to 'close' the sheet requires close attention; over-much shake would cause the sheet to look cloudy, wild or crushed; lifting the deckle off the mould too quickly, or too slowly, or at the wrong angle, will cause drops to fall on the sheet and spoil it.

The rhythm set by the vatman is entered into by the coucher, both men having to work in perfect unison and speed. The coucher transfers the layer of pulp from the mould to the felt: his movements are a series of pull, raise, drain, flip, raise, catch, pitch, throw, swing, drop, roll and press – each one crucial to the end result; even water from the finger-tips dripped on to the couched sheet will cause thin places.

Commonplace words take on special significance in paper-making: a pile of felts and sheets interleaved is known as a 'post', and exceptionally as a 'lump'. A 'pack', on the other hand, is a pile of wet paper after it has been separated from the felts; a 'wad' is the sandwich of paper and zinc plates that is put into the glazing rolls. The coucher completes his post and lays the 'pilcher' (a wad of three or four felts sewn together) on top. He then assists the layer in taking the post to the press.

The layer operates the pumps with a wary eye open for absolutely correct pressure. After pressing, the post is pulled out by the layer who throws the top felt onto the felt board. A relatively simple-sounding job of picking up the sheet from the felt requires practice, for it is all too easy to pull off the corner. It must come off the felt flat, a slight buckle or ridge will cause a vein in the finished sheet.

Each type of paper requires specialized treatment: too much pressure reduces the packs to solid blocks, too little results in the surface grain being coarse; an eggshell finish for special drawing papers requires yet another application of pressure. The protracted processes of drying, maturing and glazing have yet to be followed through before the paper is ready for sale. About five hundredweight of a thin strong paper, or as much as a ton of thick Imperial, can be made in a week by a vat crew which will comprise the vatman, coucher, with perhaps an upper-end boy (who assists the coucher at the upper end of the mould when specific sizes are made), and maybe a slice boy (who assists the layer when a very thin type of paper is being made.

The slice boy steadies the sheet laid by the layer by placing a slice – or thin wooden strip – on each as it is assembled for pressing).

Although the vat crew is the principal set of craftsmen involved in making paper by hand, there are, of course, others at work in the mill involved in the numerous processes, equally experienced at their particular jobs. Specially crafted equipment is also essential: mould-making, and hand-felting are two specialized crafts in themselves.

An apprentice paper-maker used to serve for seven years, he then received his Card of Freedom as a journeyman and was entitled to visit mills in search of work.

The apprenticeship system has been abolished by Simon Barcham Green, who does not consider the old schemes socially acceptable in these days. Since the new company was formed it has been able to recruit sufficient young people, despite there being something of a labour shortage in the Maidstone area, and they start off learning the various aspects of the craft, with their salaries increased as they become more experienced and skilled.

Hand-made paper manufacture attracts a fair amount of academic interest, which often wanes as just how much hard work is involved is revealed. There is no longer a Paper-makers' Guild, the original society having folded up many years ago, and the suggestion that hand-made paper manufacture could be classified in the fine arts group is strongly refuted, but they are very proud at Hayle Mill to be a craft industry supplying artists.

There has recently been a very big increase in demand for vellum for writing and illuminating in the United States, and they are now printing their own magazine called *Calligrafree*. Italy has also requested vellum for printing. In fact, there has been quite a demand for high-class bindings of late, notably in Europe. Hand-made sheepskin parchment and all types of vellum are finding their way to all parts of the world from H. Band & Co. of Middlesex, who also make quill pens.

The craft of calligraphy is one which suffered drastically with the advent of printing, but its influence and practice became re-established with the formation of the Society of Scribes and Illuminators (p. 198), whose goals are the same today as they were over fifty years ago; fostering a sincere and vital endeavour to encourage the practice of calligraphy, rather than of sheer technical accomplishment. Techniques are discussed and demonstrations are held at quarterly meetings. Visits to libraries and museums are arranged to study historical manuscripts and a conducted 'Calligraphic tour of London' to see twentieth-century manuscripts has been a recent and popular innovation. There are currently some 71 craft members, with 370 lay members: interest is gaining momentum as lettering is projected into an art form on its own merits of scale and design, which can give it an exciting visual impact. A travelling exhibition of contemporary manuscripts is continually on its rounds, taking the work of today's craftsmen to an even wider public.

Closely associated with the art of gilding is the craft of tempera painting, the technique depending as much on the actual construction – the making of parchment size, blending of varnishes and so on – as the personal vision of the artist. All the relevant skills are taught by the Society of Painters in Tempera as an essential means of acquiring a professional standard of work.

SOCIETIES

THE SOCIETY OF MASTER SADDLERS LTD, 82 Borough High Street, London SE1. Tel: 01–407 1582
> Membership is open to all bona fide and experienced saddlers and retailers of saddlery.

SOCIETY OF DESIGNER BOOKBINDERS, 6 Queen Square, London WC1N 3AR
> Membership is of three categories: professional for practising designer bookbinders; associates who support the aims of the society, and honorary. The declared aims are to promote and exhibit the art of the hand-bound book and to seek to exert a progressive influence on the design and technique of book-binding. An illustrated directory of members and their work, and directories of suppliers are also published.

THE WESSEX GUILD OF BOOKBINDERS, Hon. Sec: Miss W. Allen, 10 Denby Road, Poole, Dorset
> A society of amateurs who practise the craft, and exhibit at the Dorset County Exhibition.

LEATHER INSTITUTE, Leather Trade House, 82 Borough High Street, London SE1 1LL. Tel: 01–407 1582
> The public relations division of the leather industry. Bursaries and awards to students of fashion-design in leather.

TRAINING COURSES

CORDWAINERS TECHNICAL COLLEGE, Mare Street, Hackney, London E8 3RE. Tel: 01–985 0273
> Saddlery and leatherwear courses.

NATIONAL LEATHERSELLERS' COLLEGE, 176 Tower Bridge Road, London SE1. Tel: 01–407 2544
> Many colleges have courses in leather and furs within a broader curriculum; the City of Leicester Polytechnic, for instance, runs a post-graduate course in footwear-design.
> *See also* COSIRA.

USEFUL PUBLICATIONS

Leather and leathergoods directories, published by Benn Bros Ltd, Bouverie

House, Fleet Street, London EC4. Tel: 01–583 0807
  Comprehensive references – leather-producers, agents, hide-markets, etc.
    European leather guides and trade magazines, published by Benn Bros
  Ltd, Lyon House, 125 High Street, Colliers Wood, London SW19. Tel:
  01–542 8575

THE SOCIETY OF SCRIBES AND ILLUMINATORS, Sec: John Cackett, 6 Queen
Square, London WC1
    Founded in 1921 for "the advancement of the crafts of writing and illumi-
  nation by the practice of these for themselves alone. The aim of the Society
  should be directed towards the production of books and documents wholly
  handmade, regarding other application as subordinate but not excluding
  it". Membership: craft, honorary, lay and honorary lay members. Craft
  membership is limited to those whose practice of calligraphy, lettering and
  illumination reach the high standard required for election. Candidates
  submit at least three original pieces of recent work which, it is suggested,
  should comprise vellum, manuscript book or substantial part thereof, decor-
  ation-heraldry, line-drawing or illumination, raised and burnished gilding.
  Exhibitions of members' work, an annual lecture by a distinguished speaker
  and study tours are supplemented by regular meetings and a newsletter.
  Commissions are dealt with through the society's secretary who will recommend suitable members to carry out the work.

SOCIETY OF PAINTERS IN TEMPERA, Hon. Sec: Miss R. Borradaile, 28 Eldon
Road, London W8 5PT
    The society, founded in 1901, is a small group of specialists who are carrying
  out the traditions of tempera painting as taught by the early Masters. Experience in this exacting craft is recognized as essential and practical studio
  work by members is arranged for by study courses from time to time.

SADDLERS

Note: *M.S.* denotes Master Saddler Member of the Society of Master Saddlers. These are members who are defined by the society as "Saddlers, that is to
say persons, firms or companies who in the opinion of the executive committee
have skilled employees or are skilled in their own right in the manufacture,
repair and maintenance of saddlery and harness and sell such goods by retail".

A. ADAMS, 19 The Broadway, Newbury, Berks. Tel: Newbury 3329 (*M.S.*)

GEORGE ALDRIDGE AND SON, 90 Friar Street, Reading, Berks. RG1 1EN. Tel:
(0734) 52383 (*M.S.*)

ALRESFORD SADDLERY, 16 West Street, Alresford, Hants, Tel: Alresford 2277
(*M.S.*)

W. R. BAILEY, Bridge House, Congresbury, Nr. Bristol. Tel: (0934 83) 2240
(*M.S.*)

ROY A. BAKER, 93a St Giles Street, Norwich, Norfolk. Tel: (0603) 27850 (*M.S.*)

BARRETS OF FECKENHAM, Feckenham, nr Redditch, Worcs. B96 6HQ. Tel: Astwood Bank 2935/6 (*M.S.*)

T. BARRINGTON AND SON, 253 Grandstand Road, Westfields, Herefordshire. Tel: Westfields 4927 (*M.S.*)

A. E. BATCHELOR AND SON (Epping) LTD, 269 High Street, Epping, Essex. Tel: Epping 2181 (*M.S.*)

ARTHUR BENN LTD, 7 Yorkshire Street, Burnley, Lancs. Tel: (02820) 22546 (*M.S.*)

BENNETT AND SON, 266 High Street, Cottenham, Cambs. CB4 4RZ. Tel: (0954 50) 251 (*M.S.*)

BLACKS OF MACCLESFIELD, 8 Market Place, Macclesfield, Cheshire. Tel: (0625) 22556 (*M.S.*)

BLACKBURN'S, 420 Stenson Road, Littleover, Derby. Tel: Derby 23864 (*M.S.*)

THOMAS BOWERS AND SON, 264–6 Stamford Street, Ashton-under-Lyne, Lancs. (*M.S.*)

E. W. BOWLES AND SON, 91 Glisson Road, Cambridge. Tel: Cambridge 53343 (*M.S.*)

A. BRETON AND SON LTD, 5 Norfolk House, Wellesley Road, Croydon, Surrey CRO 1LH. Tel: 01–688 1678 (*M.S.*)

BRIDLEWAYS LTD, 53 Quarry Street, Guildford, Surrey. Tel: Guildford 642 96 (*M.S.*)

BRIDLEWAYS OF GUILDFORD LTD, 176 East Street, Epsom, Surrey. Tel: Epsom 25420 (*M.S.*)

L. BROOKS AND SON, 20 Hartfield Road, Wimbledon, SW19. Tel: 01–946 1574 (*M.S.*)

BURCHNELL'S, 14/16 West Street, Bourne, Lincs. Tel: Bourne 3430 (*M.S.*)

DON CARNEY, 17 Catherine Street, Macclesfield, Cheshire. Tel: Macclesfield 20044 (*M.S.*)

G. M. CATTERALL, Saddlery Stores, High Street, Staplehurst, Tonbridge, Kent. Tel: Staplehurst 891423 (*M.S.*)

FREDK. J. CHANDLER (Saddler) LTD, Stonebridge, Marlborough, Wilts. Tel: (067–25) 2633
  Racing and hunting saddlers since 1796, supplying many of the leading jockeys and race-horse-trainers in the United Kingdom. Repairs undertaken and horse-clothing manufactured. By appointment to HM the Queen. (*M.S.*)

A. F. CHANTER, High Street, Dulverton, Somerset. Tel: Dulverton 208 (*M.S.*)

W. CLARKE, 103 High Street, Eton, nr Windsor, Berks. Tel: Windsor 62824 (*M.S.*)

JAMES CLIFFORD AND SONS, LTD, 63–5 High Street, Sevenoaks, Kent. (*M.S.*)

COLNE SADDLERY (B. Emtage), 3 St Oswalds Road, Gloucester. Tel: Andoversford 293 (*A.M.*)
  Retail outlet for saddlery made by his son Maurice Emtage, Master

Saddler's award-winner at Cordwainers College. All English hides used.

LEONARD COOMBE, 13 Highweek Street, Newton Abbot, Devon. Tel: Newton Abbot 4099 (*M.S.*)

S. AND J. M. COOPER, 24 Market Place, Faringdon, Berks. Tel: Faringdon 3117 (*M.S.*)

COUNTRY FAIR, 94 High Street, Edenbridge, Kent (*M.S.*)

W. COX, 23 High Street, Chesham, Bucks. Tel: (02405) 71340 (*M.S.*)

CURTIS LLOYD CO., 2 Station Road, Lewes, Sussex. Tel: Lewes 4991 (*M.S.*)

DANIELS AND SON, Hungate Street, Aylsham, Norfolk (*M.S.*)

H. V. DAVIES LTD, Old Woolpack Buildings, Low Lane, Horsforth, Leeds. Tel: Horsforth 87156 (*M.S.*)

W. DEARDS, 34 High Street, Welwyn, Herts. Tel: (0438 71) 4074 (*M.S.*)

DENIS'S (SADDLERY AND RIDING WEAR) LTD, 75 High Street, Aylesbury, Bucks. Tel: Aylesbury 84752 (*M.S.*)

G. DODMAN, Stowmarket Road, Ixworth, Suffolk. Tel: (0359) 30877 (*M.S.*)

W. H. EATON, Mar Road, South Ockendon, Essex RM15 6QT. Tel: (50) 2245 (*M.S.*)

G. ELLIOTT, North Newington, Banbury, Oxon. OX15 6AJ. Tel: Wroxton 216
One man saddlery producing hand-sewn leather saddles.

D. L. ELLIS AND SON, 9 Commercial Street, Hereford. Tel: (0432) 2457 (*M.S.*)

EQUINE HEALTH SADDLE CENTRE, 72 Wincheap, Canterbury, Kent. Tel: Canterbury 66366 (*M.S.*)

ESSEX SADDLERY CO., 25–31 Head Street, Halstead, Essex. Tel: Halstead 2813 (*M.S.*)

FOX (SADDLERS) LTD, Northgates, Wetherby, Yorks. Tel: Wetherby 2387 (*M.S.*)

J. FREMANTLE AND SON LTD, 132 High Street, Southampton, Hants. Tel: (0703) 26678 (*M.S.*)

W. E. GARRETT (SADDLERS) The Street, Draycott, Nr Cheddar, Somerset. Tel: Cheddar 742367 (*M.S.*)

A. R. GEDGE, Edingthorpe, nr Walsham, Norfolk (*M.S.*)

GIBSON (SADDLERS) LTD, Sales Paddock Lane, Newmarket, Suffolk. Tel: (0638) 2330 (*M.S.*)

GEOFFREY H. GIBSON, Fersfield, Norfolk 1P22 2BL. Tel: Bressingham 426 (*M.S.*)

D. GILBERT AND SON, 13 High Street, Newmarket, Suffolk. Tel: Newmarket 2958 (*M.S.*)

GLOIN'S (THE WHITE HORSE SADDLERY STORES), 56 Lodge Lane, Liverpool L8 0UL. Tel: (051–709) 3179 (*M.S.*)

SIDNEY F. GODDEN, 1 East Street, Warminster, Wilts. Tel: Warminster 2439 (*M.S.*)

GRANT BARNES AND SON, The Horsefair, Malmesbury, Wilts. SN16 0AP. Tel:

Malmesbury 2316 (*M.S.*)

JOHN GRIFFIN, 55 Thoroughfare, Woodbridge, Suffolk 1P12 1AH. Tel: Woodbridge 3199 (*M.S.*)

HARRY HALL LTD, 103/113 Regent Street, London W1. Tel: 01–734 6789 (*M.S.*)

JOHN HARLEIGH, 19 Spittal Street, Marlow, Bucks. Tel: Marlow 4183 (*M.S.*)

HARRISON AND WILSON, 32 Norfolk Street, King's Lynn, Norfolk. Tel: (0553) 2167 (*M.S.*)

W. G. HAYES AND SON LTD, 6 and 8 Dyer Street, Cirencester, Glos. Tel: Cirencester 3198
Saddlers covering all aspects of astride riding, with the exception of lightweight flat-race saddlery. The saddles are designed by S. G. Hayes and contracted out to specialist makers, although repairs are carried out in their own workshops where new items of bridle work either to pattern or customers' specifications are made. Speciality saddles include a fairly unusual suede-covered showing-saddle. Dog-equipment in leather also designed and made: among which has been a single lead branching off into six separate sections so that six matching Great Danes could be shown standing side by side in front of the owner and controlled by one hand-lead. (*M.S.*)

C. HILLYER, 178 West Street, Fareham, Hants. Tel: Fareham 4017 (*M.S.*)

G. H. AND H. E. HOLDSWORTH, Three Counties Arcade, Bawtry, Yorks. (*M.S.*)

E. HOLLINGSHEAD AND SON, 36 Nottingham Street, Melton Mowbray, Leics. Tel: Melton Mowbray 2177 (*M.S.*)

GEORGE HOLLOWAY LTD, 16 Old Street, Ashton-under-Lyne, Lancs. Tel: (061–330) 1482 (*M.S.*)

M. E. HOWITT, 2 and 4 Turk Street, Alton, Hants. Tel: (0420) 83049 (*M.S.*)

S. M. HUDSON AND SONS LTD, 68 Victoria Street, Wolverhampton, Staffs. WV1 3PG. Tel: (0902) 21803/20977 (*M.S.*)

HUMBERSIDE SADDLERY, 9 Dock Street, Queen Gardens, Hull, Yorks. Tel: (0482) 35771 (*M.S.*)

F. H. HYDE, 178 High Street, Egham, Surrey. Tel: Egham 2391 (*M.S.*)

SYDNEY INGRAM AND SON, 44 Catherine Street, Salisbury, Wilts. Tel: (0722) 3802 (*M.S.*)

D. F. JACKSON LTD, 17 High Street, Hitchin, Herts. Tel: Hitchin 4117 (*M.S.*)

JOHN JOBSON AND SONS, 15 Market Place, Morpeth, Northumberland. Tel: (06070) 3248 (*M.S.*)

R. L. JOBSON AND SON, The Tower Showrooms, Alnwick, Northumberland. Tel: Alnwick 2135 (*M.S.*)

W. T. JOHNS AND SON, 17 Buttgarden Street, Bideford, Devon. Tel: Bideford 2950 (*M.S.*)

J. KEETLEY AND SON, 54 King Street, Southwell, Notts. (*M.S.*)

W. LANCASTER AND SON, 15 Little Dockray, Penrith, Cumberland. Tel: Penrith 2363 (*M.S.*)

K. LANGFORD (SADDLER), 21 Oxford Street, Woodstock, Oxon. Tel: (0993) 812100 (*M.S.*)

LARKIN THE SADDLER, 40 South Street, Eastbourne, Sussex. Tel: (0323) 34442 (*M.S.*)

LETHERS, 56 Nutfield Road, Mersham, Surrey. Tel: Mersham 4508 (*M.S.*)

G. H. LEWIS, 54a High Street, Whitchurch, Salop (*M.S.*)

A. E. LEWIN AND SONS LTD, 1652 High Street, Knowle, Warks. Tel: (056–45) 4738 (*M.S.*)

C. LINNEY AND SON, 13 and 15 Lake Street, Leighton Buzzard, Beds. Tel: (052 53) 3159 (*M.S.*)

LYNE'S ROPERY CO., 6 Wrawby Street, Brigg, Lincs. Tel: (06522) 2212 (*M.S.*)

M. A. MACCURTAIN, 106 Milton Street, Northampton NN2 7JF. Tel: Northampton 35443 (*M.S.*)

MOSS BROS LTD, Bedford Street, Covent Garden, WC2E 8JB. Tel: 01–240 4567 (*M.S.*)

D. MURRAY, 64 High Street, Winslow, Bletchley, Bucks. Tel: Winslow 2555 (*M.S.*)

HARRY R. NELSON LTD, The Leather Works, Kimblesworth, Chester-le-Street, Durham. Tel: Sacriston 291 (*M.S.*)

J. NEWMAN (Chippenham), 20 High Street, Chippenham, Wilts. Tel: Chippenham 2209 (*M.S.*)

OLD ALMSHOUSE SADDLERY, South Cockerington, nr Louth, Lincs.
Two fully-trained saddlers producing hand-stitched riding-tack, driving-harness and saddles. Specialist restoration work undertaken on the old farmhorse-type harness. Unusual lines are sometimes taken for such articles as goat-harness, hand-made ammunition-bags and fleece-lined shotgun-cases. No small items such as pouches and wallets.

OSIER SADDLERY (Gay and Tony Russell), The Old Mill, Gravenhurst, Beds. MK45 4JE. Tel: (0472 77) 269
Rural saddlers in the widest sense: fine quality show equipment and driving-harness made on the premises and sold through comprehensively stocked retail shop on site. The hide used is entirely hand-stained and curried, and all stitching is by hand using well-waxed thread, and in the case of stirrup leathers the thread is also hand-made for maximum strength and durability. While exhibiting at various horse-shows, the Osier Saddlery is prepared to carry out repairs on the show ground. Special orders for repairs have ranged to bellows, guncases and antique rocking-horses. (*M.S.*)

GEORGE G. PEMBERTON, Rupert House, Marston, York YO5 8NG
One-man saddler producing hand-sewn saddlery, bridles and leatherwork to order.

H. A. PHILLIPS, 10 South Street, Leominster, Herefordshire (*M.S.*)

J. W. POWELL (Fakenham), 5 Oak Street, Fakenham, Norfolk. Tel: Fakenham 2232 (*M.S.*)

E. C. PRATT (SADDLERS), 16 Station Road, Sheringham, Norfolk. Tel: Sheringham 3241 (*M.S.*)

T. PRIDHAM AND SON, 4 Grenville Street, Bideford, Devon. Tel: (02372) 2732 (*M.S.*)

G. W. PUGH AND SON, The Square, Market Harborough, Leics. Tel: Market Harborough 2200 (*M.S.*)

RAPLEY AND SON, 43 High Street, Arundel, Sussex (*M.S.*)

RAWLE AND SON LTD, Blackfriars Works, 30 Langton Road, SW9. Tel: 01–735 2299 (*M.S.*)

RED RAE SADDLERY, 25 Amwell End, Ware, Herts. Tel: (09200) 3170 (*M.S.*)

G. W. REVILL LTD, 28 Upgate, Louth, Lincs. Tel: Louth 2291 (*M.S.*)

A. W. RHOADES AND SON, 52 Waterloo Street, Market Rasen, Lincs. Tel: (2219) 3373 (*M.S.*)

RICE BROTHERS, 1 High Street, Lewes, Sussex. Tel: (079 16) 2176 (*M.S.*)

RICE BROS LTD, Cantelupe Road, East Grinstead, Sussex. Tel: (0342) 23009 (*M.S.*)

RICH BROS, 35 Fore Street, North Petherton, Somerset. Tel: North Petherton 337 (*M.S.*)

J. F. RIMMELL, Newbold on Stour, Stratford-on-Avon, Warks. (*M.S.*)

ROBERTSONS OF EXETER, 2 Okehampton Street, Exeter, Devon. Tel: Exeter 71141 (*M.S.*)

T. AND C. ROBINSON, Kesteven House, Tattershall Road, Billinghay, Lincs. LN4 4DD. Tel: (025–66) 436/7 (*M.S.*)

ROBINSON'S SADDLERY, 55a Wellgate, Wigan, Lancs. Tel: Wigan 45061 (*M.S.*)

ROBSON AND COOPER, 14 Lendal, York YO1 2AA. Tel: (0940) 235 88 (*M.S.*)

R. H. RYDER, 10 St John's Hill, Shrewsbury, Salop. Tel: (0743) 53552 (*M.S.*)

THE SADDLERS (LYNDHURST) LTD, 6–8 High street, Lyndhurst, Hants. (*M.S.*)

SANDON SADDLERY CO:; Woburn, Milton Keynes, Beds. Tel: (052 525) 647 (*M.S.*)

SANDON SADDLERY CO., Sandon, Buntingford, Herts. Tel: (076 387) 247/8 (*M.S.*)

SANDON SADDLERY CO., Lees Yard, Holt, Norfolk. Tel: (026 371) 3480 (*M.S.*)

SANDON SADDLERY CO., Brandeston, Woodbridge, Suffolk. Tel: (072 882) 444 (*M.S.*)

W. W. SCOTT AND SONS, 49 Market Place, Thirsk, Yorks. YO7 1HA. Tel: Thirsk 2048 (*M.S.*)

SEAL SEAM (THAME) LTD, Chestnuts Yard, Upper High Street, Thame, Oxon. Tel: Thame 2129 (*M.S.*)

W. J. AND B. R. SELWOOD, 103 Broad Street, Swindon Wilts. Tel: (0793) 5884 (*M.S.*)

JOHN SHARP LTD, 80/82 West Street, Erith, Kent. Tel: Erith 33208 (*M.S.*)

O. SHEPHERD AND SON, 6 Bridge Street, Brackley, Northants. Tel: (028 03) 2224 (*M.S.*)

SIMES AND SONS (SADDLERS) LTD, 132 Victoria Road, Aldershot, Hants. Tel: (0252) 20111 (*M.S.*)

SIMPSON BROS LTD, 27 River Street, Truro, Cornwall. Tel: (0872) 2320 (*M.S.*)

SMITH ENGLEFIELD AND CO. LTD, Parliament Street and Trinity Walk Corner, Nottingham. Tel: (0636) 812174 (*M.S.*)

J. SNOWBALL, BART LTD, 44 Dean Street, Newcastle-upon-Tyne NE1 1PG. Tel: (0632) 22894 (*M.S.*)

LEONARD STEVENS, 29 Seaside and 16 Crown Street, Eastbourne, Sussex. Tel: Eastbourne 23988 and 34496 (*M.S.*)

STEVENS, LESLIE GORDON AND CO. LTD, 424/426 Garratt Lane, Earlsfield, SW18. Tel: 01–946 6279 (*M.S.*)

D. R. STONE, Saddler's Shop, 6 North Road, Brighton, Sussex. Tel: Brighton 67429 (*M.S.*)

H. A. SWANN (WATFORD) LTD, 193 High Street, Watford, Herts. Tel: Watford 25559 (*M.S.*)

H. TILL AND SON, 16–17 Brown Street, Salisbury, Wilts. Tel: (0722) 22306 (*M.S.*)

W. G. TODD AND SONS, 27 Allhallows Lane, Kendal, Westmorland. Tel: Kendal 275 (*M.S.*)

T. TROTT, 19 Fore Street, Okehampton, Devon. Tel: Sticklepath 401 (*M.S.*)

TURF AND TRAVEL (INC. THE EMSTON SADDLERY CO.,) Gerrards Cross, Bucks. Tel: Gerrards Cross 83183 (*M.S.*)

TURNER AND BRIDGAR, 21 Wallingford Road, Goring-on-Thames, Berks. (*M.S.*)

WALKER AND ALDRIDGE, 8 Church Street, Huddersfield, Yorks HD1 1DH. Tel: (0484) 30650 (*M.S.*)

STAN WARD, East Ilsley, Newbury, Berks. Tel: East Ilsley 226 (*M.S.*)

W. A. WELCH AND SON, 2E High Street, Eastleigh, Hants. Tel: Eastleigh 2170 (*M.S.*)

E. J. WICKS, 1 Newbury Street, Lambourn, Berks. Tel: Lambourn 71766
   High-class saddlery made by and under the direction of A. W. Crofts, President of Master Saddlers' Society. Specializing in lightweight racing-saddles, Mr Crofts has now registered the design of the Badminton Mark I saddle which he made for Princess Anne as a wedding gift on behalf of E. J. Wicks Saddlery of Lambourn. Comprehensively stocked shop on site. (*M.S.*)

F. WILDING AND SON, 7 West Street, Prittlewell, Southend-on-Sea, Essex. Tel: (0702) 46924 (*M.S.*)

J. W. WILKINSON AND CO. LTD, Newin Works, Highgate, Kendal, Westmorland. Tel: (0539) 20013 (*M.S.*)

WILKINSONS (NORWICH) LTD, 1 Guildhall, Norwich NOR 14E. Tel: (0603) 20951 (*M.S.*)

C. W. WILLIAMS, 2 High Street, Rye, Sussex TN31 7JE. Tel: (079 73) 3360 (*M.S.*)

JOHN WILLIE'S SADDLE ROOM, 1/3 Ringwood Road, Burley, Hants. Tel: (04 253) 2386 (*M.S.*)

WRIGHT BROS (ASHFORD), 38 Bank Street, Ashford, Kent. Tel: Ashford 20085 (*M.S.*)

WRIGHT (BEDALE) LTD, 37 North End, Bedale, Yorks. Tel: (06772) 2213 (*M.S.*)

J. W. WYCHERLEY AND SON, Saddlers, Church Street, Malpas, Cheshire SY14 8NO. Tel: Malpas 316
   Saddlers since 1859, producing high-class hand-sewn saddles and riding-equipment. (*M.S.*)

H. YENDELL AND SON, 102 Boutport Street, Barnstaple, Devon. Tel: Barnstaple 2873 (*M.S.*)

BOOT- AND SHOEMAKERS

HORACE BATTEN, (office) Coton Road, Ravensthorpe, Northampton. Tel: East Haddon 287
   Hunting- and riding-boots made to measure by hand. Specializing in show-jumping-boots, most of the famous showjumping people are customers of Horace Batten.

CHURCH AND CO., (FOOTWEAR) LTD, St James, Northampton NN5 5JB. Tel: Northampton 51251
   A firm which has established its reputation for famous English shoes for over a century, still producing quality shoes in leather in which hand crafts-manship plays a big part.

JOHN LOBB LTD, 9 St James's Street, London SW1A 1EF. Tel: 01–930 3664–5
   For over 120 years the family firm of Lobb of St James's have hand-made boots and shoes, making to measure footwear for royalty. Highest award-winners at several exhibitions, John Lobb designs are deemed the classic English style which never dates. Individual designs and materials are worked to special order by arrangement.

R. E. TRICKER LTD, St Michael's Road, Northampton NN1 3JX. Tel: Northampton 30595
   Hand-made shoes and sandals. Customers' individual lasts are made by hand by this firm, which has made hand-sewn shoes for about 145 years. Their speciality line appears to be the heavy 'tramping' shoe, which has a half-inch leather sole made to the same pattern for over half a century.

OTHER LEATHER CRAFTSMEN

BURROWS LEATHERCRAFT (B. P. Burrows), Thorncombe, Chard, Somerset. Tel: Winsham 444
  Craftsman who, with specialized help from a few outworkers, makes hand-carved leather goods: stools, handbags, belts and small items. Sales are direct and at exhibitions and agricultural shows.

H. COXEN, Ochiltree Cottage, Upper Park Road, Camberley, Surrey. Tel: Camberley 64074
  Leatherworker specializing in making scabbards. Probably the only crafts-man making these entirely by hand. Mr Coxen has undertaken commissions for the scabbard for the sword of the Prince of Wales.

JOHN GREY, Sloop Craft Market, St Ives, Cornwall. Tel: St Ives 6051
  Craftsman producing hand-made leather belts, bags, guitar-straps and similar accessories.

IAN HAWKWORTH (Hawk of York Leatherwork), 7a Clifford Street, York
  A husband and wife team producing leather goods, the style is influenced by the tooled and embossed designs of leathercraft from Spain, where they pre-viously worked. Sales are direct from their showrooms and through selected retail shops in the north of England.

HILCOT CRAFTS, Lynne and Charlie Blatch, Hilcot, Far End Lane, Sheeps-combe, nr Stroud, Glos. Tel: Painswick 813460
  Hand-made leather goods.

D. WATTS, Upper Meadow Cottage, Kencott, Lechlade, Glos.
  Hand-made leather goods, speciality 'black jacks'.

NEIL MACGREGOR, 9 Blackhill, Malmesbury, Wilts.
  Hand-engraved leatherwork. Member of Craftsmen of Gloucestershire.

MERLIN LEATHER, Cam Houses (Head office), Oughtershaw, Skipton, North Yorks. BO 235 JT
  A small group of leather craftsmen working in the remote Cam Houses Community at Buckden, high up in the North Yorkshire Pennines.

LIZ PEARSON, 3 Glyn Terrace, Middle Road, Thrupp, Stroud, Glos.
  Hand-tooled leathercraft: bags, belts, sandals, etc.

JOHN WILLIAMS, 69 London Road, Canterbury, Kent
  A craftsman whose fine art training is expressed in leatherwork, John Wil-liams specializes in fashionable decorated belts, cutting the leather himself, stitching by hand. The buckles also are shaped up and polished by him. Other small leather items, such as folders, are also made. Painted furniture to special order.

MARION POWELL, (FAIRCRAFT), 59 Sibley Avenue, Harpenden, Herts. AL5 1HF. Tel: Harpenden 4893
Hand-sewn and trimmed suede shearling mittens, baby-shoes, muffs and cushions. Direct sales.

S. SANDERS AND SON LTD, Pilton Bridge, Barnstaple, Devon. Tel: Barnstaple 2335
An old established firm of sheepskin-dressers, hide and skin merchants whose craftsmen have been producing sheepskin coats, rugs, gloves, slippers, etc., for over 200 years.

JOHN WOOD AND SON (EXMOOR) LTD, Linton, Old Cleeve, Minehead, Somerset TA24 6HT. Tel: Washford (098–44) 291
A cottage industry type of organization where outworkers, specially trained by the firm, hand-stitch moccasins, mittens, gloves, toys, jerkins and fancy goods from sheepskins – obtained generally from the west of England and processed in the firm's own workshops. Speciality lines are a sheepskin moccasin with a particularly long wool natural sheepskin lining, sold generally through craft shops, and shaped natural floor-rugs. Commissions are undertaken by arrangement for the dressing of a wide range of animal-skins for customers who have collected them from overseas, private zoos, farms or from wild animals.

BOOKBINDERS

FRANK BROWN, The Bookshop, 8 Church Street, Dorchester, Dorset
Bookbinder, designing and executing new bindings as well as restoration and repairwork on old and rare books. Commissions undertaken.

THE EDDINGTON BINDERY LTD, Hungerford, Berks RG17 0PL. Tel: Hungerford 2275
Under the management of James Brockman, a member of the Society of Designer-Bookbinders, the Eddington Bindery has built up an excellent reputation for skilful and high-class work by its quartet of craftsmen. The first major binding undertaken was five volumes of the Bible, the finest work produced at the Doves Press. Bound in Oasis Morocco with suede onlays and suede flyleafs, the books were housed in a wooden, morocco-covered, velvet-lined box with a compartment for the original vellum case. Milton's *Paradise Lost* and *Paradise Regained*, printed on vellum, and a Kelmscott Press edition of a William Morris book are also examples of the bindery's work, photographs of which are available for inspection from the bindery. As well as traditional and contemporary bindings, commissions are undertaken for all aspects of restoration of a large cross-section of items relating to books, e.g., globes, scrolls, prints, charters and manuscripts. Among the most interesting of all their interesting commissions was a sixteenth-century printed vellum scroll 37 feet long, which was cleaned, repaired, mounted on scroll pins and boxed. Currently developing the revival of oak boards and metalwork on bindings, which have been used on several of their modern binding commissions.

CATHERINE LOUISE HODGSON, 110 Cranworth Gardens, London SW9 0NT. Tel: 01–582 0597

Designer-bookbinder – modern bindings of leather or cloth. Restoration work also undertaken.

NOREEN LITTLETON (Miss), Frocester House, Grange Court, Westbury-on-Severn, Glos. Tel: Westbury-on-Severn 217

Bookbinder and letterer. Member of Guild of Gloucestershire Craftsmen.

DENISE LUBETT, 2 Oakwood Mansions, London W14. Tel: 01–602 2134

Designer-bookbinder specializing in modern designs of her own creation, in full leather, onlays, inlays, gold or blind tooling. No repair work. Member of Society of Designer-Bookbinders.

THEO MERRETT, Round Tower Crafts, St Kevin's, Far Oakridge, nr Stroud, Glos. Tel: Frampton Mansell 384

Designer-bookbinder whose skill with leather extends to individually designed leather-covered boxes. Presentation volumes, address-books, etc. Among his interesting commissions, Theo Merrett made the Severn Bridge Visitors' Book which was signed at the opening ceremony by the Queen, and rebound a 1632 edition of Shakespeare's works for the late Dame Edith Sitwell. Member of Guild of Gloucestershire Craftsmen.

GEMMA O'CONNOR, Studio Bindery, 57b High Street, Oxford OX1 4AS. Tel: (Studio) Oxford 44193, (Home) Oxford 54058

In partnership with Ivor Robinson, under whose direction she studied bookbinding, Gemma O'Connor is a part-time assistant in project production to the printing, bookbinding, and publishing sections of the Department of Design, Oxford Polytechnic, and is an Associate Member of the Society of Designer-Bookbinders. (For commissions see entry under Ivor Robinson.)

ROGER POWELL, HON. MA, (Dublin), The Slade, Foxfield, Petersfield, Hants. Tel: Hawkley (073084) 229

Bookbinding and restoration of early vellum books. Roger Powell's work is to be found among the collectors' pieces. His commissions have included repairing and rebinding the Book of Kells among the many antiquarian books which he has worked on for Trinity College, Dublin.

IVOR ROBINSON, MDE, FRSA, Studio-bindery, 57b High Street, Oxford OX1 4AS. Tel: Oxford 44193 (Entrance from Longwall Street) (Home) Oxford 735 411

Ivor Robinson was President of the Society of Designer-Bookbinders 1968–1973. His work is represented in British royal collections, Danish and Swedish Royal Libraries, and in the special collections of the British Museum, Victoria and Albert Museum, Bodleian Library, Hornby Library, the Rohsska Museum and major private collections in Great Britain and overseas.

Silver medallist and double bronze medallist in the Prix Paul Bonet

International Bookbinding Competition, Switzerland 1971. Author of *Introducing Bookbinding* (Batsford), overseas lecturer and representative; widely exhibited and featured in major national and international publications.

Ivor Robinson is in partnership with Gemma O'Connor at the studio-bindery and commissions will be accepted by the partners, jointly or individually, for fine bookbinding, antiquarian book restoration, library and miscellaneous binding, and associated craft and design services.

C. PHILIP SMITH, ARCA, MSIA, MDE, Southcote House, 83 Nutfield Road, South Merstham, Redhill, Surrey RH1 3HD. Tel: Merstham (073 74) 2627
In his one-man studio-bindery Philip Smith specializes in original works of art, inventing ways to improve the design, durability of the binding, and efficiency in the application of the craft. Among these are the technique of maril bindings and the concept of the book wall – produced nowhere else. Among his many interesting commissions was the binding of a signed copy of Professor Tolkien's *The Lord of the Rings* for presentation to HRH the Duke of Edinburgh. Widely exhibited in Europe, North and South America, examples of Philip Smith's work are held in major public and private collections. Author of *New Directions in Bookbinding* (Studio Vista).

SALLY LOU SMITH, 42a Camden High Street, London NW1. Tel: 01–387 0370
Designer-bookbinder who won an Open Award in the Thomas Harrison Memorial Competition 1961 and 1962, and a Special Award the following year. Mrs Smith's first binding was purchased by the Victoria and Albert Museum. Widely exhibited both in England and overseas. Member of Designer-Bookbinders.

ALAN WINSTANLEY (Salisbury Bookbinders), 213 Devizes Road, Salisbury, Wilts. SP2 9LT. Tel: Salisbury 4998
Designer-bookbinder who undertakes any commissions in the field of bookbinding by hand. Alan Winstanley's undertakings vary from binding a stiff cover on a favoured paper-back to designing and binding a rare printed edition for an enthusiastic bibliophile: from repairing a puppy-chewed library-book to the restoration of rare archival tomes. Exclusive limited editions bound.

TANNERS AND DRESSERS, SHEEPSKIN PRODUCTS

WALTER CHAPMAN AND SON, Mill House, Tutbury, Burton-on-Trent DE13 9HA
Old established tanners and dressers of hides. One of the few craftsmen who have practised this craft since tanning with alum. All types of tanning and dressing skins with the hair on are undertaken: cowhides, lion skin, leopard skin, seal skin, kangaroo skin – from the ordinary to the exotic.

CITY OF LONDON HIDE AND SKIN CO., LTD, Willand, Cullompton, Devon EX15

2QE. Tel: Sampford Peverell (0884) 820567
Woolled sheepskin tanners, manufacturers of sheepskin sueded shearlings and sheepskin rugs. Coats, car-seat covers, slippers and gloves in sheepskin; leather shoulder bags; pictures (animals depicted in fur), and calfskins. Suppliers to the trade.

HENRY GILLING AND CO., LTD, Sowerby, Thirsk, Yorks. YO7 1JT. Tel: Thirsk 23138
A very old established firm of curriers who re-tan and dress various types of leather to special requirements, some for the shoe trade, but principally for the bridle and harness trade, also for belts.

THE LYNTON SHEEPSKIN SHOPPE LTD, 2 Lee Road, Lynton, Devon. Tel: (059 85) 2226
Sheepskin coats, hats and mittens made to measure; moccasins and toys.

HAND-MADE PAPER

BARCHAM GREEN AND CO., LTD, Hayle Mill, Maidstone, Kent ME15 6XQ. Tel: Maidstone (0622) 674343
Hand-made paper for watercolour painting, printing, print-making, document repair, etc. Special shades of certain papers can be made to customers' requirements, and special watermarks incorporated in any paper, to a minimum order of 2,000 sheets.

PARCHMENT AND VELLUM

H. BAND AND CO., LTD, Brent Way, High Street, Brentford, Middx. TW8 8ET. Tel: 01–560 2025–7
Light leather-tanners and dressers. Hand-made sheepskin parchment and all types of vellum. Quill pens. Recent special orders have included the vellum for binding the new Churchill Books. Suppliers to the College of Arms for Grants of Arms.

LETTERERS AND ILLUSTRATORS

MYRTLE BARTER, Church Cottage, Walkley Hill, Rodborough, nr Stroud, Glos.
Artist-illustrator: book illustration, cards and bookmarks.

GEORGE BROTHERTON, Hambutts Barn, Edge Lane, Painswick, Glos. Tel: Painswick 813559
Letterer, decorative map-maker and heraldic artist. Member of Guild of Gloucestershire Craftsmen.

JOHN F. DAVIS, 36 Hollis Gardens, Up Hatherley, Cheltenham, Glos. Tel: Cheltenham 20400
Letterer. Member of Guild of Gloucestershire Craftsmen.

Self-employed craftsmen cannot afford to stop work for a heatwave as Yorkshire weaver Rod Taylor demonstrates

(*right*) Feeding the silk-worms at Lullingstone Silk Farm, the only one of its kind in Europe

(*below*) Strusa or hand-waste, basin-waste, and a skein of raw silk

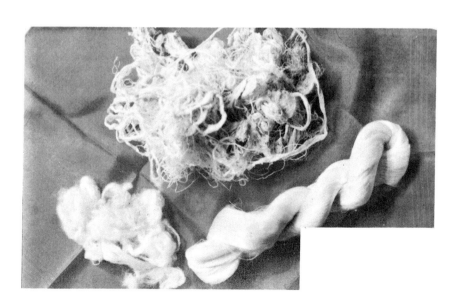

Shoe-maker of Lobb's of St James's splicing a bristle onto a
well-waxed thread with which he stitches the shoe

A. W. Crofts of Wicks Saddlery works in Lambourn, in the
heart of racehorse-training country

Lillian Delevoryas of Weatherall Workshops at work on her
prize-winning Art in Needlework pieces

Margaret Charlett practising the intricate craft of lace-making

This twelfth-century illuminated vellum was completely taken
to pieces then re-bound in goatskin to James Brockman's design
at the Eddington Bindery

Alan Winstanley tooling a facsimile of a book produced in the
last century

(right) An internal door with hand-forged animal decoration – one example of the artistic ironwork wrought by Richard Quinnell's craftsmen

(below) Vatman, Norman Peters, a veteran paper-maker with some fifty years' experience at Barcham Green & Co., throws off the wave to *close* the sheet

Champion blacksmith James Rathbone at work in his forge

11

Hornwork

Horn, in its widest sense, embraces a whole range of horny growth on animal and fowl: fingernails and claws, tortoise-shells and quills, hooves and hair shafts are, in varying degrees, of horny substance as well as horns proper – those fierce and noble appendages adorning the heads of beasts. The potential of horn as a material was realized very early in history when primitive man made his first drinking vessel of the hollow horn of his cattle. The rhinoceros is the only beast to grow a solid horn.

Traditionally centred at the termini of the old cattle drovers' routes, hornworks were among the industries which sprang up to use the by-products of the cattle trade. The peculiar properties of horn make it eminently suitable for a whole range of products. It is tough enough to be sawn, will become malleable under heat, retains a permanent polish and never tarnishes.

The principal horn works of England is the Abbey Hornworks in Westmorland. Its monastic appellation is derived from its association with Llanthony Abbey, where the monks worked horn in the seventeenth century. Within easy reach of the beautiful horned cattle of Herefordshire, trade flourished and the wide range of household ware was extended to meet the demand for powder horns for the eighteenth-century wars. It was some measure of the firm's business acumen, rather than political allegiance, that they traded with both sides during the American War of Independence.

There are only a dozen or so horners working in the Lakeland area and they hold the proud record of being the only people in the world to make shoe-horns three feet long.

As with so many crafts, the fashion and economics of one trade affect others: modern farmers tend to breed hornless cattle, and soaring labour costs make the proper removal of horns from slaughtered beasts a very expensive business. Much of the horn is therefore imported from the African continent – Nigeria, the Congo, the Cameroons, Rhodesia and the Cape. The fearsome horns of Ankole cattle, being long and fairly straight, are particularly suitable. The rich quality and scarcity of English and Scottish types of horn make them highly prized. Mainly cow-horn is used, as bull-horn tends to be somewhat thinner.

After careful sorting for size, quality, grain and colour, the horn is sawn by those experienced in determining the potential of each piece. Straightening is done by passing it through a gas flame at the same speed as the flame burns. Infra-red heat is used in processing moulded items. Green horn is first pressed in hot tallow to become a homogenous mass.

Often described as man's first plastic, it was certainly his first glass. After heating it can be pressed out into beautiful translucent sheets, and was used for windows and lanterns (the old *Lanthorn* being so named because of its horn glazing).

The art of making horn windows and lanthorn leaves has not been lost to the Lakeland horners, for the Americans' love of history has resulted in orders for horn articles for the reproduction villages and their furnishing. There is a standing order from the city of Dallas for the largest shoe-horn in the world.

Apart from producing something like 30,000 shoe-horns a year, the horners make spoons, handles for cutlery, brushes and corkscrews, decorative jewellery, buttons and beads, ornaments, and a whole range of domestic ware. Horn is unaffected by chemicals, mild acids and powders, and can be washed until sterile in luke-warm water so is used for a great number of laboratory items. Its other virtue is that it does not stick to other substances and is therefore ideal for potters for shaping their clay.

After the shaping comes the removal of the 'burring' – the surface burning which occurs during the heating process. Abrasive discs are used for refining the shapes, then removal of the 'schoring' caused by the abrasives. Polishing also involves various processes, the latter stages being the buffing with linen and finally with swansdown.

Exports to the Continent and America are on the increase as more customers are regarding horn as something of a semi-precious material. Likened to fingerprints, whereby no two are ever alike, each piece of horn is unique, with its own distinctive markings.

Retail outlet of the products of THE ABBEY HORNWORKS, is THE HORN SHOP, 94 Stricklandgate, Kendal, Westmorland. Tel: Kendal 20291

12

Metal

Metal, strong and malleable, has almost unlimited use and forms the spine of traditional craftwork. Its potential is realized in many shapes and forms. Because the iron and steel industries were once sustained by the charcoal from our woodlands, the activities of the iron-masters were held in check by Elizabeth I in the mid-sixteenth century, to conserve the London's firewood supplies and preserve the heavier timber for the shipwrights; and the Sussex area, abounding in wood and iron, became a veritable storehouse for the naval equipment of the Tudor period.

The woodlands of the northern ironstone districts did not benefit so readily from royal protection, and the anxiety about the dwindling English forest was not relieved until coke superseded charcoal as a fuel in the eighteenth century. The sites of the old ironworks were marked by massive masses called 'blooms' – the industrial waste of fused metal from the bloomaries, the forerunners of the modern blast-furnaces. Sheffield, still world-famous for its cutlery, discovered its iron ore, smelted it and shaped the resultant steel from it as far back as at least the fourteenth century; Chaucer's miller carried "a Sheffield thwytel in his hose" in *The Canterbury Tales*.

From Homer to Dickens, it is the worker of metal who has captured the writer's fancy, but few portraits of the smith can equal the following evocative lines from the apocrypha of the Old Testament:

> . . . sitting by the anvil,
> And considering the iron work,
> The vapour of the fire wasted his flesh,
> And he fighteth with the heat of the furnace;
> The noise of the hammer and anvil is ever in his ears,
> And his eyes look still upon the pattern of the thing that he
>   maketh;
> He setteth his mind to finish his work,
> And watcheth to polish it perfectly.

SMITHCRAFT AND FARRIERY

James Rathbone's services to smithcraft received royal recognition in 1963, an apex to a career punctuated by prize winning. Three times champion blacksmith, Mr Rathbone now judges at the Royal Show.

The walls of his forge are papered with a lifetime's chronicle of competitions: curly-edged certificates testifying to his craftsmanship, which started over half a century ago at the age of 13, when he worked for two years for nothing other than the privilege of learning a time-honoured skill. "I had to notch a whole scythe blade along for a hack-saw in the early days," he recalls without rancour, "I've trained my two sons to be clean workmen too, no hammer marks."

Both his sons have won numerous awards and wrought iron as sensitively as sculptors. Sheaves of corn finials contain some 85 individual iron cornstalks in each sheaf; and a pair of gates used some 600 delicate flowers in its design. The ability to give the impression that the foliage has actually grown out of the design is the criterion by which the true artist in ironwork is judged; there is no margin for error, the slightest misplaced piece upsets the symmetry of the whole.

That a village blacksmith was chosen to make the new gates for the Royal Enclosure at Ascot is proof of the immense skill that James Rathbone acquired in his transition from shoeing the horses of the Oxfordshire countryside to working iron into artistic furnishings. It is reported that both the Queen and Prince Philip have definite views on wrought-ironwork, so it was no mere formality when the designs, drawn up by COSIRA, were approved; the Queen making several visits to Ascot while James Rathbone and his two sons worked on the gates. Some 15 feet high and covering an opening of $14\frac{1}{2}$ feet, the gates weighed well over a ton and used some 1,500 feet of iron in their construction.

Immense strength is the physical feature of the village blacksmith, his virility is indisputable. "I saw my father lift a 3 cwt anvil up in his hands even though a heart attack was supposed to limit his life span to 10 years – 29 years ago", says Walter Moulsley, a Devon blacksmith whose long and hard apprenticeship started in the days when a young smith had to turn up in spotless white corduroys and clean boots, polish the anvil, watch his language and saw wood properly and cheerfully. "It was a long time before you touched the fire; you never touch another man's fire. Bellows are still the best way to get the feel of the forge. I reckon I have done some 30,000 picks in my time, and my father once made 30 shoes in 30 minutes for a five-shilling bet – with seven shoes in the fire at a time."

Universally acknowledged as King of Craftsmen, the smith has been farrier and ironworker since iron was first wrought. And few today, like the lame Vulcan, have escaped injury for all their might and skill; especially when a horse weighing nearly a ton transfers all his weight onto one leg, the one which the smith is holding up. But a light horse, because of its quickness, may be just as much a strain as a carthorse.

Charlie Bartlett lost his eye while shoeing horses and high-kicking mules for the Army. The old smith has turned his hand to many things since then, but never thought he would end up making trailers and fire-irons and gates and such like. He is proud of the fact that he never had to ask for a job, or advertise, and that his handiwork is still there at Rodmarton Manor, seeing it as a kind of a memorial to the old Cotswold craftsmen – the brothers Barnsley and Gimson.

The gateway to his blacksmith's shop is flanked by a little spinney of artful shapes of country life: Charlie's weathervanes signal the wind directions in all four corners of the world. Symbolic of the universal importance of the smith's craft, a weathervane – iron wrought into slender fingers pointing to the four cardinal points – was the test piece by which the old guildmasters assessed an apprentice's ability to practise.

The vital interdependence between crafts and the land sustained the rural economy from the Middle Ages, and the craftsmen and the farmers were bonded together for the common weal; but a disturbing shadow now tinges the pastoral scene, for many smiths complain that some affluent farmers cause extreme hardship to the smith because they can get grants to put up new buildings and often use a corner of these as an unregistered workshop where they do their own welding and blacksmithing of a sort.

"It is no wonder so few people take up the craft professionally, next to the Inland Revenue officer the smith is probably the most cheated individual and has to wait as long for his money," one smith remarked. He had sent his wife to evening-classes to learn about metalwork, as he was desperate for a helper. She found about fifteen young farmers actually taking work off their farms to do there – work which could have gone to the local smith. There also are quite a few 'backyard blacksmiths' from industry, taking work from the smith – people who would strike if a non-union man did their job.

The pirate who really upsets the smith is the 'barnyard farrier', who might think he is able to shoe his own horse, but can easily alter the natural action of the leg so the horse walks around in constant pain.

"Preserving of horses" was one of the duties of the Royal Charter granted by Charles II to the Worshipful Company of Farriers, a guild which was in existence in 1356. Still actively engaged in the craft for which it was formed over 600 years ago, the company was instrumental in getting the Farriers (Registration) Act through Parliament. This received the Royal Assent 22nd May 1975, and now ensures that the shoeing of horses is undertaken only by competent farriers, thereby protecting the horse from cruelty and the horseowner from exploitation. A registration scheme for smiths who practise shoeing was inaugurated by the company as far back as 1890. Supervised by a Registration Committee, it holds examinations at different levels to test the proficiency of farriers and since its introduction some 10,500 have qualified for registration.

Over the last twenty years, however, the dearth of farriers in the countryside has been made noticeable by the increasing horse population, as more people turn to the equestrian field for recreation and sport. The village blacksmith's ability to produce artistic wrought-ironwork attracts a different kind of customer: designs of an advanced character were demanded as fine craft commissions replaced the local farmers' farriery. A four-year apprenticeship scheme, sponsored by the company in 1958, has grown, so that the number undergoing instruction at any one time is now over 100. To cope with the estimated 400,000 horses in Great Britain today, there are some 1,200 shoeing smiths, many of them elderly. The number needed is around 1,500. An appeal, launched in 1969 by the Duke of Beaufort, Master of the Horse, received royal patronage and finances the expanding training scheme.

COSIRA contributes to the educational programme, is represented on the Registration Committee and collaborates with the company in the training courses at the Royal Army Veterinary Corps Centre, and retains eminent farriers as consultants. COSIRA also offers helpful short courses in special aspects of smithery and these augment the training offered in individual workshops, but many smiths view apprenticeship with caution and prefer to employ men with experience who have made a mature decision to enter the craft. Figures for 1972 showed a decline in employment: 2·2 per cent blacksmiths.

S. C. Pearce and Sons Ltd, of Suffolk, although forced by the general economic situation to reduce their number of craftsmen, operate both an indentured apprenticeship scheme and accept boys on day release from the local schools. But braver still, perhaps, is their acceptance of parties of school-children who come to see the smiths hand-forging iron, for this has a purely educational function, providing an invaluable demonstration of an ancient art which has continued to exist as a technical craft: different ethics entirely from those firms who invite the public into their forges only to boost sales.

Direct contact between craftsman and customer is of great importance in this crafts field, more, perhaps, than any other. Few smiths belong to general craft associations and find formal exhibitions too art-orientated for their liking. Abhorring the social side of the craft associations, and the publicity, they remain the last bastions of all that the rural craftsmen stand for. They maintain a rich rapport with their clients, who are generally farmers or members of the local hunt or the 'big house'. Meeting a smith on his own ground can be a revelation – especially if the blacksmith is a woman. One shop has a mother and five daughters as blacksmiths!

F. C. Harriss of Witney assigns to his young daughter, Janet, the task of pumping the giant bellows when he is demonstrating the craft at steam engine rallies. Now the only smith in an area where there were once five, he covers a variety of work, repairing things from blanket factory machinery to engine boilers, as well as hand-forging shoes.

Not only the products, but also the method of producing power has changed in the blacksmith shops throughout England, but Hector Cole of Great Somerford in the famous Badminton horse country still works in the truly traditional manner, using hand-pumped bellows. Pieces are joined by fire-welding, riveting or bolting, never arc-welded. Gas welding is only resorted to where very concentrated heat is needed that cannot be achieved on the forge.

A Cotswold blacksmith, John McCormick, has just set off with anvil, full set of tools and a ton of coal, to equip a forge and train local men in the craft of shoeing at the first ever blacksmith's shop to be set up on the Indonesian island of Brunei, so that the Sultan may start up a polo club there.

Sean Black studied smithery under a government vocational training scheme and rescued a derelict forge in the Sussex countryside. Personifying the traditional image of the village blacksmith, he revived production of the local Pyecombe sheep crook, sometimes for use by shepherds, sometimes for symbolic use in churches. But orders take many forms – from delicate iron jewellery to robust staircases.

It is a popular misconception that it is only in recent years that the smith has turned his hand to making objects both decorative and functional, for many a church clock was the work of the village blacksmith, the original pioneer of engineering. Just how versatile and vital his work has been can best be summed up by one old smith's remarks:

> If old Hitler had known how dependent the aircraft industry was on the village blacksmith, he'd have bombed the lot of us – I've known when we've worked all through the night to get a job done for a ship lying 40 miles away. When I first started we repaired a lot of irons for legs of men injured in the Great War – we even made a wooden leg for one of the chaps.

Metrication has presented problems to the village smith. The steel industry seems to have cut down on the range of sizes, catering primarily for the standardized requirements of mass-production. Iron, as opposed to mild steel, is practically impossible to get. Resolute smiths, like Hector Cole, salvage and recycle old gates and railings to meet the demands of special orders where it is essential to use wrought-iron; whereas Garratt's of Sheffield say they wrought mild steel quite successfully, in exactly the same way as iron, preserving both the craftsmanship and non-corrosive properties by the final treatment of the finished product. Unprotected steel rusts rapidly and is usually treated with zinc-based paint.

Michael Roberts is one of the few – if not the only craftsman – to forge aluminium by hand. Britain was represented for the first time in 1974 by him and Alan Knight at Lindau in Germany, at the largest metalwork exhibition in Europe which is held every five years. Some measure of the competition can be gauged by the fact that from 1,800 entries submitted from eight countries, Michael produced six of the 170 items selected.

One of the largest firms specializing in high quality hand-forged ornamental wrought-ironwork and other metalwork is Richard Quinnell Ltd of Surrey, which has a productive staff of ten craftsmen.

Small workshops cannot cope with big projects so when twenty-two West Country blacksmiths staged an exhibition of wrought-ironwork at the Building Centre in London in 1966, and a Cornish smith was commissioned to make five large sets of gates and about 170 feet of railing for Virginia's National Memorial Park, the order had to be subcontracted to meet the time limit. Groups were formed in the five counties and a network plan for the production was evolved, with the help of COSIRA's design and planning services. Not only had the aim of introducing the skills of the craftsmen to eminent architects been achieved, but the major outcome was the formation of the Wessex Guild of Wrought-Ironwork Craftsmen.

Like the members of the Northumbria Guild, the smiths work at their own forges, using skills and tools which have remained unchanged for centuries. The guild promotes the smiths' work and ensures that the matters of pricing, delivery and documentation (in the case of export orders) are handled expeditiously, with a close watch on standards.

BELL-FOUNDING

The iron tongue of England's bells has spoken through the ages across city streets and country meadows, calling, warning, rejoicing and mourning. When a bell cracks it is melted and recast; the continuity is preserved; the same metal rings.

There are only two bell-foundries in the whole of England; each following the tradition of its early foundation. The bell shape, which was developed in the Middle Ages, has remained the same to this day, the only modifications being in the adjusting of the harmonics, but the founding process of "making by melting" still exacts the same skills. The foundries have to recruit and train their own craftsmen.

There are no short cuts in this craft industry, in which each bell is individually made. A core of brick is built up and a thick, messy mixture of sand, clay, horse manure and chopped hair or straw is plastered over it, moulded to the correct shape by hand, and smoothed to the right dimensions. Dried in the oven, it is coated with graphite and polished to a smooth finish. The cope, or outer shape, is similarly formed inside a cast-iron moulding-case, any inscription being impressed before drying out. *Closing down* is the process of lowering the cope over the core and securing the two moulds together. Casting is the actual pouring in of the molten metal (an alloy of approximately 77 per cent copper and 23 per cent tin) from the furnace on a gigantic ladle to run at exactly the right temperature into the space between the moulds. Cooling can take up to over a week. The bell is then cleaned of any adhering clay, or pared of excess metal, and is then ready for the intricate art of tuning.

Whitechapel Bell Foundry, employing thirty-six people, has a long and interesting history. Recent evidence asserts their foundation as 1420; but through the incorporation and acquisition of other foundries, notably Rudhalls of Gloucester, it can claim an indirect succession from about 1270. Like other crafts, the founders' skills were utilized in the war-torn years, casting cannon for the Tudor navy and precision casting for the Admiralty in 1940. Breaking its tradition of casting each bell individually, Whitechapel cast the 2,400 replicas of America's Liberty Bell — one for each month of freedom — in clay moulds round wax patterns, as was done over a thousand years ago.

The Taylor Bell Foundry of Loughborough can trace its business back to the mid-fourteenth century, acquiring and subsequently dropping clock-making on the way. Many noble and famous peals punctuate their order books, including 'Great Paul' of St Paul's, the largest bell in the British Commonwealth, cast in 1881.

Lack of space prohibits the inclusion of the craftwork involved in church bell hanging, a specialist trade in which fittings and frames, wheels and headstocks are made.

13

Gold and Silversmithing

"A distinguished craftsman who has attained to a splendid position among the silversmiths of our age", was how Leslie Durbin was introduced at the presentation of honorary degrees. His sensitive skills earned him indefinite leave from the RAF to make the gold and silver-work on the famous Sword of Stalingrad, King George VI's gift, on behalf of the British people, to the heroic defenders of that city; Professor Gleadowe, the designer, and Leslie Durbin, the craftsman, were both honoured by the King on its completion, receiving the Royal Victorian Order. His fine craftsmanship served the country at that time in less auspicious but monumentally important circumstances when he supplied the Air Force with delicately constructed models.

"All my work," he says, "seems to be unusual and for unusual people," and adds that his small workshop where he is aided by two assistants will "take on anything from a medal to a church screen". He has taught the traditional skills to students at the Royal College of Art and to four of his apprentices who have now launched out on their own. His respect for the Goldsmiths' Company, and theirs for him, is mutual.

The Worshipful Company of Goldsmiths has given its patronage and support to craftsmen since 1180; and has provided since 1300 the most ancient form of consumer protection by hallmarking gold, silverware, and (from 1st January 1975) platinum. An international convention on the control and marking of precious metals came into operation in the United Kingdom on 1st June 1976, open only to those countries with an independent assay system; hallmarking practices differ between countries so EEC directives have yet to be ratified. Changes are inevitable: one which saw the end of an 800-year-old tradition was the first-ever selling exhibition staged in 1975 at the Goldsmiths' Hall, when over 2,000 pieces were exhibited by some 300 silversmiths and jewellers.

The company promotes research through the Technical Advisory Committee, forming the first centre to combine both design and research in 1946, following trade meetings called by the Goldsmiths' Company. The resultant Design and Research Centre (DRC) was initially financed by the company and trade associations but was compelled three years later to become a section of the Jewellery and Silverware Council, set up under government legislation. The Council was dissolved in 1952 and grants diminished as a consequence. Re-organized, the DRC is a non-profit distributing body; ploughing back its income into developing its work towards improved design; promoting and funding its main design exhibition and competition projects in association with the Design Council; and fulfilling many of its research aspirations in a practical way in close co-operation with the Goldsmiths' Company. Covering the whole spectrum of the craft-based industry, membership of the DRC consists of approximately 40 per cent who are hand craftsmen or designer-craftsmen jewellers and silversmiths, who prove a very active section indeed.

Certainly the news bulletins issued by the company's Technical Advisory Service are appreciated by progressive craftsmen who wish to keep abreast of new ideas and take advantage of the technical developments which enable the craftsman, as manufacturer, to benefit from industry's experiments.

Whilst most designer-craftsmen see their role and that of industry's as incompatible, several silversmiths have achieved success by providing a design service for industry. This enables the silversmith to make the one-off pieces which a craftsman likes to do, and thus to realize his own potential, whilst releasing him from personally having to repeat certain lines to establish a commercially viable concern, but extending his responsibility so that he becomes conversant with factory techniques, while his own facility to use hand-skills and handle numerous materials enables him to design and produce accurate prototypes for subsequent manufacture. The value of a craftsman-designer, what he does and how he can contribute to the design of the product, can only be appreciated through closer liaison between crafts and industry and could benefit both. After all, artists earn commissions to design all kinds of things from seed packets and stationery to silk scarves. The essential interplay between the design and the materials is denied to the designer whose drawings are given to someone else to make up, creating the schism between designer and craftsman which, so many insist, exists in modern silversmithing. It would be interesting to know how many industrialists ever attend the important craft exhibitions!

The Cotswolds is a region traditionally associated with fine architectural craftsmanship. Chipping Campden developed as an enclave of the art-crafts and became the home of the famous Guild of Handicraft when C. R. Ashbee and his East End craftsmen descended upon it in the 1880s.

David Hart, whose grandfather took over the workshop after Ashbee's guild broke up in 1908, says that the type of article produced has changed drastically over the last five years from the ecclesiastical work, in which his grandfather almost entirely specialized, to an output of 90 per cent domestic silverware. It is a small workshop (of some four or five gold- and silversmiths) with a great reputation and has always taken apprentices.

Robert Welch established his silversmithing workshop in a silk-mill also previously occupied by one of the Ashbee Guild handcrafts. Production is purposely kept small and specialized, the pieces are made from start to finish by the same craftsman. Robert Welch is also an eminently successful industrial designer.

Rarely can the history of a country's crafts be divorced from its social customs and politics: Stuart silver was initially regarded as monetary reserve to pay war expenses; consequently little ornamentation was needed on the plate, which invariably ended up in the melting-pot to help out with the royal house-keeping. Cromwell further reduced England's royal plate by sheer destruction. The Restoration, however, embraced the art crafts and the silversmiths were patronized. To them Charles II turned for the exquisite gifts which he lavished upon his mistresses: Nell Gwyn received a silver bed.

The decline of some ceremonial functions and the rise of others was reflected in the changes in the type of objects produced by the smiths. But it was the attempt to recapture elements of the design of the medieval age, when craftsmanship was worthy of its material, that made the next noticeable impact on silversmithery. The Morris doctrines were taking shape through the initiative of guilds formed at the turn of the century, endeavouring to reunite designer and smith. Even industrialized Sheffield had its Art Craft Guild and Birmingham its Guild of Handicraft, which flourished during the emancipated Edwardian era.

It was at this time that silver was acquiring colour; although the exacting techniques of enamelling have obviously excluded many from attempting it. Enamel is an unpredictable material under stress, and the process of enamelling can involve more than a dozen separate firings. One of the few exponents of this technically difficult craft is Gerald Benney, whose quarter of a century of silver-smithing was honoured by a one-man exhibition at Goldsmiths' Hall, where the public was able to appreciate what could be the rebirth of an art as his enamelled silver was displayed. Whereas the enamelling process was painstakingly researched, his surface texturing developed almost accidentally. Silver plate struck unintentionally with a chipped hammer would have sent a lesser artist into a frenzy, but Gerald Benney's interest was aroused, and this opened up a wider spectrum from which he has developed a whole range of refined surface markings; a technique that has been enthusiastically adopted by other silversmiths.

The emergence of newly independent countries and an upsurge of university buildings in the 1960s created a new heyday for silver design; commissions for academic and civic institutions outweighed those of the old patron, the Church. And now, with an economic depression and monetary values inflated, people are investing in top quality well-designed gold and silverware, enjoying its beauty and confident of its assured and increasing value as an heirloom for their children.

Silversmithery, traditionally a craft of the city, with its concentrated population and network of retail outlets, has, of late, found its way into the country. Philip Lowery works in a truly rural environment, his cottage workshop lies at the end of a bramble-tangled farm track, the sole survivor of the Taena Community which started off as a religious fraternity under the shadow of the venerable Benedictine abbey. Instead of decrying public taste and industrial waste he sees both the craftworker and industry having their own place in an advanced society and admires the really excellent results which industry can achieve. Being of a practical nature, Philip makes a tool to fit the job in hand; "I started with three hammers," he says, "I now have over eighty. I have made, exchanged and inherited most of the heads, and many have changed their shape during their working life here." Angela, his wife, is a woodcarver and is able to help with modelling the wood for the piece he later casts in grey iron before he uses the hammer on the silver.

An essential feature of the silversmith's craft is the manner in which the silver is raised to a three-dimensional effect by means of shaped metal stakes and various raising and planishing hammers. There appears to have been no appreciable change in this aspect of the craft since the Bronze Age, therefore silversmithery remains one of the very few handcrafts where a basic material undergoes its major change of form without the intervention of the machine.

SOCIETIES

WORSHIPFUL COMPANY OF BLACKSMITHS, 41 Tabernacle Street, London EC2. Tel: 01–251 0203

THE WORSHIPFUL COMPANY OF FARRIERS, Clerk and Registrar: F. E. Birch, 3 Hamilton Road, Cockfosters, Barnet, Herts. EN4 9EU. Tel: 01–449 5491
Apprenticeship and registration schemes for smiths specializing in shoeing. The company is actively engaged in continuing the improvement of standards of farriery by means of education, promotion of competitions and the award of medals.

NORTHUMBRIA GUILD OF WROUGHT IRON CRAFTSMEN, Sec: I. Atkinson, Hallgarth House, Hallgarth Street, Durham. Tel: Durham 3511
Enquiries through the secretary. Restoration work is one of the guild's important activities. All items thoroughly protected against rust, inspected by an officer of the guild and stamped.

THE GUILD OF WROUGHT IRONWORK CRAFTSMEN OF WESSEX, Sec: Angus Newton, County Hall, Exeter, Devon. Tel: Exeter 77977
Enquiries to the secretary, who reserves the right to distribute work among guild members at his discretion to maintain the standards of workmanship and ensure that delivery dates are met. Each article bought through the

guild is thoroughly protected against rust and other deterioration, inspected by an officer of the guild, and is accompanied by a certificate of origin.

BRISTOL CRAFT JEWELLERS GUILD, Harold Hedges, 47 Princess Victoria Street, Clifton, Bristol
The three other members are: Nick Croome, Carol Mayne and Dick Richards.

DESIGN AND RESEARCH CENTRE FOR THE GOLD, SILVER AND JEWELLERY INDUSTRIES, St Dunstan's House, Carey Lane, London EC2V 8AE. Tel: 01–606 7260
The DRC represents the whole spectrum of these craft-based industries by encouraging research in the development and application of new manufacturing methods and materials, and serving the interests of designers, craftsmen, traders and teachers by exhibitions, lectures, seminars, competitions and publicity through its regional centres. An advisory service and record of designers are available. Membership fees are graduated according to size of firm. Technical reports are available to members upon application, particulars are published in the newsheet.

WORSHIPFUL COMPANY OF GOLDSMITHS, Goldsmiths' Hall, Foster Lane, London EC2. Tel: 01–606 8971
Hallmarks precious metals through its assay offices: Goldsmiths' Hall, Gutter Lane, London EC2; 137 Portobello Road, Sheffield; Newhall Street, Birmingham 3 (and Edinburgh). Promotes research through TAC. A leaflet on hallmarking is obtainable from the Assay Office of Great Britain on receipt of a SAE: Assay Office, Goldsmith's Hall, Gutter Lane, London EC2V 8AQ.

TECHNICAL ADVISORY COMMITTEE (TAC), Directors: P. Gainsbury, Worshipful Company of Goldsmiths, Central House, Whitechapel High Street, London EC1. Tel: 01–283 1030 ext. 219
Publishes special reports, bulletins and a newsheet.

PUBLICATIONS

Gem Craft, published by Model and Allied Publications Ltd P.O. Box 35, Bridge Street, Hemel Hempstead, Herts. HP1 1EE
Competitions and exhibitions. *Gem Craft* is the only monthly magazine in the country dealing in depth with lapidary and allied crafts.

The Convention on the Control and Marking of Precious Metals is available from Government Bookshops.

IRON AND METALWORK

H. AMOS AND SON, Heddon on the Wall, Newcastle upon Tyne.
Member Northumbria Guild of Wrought-Iron Craftsmen.

C. A. BARTLETT, The Forge, Coln St Aldwyns, nr Cirencester, Glos. Tel: Coln St Aldwyns 346
General iron and metalwork to order. Range extends from fire-baskets and guards, gates and weather-vanes to two-wheel trailers. Agricultural and general implement repairs.

L. AND J. BATY, Hexham
Member Northumbria Guild of Wrought-Iron Craftsmen.

N. A. BIRD, The Forge, Radway Street, Bishopsteignton, Teignmouth, Devon
Member Guild of Wrought-Ironwork Craftsmen of Wessex.

SEAN BLACK, The Forge, Pyecombe, Sussex. Tel: Hassocks 2272
Ironwork and metal sculpture. Extensive range from the famous Pyecombe shepherd's crook to wrought-iron staircases and jewellery.

T. E. BROWN AND SON, Dragonville
Member Northumbria Guild of Wrought-Iron Craftsmen.

M. J. CLARK, FWCF. The Forge, Great Haseley, Oxford. Tel: Great Milton 25
General smith.

P. CLARKE AND SON LTD, Harepath Road, Seaton, Devon
Member Guild of Wrought-Ironwork Craftsmen of Wessex.

J. COE, Fitzhead Forge, Fitzhead, Taunton, Somerset
Member Guild of Wrought-Ironwork Craftsmen of Wessex.

HECTOR COLE, The Mead, Great Somerford, Chippenham, Wilts.
Ironworker using hand-pumped bellows forge Hearth furniture, fire-baskets, chestnut-roasters, light-fittings, stands, brackets, gates, etc., and repairs to antiques in most metals. Exhibitor at Badminton Horse Trials.

T. H. CONIBEAR, 3 Gregory Terrace, Hartland, Bideford, Devon
Member Guild of Wrought-Ironwork Craftsmen of Wessex.

G. P. COX, Giltina Forge, Lower Southayes, Dunkeswell, nr Honiton, Devon. Tel: Luppitt 632
Commissioned work only: speciality line in bed-heads.

W. F. DAY, The Forge, West Monkton, Taunton, Somerset
Member Guild of Wrought-Ironwork Craftsmen of Wessex.

LUCA D'ONOFRIO, Shepherd's Close, Kingston Stert, Chinnor, Oxford OX9 4NL
Craftsman specializing in wrought-ironwork. Range is extensive – gates, chairs, tables, candlesticks, etc. to special order.

W. GARRATT AND SON LTD, Classic Forge, Kirk Street, Sheffield S4 7JX. Tel: (0742) 77382

In addition to the normal run of architectural metalwork, this company produces wrought-ironwork. Mild steel is wrought in the same way as wrought-iron, with a final treatment which preserves both the craftsmanship and also the non-corrosive properties of the material.

GLENDALE FORGE (F. M. TUCKER), Glendale, Monk Street, nr Thaxted, Essex. Tel: Thaxted 466

A small forge of four craftsmen whose range extends from producing hand-wrought ironwork, like that made by Jean Tijou in the eighteenth century, to the more progressive work demanded by modern architects in forged sculptural design. In addition, they produce a complete range of black-smith's tools for the artist-craftsmen and educational authorities for use in schools and colleges. Apprentices under their own special scheme.

GOMMES FORGE LTD, Foundry Lane, Loosley Row, Princes Risborough, Bucks. Tel: Princes Risborough 5546

A very small family business with a wide range of work, including fireplaces. Many unusual commissions for both home and overseas buyers.

F. R. GRANTHAM AND SONS, The Forge, Ashurst Wood, East Grinstead, Sussex RH19 3TQ

Designers and makers specializing in traditional hand-forged ironwork. Bronze medal presented by the Worshipful Company of Blacksmiths, 1959; silver medal for outstanding merit, 1966. Member of the Guild of Wrought-Ironwork Craftsmen of Wessex.

J. L. J. GREENSLADE, The Forge, Pennymoor, Tiverton, Devon.
Member Guild of Wrought-Ironwork Craftsmen of Wessex.

W. R. HALL, The Forge, Great Barrington, Glos. Tel: Great Barrington 219
General smith; wrought-ironwork to order. Agricultural repairs.

F. C. HARRISS, Newland, Witney, Oxon.
General smith; hand-forged horse-shoes. Ornamental ironwork, machinery and engine boiler repairs. Mr Harriss has won numerous prizes for shoeing and ornamental ironwork and has demonstrated his craft in front of the Queen at Windsor Great Park. Member Worshipful Company of Farriers.

TONY HODGSON, The Forge, 23 Marshland Street, Terrington St Clement, Kings Lynn, Norfolk. Tel: Terrington St Clement 361

Winning the National Championship of Great Britain in wrought-ironwork, Tony Hodgson was brought up as a smith from two generations of blacksmiths and specializes in genuine hand-forged work. A wide range of work, exhibited at the main Royal Shows and available from stock, is extended to meet individual special orders. Recent commissions have included the renovation of all the gates at Sennowe Park in Norfolk.

JOHN HORLICK, 69 Didbrook, Cheltenham, Glos. GL54 5PF. Tel: Toddington 325
Ornamental and general metalwork. Member of the Craftsmen of Gloucestershire.

H. AND J. HORROBIN, Crafts Workshop. Roadwater, Watchet, Somerset TA23 0RB. Tel: Washford 342
Ornamental ironwork produced by two craftsmen: mainly hearth furniture, and domestic fittings, ranging from decorative wall-plaques to church candelabras. Open for commissions. Member of county guilds and Society of Designer Craftsmen.

HYDERS LTD, Plaxtol, nr Sevenoaks, Kent TN15 0QR. Tel: Plaxtol 215/6
Specialists in hand-forged wrought-ironwork. Artistic metal workers. Comprehensive range: balustrades, wellheads, gates, garden and house furniture, electrical fittings, firemesh curtains; everything from a weather-vane to a royal coat of arms attractively displayed in extensive showrooms. Many commissions for restoration of old wrought-iron gates and railings for historically important buildings.

IRONCRAFTS (STOTFOLD) LTD, Rooktree Forge, Baldock Road, Stotfold, Hitchin, Herts. SG5 4PA Tel: Hitchin 730671
A relatively small firm producing high quality ironwork: memorial gates, spiral staircases, balustrading, gates etc.

G. HARRISON, Downs Cottage, South Cerney, Glos. Tel: South Cerney 416
Ironwork: fire-baskets and hearth furniture.

JOHN STUART JACKSON, 174 Allendale Avenue, Aspley, Notts.
Sculptor working in stainless steel. Exhibited in London and Paris, one sculpture purchased by Jamaican High Commission.

H. JORDAN, The Forge, Commercial Road, Penryn, Cornwall
Member Guild of Wrought-Ironwork Craftsmen of Wessex.

P. KITCHIN, Graythorpes
Member Northumbria Guild of Wrought-Iron Craftsmen.

ALAN KNIGHT, Mullion Cottage, 27 Licky Square, Rednal, Birmingham
Ironworker. Member the Craftsmen of Gloucestershire.

R. L. LAMBOURNE, The Homestead, Marsh Gibbon, nr Bicester, Oxon. OX6 0AP. Tel: Stratton Audley 284
Smith producing wrought-iron work and carrying out the ancient craft of hand working metal. Using age-old methods and skills, both traditional and modern designs are created. Ecclesiastical commissions, hearth and door furniture, weather-vanes, gates: the range is fully comprehensive.

F. LANDON, The Forge, Mount Pleasant Road, Jarvis Brook, Crowborough, Sussex. Tel: Crowborough 3789
   Ornamental and general smith.

G. E. LAWRENCE, The Forge, Church Lane, Frithelstock, Torrington, Devon
   Member Guild of Wrought-Ironwork Craftsmen of Wessex.

LLAD ENGINEERING (JOHN DALL), 19 Middlegates, St Agnes, Cornwall. Tel: St Agnes 2872
   A local engineer and blacksmith producing a wide range of work from commissioned ornamental ironwork to marine and agricultural repairs. Metal relief plaques for the fine art gift trade. Well-known model-maker.

J. S. LUNN AND SON, Red Row, Morpeth, Northumberland
   Member Northumbria Guild of Wrought-Iron Craftsmen.

J. F. MCCORMICK, Forge House, Daglingworth, Glos. Tel: Cirencester 2486
   High-class ornamental iron, brass and copper work. Shoeing smith. Welding and fabrication engineer.

J. MALE AND SON, St Buryan, Penzance, Cornwall
   Member Guild of Wrought-Ironwork Craftsmen of Wessex.

MERCER AND THOMAS, The Mill Forge, Bibury, Cirencester, Glos. Tel: Bibury 391
   High-class shoeing smiths. Frank Mercer made all the shoes for the British team when they won the Gold Medal at the Mexico Olympics. Wrought-ironwork to order.

H. G. MIDDLETON AND SONS, 31 Broadstone, Dartmouth, Devon
   Member Guild of Wrought-Ironwork Craftsmen of Wessex.

W. H. MOULSLEY, Petrockstow Forge, Petrockstow, Okehampton, Devon EX20 3HW. Tel: Hatherleigh 358
   Quality ornamental ironwork and general smith. Restoration work for churches and houses, contractors' tools maintained, builders' ironwork, agricultural repairs. Member Guild of Wrought-Ironwork Craftsmen of Wessex.

A. V. NICHOLLS, The Old Smithy, Lower Swell, Stow-on-the-Wold, Glos. GL54 1LF. Tel: Stow-on-the-Wold 30041
   Specialist in antique and modern wrought-iron. Range includes Adam-style steel grates, light fittings in bronze and brass, and water clocks, as well as the usual run of ornamental ironwork. Very specialized work, to special commission both at home and overseas, includes a wind dial, Haddon Hall and Louis XIV-style wall-lights, and brass Queen Anne lanterns.

W. NORRIS, Trebyan Forge, Lanhydrock, Bodmin, Cornwall

Smith producing wrought-iron work, ecclesiastical, architectural and domestic metalwork, restoration and répoussé. Member Guild of Wrought-Ironwork Craftsmen of Wessex.

S. C. PEARCE, AND SONS LTD, Bredfield Ironworks, Woodbridge, Suffolk IP13 6AE. Tel: Woodbridge 2514
High quality hand-forged gates and other ironwork. Exhibitions have included the Chelsea Flower Show, and HM Queen Elizabeth the Queen Mother counted among the customers. Contractors to Department of the Environment, County Councils and leading landscape gardeners.

J. T. PEGG AND SONS LTD, 29 Park Road, Aldeburgh, Suffolk IP15 5EU. Tel: Aldeburgh 2281
A family firm whose work of three generations is to be seen in churches, hotels and many public places. Range includes the *de luxe* peacock fire-screen which won first prize for design workmanship at the Royal Show in 1964, unique house signs, antique doors, hearths, garden and house furniture and fittings. The firm's own retail shop, Ironcraft, is at 187 High Street, Aldeburgh.

D. M. PROCTOR, The Elstree Forge, 21 High Street, Elstree, Herts. WD6 3EZ. Tel: 01–953 2553
Quality ironwork forged to customer's requirements. The traditional arts of the blacksmith are enlarged upon to meet the exacting demands of modern designs. Member National Master Farriers, Blacksmiths and Agricultural Engineers Association.

WALENTY PYTEL, Terrace Hall, Woolhope, Hereford. Tel: Fownhope 373
Sculptures of birds and animals in welded steel. Private commissions undertaken.

RICHARD QUINNELL LTD, Rowhurst Forge, Oxsholt Road, Leatherhead, Surrey KT22 0EN. Tel: Leatherhead 75148/9
Master craftsmen working in iron. One of the largest firms specializing in ornamental, hand-forged wrought-ironwork of the highest quality. Commissions also undertaken for work of widely differing kinds in other metals. Stock items such as flower pedestals for churches, fire-baskets and hearth furnishings are available. Recent important commissions range from a sculptured steel ventilator for Queens College, Oxford, to a heraldic four-poster bed. Restoration work includes the Venetian gates at Syon Park and the 'Golden Gates' at Ascot Race-course. Contractors to Government departments, local authorities and leading architects.

J. RATHBONE, MBE, FWCF, AND SONS, The Forge, Kingham, Oxon. Tel: Kingham 431
A family business comprising father (awarded MBE for his services as smith and three times champion blacksmith of Great Britain) and his sons – many times prize-winners themselves. Highest quality ornamental ironwork to order. Important commissions have included the gates of the Royal

Enclosure at Ascot. Agricultural engineering and welding.

MICHAEL E. ROBERTS, Sudgrove House, Miserden, nr Stroud, Glos. Tel: Miserden 244 (Workshop)
Hand-made iron and metalwork. Only known hand-forger of aluminium. Represented England, with Alan Knight, in the Lindau Lake Constance Exhibition, the largest of its kind in Europe. Member of the Craftsmen of Gloucestershire.

H. ROBINSON, Longhoughton, Alnwick, Northumberland
Member Northumbria Guild of Wrought-Iron Craftsmen.

W. ROBINSON, Longhoughton, Alnwick, Northumberland.
Member Northumbria Guild of Wrought-Iron Craftsmen.

A. AND J. ROGERSON, Stocksfield, Northumberland
Member Northumbria Guild of Wrought-Iron Craftsmen.

R. STEPHENSON, Beamish
Member Northumbria Guild of Wrought-Iron Craftsmen.

E. TAYLOR, Hetton le Hole
Member Northumbria Guild of Wrought-Iron Craftsmen.

W. R. TOMS, 11 Tywardreath Highway, Par, Cornwall. Tel: Par 2658
General blacksmith (forge at Castledore, Par): ornamental ironwork includes gates and railings, hearth furniture, flower-baskets and boat-anchors; produces new and repairs old agricultural implements; special attention is given to riveted work, as opposed to the more general welded type.

R. TRINDER AND SON, The Forge, Filkins, Lechlade, Glos. Tel: Lechlade 52244
All kinds of ironwork, balustrades, railings, fire-baskets, hearth furniture, pedestals, candlesticks and weather-vanes. Commissions are dealt with promptly by this father and son partnership in traditional manner.

LUCIEN VARWELL, Bounds Forge, Ebbesbourne Wake, Salisbury, Wilts. Tel: Broad Chalke 288
Fire-guards, hearth and door furniture, brackets, lamps, etc. Member Guild of Wrought-Ironwork Craftsmen of Wessex.

WENDRON FORGE LTD, Wendron, Helston, Cornwall. Tel: Helston 3531
A firm of designer-craftsmen producing a range of clocks, and stainless steel pictures made by screen-printing and chemical catalysis, special commissions have included large copper-etched wall murals and small club plaques. There is also a blacksmith in a 'preserved' forge who works on a bespoke basis to customers' orders. Wooden furniture is also produced on a small scale.

W. S. WHITE, Haggerston
Member Northumbria Guild of Wrought-Iron Craftsmen

A. WILSON AND SON, Millfield
Member Northumbria Guild of Wrought-Iron Craftsmen.

DEREK WEBB, 1 Vines Row, Fairford, Glos. Tel: Fairford 712674
  Ornamental ironwork.

BELL FOUNDRIES AND HANGER

JOHN TAYLOR AND CO. The Bell Foundry, Loughborough, Leics. LE11 1AR.
Tel: Loughborough 2241
  Bells across the world, from York Minster to Harvard University, and
  Britain's gift of the Canberra Carillon to the Australian people, have been
  cast by this old established foundry.

WHITECHAPEL BELL FOUNDRY LTD, 32 and 34 Whitechapel Road, London E1
1DY. Tel: 01–247 2599
  Out of the famous bells that have been cast at this notable foundry are Big
  Ben and the Liberty Bell.

F. A. WHITE, Appleton, Abingdon, Oxon OX13 5JJ. Tel: Cumnor 2549
  Church bell-hanger whose craft embraces lowering the bells and sending to
  the foundry for tuning or re-casting, making and repairing fittings (bell-
  frames of wood or metal) and all supporting ironwork necessary to the working of a ringing bell.

JEWELLERY

"I taught myself metalwork," says Helen Newman, "applying principles of design acquired for use in other techniques," but she admits
that the technical side is very involved and time-consuming. Certainly
the importance of a knowledge of metal chemistry cannot be underestimated. Under the all-embracing titles of metalworker and jeweller,
Helen covers a wide range of artistic interpretation through a broad
field of design in painting, sculpture, textiles, collage and wrought
metals. Like most artists, she enjoys a challenge, and will cheerfully
make a bishop's ring, a film star's brass bra and belt, a casing for a vin-
tage motor or a set of dress jewellery.

Precious metals have been fashioned into jewellery since the Celts
bedecked themselves with ornaments as an expression of their wealth.
The opulent Romans preferred the more dramatic designs, yet most of
their pieces served a functional as well as decorative purpose, for the
loosely flowing togas were caught in place with bold brooch-like fastenings: whereas the farming Anglo-Saxons produced quite delicate and

sensitive trinkets, the Birdlip mirror being an outstanding example of the craftsmanship of that period.

Cire perdue (lost-wax casting) is a revival craft which is gaining popularity with jewellers. It is known to have been practised by the Incas and was used extensively as a method of casting medallions and brooches by the Romans. Basically, it is a technique by which a model is made in a special wax which is placed into a plaster of Paris mould and heated. The wax is lost during the heating process (hence the name), leaving a faithful replica of the model cast into the plaster mould. Molten metal is then poured into the mould and takes on the shape and characteristic marking of the original model. Modelling of the wax itself is delicate work and the whole process more exacting than a simple description implies.

After the Norman Conquest there was a marked degree of French influence in the design of the jewellery worn by the English; immigrant craftsmen in later centuries brought their techniques and skills with them and furthered the continental influence. But always, with a total disregard for what was fashionable in any period, there existed the lucky charms and amulets such as those worn by primitive people as talismans against the evil eye. Acknowledgment has already been made to the long-standing belief that the blacksmith was endowed with special powers and imparted a measure of this mystique into the things he fashioned. It has been recorded that the makers of horseshoe-nails always dined at a separate table at the general nailmakers' annual dinners.

Romany gypsies, epitomizing mystery, magic and superstition, traded in love potions, spells and charms and in the fifteenth century they fashioned Toltek horseshoe-nail pendants and jewellery as symbols of chastity. If the recipient of such jewellery proved to be an unfaithful lover, the nails would straighten out and pierce them through the heart. Jean Davis has become famous for her intricate jewellery fashioned from genuine craft-forged horseshoe-nails. The design permutations are almost endless and other components such as wire, beads, nuts, buttons, washers and tube are incorporated in the wide range. The results are attractive and sell easily. Jean sees it as an ideal craft for revival, although it is hard on the hands, and the horseshoe-nails need immediate special treatment to stop them rusting. There is a strong humanitarian element in Jean Davies Craft Ltd; socially handicapped people, particularly ex-criminals, are taught the skills and become involved in the artistic activities.

Jet, a material favoured for personal ornament since the Bronze Age, was also considered a potent charm against the evil eye and hung on the witch-posts of Yorkshire houses. Whitby jet, a kind of lignite or anthracite, with a greater tenacity and elasticity than other kinds, is the finest in the world. When it was discovered that this hard, coal-like substance could be turned on a lathe, the first jet workshop was founded at the beginning of the nineteenth century. By 1873 no fewer than 200 were employing some 1,400 men and boys. Its zenith was reached when Queen Victoria, after the death of the Prince Consort, decreed that no jewellery other than that fashioned from jet should be worn by the ladies presented to her. French jet, bog oak and vulcanite (a mixture of India rubber and sulphur) vied with Yorkshire's coastal fossil, but none could match the brilliance of that from Whitby.

Roy Jay is the sole surviving craftsman of the jet industry, which collapsed dramatically after Victoria's reign. He served four years apprenticeship to the last of the old remaining jet workers who died before Roy could officially complete his extensive training. Having acquired the basic skills by then, Roy is conscious of the vocational dedication required in preserving the old and important craft, and manages a steady output using traditional methods and mixing his own polishes.

Rock-hunting has suddenly become a national pastime, almost an obsession; yet it is only recently that England has looked at her minerals with a jeweller's eye – whereas mineral exhibitions have been staged on the Continent for many years. Organic materials are now accounting for a high proportion of the substances used to make modern jewellery. Tumbling, cutting, faceting and fixing on findings have given rise to an extraordinary number of lapidary suppliers, courses and publications. *Gem Craft*, the most comprehensive magazine dealing with all aspects of lapidary, mounted Britain's first exhibition, to which over 8,000 enthusiasts flocked within three days.

The official information centre for the jewellery and allied industries is the Jewellery Information Centre but this deals with "mainly Press information and is not really concerned with individual craftsmen".

The British Jewellery and Giftware Federation Ltd, originally formed as the British Joint Association of Gold, Silver and Allied Trades, comprises six trade associations including the British Jewellers' Association. Craftsmen engaged in the jewellery and art metalware sections of the BJA are usually members of the National Union of Gold, Silver and Allied Trades. Essentially a manufacturer's association, the BJA also makes awards to individual jewellers.

Harold Hedges, who earned a BJA award for his work while in London, has recently, with three fellow craftsmen, formed the Bristol Craft Jewellers' Guild. To say that Bristol could compete with the capital as the country's craft jewellery centre seems a somewhat sweeping prediction, but is justified by one of the major bullion dealers being convinced of a marked movement of craft dealers from London to the West Country. Harold works in all the precious metals, but delights in 18-carat gold. His commissions have ranged from the beautiful to the bizarre; from a sapphire-studded silver tiara to human teeth set in rings.

For all but the top names, those who make jewellery, like craftsmen in other fields, have to make a continual compromise between the inexpensive pieces, relatively easy and quick to make and sell readily – the 'bread and butter' lines – and those which exact every ounce of their artistry and skill. Sameer Bowyer lets off his creative steam by producing some flamboyant ornamentation which, he says, will probably never sell but serves as "an eye-catcher". He enjoys designing pieces with dramatic appeal and has made all the jewellery for Alvin Stardust. Rings seem to be the most popular item, accounting for 50 per cent of Sameer's output; with bracelets 25 per cent; pendants and necklaces 15 per cent; and ear-rings 10 per cent.

For those who work exclusively in gold and silver the capital outlay is astronomical: some thousands of pounds are tied up with stock materials of various shapes and sizes: in sheet or tube; in the square or in the round; in wire or grain. Gold may have to be held in various carat values, and possibly colours. On top of which is the expense of adequate security precautions – by no means a cheap venture. There may be some crumbs of consolation in the fact that if a piece does not sell it can be recycled. Until January 1975 it was not legally possible to use a precious with a non-precious metal. Silver, for instance, could not be described as silver unless it was hallmarked, and could not be assayed if used with a non-precious metal. Now this obstacle is out of the way, jewellery can be made using titanium and 'a silver-coloured metal'.

Whereas the intrinsic value of precious jewellery is embodied in the raw materials, the other form of personal decoration, medals, are fashioned almost as a token issue; the notable exception being the Victoria Cross, hand-fashioned by craftsmen jewellers from Russian guns captured during the Crimean War, the metal having been kept by the Mint.

Jewellery created to express nothing other than great wealth and representing investment value is rarely seen; too valuable to wear, the pieces are hidden in a bank vault, with a duplicate copy in paste for the owner to wear. Such articles are usually made to hold priceless gems and the smithwork becomes an unobtrusive setting for them. Modern craft jewellers are aiming at more congruity between materials and composition, but British pearls, prized since the Phoenicians discovered the wealth of our fresh waters, although studded in crown regalia across the length and breadth of Europe, almost always stand on their own, strung together as a necklace.

Bill Abernethy is the only full-time professional pearl-fisher in Europe; indeed, as the East turns to a more lucrative and less hazardous mode of extractive industry on the rich oil-fields, he may be the only one in the world. The Uhio mussel-pearl yielded from British rivers was traditionally a feature of Scottish jewellery, but met fierce competition from the great Japanese pearl-farming industry. The cultured pearl swamped the world market and created such a stir in the 1920s that the London Chamber of Commerce founded its Pearl and Precious Stone Laboratory in Hatton Garden. Simulation of the pearl has developed over the years in this country into an acceptable, and certainly plausible, substitute for the real thing, although this is not entirely a new thing, for two hundred years ago Thames fishermen were encouraging a lively trade in the sale of "fish-scales from which to make beads".

So many factors can influence a craftsman's method of production; often he tries to work to an ideal rather than a realistic situation. For a designer-craftsman to survive, let alone prosper, he must find which market-place suits his personality and how best he can apply his particular skills. Having completed a lengthy training, which can often be rated alongside that of the medical profession, he is then faced with the question of how to find a slot into which his trained talent will fit, invariably this results in adapting to the situation in which he finds himself, which is often different from that for which he trained.

Duncan James, like many other craftsmen, works in relative isolation and acknowledges that as a result the isolated artist has special difficulties, so there is a degree of subjectivity in any one person's remarks but, in this case, they reflect the tenor of remarks made by many others who also say that many craftsmen use the term *hand-made* as if it somehow dignifies the work and should automatically command a higher price. A long and involved treatise could be written expounding the limitations, meaning and qualification for, both the terms *hand-made* and *craft*, an argument by no means confined to jewellery. Suffice it to say that the ethics or desirability or sensibility of using the terms can safely be left to the integrity of a sensitive artist who will not resort to mass-production, the very antithesis of craftwork; so it is up to the individual to decide upon his position in a money-orientated society. Duncan James says:

> Both terms, can be applied to the more expensive items stocked in any High Street jeweller's. Craftsmen in the trade at Hatton Garden, for instance, could teach some so-called craft jewellers great *depth* of skill. The difference, however, lies in *breadth* of skill. The jeweller working on his own must embrace many skills.

The difference therefore lies between the jeweller who specializes within the trade, and the artist-craftsman who designs and makes his own work. How to apportion the time between the two aspects is governed by the individual's economic position. Work entirely composed of unique designs means limited output and high prices – so he is ruled by his client's purse. Also, Duncan makes a further point:

> I think it a shame *not* to reproduce a good jewellery design a few times at

least, after all there are a lot of people in the world. Repetition also gives one a chance to perfect every aspect and get structural and aesthetic proportions exactly right. But I only repeat a design which qualifies on a variety of counts.

There is an encouraging swing towards craft jewellery, which seems to be the public's way of expressing discontent with the quality and design of the mass-produced pieces, and there is some evidence that it is the artist-craftsman who now represents the contemporary scene in jewellery, and that where he goes in terms of design, the trade manufacturers are endeavouring to follow. Levelled against this, however, is the feeling that craft jewellery is being elevated out of all proportion from its natural function to become fine art. Many craftsmen feel strongly on this point and whilst they admire the genuine artistry and skill involved they see the fragile and sometimes virtually unwearable pieces receiving a disproportionately large amount of financial support and publicity.

The more robust jewellery is becoming increasingly akin to miniature sculpture, for many craft jewellers are also talented sculptors. This is reflected in the way in which galleries are displaying jewellery in more sympathetic surroundings, where pieces can be considered not solely for their material content but also for their visual and sensory qualities.

Marion Watson is an artist whose philosophy of life is expressed in her jewellery: warmth, sensuality and colour reflect her personality in the pieces she fashions.

Clare Street, like most artists, takes inspiration from the study of past civilizations and their techniques, interpreting them through her own modern designs. She uses hand-engraving (probably the most ancient of all art-crafts, for records aver that the Scriptures were first engraved on precious jewels) for textural effect as well as for executing portraits on precious plate, as was favourable a century or more ago, and creates a three-dimensional design which is punched out from a flat sheet of metal – a method much used by the Incas.

Three jeweller-silversmiths who work individually but in a communal workshop derive benefit from their combined experiences as far as contacts and sharing equipment are concerned, but each follows a distinctive path in design and development. Michael Wood combines materials such as glass beads and resin with his silver to produce precise, rather diagrammatic designs; Pamela Martin characterizes her jewellery by using three-dimensional tubular forms; and Peter Chatwin is researching into combining silver with laminated veneers of dyed wood – an idea which has yet to realize its full potential.

Research and experiment are very much part of the serious artist-craftsman's work.

It is ironic that as the trend is towards more use of animal, plant and organic materials the urgent need for conservation increases. The mineral hunting grounds of England are fast becoming protected by preservation orders, or sealed under motorways. A deposit of 'Bristol Diamonds' – exquisite quartz crystals upon which a thriving West Country jewellery industry once relied – is now buried under the M5.

GOLD, SILVER, OTHER METALS AND JEWELLERY

MICHAEL AND HEATHER ACKLAND, Coniston House, New Street, Deddington, Oxon. OX5 4SP. Tel: Deddington 241
  Design team of husband and wife making gold and silver modern jewellery by hand. Especially interested in developing commissioned work, i.e., engagement-rings to individual design in consultation with customer. Some retail outlets in the south of England for jewellery, made by the lost-wax process.

PETER BALL, Bandits Retreat, High Street, Newent, Glos. Tel: Newent 820466
  Gold and silver jewellery. Member of Craftsmen of Gloucestershire.

PETER JON BARNETT, M.Coll.H, Havenfield Cottage, Aylesbury Road, Great Missenden, Bucks.
  Artist-craftsman working in silver, gold and semi-precious stones. Specializing in designing and making rings to private commission, Peter Barnett also lectures and instructs on the craft of jewellery-making.

GERALD BENNEY, 36 Bear Lane, Southwark, London SE1 0UH. Tel: 01–928 6409
  Goldsmith and silversmith firm by appointment to HM the Queen, specializing in hand-made commissioned silver pieces. Unusual commissions have included making an enamelled box in the form of an eye to store false eyelashes or contact lenses.

DEREK BIRCH, 34½ Hungate, Lincoln LN1 1ET Tel: Lincoln 30120
  Silversmith whose work is entirely commissioned pieces: for households, municipal buildings and churches, jewellery, in precious metals. Member of the Society of Industrial Artists and Designers, and Society of Designer-Craftsmen.

SAMEER BOWYER, 7 Parkside Road, Sunningdale, Berks.
  Sterling silver jewellery incorporating semi-precious stones which can range from beach pebbles to opals. Particularly interested in designing theatrical jewellery, many commissions from pop stars and has made, to date, all the jewellery for Alvin Stardust. Retail outlets include The Great Frog, Harrods, Way In, Biba, Selfridges, and on Sundays at the open-air Art Exhibition in the Bayswater Road.

RICHARD BRADLEY, Billingford, nr Dereham, Norfolk NR20 4AJ. Tel: Elmham
353
  A small firm of half a dozen craftsmen producing exclusively bench-made
  jewellery mainly to the trade, but some direct retail. Commissions for individually designed pieces are undertaken. Necklets, bracelets, earrings:
  speciality design is for a neck torque reminiscent of early Celtic work – not
  copies.

ANDREW BRAY, DES. RCA, Dyad Associates, Smarden, Ashford, Kent TN27
8ND. Tel: Smarden 266
  Designer-craftsman, with specialist training as a silversmith, who can provide a design and designer craftsman service for individual clients by executing the one-off commissioned pieces in silver, gold, and other materials, and
  industry by making prototypes for subsequent quantity or mass production.

DI BROOKE AND PENNY PRICE, Design Brokers (Holdings) Ltd, 90 Lots Road,
London SW10. Tel: 01–352 7454
  Design and production of jewellery in precious and semi-precious metals.
  Commissions accepted by arrangement.

B. M. BRUCE (MRS), 7 Fox Lane, Little Bookham, Leatherhead, Surrey KT23
3AT
  Pewter repoussé work – jewellery-boxes, picture and commemorative
  plates. Tutor at Further Education classes. Commissions undertaken.

PETER CHATWIN, Factory Site, Wayside, Rengstone, Loughborough, Leics.
LE12 6RQ
  Jewellery incorporating silver and laminated veneers of dyed wood. Main
  retail outlet is Booty Jewellery, London. Part-time lecturer.

GERDA CUNDELL (MRS), Haydon Hayes, Washfield, Tiverton, Devon Tel: Oak-
ford 288
  Jewellery in rolled gold made to her own designs. Produced and displayed at
  Bickleigh Mill Crafts Ltd.

MAUREEN CARSWELL, Gemini, 20d Castle Gates, Shrewsbury, Salop Tel:
Shrewsbury 61765
  Commissioned work of drawing on enamel, mostly scenes or buildings from
  photographs. Supplier of jewellery-making equipment.

JEAN DAVIES CRAFTS LTD, Burnbake, Wilton, Salisbury, Wilts. SP2 0ES. Tel:
Wilton 2553
  Art jewellery fashioned by skilled craftsmen. Specialist designs of Toltek
  horseshoe-nail jewellery as made by fifteenth-century Romany Gypsies.

LYS DE BRAY, FLS, Turnpike Cottage, 8 Leigh Road, Wimborne Minster,
Dorset BH21 1AB
  Designer: jewellery from semi-precious agates, etc., with a character or

flower plaque affixed to make a pendant. Graphic designer using botanical subjects for a wide variety of speciality lines, under contract.

JOËL DEGAN, 31 Willow Road, London NW3. Tel: 01–435 5186
Jewellery designer working in a diversity of materials.

LESLIE DURBIN, 62 Rochester Place, London NW1 9JX. Tel: 01–485 5192
Leslie Durbin, MVO, is a master silversmith whose distinctive works range from the personal to the ceremonial. "A craftsman inspired by Minerva", is how the orator of the presentation of Honorary Degrees, University of Cambridge, presented him in 1963. His distinguished career is punctuated with scholarship successes; achievements which came to fruition in the shape of countless works of art. Ecclesiastical and civic dignity emblems – St Michael's staff in Gloucester Cathedral, cups, chalices, crosses, sculpture and candelabra in churches and universities throughout the country; the silver-gilt engagement-card-holder used daily by HM the Queen (a gift from members of the Royal Family on the occasion of her coronation), all testify to the skill of this designer-craftsman who, with his two assistants, undertakes commissions for anything from a medal to a church screen.

NIGEL EDMONDSON, 429 Blackburn Road, Higher Wheelton, Chorley PR6 8HY. Tel: Brinscall 830035
Individually made cast-pewter pendants. Exhibited at Design Centre. Main retail outlet through Thornthwaite Gallery, Keswick.

JESSICA FAGIN, Flat 2, 28 Chesterford Gardens, London NW3
Jewellery of silver, semi-precious stones and beads of all sorts.

ANN FERRIDAY, 56 Redhill Road, Rowlands Castle, Hants. PO6 9DF
Designer working mainly on jewellery in gold and silver, also small boxes and sets of boxes decorated with stones or gold embellishments. Member of Society of Designer-Craftsmen.

FIVE JEWELLERS (Jackie Jones, Karen Lawrence, David Taylor, Beverley Phillips, Susan Hines), Camden Lock, Commercial Place, London NW1 8AF
Jewellery.

PETER J. GOODENOUGH, Malverleys, 1 Greenway Park, Chippenham, Wilts. SN15 1QG. Tel: Chippenham 2344
Specializing in designing and making modern jewellery, Peter Goodenough also undertakes restoration of antique clock-dials. Recently commissioned work has been restoration on eighteenth-century clock-dials, enamel on beaten copper forms.

G. W. M. GREEN, 35 Marshalls Way, Wheathampstead, Herts. Tel: Harpenden 60593
Craftsman working in hand-beaten metal, chiefly brass, copper and pewter. Exhibits locally.

GEOFFREY HARDING, 31 The Green, Steventon, Oxon OX13 6RR. Tel: Steventon (023–584) 371
Designer-silversmith specializing in simple, elegant shapes. Contemporary designs, but never gimmicky or provocative. Church silverware, particularly chalices, undertaken to commission.

DAVID T. HART, Trinder House, High Street, Chipping Campden, Glos. Tel: Evesham 840443
Designer-craftsman in gold and silver carrying on the tradition of fine workmanship founded by his grandfather at the turn of the century under the noted C. R. Ashbee Guild. The Hart workshop has been famed for ecclesiastical work, but domestic silverware is also undertaken to commission, as are civic and military emblems.

PETER B. HARWOOD, 27 Church Road, Bishops Cleave, Glos. GL52 4LR. Tel: Bishops Cleave 2378
Designer and craftsman principally in gold and silver whose platinum pendant won fourth place in the Johnson Matthey Competition 1974. Domestic, church, and civic plate and regalia to order. Scale models. Engraving. Antique silver of all descriptions restored. Member of Craftsmen of Gloucestershire.

CHRISTOPHER HAYWARD, 1 The Rylands, Ash Lane, Randwick, Stroud, Glos. Tel: Stroud 3458
Silversmith. Associate member of Guild of Gloucestershire Craftsmen.

DUNCAN JAMES, 49 Banbury Road, Brackley, Northants. NN13 6BA Tel: Brackley 2948
Designer-jeweller working in gold and silver, mostly without gemstones.

ROY JAY, Abbey Gift Shop, 155–156 Church Street, Whitby, Yorks. Tel: Whitby 3525
Possibly the last apprenticed jet-turner in Britain. Jewellery, ornaments and bric-à-brac. Commissioned work has included pieces for royalty.

LAKELAND RURAL INDUSTRIES, The Old Smithy, Cartmel, nr Grange-over-Sands, Cumbria LA11 6PZ: Tel: Cartmel (044 854) 362
Attractive hand-beaten stainless steel and copper tableware and church pieces. Simplicity of design and practical shapes make for a variety of possible uses. Engraving and special designs to order.

GORDON LAWRIE, Penfold Cottage, 30 High Street, Steyning, Sussex BN4 3GG. Tel: Steyning 814056
Artist-jeweller who makes individual jewellery, the pieces are usually inspired from plant forms and natural objects from the Downs and seashore. Similar work, including small sculptured pieces, in silver or gold, to commission. Permanent exhibition of jewellery. Member of the Guild of Sussex Craftsmen, and Society of Designer-Craftsmen. Exhibited at the Design Centre.

PHILIP LOWERY, Taena Workshop, Whitley Court, Upton St Leonards, Gloucester. Tel: Gloucester 66669
Designer-silversmith. Member Guild of Gloucestershire Craftsmen.

PAOLO LURATI, Camden Lock, Commercial Place, London NW1 8AF
Silversmith and jewellery.

SHEILA MADDOCK, Vale View Cottage, Hyde, Stroud, Glos. Tel: Brimscombe 3885
Gemstone jewellery to order.

STEPHEN MAER, 18 Yerbury Road, London N19 4RJ. Tel: 01–272 9074
Designer-jeweller making individual pieces and limited editions in silver and 18-carat gold, usually incorporating stones. Member of the British Crafts Centre, Society of Designer-Craftsmen, Design and Research Centre for the Gold, Silver and Jewellery Industries, and Design Council Record of Designers. Commissions occasionally accepted for design for industry. Retail direct and through galleries.

MAGNUS MAXIMUS DESIGNS, Frizington Road, Rowrah, Cumbria. Tel: Lamplugh 491
One of the country's leading manufacturers of silver jewellery. Craft, gem stone, and natural stone jewellery. Great Britain's leading cutters of British marble, serpentine, slate, etc., which are hand-made on the premises into desk-sets, jewellery, plinths, cutlery handles, etc. Showroom.

PAMELA MARTIN, Factory Site, Wayside, Rengstone, Loughborough, Leics. LE12 6RQ
Highly individual designs developed from three-dimensional tubular form in jewellery to small pieces of hollow-ware; intending to develop enamelling to produce colour in her work. Exhibited at Victoria and Albert Museum and Cameo Corner. Part-time art college lecturer.

IAN AND RHONA MATHEWS, Yew Tree House, Crosby Garret, Kirkby Stephen, Cumbria. Tel: Kirkby Stephen 436
Husband and wife partnership designing and producing jewellery using Lakeland slate. Other stone products are dominoes and studies of animals and birds.

JACQUELINE MINA, DES.RCA, 122 Church Road, Teddington, Middx. Tel: 01–977 4742
Jewellery designer who has developed a unique style showing traces of the influence of ancient Egyptian and Etruscan jewellery. Basically working in gold, but with a wide range of other materials, precious and semi-precious stones, even shells and beads, as dictated by the design. Widely exhibited in America and Europe, customers include princes from the Middle East, actors and musicians.

JOYCE MOLD, St Cyril's Lodge, Stonehouse, Glos. Tel: Stonehouse 3378
Pewter jewellery.

LUCILLE MOORE, Mythe Crest, Tewkesbury, Glos. Tel: Tewkesbury 294003
Jewellery-designer working in gold and silver and semi-precious stones to
create individual pieces of jewellery. Specialist in designing necklaces. Exhibited at the Design Centre. Member of Guild of Gloucestershire Craftsmen.

GLYN AND DIANE MORRIS, Glydwr Copper, Goulter's Mill, Nettleton, Chippenham, Wilts.
Hand-worked copper: jewellery, trays, etc.

GEORGE AND MARY NEED, The Sloop Craft Market, St Ives, Cornwall.
Silversmithery and copperwork.

HELEN NEWMAN, Avenis Studio, Bournes Green, Oakridge, Glos. Tel: Bisley
407
A designer whose creative talent is realized through her skill as a craftswoman. Under the all-embracing nomenclature of metal-worker, Helen
Newman designs and makes jewellery and silverware. Retails through
galleries, exhibitions and the occasional boutique. Commissions are dealt
with at the studio. Member Guild of Gloucestershire Craftsmen.

ANN O'DONNELL, 56 Cliff Road, Leeds LS6 2EZ. Tel: (0532) 785254
Jewellery-designer whose interest lies mainly in gemology and lapidary.
Uncut minerals or cut stones often incorporated into the design. Sales are
made mainly through exhibitions.

M. PETTIT, Ashdown, Brightling Road, Robertsbridge, Sussex
Silversmith.

DON PORRITT, MSIA, 129 Main Street, Menston, Ilkley, Yorks. LS29 6HT. Tel:
Menston 4736
Practising designer-sculptor and silversmith producing designs of modern
domestic silver and carrying out commissions to individual requirements.
Commissions for special awards and presentations have included the
Sportsman of the Year Award – from Yorkshire Television; the John Hunt
Award – from Countrywide Holidays Association; and the B.P. Trophy –
from Inland Waterways Association.

ELSIE M. RAMSAY, The White House, Worlaby, Brigg, Lincs. Tel: Saxby-all-
Saints 341
Designer-craftswoman in gold, silver, pewter and enamel; mainly personal
jewellery. Direct retail to the customer on the whole, although some sales
are made through exhibitions and the Lincs. and South Humberside Arts
regional craft centre. Commissions have included christening-spoons, a
school trophy bowl, and special twenty-first birthday rings.

ZOË RAWLINS, Tan Yard Bank, Castle Street, Winchcombe, Glos. GL54 5JA.

Tel: Winchcombe 602782

Silversmith and metalworker who specializes in designing and making small boxes for pills, snuff, rings, cigarettes and matches. Lockets in a variety of shapes and sizes also made. Member of Guild of Gloucestershire Craftsmen.

GEOFF AND IRIS RICHES (Kerrow Enamels), The Sloop Craft Market, St Ives, Cornwall

Copper, pewter and bead jewellery.

ROCKCRAFT, 6a Northgate, Chichester, Sussex PO19 1BA. Tel: Chichester 82766

Majority of jewellery work is commissioned to customers' own designs in either silver or gold with precious or semi-precious stones. Stones cut and polished. Lapidary supplies, from rocks and minerals to tools.

RAY SEMPLE, DES.RCA, MSD-C, MSIA, Ashley Cottage, 374 Pensby Road, Heswall, Wirral, Merseyside

Designer-craftsman whose commissions range from domestic, ecclesiastical and ceremonial plate to numerous jewellery pieces. Recent work has included a suite of jewellery for a newly consecrated bishop, church plate for Manchester Cathedral, and the 1975 Topham Trophy. Industrial designs have been in the fields of furniture, light fittings – including those for *QE2* – hollow-ware and cutlery.

ANN MARIE SHILLITO, 29 Thick Hollins, Meltham, Huddersfield, Yorks. HD7 3DQ Tel: (0484) 850265

Jewellery-designer working mainly in non-precious metals to satisfy the demand for well-designed pieces in the lower price range. In direct contrast to this is Ann Shillito's recently explored field of setting ammonite fossils in silver and gold. One of her most unusual commissions was from British Steel for the designing and making of a crown, sceptre and cape in steel, to be used for beauty contests. Part-time tutor.

DOUGLAS SIBBALD, Manor Cottage, Througham, Camp, Stroud, Glos.

Designer and maker of jewellery in silver and gold. Repairs and recycling also undertaken.

RED AND RUTH SIMPSON, The Sloop Craft Market, St Ives, Cornwall

Silver and gold jewellery and copperwork.

JANET SLACK, Sycamore Cottage, St Ives, Cornwall. Tel: St Ives 5067

Gold and silver jewellery of all kinds, also some spoons. Member of the Society of Craftsmen at Hereford, and the Cornwall Craft Society.

I. R. SMITH, Old Forge House, Ravensthorpe, Northampton. Tel: East Haddon 284

Designer of silver jewellery; Mr Smith is also a potter.

JACQUELINE STIEGER, Welton Garth, Welton, nr Brough, E. Yorks. Tel: Hull 668323

Sculpture, jewellery; works in bronze, gold and silver. Commissioned pieces include a silver chalice with amethysts; church windows with etched reliefs by special technique in several European countries; church interior furnishing and glass madonna for St Margaret's, Glasgow; fountain at Dr Barnado's in Ilford, Essex; two gold cups with emeralds, and Benson and Hedges gold cup trophy, York. Numerous exhibitions in this country and abroad; awarded first prize at "Revival of the Medal 1974" exhibition in Paris. Jacqueline Stieger's jewellery is retailed at Blooms, Bond Street, London; Galerie Riehentor, Basle, Switzerland, and the British Craft Centre. Special commissions undertaken, by arrangement.

CLARE STREET, Little Offley Farm, Hitchin, Herts. SG5 3BU. Tel: Offley 202

Designer of modern jewellery who specializes in three old techniques: classical grain setting of precious stones, as seen in the conventional eternity ring; répoussé and chasing; and hand-engraving. Good tumble stones also used in precious and semi-precious materials. Clare Street is probably the only jewellery-maker who carries out the old craft of hand-engraving miniature portraits on copper, silver or gold plate – this can be carried out from a customer's photograph.

GILLIAN TAIT, 54 St Martin's Hill, Canterbury, Kent

Jewellery-designer and goldsmith. Individual to special commission and one-off exhibition pieces.

ANN THOMSON, 21 St Stephen's Road, Cheltenham, Glos.

Silversmith specializing in small boxes incorporating ivory, tortoiseshell and ebony; small pots of flowers and foliage wrought in silver; pictorial jewellery in mixed media, and men's jewellery. Member of Society of Designer-Craftsmen.

TIKI (Iris Radway), 6 Well Walk, Cheltenham, Glos. Tel: Cheltenham 53639

Gemstone jeweller who will also polish stones for customers who are keen to make up their own jewellery. Full range of equipment available at the above shop from minerals, rocks, and hammers to tumble polishers and craft books.

MAJOR G. N. TURNER (Retd), Maytrees, 3 Rances Lane, Wokingham, Berks RG11 2LG. Tel: Wokingham 782679

Silversmith producing salvers, spoons, beakers, goblets, and jewellery. Embossed pewterware – pictures, jewellery, boxes and plates. Commissions undertaken.

GRAHAM WATLING, 23 Church Street, Lacock, Wilts. Tel: Lacock 422

Designer-craftsman of gold and silverware including ecclesiastical pieces and jewellery. A continuous and changing display of work is always on exhibition in the shop.

MARION WATSON, 48 Swinbrook Road, London W10

Craftswoman who works intuitively with precious metals. Sales are direct from her own studio or through Casson Gallery, 96 New Cavendish Street, London W1.

ROBERT WELCH, The Mill, Chipping Campden, Glos. Tel: Evesham (0386) 840522

Designer and silversmith whose hand-made silver has been featured many times in national newspapers. Well known also for his industrial designs, particularly his work for Old Hall, including the Alveston designs which won a Design Centre Award in 1965 and were chosen by the British Government for presentation to Russian Heads of State. Robert Welch's commissioned work for individual pieces, ecclesiastical, civic, and ceremonial plate is to be found in many churches, universities and company buildings throughout the country, as well as private collections. His Studio Shop in Sheep Street (a few yards away from the workshop) with exhibition gallery, is the principal retail outlet.

K. P. WILLIAMS, Hafren, Loop Road, Beachley, Chepstow. Tel: Chepstow 3395

Lapidary and jewellery. Member of Guild of Gloucestershire Craftsmen.

MICHAEL WOOD, Factory Site, Wayside, Rengstone, Loughborough, Leics. LE12 6RQ

Designer-silversmith whose work has been mainly to commission, but now making a collection of jewellery combining silver with various materials. Part-time lecturer.

FAY YOUNGBERG, Apple Tree Cottage, Tuttors Hill, Cheddar, Somerset. Tel: Cheddar 742884

Hand-beaten English pewter jewellery retailed in craft shop in Cheddar Gorge.

MICHAEL BURTON, Osborne Cottage, Hurst, Mortlock, Somerset

Craftsman working in silver and ivory.

ALAN EVANS, Makins, Whiteway, nr Stroud, Glos.
Tel: Miserden 366

All pieces individually designed and made to order; Hand-raised silverware. Stones re-set.

MICHAEL MURRAY, 27 Old Street, London EC1

Craftsman-silversmith: founder of the Clerkenwell Green Association for craftsmen.

PHIL STEPHENS, Sheephouse Cottage, Ampney, nr Cirencester, Glos.

Silversmith and goldsmith.

COLIN STEPHENSON AND MICHAEL KARR, Design Brokers Ltd, 90 Lots Road, London SW10

Silversmiths.

MARGARET STOCKEN, 54 Overhill Road, Stratton, Cirencester, Glos. Tel: Cirencester 2410
   Polished stones.

OWEN SWINDALE, The Jewellery Workshop, 64 Worcester Road, Malvern, Worcs. Tel: Malvern 61342
   Gem-cutter and jewellery-maker.

CLIFF WHEELER, 'Triana', Bread Street, Ruscombe, Glos.
   Horseshoe-nail jewellery.

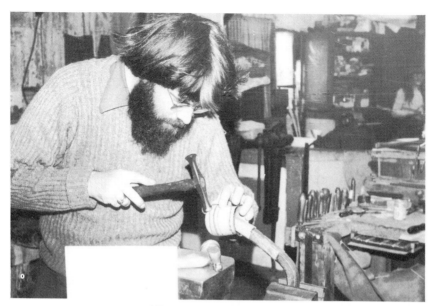

Silversmith Philip Lowery

Metalworker Helen Newman has become well-known for her
jewellery designs

The Churchill Goblet, showing Chartwell from across the large lake, designed and diamond-point engraved by Honoria D. Marsh

The Churchill Plate, a limited edition of twenty-five designed and engraved by Bernard M. York

Adding molten glass to make a stem at Dartington Glassworks

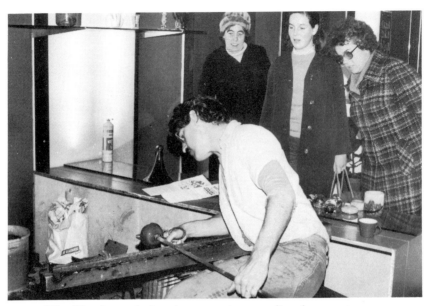

The Glasshouse in London – a unique studio where customers can watch the craftsmen at work

(*below*) Edward Payne works his designs out first as full-size cartoons and paper sculptures

(*opposite*) the finished stained glass church window

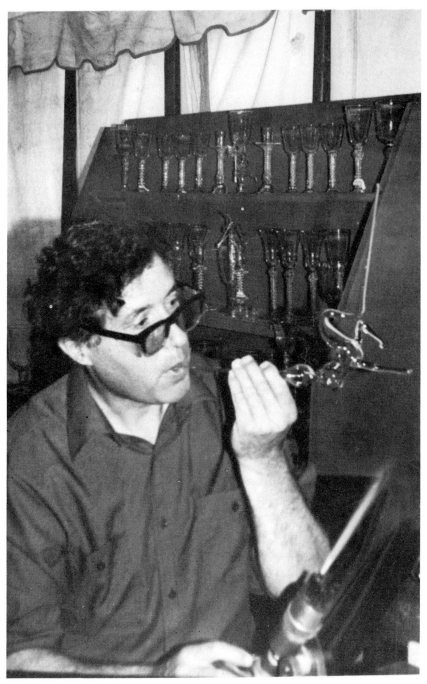

John Akers demonstrates how glass tubing can be blown into
the shape of a dancing horse with the aid of a blow-torch

Ceramic sculptress Marjorie Smith

Yorkshire potter, Peter Dick, unpacking his wood-fired kiln

(*left*) The world-famous Roman mosaic Woodchester Pavement recreated by Katie Woollatt, seen here with Robert Woodward, who headed the project

(*below*) James English – the last of the Brandon flint-knappers, and perhaps the last professional flint-knapper in the world

14

Glass

Glass is literally as old as the hills, since vitreous metal is found in the form of obsidian, a dark volcanic substance very like that of bottle-glass. The craft of glass-making goes back to the ancient East where it evolved almost by accident, by potters fusing sand and minerals on ceramic beads. Pliny the Elder told of Phoenicians discovering glass accidentally in the ashes of a sailors' camp fire on a beach in which a form of soda, used to prop up their cooking-pot, had fused with the sand in shapeless lumps of glass.

The basic ingredient of glass is silica, which occurs in a natural state in the form of flint, quartz, or sand. When mixed with potash or soda and subjected to great heat, the compound becomes a molten metal, so flexible that it can be twisted and rolled, stretched and shaped into any form, or blown into bubbles so light that they float in the air.

Glass was made in England from the Roman occupation but the art of the Venetians was never rivalled. Although some window glass was made in the thirteenth century, it was not until the 'gentlemen glass-makers' from Lorraine in Northern France came to this country in the sixteenth century that glass-making became established. Initially settling in the well-wooded Kentish Weald, the Huguenot glass-makers migrated north to work the new fuel – coal, when the law prohibited the use of wood as furnace fuel, and Stourbridge was thrust into prominence as a glass-making centre.

English craftsmen became important in glass history as the originators of flint glass (launched in the 1670s), the famous and lovely lead crystal which was vastly different from the frail Continental soda glass, and the envy of the world between the seventeenth and eighteenth centuries. Tax by weight was a heavy burden borne by English glass-makers, and the Irish took advantage of their exemption to flood the market with their massive pieces, until they too were caught in the excise collector's net in 1825.

By the time the tax was abolished in 1845 designs had taken on diverse guises. To combat the fierce competition from the Continental glass-makers, who turned to using colour when the brilliance of English flint glass could not be equalled, a decidedly thinner and therefore lighter glass was made and gave rise to the delicate air-twist and spiral stems with which the Jacobite period is associated. The limpid beauty of the elegant drinking-glasses of the early eighteenth century reflects the social habits of the times; as port became the fashionable drink the gentry sought transparent vessels for it and decanters made an appearance. Colour was confined to the less-taxed bottle-glass, resulting in an ethnic era in which Nailsea developed its own distinct, rather unsophisticated, marbled and trailed patterns.

Although often indiscriminately applied to all blue glass, the term *Bristol blue* referred to an earlier development in coloured glass when only one Bristol dealer could profit from the scarcity of Saxon cobalt oxide during the Seven Years' War. It was not until the tax on flint glass was removed that the use of colour in glasswork was developed. Decoration took many forms, even to the extent of overall painting, so disguising glass that it took on the appearance of porcelain; the limits extended as the vogue for anything remotely oriental reached enthusiastic heights in the 1870s. The secrets of ornamentation were zealously guarded, and much glassware between 1842 and 1883 was registered by the Patent Office to prevent piracy of designs. The Victorians' love of the exquisitive and the marvellous produced incredible creations of spun glass, to be exhibited under domed glass covers. A number of these works were produced not in the confines of industry but by individual extrovert craftsmen who performed before an admiring audience, often on a street corner, their wondrous feats of weaving hot glass threads into subtle shapes and fancy forms. It is still possible to recapture something of those days at an agricultural show or crafts demonstration where an artist like John Akers will fashion dainty dancing horses from glass rods over a bunsen-burner; but will devote his serious study time to copying the air-twist stemmed drinking-glasses of an earlier period.

GLASS-MAKING

> The Glasshouse is a workshop and gallery combined where anyone can come in and watch glass being blown. We work here as a co-operative, a percentage of our sales being put back into the studio to cover our expenses. We are particularly interested in extending the tuition courses which are offered here.
>
> *Annette Meech, The Glasshouse*

Free-blown glass made in the studio is still in its infancy in Europe. The cost of small furnace workshops is too high to be borne by the individual so the glass-making facilities afforded to craftsmen of other countries have just not been available to the British, who often had little physical contact with the medium for which they were designing. The drawing board and the glasshouse were quite separate entities and contributed to the stagnation in the design of much British glass as far as individual expression was concerned. Not, of course, in the industry as a whole, for the leading glasshouses have a long and honoured history in which hand craftsmanship still plays a vital role.

The 'gentlemen glass-makers' settled in Stourbridge and married into the most notable of the local families; one of the last of the Henzeys wed the daughter of Mr Honeybourne, the glass-maker of Briar Lea Hill in the Pensnett Chase, from whom the glasshouse was leased to Joseph Silvers, the first of the family line of Stevens and Williams Ltd, the makers of Royal Brierley Crystal. Full lead crystal, such as Royal Brierley, contains 30 per cent lead, mixed and melted with a silica in oxide form, and gives the glass its great brilliance, strength and durability.

Hand-made crystal is also made by Whitefriars, whose furnaces have been burning unquenched since 1680. In keeping with many traditions of this ancient craft, a brazier from the old works on the site of a Carmelite monastery was carried to Harrow to ignite the first furnace in the company's present Wealdstone glassworks.

Glass-making is a fascinating activity with ancient names for each key worker and process. Molten glass is withdrawn from the melting pots which are set around the furnace. The *footmaker* takes a *gather* of glass on to the end of the *blowing-iron*, *marvers* (rolls) the blob of glass on a solid steel sheet and centres it on the blowing iron to give it a smooth, even shape. *Takers-in* are kept busy, dashing backwards and forwards to the furnace with glass for re-heating. The *servitors* blow the red-hot glass into a bubble which can be extended and varied by swinging and weaving, and all the time the fiery knob is assuming shape and substance. Sitting in his chair, surrounded by the tools of his trade which have remained unchanged for three centuries, the glass-maker – usually called the *gaffer* – rolls the rod along the narrow board arm, coaxing the fiery orb by squeezing, spinning, pulling or snipping it into a preconceived shape. Cooling is carried out by the carefully conditioned process of annealing, in which the glass travels on an endless belt from the hot end of the tunnel kiln until it is cold.

The fireclay melting pots, each of which will hold up to almost a ton of molten glass, are hand-made by Whitefriars' own pot-makers. Subjected to a constant heat of about 1400°C, the pots last about fifteen weeks. Putting a new pot into the furnace calls for the men's oldest clothes which often smoulder under the intense heat. Once lit, a furnace is never extinguished during its lifetime; the high temperature is maintained throughout. The fires of Whitefriars have burnt continuously through fifteen reigns and the craft skills have not changed, gathering around them a vocabulary of their own. A 'frigger', for example, is an artistic trifle worked in glass by a glass-blower in his spare time for the amusement of his friends or as an experiment.

Ever ready to realize the potential of glass, Whitefriars' craftsmen have turned their skills to make such diverse objects as sparkling glass eyes, optical glass for gun-sights, miners' lamp glass, vacuum flasks and thermometer tubing – which, until their designers conceived the idea of an electronically controlled tower, was made by two men walking slowly apart pulling a gather of molten glass into an extended tube.

This old method is still used for drawing out the canes of coloured and 'lace twisted' glass from which the magnificent *millefiore* patterns are assembled. About half a dozen of Whitefriars craftsmen spend some time of every week making 'a thousand flowers' from the glass rods which are cut up into tiny stubs when cold. Bedded into a base in a ceaseless permutation of colour and pattern, the designs differ from one another so that each piece, whether a paperweight under a dimpled dome, a dish or a bottle, is individual. Highly prized by collectors since they started making them in 1840, Whitefriars' paperweights now have the insignia and date hidden deep in the midst of the *millefiore*, and are the only ones of any importance to be made in England today.

The setting up of The Glasshouse in London in 1969, to provide glass artists with studio facilities denied them outside industry, was a major contribution to the revival of hand-made glass. The problems inherent in being the pioneer in any field, and the particular ones peculiar to small furnace workshops, appear to have been overcome: the resident craftsmen openly acknowledge the assistance and support given to them at such times by CAC, and are resolute in their aims to make the venture completely self-sufficient. For this purpose they also sell the work of other glass-makers, thereby having a comprehensive range of glass on view. They also arrange exhibitions elsewhere in England and abroad to ensure that the work reaches a wider public, which is good business sense as The Glasshouse is a little off the tourist beat, at the back of Covent Garden. The British Crafts Centre proved a good neighbour in the formative years when the small group of young glass artists, fresh from college and enamoured with the studio glass movement in the USA, took a positive step towards establishing the workshop-gallery instead of complaining about the limited prospects for their particular training.

Keen on developing the tuition courses they hold at The Glasshouse, the resident craftsmen have much to offer to beginners or practising glass-makers wishing to avail themselves of the facilities there. There is nothing quite like it anywhere else in Europe.

The Glass Manufacturers' Federation holds a watching brief on the development of craftsmanship through its close contact with the Design Centre and the colleges of art, as well as its relationship with European organizations, but is in no way a craft association in the accepted sense. Nevertheless, although it is concerned with the overall manufacture of hand-made goods, rather than the individual craftsmen, it does safeguard their well-being through safety training, general education projects and support for the City and Guilds certification.

Stourbridge College of Art, being in the traditional centre of that industry, teaches glass to degree level, and the Royal College of Art runs a postgraduate course. As far as I can discover, Sheffield is one of only two universities in the world offering glass technology.

The new visual arts expressions which developed in the late 'fifties inspired a major reappraisal of glass-making. The move towards exploiting the material rather than making it a subsidiary factor of the design had already penetrated the fields of ceramics and textiles. Designer-craftsmen were starting to build their designs into and therefore through their materials, and glass-makers looked anew at the glass-making processes in order to realize the full potential of the material as a design source. Playing with fire, literally, glass-making embodies more than an element of danger in its magic. Technically the manufacture of glass was always more suited to industry, but here and there isolated workshops are appearing in England, yet there are only a mere couple of books devoted to the single craft glasshouse set-up. Technical treatises relate more to the industrial scene, so each studio glass-maker seems to take on the role of a pioneer in the craft.

GLASS-ENGRAVING

The art of glass engraving, after some 3,000 years of history, is perhaps nowhere so alive today as in Great Britain.

Guild of Glass-Engravers

Back to the Egyptians again. It seems that engraved glass was practised and used by the Ancients, so no doubt we acquired its practitioners through the usual drift from east to west. There has been a remarkable revival of the craft this century and to promote the highest quality of creative designs and craftsmanship the Guild of Glass-Engravers was formed in 1975. The first in its field for 3,000 years!

Commemorative glass has been presented over the centuries marking national and personal milestones, but there is now a growing demand for engraved windows for churches and public buildings. The potential of the engraver's art is only just being realized. The very essence of the art form is a synthesis of light and shade, depths and tones which depend on the skill of the artist. Devoid of colour, the design has to emphasize the transparency of the glass, transmitting light without diffusing it. Because of these special demands, engraved glass has presented its own peculiar problems in its display. The paramount importance of stimulating and absolutely correct lighting of pieces for exhibition is fully appreciated by the guild.

It is not a craft for the timorous. If the fragility of the medium (the hazards of actually working the design with the dread of dropping the thing) is not an initial deterrent, there is also the problem that errors become magnified and cannot be erased or easily disguised. Added to which, the back-to-front kind of approach – drawing in reverse, so that the design is viewed through the unengraved side – is further complicated by drawing in the round, as it were, cylindrical shapes being the most widely used in the form of glasses and bowls. But the dedicated are never daunted, this achromatic art holds for its craftsmen an exciting challenge in which they become totally involved. The full implication of this may be easier understood as one enters an exhibition area where carefully lit engraved glass makes an impressive sight in a dark void.

Different artists choose different tools and techniques. The main methods are carried out entirely by hand, using a diamond – a small diamond set in a pencil-like holder – or a steel point; copper wheel – one of the oldest forms, where the glass is held to the revolving wheel; a power-driven drill; acid-etching, and sand-blasting. Each exacts a different type of dexterity from the craftsman; each evokes a different response from the glass. Although the art of cutting diamonds has existed for centuries, it was not until the mid-1700s that the flint glass masters experimented in applying flat facets cut into their crystal with a stone wheel rotated by means of a foot treadle. The motive power of the lathe, the type of wheel and abrasive have changed, but not the degree of individual craftsmanship required to hand cut the crystal in order to release its myriads of dancing, dazzling lights.

Individual glass artists tend to veer towards engraving but rarely train specifically for it. Most come to the craft through other artistic fields such as sculpture or architecture.

David Peace, chairman of the guild, uses calligraphic art to immense effect in his work as sculptural symbols, whereas the president of the guild, Lawrence Whistler, is eminent in the field of pictorial art. Both have profound influence on the designs and techniques of the glass artists today.

Bryant Fedden is a craftsman of great versatility and distinct personality. Within his classification of sculptor, letter-cutter and glass engraver is an extensive skill expressed through many media. Stone, wood and glass are extended to the limits of their capabilities in the same way as he extends his own skilful dexterity. His attitude to craftwork generally is gregarious; he is very much in favour of corporate craftsmanship where individual talents are combined to meet special commissions. The outstanding results of this are to be seen in the work which is produced at Tan Yard Bank, where he and Keith and Joan Jameson work together. It is characteristic of him to accept challenges as he feels that glass has been somewhat undervalued as a display material and has used it in many forms: as kinetic sculpture in Newton Abbot Race-course restaurant decor, set in stone to create table sculptures, and engraved for cathedral windows. He often engraves wine goblets with a dentist's drill submerged in a bath of water to counteract dust and heat problems.

David Monkman, like the majority of glass-engravers, is self-taught, for there are relatively few places where glass-engraving can be studied; but he numbers international personalities among his customers. "Engraving names on cheap glasses at markets and fairs pays the rent," he acknowledges. He uses a dentist's drill for speed when at an agricultural show, to satisfy the immediate customer who wants to buy a personalized present. The diamond-point work, however, demands total concentration and a lot of time.

Just how much time is involved can be gauged by the fact that stipple engraving means building up a design by dotting many thousand minute indentations on the glass surface, variations in tone are achieved by altering the spacing of the dots. Pricing such work is the part most artists dislike, relating time and cost takes them to that decisive point where their craft must become a viable business.

"Meeting people for whom I am to design a piece is part of the pleasure of my work," Stephen Proctor says. Like most engravers, his is the role of translator of the client's initial idea into the final pictorial presentation which has to convey so much in such a small, usually spherical, space. Danek Piechowiak, on the other hand, finds that most of his orders are for making graven images from photographs; something which does not fit into Stephen Richard's concept of craftsmanship. His twenty-three years in the craft have brought him some remarkable challenges and must have underlined how little is comprehended by the customer of the work involved.

A prima donna was once asked to vet his trial engraving of a dancer and suggested that the fingers should be fractionally closer together. The whole figure was less than two inches high so it is not difficult to imagine the size of the fingers, or the complications involved.

Most engravers work on 'biographical' design; making a coherent whole out of a list of relevant headings – school, regiment, interests, work or peculiar circumstances. These are usually anniversary pieces and are therefore required on a specific date. Working with such a delicate and expensive medium imposes a great responsibility on the craftsman to keep within his own artistic limitations.

Bernard York is a relative newcomer to the craft in a full-time capacity and sees the market as wide, "world-wide – almost beyond computation if one raises one's sights, but the problem is to let the public know that the products are available". That is a problem common to most crafts, but the glass-engravers have rather special ones related to their total dependence on a primary producer of their basic material.

It is unfortunate, in some ways, that the best crystal for engraving should be English, for such is the export demand for it that English artists have to wait, sometimes up to a year, to get the pieces they require; by which time prices have escalated, wrecking their original quotations for commissions and ruining their carefully budgeted programmes. One craftsman had indicated that the only way to overcome this was to "hire a chair" (a team of glass-makers) one's self or as a group, but the leading glass-manufacturers had not heard of this being done in England, although it is sometimes done on the Continent. Hiring a team of glass-makers would, in any case, they say, be an extremely expensive venture. The patriotic see it as an ironic situation in which, in an endeavour to earn export orders, they have to buy imported glass on which to work. Moreover, importers – the craftsmen say – offer glass at trade price if it is purchased in reasonable amounts, whereas English glass has to be bought through retail channels, thus adding to the expense.

Such is the glass-engravers' current situation – whereby some 95 per cent are so adamant in their belief that the manufacturers were inimical to the interests of artist-craftsmen – that I put this viewpoint to the Managing Director of Stevens & Williams Ltd, makers of the world-famous Royal Brierley Crystal in the Stourbridge glass-making centre.

The chief complaints levelled against English manufacturers are:

1 there is a definite shortage of good quality interesting pieces on sale;
2 companies are too busy to produce or put such high prices on 'specials' that they price them out of the market for the single craftsman;
3 there is little interest from the English glasshouses to supply blanks specially for outsiders; they use all their best glass for their own cutting, and are not prepared to deal with the small orders, which of necessity the single unit business can place.

It was agreed that the three points were valid and correct, but it is also true that they are interconnected. There is, however, absolutely no antipathy with individual craft engravers and the company wishes to encourage them in every way possible.

When I discovered that the five member companies of the Stourbridge Crystal Glass Association employ over 2,000 people between them, one can appreciate the size of the problem from the manufacturers' point of view, especially within their industry, which is craft-orientated, with its own artist-craftsmen for deep-cutting and engraving crystal.

One of the declared aims of the Guild of Glass-Engravers is to strengthen the links with the glass industry. Advocacy must obviously be made through a properly constituted body and spearheaded by professionals who wish to resolve these problems for its 200 members.

STAINED GLASS

> Stained glass artistry is largely a matter of calculating the effect of colours together. Seen from a distance, colours sometimes neutralize each other; only experience can anticipate the result.
>
> *Edward Payne*

Stained glass is part of our national heritage; its conservation is constantly exercising the skill of the most talented specialists who, whether they be chemist, scientist, historian, artist or craftsman, are custodians of the antique "storied windows – casting a dim religious light" into our religious houses. The writings of the Venerable Bede in 647 tell us that the craft of glazing was unknown in this country at that time. By the twelfth and thirteenth centuries, however, England was leading the field, and it is during that period that glass artwork became an integral part of the structure of the church. As an architectural element it has hardly ever been dissociated from its ecclesiastical foundations, and so it is to the lofty cathedrals and the humble churches that students of stained glass go to study the great masters.

In times of national danger, the irreplaceable windows were removed and hidden for safety, as part of the country's art treasures. The opportunity of cleaning and repairing some eighty of York Minster's windows during the last war resulted in the accumulation of unique store of knowledge, which materialized in 1966 in the York Glaziers' Trust. Financially aided by the Pilgrim Trust, and having the status of a charity, the trust was primarily established to repair and preserve the glass of York Minster (England's largest medieval window depository), but any stained glass of merit will be treated, with the needs of the Minster taking precedence. Its interests are neither confined to medieval nor just English glass: some interesting nineteenth-century pieces find their way to the Minster workshop, and there is international exchange of study, research and reports.

The strong link between the University of York and the Glaziers' Trust bridges the gap between science and art-craftsmanship to make this a centre unrivalled anywhere else in the world. Its object is to provide a scholarly and technical expertise not readily available from any other single source and was not set up as competitor to other firms.

Most conservation workshops are centred around the cathedrals, and run their own apprenticeship schemes. Canterbury has its own centre but currently strives to attract a new generation to the craft through its training scheme based on the preservation of its ancient glass, which is now in a parlous state. The problem is immediate.

Dr Roy Newton, recently of the British Glass Industry Research Association, now an honorary visiting professor of the University of York, helping with their research on the Minster glass, says of the training of glaziers:

the situation is even worse for students of conservation techniques [than for art students]. At the moment perhaps half a dozen are urgently needed at Canterbury, York and elsewhere, but by the time a *viable* class (perhaps fifteen students) had been launched on the world in three years' time, would there be any jobs for them?

One of the larger firms reported that despite being extremely busy, 70 per cent of its work was restoration and releading which called for even greater expertise and was "certainly not the type of work one could trust to an apprentice". The general demand for stained glass is so very unpredictable and inconsistent that until firms see some kind of continuity of orders they are reluctant to take on any more staff – let alone train them for an uncertain future.

Even big firms with international reputations have failed to survive the vagaries of stained-glass fashion: Whitefriars have recently closed their studios after 140 years, during which time cathedrals and churches, from St Paul's in London to ones in New Zealand, were glazed by their artists. Burne-Jones was one of their early designers; Alfred Fisher their last.

Wishing to return to the practical side of the craft, Alfred Fisher and Peter Archer of Chapel Studio carry out stained glass work in its widest sense in the belief that only by being comprehensive can one survive in this particular field; their work thus ranges from new stained glass windows, engraving and other decorative techniques, as well as the highly specialized restoration of Victorian glass, particularly Pre-Raphaelite work.

The Worshipful Company of Glaziers offer an annual prize and a travelling scholarship. A new Glaziers' hall, opened in 1975 off London Bridge on the South Bank, has done something towards establishing a national centre where conferences, film shows and courses are held.

The British Society of Master Glass-Painters, inaugurated by Charter in 1921 to advance the art of stained glass and to promote scholarly study of the subject, has a membership of some fifty fellows and eighty craft members. Its scope has been extended to cover all forms of decorative glass used in architecture; its exhibitions have illustrated this, the new techniques of fusing and copper foil being represented alongside the traditional leaded pieces.

Stained glass is rapidly appearing in more secular spheres. Jane Grey, who worked on the nave windows for Coventry Cathedral when she was assistant to Lawrence Lee, now specializes in panels for interior design and uses both the traditional leaded method and the more recently introduced appliqué technique – rather like a transparent mosaic. From her garden-shed studio, with a small kiln accommodated in a converted coalbunker, all kinds of interesting commissions emerge, including a minutely detailed study door for an author, incorporating wild flowers, insects and initials into the design, composed of mainly flashed glass which has dissolved away by acid leaving small areas of colour.

Edward Payne studied under his father, Henry A. Payne, a great stained glass artist, and therefore sees his own work as following in the tradition of Christopher Whall, his father's tutor. Exerting a mastery over all processes, Edward Payne both designs and makes stained glass windows, producing two or three a year with "the help of one faithful assistant". Maintaining a steady flow of work from his studio since 1946 has meant taking on a variety of orders: restoration, releading, portraits and giving some tuition in drawing.

Often discarding his initial idea, Edward Payne interprets a subject by linking motifs together, making studies from nature and using live people for his models. He makes a full-size cartoon before sketching on the specially made glass. Every detail demands minute attention, so for one design he sculpted a three-dimensional paper model of the first English Bible and pinned it to the wall to study the depth of light and shadow from which to make the drawing.

Stained glass is vastly different from painted glass: the monochrome enamel paint becomes a form of glass when heated and made permanent in the kiln. Its dramatic beauty depends on transmitted light. Definition is given to the glass and the transition from one colour to another is eased by the distinctive outlines; leads, in the same way, have to be decorative as well as functional.

The stained glass artist's relationship with his client has invariably been a gentleman's agreement, but puts the artist in a precarious position; ecclesiastical commissions depend on committee approval – and not all committees are decisive bodies. In the event of a misunderstanding, or a breakdown in communications, the artist can lose heavily. A window designed for one church can not be easily sold or made to fit elsewhere.

Such legal matters as contracts, copyright and rates of pay are among the interests of the profession protected by the British Society of Master Glass-Painters. The society has been instrumental in promoting major exhibitions, where architects and planners are given a chance to view at least samples of the work of both new and established artists. Members are also afforded a look at their contemporaries' glass, which has to be inserted in some far-off building once it has left the studio, for windows, particularly, are too large and cumbersome and costly to have lying around one's workshop.

A handy guide to the work of leading artists is published by the society and may go some way to introducing architects to the possibility of using stained glass within domestic and civic buildings. The survival of stained glass as an art-craft must surely depend on its achieving a strengthened place in secular work. It cannot be dominated by its glorious past; its aged patron, the Church, is no longer a wealthy master, but it would help the living tradition if as much mention were given to those craftsmen who design, make and restore the wondrous windows as is given by the authors of the small printed church guides to the anonymous craftsmen of ancient times.

SOCIETIES

GUILD OF GLASS-ENGRAVERS, Hon. Sec: Mrs E. Freed, Wilmer House, Church Road, Ham Common, Surrey TW10 5HL. Tel: 01–940 9000; Membership: Mrs E. Eliades, 100 Haven Green Court, London W5 2UY. Tel: 01–997 2579
  Formed in 1975 to promote the highest quality of creative design and craftsmanship among glass-engravers, the guild serves to assist them on technical matters and to spread a knowledge of engraving methods among its lay members who seek a wider appreciation and understanding of the craft. Its main objectives are: to stimulate imaginative work; to make known to clients those craftsmen who undertake commissions; to act as a forum for interchange of ideas, designs and markets; to strengthen links with the glass industry and interested bodies; and to ensure that exhibitions of members' work are judiciously presented in appropriate lighting.

THE BRITISH SOCIETY OF MASTER GLASS-PAINTERS, 6 Queen Square, London WC1N 3AR; Hon. Sec: Mrs Caroline Swash, 88 Woodwarde Road, London SE22. Tel: 01–693 5674
  Its aims are to advance the art of stained glass, promote its scholarly study, protect the interests of its members and further the interests in and of the craft by demonstrations, exhibitions and publications. Articles of historical interest and international current news are included in the annual journal; the quarterly news sheet is designed especially for craftsmen in the provinces, to keep members in touch with the society, and advertises jobs, discusses new equipment and technical problems, as well as publicizing exhibitions and courses and information from BCF and CAC.

WORSHIPFUL COMPANY OF GLAZIERS AND PAINTERS OF GLASS, The Rectory, St Mary at Hill, London EC3. Tel: 01–283 3601
  Annual competition and travelling scholarship.

CONSERVATION AND RESTORATION

CANTERBURY CATHEDRAL STAINED GLASS STUDIO AND RESTORATIONS CENTRE, The Precincts, Canterbury, Kent. Tel: 0227 53626
  Conservation and restoration of the cathedral's windows, but work for other churches is also undertaken.

YORK GLAZIERS' TRUST, 3 Deangate, York. Tel: 0904 56846
Scholarly and technical expertise is accumulated and disseminated. Historically important glass is treated from any source although the trust's primary object is the conservation of the Minster's glass.

GLASS-MAKERS

JOHN AKERS (White Horse Vale Glass), 72 Westfield Way, Charlton Heights, Wantage, Berks. Tel: Wantage 4552
Free-blown glass – tableware and figurines. Speciality is the reproduction of fine eighteenth-century glasses with air-twist stems.

JOHN COOK, MDeSRCA, MSDC, 28 Castle Street, Whitwick, Leics. LE6 4AG
Mainly free-blown glass. Widely exhibited.

DARTINGTON GLASS LTD, Torrington, North Devon. Tel: Torrington 2321
Dartington Glass is part of the wider organization, the Dartington Hall Trust. In the few short years since production started in 1967, Dartington has become famous for the quality and design of its hand-made glass. Frank Thrower, the designer, won the Duke of Edinburgh Design Prize in 1972. Retailed through leading shops. The factory shop at Torrington sells seconds.

THE GLASSHOUSE, 27 Neal Street, London WC2. Tel: 01–836 9785
Studio-gallery offering both facilities for the designer-craftsmen in glass-making and a retail outlet.
Resident craftsmen:
DILLON CLARKE, JANE GILCHRIST, ANNETTE MEECH,
STEVEN NEWELL, PAULINE SOLVEN and FLEUR TOOKEY.

Glass-blowing courses are organized as three-week evening classes and intensive week-end classes. There are courses for beginners and advanced students in small groups.

ROYAL BRIERLEY CRYSTAL (Stevens & Williams Ltd), North Street, Brierley Hill, Staffs. DY5 3SJ. Tel: Brierley Hill 77054
Hand-made, mouth-blown 30 per cent full lead crystal glass. The first royal warrant was awarded to this company in the reign of King George V, and has been renewed by each successive monarch. The glass, the only royal brand, is retailed through glass and china shops, jewellers, and department stores throughout the world.

WHITEFRIARS GLASS LTD, Tudor Road, Wealdstone, Middx. HA3 5PF. Tel: 01–427 1527
Still employing the traditional methods which Pepys would have recognized, a vast range of fine hand-made crystal is made; a small symbolic white friar is the trade-mark on the exports which go to many parts of the globe. Limited editions of hand-engraved commemorative goblets to mark important historical occasions are also made. The ancient processes of creating *millefiore* are perfected by the master glass-makers to capture 'a

thousand flowers' in exquisite paperweights. Whitefriars Glass is retailed through leading shops.

GLASS-ENGRAVERS

T. A. APPLEYARD, "Keepers", Church Lane, Bury, Pulborough, Sussex. Tel: Bury 669
Diamond-point engraving mainly to commissioned orders. Exhibiting associate member Guild of Sussex Craftsmen.

FRED BEAMES, Moors Cottage, Swellshill, Brimscombe, Glos.
Glass-engraver.

DOROTHY BROWN, 115 Home Park Road, Wimbledon, London SW19
Glass-engraving by copper wheel. Speciality line is the development of a cameo-cutting technique. Individual pieces to special commission by this long established artist-craftswoman, at whose first exhibition the Queen Mother purchased a pair of glasses.

JOHN CLIFFORD, 15 Springfield Road, Gorleston, Great Yarmouth, Norfolk
Glass-engraving. Member of Great Yarmouth Guild of Artists and Craftsmen.

E. M. DINKEL, The Grange, Bussage, Stroud, Glos. Tel: Brimscombe 2368
Glass-engraver. Member of Guild of Gloucestershire Craftsmen.

BRYANT FEDDEN, Tan Yard Bank, Castle Street, Winchcombe, Glos. GL54 5JA. Tel: Winchcombe 602782
Artist-craftsman whose skill ranges from glass-engraving and letter-cutting in stone to kinetic sculpture. Most work is commissioned and has included engraving windows for Bristol Cathedral. Member of Guild of Gloucestershire Craftsmen.

JOAN JAMESON, 19 Hailes Street, Winchcombe, Glos. Tel: Winchcombe 602549
Glass-engraver whose range extends from designs on table-glass to door-panels and sculptured jewellery. Wildlife is Mrs Jameson's forte but she will quite happily engrave abstract designs, lettering, buildings and crests as meticulously as animals, flowers or butterflies. Associate Member of Guild of Gloucestershire Craftsmen.

HONORIA D. MARSH (Miss), Brigge House, Broughton, Stockbridge, Hants. SO20 8AE. Tel: Broughton 369
Distinguished artist whose major works never number more than three or four engravings a year. Some commissions, such as the Churchill Goblet, showing Chartwell across the wide lake, take almost a year to complete. Engravings are always carried out with diamond-point tools specially made for her. Recent commission is the Royal Air Force Goblet.

WILLIAM MEADOWS, The Old House, Milverton, Taunton, Somerset. Tel: Milverton 369
Engraving by diamond-point stipple on glass goblets which the artist designs and has made specially for his commissioned work.

DAVID H. MONKMAN, c/o Swan Hotel, Hay on Wye, via Hereford HR3 5AE
Diamond-point glass-engraving. Sign-writing.

STEFAN OLIVER, Broadgate, Whepstead, nr Bury St Edmunds, Suffolk 1P29 4YB. Tel: Horringer 404
Glass-engraver working mainly to commissioned orders. Widely exhibited.

DAVID PEACE, Abbots End, Hemingford Abbots, Hunts. PE18 9AA. Tel: St Ives 62472
Glass engraver specializing in presentation glass, calligraphy, heraldry and windows. Master of the Art Workers' Guild 1973 and Chairman of the Guild of Glass Engravers, this artist's work is in many public collections, including the Victoria and Albert Museum and Corning Museum of glass in the USA.

DANEK PIECHOWIAK, Kingslea Cottage, Kemerton, Tewkesbury, Glos. Tel: Overbury 359
Diamond-point hand-engraved glass. Any subject can be engraved to order on glasses, decanters or fruit bowls, from photographs or illustrations. Sets of glasses or individual pieces, commemorative or presentation items – quotations and designs will be submitted on request. Member of the Craftsmen of Gloucestershire.

STEPHEN PROCTOR, Brimbles, Bowdley Hill, Ashburton, Devon
Glass-engraver. Specialist detailed pictorial studies in diamond-point on goblets and decanters. Commissions accepted. Member Devon Guild of Craftsmen.

STEPHEN RICKARD, The Old Vicarage, Vicarage Park, Plumstead, London SE18 7SX. Tel: 01–854 3310
Artist-engraver on glass. Each piece is signed and dated. Commissioned work, executed by promised date, has included presentation pieces to the Royal Family, Heads of State and civic bodies, as well as to business houses and private individuals. Fellow of the Society of Designer-Craftsmen.

JAMES WATKINS, Summerleaze, Trowbridge, Wilts. Tel: Trowbridge 62139
Diamond-point engraving on good quality glass.

BERNARD M. YORK, 10 Tellisford Lane, Norton St Philip, nr Bath, Avon BA3 6LL. Tel: Faulkland 318
Glass-engraving by hand. This artist's work has been sold all over the world and appears in the Museum of Applied Arts and Sciences, Sydney, Australia, Collection of Flinders University, Adelaide, Australia, and the Museum of Lincolnshire Life, Lincoln. Presentation plate by the Fleet Air Arm at the

sixtieth anniversary exhibition to HRH Princess Anne; pieces for the Prince of Wales Investiture and commemorative items as well as commissions for private individuals.

STAINED GLASS ARTISTS

ANN BOOTH (Mrs), Clarage House, High Street, Kingston Blount, Oxon.
Designer-craftswoman of stained glass hangings, screens and windows. Mainly bonded stained glass but some leaded. Commissions undertaken, small pieces sometimes available for sale.

ALFRED FISHER, FMGP and PETER ARCHER, AMGP, Chapel Studio, Bridge Road, Hunton Bridge, Kings Langley, Herts. WD4 8RE. Tel: Kings Langley 66386
Designers and craftsmen in stained glass work in its widest sense. Most work is commissioned and ranges from new stained glass windows for ecclesiastical and secular buildings to specialized restoration of both medieval and Victorian glass. Commissions have included windows for Canada, USA, South Africa, New Zealand, and stained glass stations of the cross for a church without walls in Sarawak. Restorations have included the medieval glass of the 'bird window' in Clothall Church. Other decorative techniques embrace glass-engraving in both small scale and architectural work, and fused glasswork.

JANE GRAY, ARCA, 117 Belmont Road, Uxbridge, Middx. Tel: Uxbridge 32717
Stained glass artist working in both the traditional leaded and the more modern appliqué methods for domestic panels, hanging frames, partitions and heraldic windows. Commissions have included all twenty-six windows in Hillingdon (Middx) hospital chapel executed in glass appliqué.

MICHAEL HARRISON and KAREN QUILÁN, 8 Brookside Road, Leigh, Wimborne, Dorset
Artists working in stained glass, primarily utilizing the copper foiling method. Speciality commissions for Tiffany-type lamp-shades.

PHILIPPA HESKETT, Malting House, Shimpling, Bury St Edmunds, Suffolk 1P29 4HS. Tel: Cockfield Green 609
Designer-artist in stained glass whose outstanding work can be seen in two west windows of the church of St Peter and St Paul at Grays Thurrock in Essex, a church in Withersfield, Suffolk, and a synagogue in Rochester. Miss Heskett also works on glass for domestic use – Zodiac and heraldic designs in leaded glass or glass mosaics, and is an annual exhibitor at the Aldeburgh Festival. Member British Society of Master Glass-Painters.

EDWARD PAYNE, Triangle, Box, nr Stroud, Glos. Tel: Nailsworth 2862
Artist-craftsman making stained glass windows to his own designs in the Christopher Whall tradition. There are many windows by Edward Payne in Gloucestershire and Lincolnshire churches. Considerably experienced in restoration work, this eminent artist is custodian of the world-famous set of

medieval windows of Fairford Church. Member of Guild of Gloucestershire Craftsmen. Member of British Society of Master Glass Painters.

HUGH B. POWELL, Farringdon Hurst, Alton, Hants. Tel: Tistead 210 (London Studio 01–736 3113)

An artist who has designed and made stained glass windows for both English and Canadian churches, with an interest in commissions for portrait painting.

15

Ceramics

The discovery that the four elements – earth, air, water and fire – could be combined to produce impermeable containers made pottery one of the earliest staple crafts of civilization. That certain clays were more suitable for the purpose than others could only be found by trial and error.

At its most primitive pottery is functional, crude but never vulgar; at its most sophisticated it is an artistic expression. The qualities of the clay are released through a combination of manipulative skill and creative craftsmanship. It is the talent, techniques or styles which distinguish the work of one potter from another. It is a craft which excites more comment, criticism and controversy than any other, mostly between the potters themselves, although it is not unusual for other people to disagree when it comes to judging what one may admire in a pot when it is viewed as an aesthetic artefact, while yet another group of people may regard the same piece simply as a plain, practical pot. But it is this acute awareness, and even ambiguity of and within the crafts medium which is vital in the perpetuation of a living tradition.

As with other crafts, research is carried out to re-discover original designs and to re-construct the methods as practised by the ancient civilizations; and so one finds a great number of potters who build pots by the coiling or slab methods. The most dramatic technical advance on the hand-built forms was the invention of the rotating wheel, on which clay can be moulded into a cylindrical shape.

It has been said that it is not commercially viable to produce pottery by the original hand-thrown method, but this has been disproved by those who have remained true to tradition, re-organizing their production line rather than changing their mode of making. Unfortunately, few customers seem to know or care about the difference between hand-made and factory-produced pieces so the prices have to be competitive, irrespective of the time spent on hand-made pieces. Time is the unseen factor which the customer is not willing to pay for, he assesses only the values of the raw material, although the younger people are the ones who buy the hand-thrown pottery.

Studio potters working on highly individual projects find it impracticable to employ assistants. They also value their independence highly. Taking on paid help involves a disruption of routine and increased responsibilities. It is an investment which shows no dividends for some time and none at all if the "apprentices" leave – as they invariably do when confident of their own abilities, to set up on their own in competition with their tutor.

Some art schools send fourth-year students out to local potteries on a grant. Other studio potters offer a 'give and take' kind of scheme whereby students can make use of the facilities, learning the craft and seeing at first hand the practical problems, in return for basic help to the general business. The Dartington Hall Trust has established its own pottery training workshop with substantial assistance from CAC. Under the direction of Peter Starkey students are given the opportunity to learn about workshop conditions.

Compromising between a fair-sized output of regular items such as plates and cups and saucers, where exact reproduction is necessary for sets, with a continual quality of finish, potteries such as Robin Welch use the semi-industrial techniques of jigger and jolleying, leaving the studio potter more time to the creation of individual pots and sculpture.

Not all potters stick to pots, of course; the Well Walk Pottery in Hampstead has developed an individual line in garden fountains, and many 'specialize' in having no speciality, but will meet the challenges as they come. The aesthetic aspect is often not the only consideration. Durability and practicability are equally important factors; there is not much scope for artistic licence in the production of a doorstep, but Bryan Newman was suitably gratified that his withstood, not the buffeting one usually has to suffer from craft critics' blows at a public exhibition, but the rigours of the stiletto heel period. He went back after two years to see how the step had fared: there was not a mark on it. He, like so many others, was once pleased to accept an order for 100 ashtrays and 300 cups and saucers for a café in Chelsea. A proposition at which many craft potters turn up their noses, but one which often keeps the struggling craftsman just solvent in that difficult first year when all his capital is spent on the necessary equipment. Once established, he can then be selective.

"Knowing when to say no is as important as responding to demands," Thomas Plowman says. With some twenty years' working experience and international exhibitions behind him he has both encountered and survived the initial difficulties of marrying artistry with practicability. The perennial problems which face successful potters are how to tailor the output to the demand, and how to manoeuvre the demand to suit the output. Expanding means losing individuality, remaining small results in working one's self to a standstill; creating one's own market is a matter of compromise and diplomacy. His commissions have ranged from requests to make copies of antique Lowestoft porcelain to 10,000 honey-containers, from church altar furniture to satisfying the complete crockery needs of a restaurant. "I won't say which I accepted or which I turned down," Thomas Plowman says, "just that I'm always approachable." He makes both a comprehensive range of domestic pottery and a considerable number of one-off pieces, including porcelain: the close combination of the two activities results in mutual benefit to both, in that the domestic pots embody an artistic craftsmanship and the individual ones are rooted in functional pottery.

Making what is wanted and what they really want to make are often thought of as two distinct forces, irreconcilable in the minds of some potters who will also only answer to the name of ceramic artists. Perhaps it is in this particular field that the schism between the arts and crafts (if one really exists!) is the more ill-defined and therefore controversial.

There is also the sobering thought put forward by one artist that of course it is easier to make a profit from producing bad pottery than to make a modest living from producing good pottery, a situation which offends the dignity of craftsmanship. Commercial and creative aspects are too often opposing forces.

Industry is the bane of some craft potters, but others feel there could be more liaison, and cite the example of Scandinavia, where designer-craftsmen are granted access to industry's studio and technical facilities, and even a modest grant. But it is not easy to compare the principles of this to those of English crafts, because Scandinavian designs, on the whole, are adapted for industry, which is understandable when one considers that only comparatively recently has the totally rural life of their communities changed to an industrialized state; whereas English craftsmen are sensitive only to the mediocrity resulting from our century of industrialization. Most feel it would be in direct opposition to the principles on which they work if there were any link-up, and prefer to create a distinct divide between industry and craft.

The idea of co-operative industrial research began during the First World War when it became evident that Britain, although as advanced as any country in the field of scientific research, had in many instances failed to apply its sciences to industry. As an immediate step to rectify the general position, the Government established the Department of Scientific and Industrial Research (DSIR). Since then it has been Government policy to encourage the establishment and growth of research associations: some fifty such institutions now serve most sections of industry. Combined, they form a great national reserve of knowledge and expertise.

Under the guidance of DSIR, two associations were formed to serve the pottery and clay building-materials industries. Amalgamated in 1948 to cover the whole ceramic field as the British Ceramic Research Association (B Ceram RA), the pottery division is the largest of the four groups. Dealing mainly with industrial ceramics, the association has little to do with the work of individual craftsmen – although such potters do make use of its testing services, particularly with regard to compliance with British Standard 4860 for metal release from tableware.

Co-existence of artistic ideals and commercial practicalities within a craft-orientated industry is evident, however, within the giant potteries of Wedgwood. The Wedgwood Group today employs some 9,000 people in about twenty factories, mostly located in North Staffordshire, accounting for about one fifth of the British ceramic tableware industry's output and about a quarter of its exports, being one of the first recipients of the Queen's Award for export achievement.

The "father of English potters", Josiah Wedgwood, founded the firm in 1759, inventing, perfecting and marketing a wide range of tableware and ornamentalware. One painted plate from the 952-piece dinner service which he made for the Empress Catherine of Russia in 1773 realized £900 in a recent sale at Sotheby's. The greatest ceramic innovator of the eighteenth century, Josiah Wedgwood was an indefatigable experimenter. Black basalt, a fine-grain stoneware in which the rich black colour is achieved by staining the body with ironstone, manganese dioxide and cobalt, he had perfected by 1768; Jasper, a hard, vitreous white stoneware which can be stained by the addition of metallic oxides to a variety of colours, with some of the qualities of porcelain, he introduced in 1774. Both are still in production. The processes have remained unchanged for over 200 years.

The European predilection for portraiture reached an unparalleled peak at this time, and Wedgwood pandered to his customers' passion by making portrait medallions. His popes did not find a very wide market in Protestant Britain, nor, for that matter, on the Catholic Continent, but a large collection of portraits of notable people was produced, generally in flattering profile – though George III seemed to be the exception. But his queen proved a prettier subject – fortunately, as she was one of Josiah Wedgwood's patrons and gave permission for the name 'Queen's Ware' to be used exclusively for Wedgwood's fine earthenware. Neo-classical designs introduced at that period are still popular, and still characterize the traditional ceramics, immediately identified as Wedgwood. A very high degree of hand craftsmanship, design and artistic skills is involved; most of the handwork is carried out at Barlaston, at the British pottery industry's most up-to-date factory where a new visitors' complex is in operation. Demonstrations of the main handcraft processes are given, and a museum, opened in July 1975, gives a panorama of the potter's art over two centuries.

Tracing the origins of pottery and the rise of the industry in North Staffordshire is made easy at the Gladstone Pottery working museum, where the distinctive bottle-shaped kilns stand as monuments to the potter's past. The skills of the craft are demonstrated to visitors and the hand-thrown products are sold in the museum's shop. The wares are fired in a modern kiln, as firing the old bottle-ovens would contravene the smoke regulations That any bottle-ovens survived the Clean Air Bill is a feat of conservation, for, built of solid brick with no internal support, it was the constant firing – keeping off destructive frosts – that was their salvation. Perhaps more than any other architectural feature, the old pot-ovens are silent epitaphs to a grim Victorian industrial existence where clay claimed its victims by anaemia, fits and paralysis, brought about by the lead and silica. The 'jiggers' and 'mould-runners' were a race of pale, diminutive children, labouring "like little slaves. With the mercury 20 degrees below freezing they run on their errands bare-footed from the atmosphere varying from 100–120 degrees where they labour from half-past five in the morning until six at night" – so states a report of 1843 on child labour. Arnold Bennett observed the relationship between the Stoke community and their clay: "the horse is less to the Arab than clay is to the Bursley man. He exists in it and by it; it fills his lungs and blanches his cheek; it keeps him alive and it kills him".

Any chimney may later be a museum-piece as smokeless zones and central heating tidy up the rooflines, but traditional salt-glaze chimney-pots are still made by Knowles of Elland who have their own clay-mines. North-west England has always had access to clay, coal and salt; and salt-glazing – a method of vapour glazing in which salt is thrown into a white-hot kiln – is a technique, made more attractive by its unpredictable results, which is a European contribution to the ancient craft of pottery.

Wood-fired kilns obviously make greater demands on labour than ones heated by oil or electricity, in that they need someone on hand to tend the fire all the time and often to cut and gather the kindling. However, the labour costs are offset by cheaper heating, and the fact that wood ash can be utilized by the potter in his glazing. It is, however, the aesthetic qualities of a wood-fired pot, with its particularly rich and satisfying glazes, which decide its use.

To determine whether it is the difference in glazes or simply a matter of different positions in the kiln, Peter Dick co-operated with Geoffrey Fulham as part of an experiment on traditional slipware, building an outdoor kiln based on archaeological evidence of seventeenth-and eighteenth-century types. They agreed that many erroneous statements had been accepted as facts through academic assumption rather than practical reasoning. No traditional kilns had been found over fire-box height so no-one can categorically state whether or not the early ones had domes. They also thought it possible that they were coal-fired, and were experimenting with coal, protecting the glaze from becoming pitted by the coal-ash by firing small pots inside larger pots.

In the same way, comparisons are made between buying prepared clay and digging one's own. The latter, of course, is very much dependent on whether one lives in a conveniently sited spot. A potter is in such close physical contact with his material that this will be the deciding factor for using clay which he has dug and prepared himself. Stephen Humm, who worked part-time while at University for David Long in Toronto, estimates that he spends as much as a third of his working time on preparing the red clay which he digs from his garden, cleaning it and mixing with sand and fire-clay to reduce shrinkage and increase heat resistance in the oven. He glazes his pots when wet and leather-hard and, having a preference for firing only once, has to take special care with the preparation of the clay so that the glaze still 'fits' when the pots dry out.

Potters, like cooks, have their closely guarded recipes. John and Margaret Harlow produce their own special glazes from their local Somerset stones: basalt, limestone and metamorphic sandstone, which are durable, heat-and craze-resistant, and totally non-poisonous. Jean Randall-Cook delves into the depths of history for a recipe like the one used in Ancient Egypt for her paste beads.

The greatest secret of art is often the technique: Lavender Groves invented her unique method of decoration and calligraphy twenty years ago, and has no intention of ever divulging the secret. There are absolutely no commercial methods employed at all in what she terms her 'old-fashioned' type of decoration which has never previously been used in the production of studio pottery.

Many craftsmen have complained of variability of raw materials; craft suppliers often do not specify types in sufficient detail, and change them without informing their customers. Carriage costs and long delays in delivery are two main problems for potters. Some overcome these by joining forces and collecting the clay themselves in a large van or trailer, sharing the petrol costs. To which, of course, one must add the real cost of the time taken for the collection, for all time is money, and time is taken up in travelling which could be devoted to the craft. But this does enable personal contact between the suppliers and craftsmen; "the Stoke-on-Trent people are very helpful to our small craft businesses", says Fiona Cutting, and most studio potters have agreed with this.

Craft consultants, Podmore and Sons, hold seminars in the very heart of the Potteries at varying levels from one-day courses on throwing and related techniques to a special two-day teaching course.

Pottery lends itself admirably to the gift trade as can be witnessed by the proliferation of potters in the tourist areas of the South-West and the Lake District. Whilst customers are essential to the craftsman's existence, it is not conducive to creativity, or practical, to have curious lookers-on lurking around the workshop "to see how it is done". It is just not fair to a craftsman to expect a performance, a practical demonstration and a step-by-step exposition of the making of a pot in return for buying one. Workshops which are open to the public advertise themselves as such, and equip themselves especially for organized parties, with excellent results.

Les and Aubrey Robinson actually invite visitors to throw a pot at their pottery, but theirs is a specially designed craft centre catering for a lot of people with lecture, demonstration and exhibition areas and pottery classes.

Douglas Phillips holds weekly courses throughout the summer at Ridge Pottery deep in the beautiful border area between Devon and Somerset. This introduces students to the many aspects of the craft and concentrates the teaching period into a sensible schedule for the potter; similar tuition is offered by other individual studios, while pottery courses punctuate every major craft centre prospectus.

Giftware potteries have mushroomed and although their first aim may have been to provide visitors with something with a local label, they have expanded to meet a wider market and have mainly mechanized their processes to cope with the demand. The fascination of seeing things being made is still an attraction, and guided tours of the works form a valuable addition to the programme.

Founded by the Countess of Leicester in 1951, Holkham Pottery was started with a thrower from the original Holkham brickworks who made vases and plant-pots for sale to visitors to the magnificent eighteenth-century Palladian mansion. From its small studio beginnings, it is now one of the three leading giftware potteries in the British Isles and exports to many countries.

Prinknash Pottery started by a providential discovery of a seam of clay during the digging of the foundations for the new abbey in 1942. Experiments proved successful and Brother Thomas started the pottery in a hut in the grounds to help with the building fund. Many thousands of tons of clay yielded to the shovel. Mainly, it fired red and had iron in it, but the seams varied and glazes changed colour. To meet the increased demand, lay employees joined the monks at the potter's wheel and it was decided to build a new pottery and modernize production. Opened in 1974, the output is now in the region of half a million pieces a year and is the abbey's main source of income, new designs are introduced, but the original creations, especially the traditional pewter-glaze tankard, are still produced. About a third of the total output is exported.

The Cotswold clay seam was exhausted by the time the new factory opened; supplies now come from Stoke-on-Trent. Brother Thomas is the chief designer, but only one other member of the community continues the tradition of working in the pottery. An element of handwork is retained, Roland Cox, who lives on the estate, and Ray Martin, the production manager, still throw on the wheel; the application of liquid gold and hand-painting are mainly Brother Thomas's prerogative.

Trainees are taught all the processes in the two to three year apprenticeship scheme. Some thirty-four lay people, including a dozen women, work in the pottery – which incorporates a visitors' viewing-gallery from where the various processes can be watched. The advantage of a majority lay labour force is that work continues throughout the day, if it was staffed completely by the Benedictine monks work would grind to a halt when they were called to prayer – as used to happen.

Decorative and functional, there have been certain local influences in design and these undoubtedly add character to the pieces, identifying them from those produced in other regions: Prinknash has a distinctive pewter-polish glaze; The Wells Pottery decorate with slip and graffito designs based on the traditional West Country ware prevalent in the seventeenth century; Maria Beckett is researching into the traditional pots of Kent; F. Fowler of Sussex applies local town and county crests to goblets and dishes; and Devon cider-mugs form part of Michael Hatfield's wide range. Adrian Lewis-Evans has a lovely line in 'Dorset Owls,' which are globular, narrow-necked, leather-thonged cider-flagons, hundreds of which go to the Plymouth Plantation, the American 'living' museum which reconstructs the living conditions of the early settlers. Two Cornish potters admit local influence on their work – Michael Truscott's stoneware reflects the rich and subtle shades of the landscape, and Peter Ellery's pots reflect the natural forms of weathered stones from the sea-shore.

Wares with historical associations, like those produced at the Pennine Pottery, are in a class above the souvenir types, and recreate distinctive designs which originated in fourteenth-century England. Hand-thrown and hand-painted, the domestic lines are hard-fired earthenware with an englobe, brushed underglaze decoration, which was once made mainly in the south, the style and technique being known as Cambridge ware. The natural lead sulphide used on medieval pots is not acceptable today, of course, so the glaze is leadless with copper and iron colouring oxides – but the shapes and colours are compatible with the period, and in great demand for medieval-style banquets. C. Peasey has obviously researched diligently into the history of his locality for he has also traced the original seal of the local dissolved Priory of Beauvale and incorporates the sprigged seal in his range.

Lavender Groves and Mark Beard make selective commemorative pieces in limited numbered editions, and a unique line in Worcestershire wildlife designs, where long-tailed fieldmice, owls and other creatures decorate small dishes.

Commemorative ware becomes a kind of hallmarked personal expression in the hands of potters. Peter Brown designs a mug for each general election; and for those who have done the Lyke Wake Walk there is the opportunity of getting a commemorative beaker made by Yorkshire's widely acclaimed Charlotte Hargreaves. Ursula Mommen numbers commemorative bowls and beer-mugs in her commissions and Mary Wondrausch has captured the headlines with hers.

Mary Wondrausch has rejected the role of the artist-potter who makes a living by teaching and creating beautiful objects for choice exhibitions to be admired by other potters. "They may think that what I am doing is terribly vulgar, but my philosophy of making pots individually for people has materialized." Looking back on what she terms her 'protected' first year, when she rented a garage behind an antique shop in which to pot, she compares the relatively low outlay with that attached to the shop she now has in a working class district. Outgrowing the garage has meant a five-fold increase in her overheads, but more shop trade than in the garage. Mary acknowledges the "marvellous spread" which *The Times* gave her, resulting in an order for 1,000 named ashtrays, and the wherewithal to buy a kiln. Most of her orders come to her as a direct result of publicity, not through exhibitions or advertising, nor from traipsing the well-tried trails leading to shops and agents. Deriving greater pleasure from her file of thank-you letters than any academic acclamation, she emphasizes that she requires her work to be of sufficient quality to be counted amongst a family's heirlooms. But, even being in the enviable position of having customers seek her out, rather than her seeking them, she is emphatic that it is marketing which presents the biggest and most pressing problem.

A new concept in marketing is that of organizing sales in private houses, on the lines of the increasingly popular type of 'Tuppaware parties'.

Exhibitions are usually the potter's favoured forum: artistically and sympathetically arranged, the pieces stand out, whereas in the High Street shops they jostle for space with mass-produced mugs and general ware. For variety, and to supplement the limited output from their own studio, potters often sell the work of others.

The Craftsmen Potters Shop at William Blake House is the London Centre of the national body serving the interests of craft potters. The Craftsmen Potters Association of Great Britain, established in 1958 for the encouragement of creative ceramics has, currently, 149 full members and about 1,200 associate members; which means a fairly immediate contact with quite a large part of the pottery world.

The full members are the sole shareholders in the non-profit-distributing organization and each has shelf-space in which to show work for sale. Exhibitions by individuals and groups are also staged. Selection is by an elected council comprising a cross-section of full members. Criticism has been levelled at the supposed bias towards stoneware and against earthenware, but this is repudiated by the committee, who say they would be only too happy to have more applications from potters producing good earthenware. There is also the fact that the attractions of high fired pottery have claimed the erstwhile earthenware potter. The members receive the sale price of the work they sell, and pay the association a fixed commission to cover running costs. Contacts with craft potters overseas are established and encouraged, and seminars at a professional level are arranged through West Dean College. Valuable contact with all that concerns the studio potter is made through the Association's excellent magazine, *Ceramic Review*. Full members are listed with their trade-marks and photographs of their work, together with workshop opening hours, in a newly published directory.

The British Stoneware Potters' Association is a small association comprising only six commercial-scale manufacturers whose output of stoneware pottery must account for 75 per cent of their total output. Despite a high degree of craftsmanship in the work, the individual potters within the companies are not, of course, identifiable as studio potters are.

The only regional potters' associations are in Buckinghamshire, Kent, and Dacorum and Chiltern. The latter, with a membership of 250 – and still growing – is headed by Murray Fieldhouse and has a positive purpose. Many other associations, in any craft field, could well be as effective. All its newsletters are released to the Press and influential people to great effect. A regular survey of all potteries in the area is undertaken and reported upon, but perhaps most valuable is the liaison with all general crafts organizations to ensure that individual work is not neglected by lack of contact between the public and the craftsmen. The remaining English potters who do not derive benefit from regional potters' associations belong to the all-craft county guilds, but 64 per cent in this survey feel they have no need of either the associations or their exhibitions. All agreed there was an increased demand for hand-made pots, and seemed to appreciate the public's awakened interest and discernment in the craft, although many feel that too much red tape inhibits much export potential in the crafts generally. Ceramics present their own problems; in particular, they require a special type of packaging to protect the fragile contents from the rough rigours of a customs and excise scrutiny.

Specialized associations and guilds can be influential in forming pressure groups to stabilize standards of manufacturers. The obvious advantage to the individual craftsmen is the forum through which ideas are exchanged and impetus is increased as fresh forms are presented by others in the same field. As one potter said: "working in isolation, or for a seasonal tourist trade, there is a danger of personal standards slipping, and so few people notice the difference!" Some potters, like Cecilia Milton, dislike repetition in their work so intensely that they build their ceramics by hand: in this way all pieces are individual. Joan Nightingale models expressive terracotta nativity figures and glazed child and animal portraits, and Marjorie Smith's sculptures are so widely collected now that she signs and dates each piece.

Generally, it is the eighteenth-century slipware and oriental stoneware which are the common models. But this is adherence to tradition which brought forth a scathing summary of the English pottery scene from the pen of an Australian, here on a scholarship study tour in 1969. "Dead, unimaginative and bound to the glorious ages past," is how the disappointed John Gilbert used to voice his opinion of our abject state in *Pottery in Australia* Vol. 10, No. 1. criticizing the contemporary potters who aped the techniques, glazes and every device of our acknowledged master potters, the man from down-under blamed them for contributing "to the relegation of pottery to the artistically inferior status of a backyard craft".

Tradition, however, is something we British are famed for, so, oblivious to such scorn, our potters still practise the old tried and true techniques with the dedication of disciples. Bernard Leach's philosophy is manifested in the simplicity of his classic style. His new book *The Potter's Challenge* puts art in craft in true perspective. And it is the traditional English pottery, no matter how it is interpreted, which sells to the foreign visitor: Americans flock to the British Crafts Centre for porcelain because few, if any, of their own potters work in this fine medium; the Japanese have been observed buying the works of several potters at once to display as a collection in their own country, and are reported as being "impressed" with English medieval-type pots. It cannot all be attributed to favourable currency exchange rates that hand-made pottery finds such a ready market. Perhaps the scope of a one or two-man studio pottery is not appreciated by overseas buyers, for some of the commissions which come to its doors would require changing over to large-scale industrial methods. "How about an order from the States for a million Grand Canyon medallion mugs?" replied Roger Irving Little when I asked about unusual projects. Making traditional Cornish pottery is one thing, signing away fifty years of his life to fulfil that sort of order is another!

Pleasantly surprised to find that things like his oven-to-table-to-storage-to-freezer stackable lidded pots "go like fun", Stephen Mills gives the impression that it is but a simple task to design such an obviously good idea, throwing by hand and firing in an unattractive but startlingly efficient gas kiln.

Several curious and unusual types of English pottery have been revived by Peter Brown at The Snake Pottery. Like the originals, they are hand-thrown from local clay which Peter digs himself, many of the glaze materials are also dug locally from below the Cotswold scarp. English puzzle-jugs are now rare and valuable. Very few potters make them, jealously guarding the rather difficult method. The jugs date back to Tudor times and are appositely named: only the initiated, and sober, can drink successfully from these large beer-mugs perforated below the rim with hearts and fleurs-de-lis – others only get wet.

Another traditional curiosity, now probably made only by Peter Brown, is the fuddlingcup – a nest of small cups stuck together, with inter-connecting holes. To drain one you must drain all, hence the name. Frog mugs (popular in the eighteenth century), tygs and Tobys made by Peter are indelibly imbued with his personality; stamped and initialled, they are eagerly sought after by collectors but, in keeping with its local origins, almost all his work is sold within the county. The Snake Pottery is a one-man, highly individual enterprise.

Enamellists, as Pat Johnson puts it, are on the border of the conventional distinction between arts and crafts, and therefore have a foot in both camps. Of great antiquity, enamels have a timeless quality. The colours remain for all time and examples of pieces over 2,000 years old are as beautiful today as when they were first made. The craft dates back some 4,000 years, but interest waxed and waned and Ruskin tried to stimulate a latent spark by offering a prize for enamelwork. English artists showed interest as Chinese enamels made their way into Europe in the mid-nineteenth century, but it remained a minor craft until the Artist-Enamellers' Society was formed in 1969, with the aim of using vitreous enamels to their fullest extent, not merely as a decorative medium, but as an art form. The society has been the main factor in promoting the recent revival in the craft, with a membership of forty, it exhibits once a year at a London gallery.

Tiles have been used as a durable and decorative building material for thousands of years; from the vividly-coloured Egyptian and Persian types, through the rich galena glazes of the medieval craftsmen, to the cool blue and white of Delftware, evolving into a high art form in recent years. Many potters produce a few tiles; few potters produce many.

Withersdale Tiles belong to the few. In their small workshop, with the help of one part-timer, they produce enough hand-decorated ceramic tiles to supply about 200 retail outlets.

The most ambitious project to be undertaken this century by English ceramic craftsmen must be the recreation of the Woodchester Pavement. One of the finest examples of Roman mosaic work north of the Alps lies buried in an old Cotswold churchyard, beneath sisal-kraft paper and tons of earth – the best known method of preserving it. It is unearthed once in ten years and some 140,000 people clamber over the tombstones to marvel at the artistry of *c.* A.D. 325. Now, thanks to the perception of Bob Woodward – who went to an auction to buy a paddock and ended up buying a disused tabernacle – the Roman Pavement is being reconstructed, the old tabernacle providing a perfect arena for the mosaic. The original Pavement will be copied exactly, inch by inch the *tesserae* is being laid, all one and a half million pieces of it – resurrecting Orpheus from his underworld at Wotton-under-Edge.

CERAMIC CONSULTANT SERVICES

THE BRITISH CERAMIC RESEARCH ASSOCIATION, Queens Road, Penkhull, Stoke-on-Trent ST4 7LQ. Tel: 0782 45431

Ordinary membership is open to individuals or firms engaged in the production, use or marketing of ceramic products, or those with an approved interest in the ceramic industry. Not geared specifically to the studio potter although even non-members can participate in research activities by arrangement.

PODMORE & SONS LTD, Shelton Works, Shelton New Road, Shelton, Stoke-on-Trent ST1 4BR. Tel: 0782 24571

Manufacturers and suppliers of comprehensive range of equipment and materials for the craft potter. Seminars, under the direction of skilled craftsmen and leading lecturers, different levels up to pottery craft teaching. Free advisory service to assist in the design of pottery departments or studios. Visiting lecture service: details from the Educational Adviser.

CERAMIC SOCIETIES

THE CRAFTSMEN POTTERS ASSOCIATION OF GREAT BRITAIN, William Blake House, Marshall Street, London, W1

Full membership is open to practising professional individual potters and potteries employing not more than thirty people. The criteria for full membership are evidence of mastery of techniques and the creation of an individual style – both essential in order to maintain professional standards. Associate membership is open to everybody interested in pottery; it entitles members to participate in the Association's activities and gives a 5 per cent discount on all goods purchased in the Potters Shop. Regular evening meetings are arranged, mainly for the benefit of Associate Members; seminars at a professional level for full members. A comprehensive selection of everyday items for the potter and selected books on ceramics always in stock. Fully illustrated directory of full members and their work, and *Ceramic Review*, a bi-monthly magazine, are published.

ARTIST ENAMELLERS SOCIETY, Sec: Mrs M. I. Shepherd, 5 Mansfield Road, Wokingham, Berks. Tel: Wokingham 784780

Membership is dependent upon production of high quality enamelwork.

THE DACORUM AND CHILTERN POTTERS GUILD, Murray Fieldhouse, Northfield Studio, Tring, Herts.

Membership is open to all: professional potters, amateurs, students, and teachers. The aims of the guild are to promote increasing awareness of the values of craft pottery and represent within the area the interests of craft potters, pottery-teachers and their students to encourage the establishment of serious part-time vocational courses. Lectures, practical demonstrations, and other activities. Publishes a newsletter and magazine.

CERAMIC ARTISTS AND POTTERS

GEORGINA ALEXANDER, St Katherine's Studio, Onmond Road, Wantage, Oxon
Small studio pottery – one potter. Hand-built stoneware. Speciality is individually moulded ceramic birds. Georgina Alexander also teaches fabric-printing: author of *Fabric-Printing and Dyeing at Home*.

BERYL BALL, Knapp House, Birdlip, Glos.
Enamelling.

VIRGINIA BAMFORD, Clock House, Pottery, Tregony, Truro. Tel: Tregony 666
Hand-thrown domestic ware. Special line: decorative thrown birds, mostly slip decorated and unglazed. Member of Society of Designer-Craftsmen.

GEOFFREY AND OLIVE BAREFOOT, The Wells Pottery, 71 St Thomas Street, Wells, Somerset BA5 2UY
Small studio pottery run by husband and wife whose speciality is earthenware. Commissions for commemorative pieces for schools, churches and presentation items to participants in TV and radio programmes.

PAT BARFOOT, 33 High Street, Martin, Lincoln LN4 3QY. Tel: Martin 234
Stoneware in a wide variety of articles, ceramic plaques, etc. Sales mainly direct from workshop where visitors are welcome. Phone-call advisable. Member of Society of Designer-Craftsmen, and Guild of Lincolnshire Craftsmen.

CLIVE BARRATT, Ceramica, Upton Lane, Upton St Leonards, Glos.
Pottery.

VAL BARRY, 86 Cecile Park, London N8 9AU. Tel: 01–340 3007
Studio potter producing individual stoneware and porcelain. Retail through the Craftsman Potters' Association, British Crafts Centre and Victoria and Albert Museum Craft Shop.

SALLY ANDERSON (Ceramics) Ltd, Parndon Mill, Harlow, Essex. Tel: Harlow 20982
Sally Anderson was largely responsible for the design of the tiles used in the renovation of St Pancras Station, and heads the ceramic design panel which operates at this recently established crafts centre.

MARIA BECKETT, Garden Cottage, Egerton House, Egerton, Ashford, Kent. Tel: Egerton 320
Pottery by Maria Beckett is produced from local red clay which she digs and prepares herself. Basically stoneware. Glazes are made to the potter's own recipes. Decoration ranges from carving to hand-painting. Whiteware from porcelaineous clay from Stoke-on-Trent, hand-painted in gilt. Talks and demonstrations given. Private tuition given by arrangement at her studio-workshop during school holidays. Member of the Kent Professional Potters' Association.

FRANK AND FRANCES BENATT, Beach Pottery, 14 The Beach, Clevedon, Avon. Tel: Clevedon 5066
Wide range of domestic stoneware and individual pots. Sales direct from own pottery shop.

MARGUERITE BETNEY, Turners Farm, Stoven, Beccles, Suffolk. Tel: Brampton 659
Limited output of pottery. Special line: salt-jars.

ELSIE BLUMER, BA, NDD, Harborne Pottery, 164 West Heath Road, Birmingham B31 3HB. Tel: 021–475 6506
Individual earthenware pots; red body, tin glaze and oxide decoration. Oxidized and reduced stoneware and porcelain. Ceramic jewellery exhibited at the Design Centre. Commissioned work includes many murals in ceramic tile and other complementary materials.

CLIVE BOWEN, Shebbear Pottery, Shebbear, Beaworthy, Devon EX21 5QZ. Tel: Shebbear 271
Wood-fired red earthenware from Fremington clays for table ware, bread-crocks, cooking-pots and storage-jars. Direct sales and some retailing through shops in Devon.

WENDY BRADSHAW, Frogmarsh Pottery, South Woodchester, Glos.
Pottery of all kinds – beads, clay sculptures.

KEITH BROLEY, The Old Bell Pottery, Lechlade, Glos. Tel: Lechlade 52608
Studio potter producing a wide range of mainly domestic ware.

PETER BROWN, The Snake Pottery, Green Street, Cottage, Cam Green, Dursley, Glos. GL11 5HW. Tel: Dursley 3260
One-man rural pottery. Wood-fired kiln produces traditional but distinctive truly local earthenware. Heraldic decoration is a speciality, also bonsai dishes. Commemorative mugs in special limited issue. Direct sale, usually at exhibitions and shows. No wholesale or mail order. Exhibiting member of the Craftsmen of Gloucestershire.

JOHN BUCHANAN, Anchor Pottery, The Sloop Craft Market, St Ives, Cornwall
Hand-thrown pottery from single cups to complete dinner services. Individual designs in stock.

A. A. CARLTON, 'Rosary', St Radigunds, Alkham, nr Dover, Kent. Tel: Kearsney 2878
Earthenware clay pottery tiles.

CERAMIC SERVICES (M. J. and D. M. Harris), School House, Dryham, Chippenham, Wilts. SN14 8HA. Tel: Abson 3443
Ceramic ware to customer's requirements, not confined to the usual table-ware; for example, commissions have included producing hand-made wall-

tiles for the exterior of a house, matching existing ones in both colour and texture. Another similar job was the making of a ceramic capping for a soil-pipe, designed and finished to blend with roof tiles. The major side of the business, however, is an equipment maintenance and installation service. Items of equipment made to customers' specifications, electric wheels also produced.

KENNETH CLARK POTTERY, Dryden Street, London WC2. Tel: 01–836 1660
Architectural ceramics, individual pottery and commissioned designs, decorative tiles and dishes.

JOHN CLIFFORD, 15 Springfield Road, Gorleston, Great Yarmouth, Norfolk
Pottery figures and scenes. Member of Great Yarmouth Guild of Artists and Craftsmen.

JOHN COLLETT, Townsend Farm, Littleton Drew, Chippenham, Wilts. Tel: Castle Combe 782441
Studio potter making individual pieces. Coloured glazed ware, which can be wiped clean and does not craze, and salt ware following the lines of Western European medieval pottery. Retail shop on the premises.

RUSSELL COLLINS, The Pottery, Netting Cottage, Netting Street, Hook Norton, Oxon. Tel: Hook Norton 414
Small pottery of three throwers producing mainly domestic ware. Individual porcelain pieces; large pots and cider-jars. Special commissions have included the mural above Harrow Corporation's Public Library. Exhibitions at Heals and Design Centre. Member of Craftsmen Potters Association.

DELAN COOKSON, 5 Mole Run, High Wycombe, Bucks. Tel: High Wycombe 34256
Ceramics falling roughly into two categories: decorative pottery, and sculpture. Recent commissions have included ceramic panels for the pub, 'Captain Coram', in Russell Square, London. Delan Cookson won a gold medal at an international exhibition at Vallauris in 1974. Fellow of the Society of Designer-Craftsmen, helping to launch its licentiateship scheme; currently Licentiateship Secretary.

EMMANUEL COOPER, Fonthill Pottery, 138 Fonthill Road, London N4 3HP. Tel: 01–272 4909
A wide range of oxidized matt oatmeal glazed stoneware, mainly tableware, is made by Emmanuel Cooper and fellow potter Hassan Hassan. Individual pieces are bowls – porcelain and stoneware. Pots for Japanese restaurants, and cream- and milk-separators have been made to special order. Individual and unusual commissions are accepted.

AUBREY COOTE, 1 Normandy Way, Poundbury, Dorchester, Dorset DT1 2PP. Tel: Dorchester 4393
Studio potter producing interesting range of mainly domestic ware.

CONNIE CRAMPTON, North Street Pottery, Ilminster, Somerset
Potter specializing in stoneware. Sales direct from own pottery shop.

TONY DAVIES, 31 New Barn Lane, Prestbury, Cheltenham, Glos. Tel: Cheltenham 28156
Potter. Member Guild of Gloucestershire Craftsmen.

RICHARD DEWAR, Yew Tree Cottage, East Street, St Briavels, Glos. Tel: St Briavels 297
Studio potter producing an interesting and ever-changing range of oven, table, and kitchen ware. Included, are such items as colanders and mixing-bowls. Member of the Hereford Society of Craftsmen.

PETER DICK, Coxwold Pottery, Coxwold, York. Tel: Coxwold 344
Hand-made pottery by Peter and Jill Dick, wood-fired to a distinctive texture. Impressed patterns and slip-trailing are used for decorating the wide range of mostly domestic ware, available direct from the pottery and through selected retail shops.

BARBARA AND RUSSI DORDI, 5 St Leonards Road, Hythe, Kent CT21 6EH
A good range of wheel-thrown tableware, slabbed platters and hand-coiled bread-crocks. Speciality lines are large stoneware coiled pots to stand on a wall or floor; porcelain frilled flower-shaped pots; electric lamps made completely of clay, including the shade; and Roman oil-lamps. Some sculpture, mainly figures and abstract shapes.

HEATHER AND MICHEL DUCOS, Acacia Cottage, West Street, Alford, Lincs. Tel: Alford 3342
Hand-thrown stoneware, matt finish, all of the 'useful' rather than purely decorative pieces. Hand-made candles also produced to fit into pots to make lanterns. Sales are direct from the Ducos's seventeenth-century thatched cottage (at the back of which is the pottery) and at the Alford Craft Market.

GEOFFREY EASTOP, Fawley Pottery, Fawley Bottom Farmhouse, nr Henley, Oxon.
Small pottery specializing in large orange and red glazed dishes with wax-resist surface treatment, and tiled murals in rich earthenware colours. Main production is a range of oxidized stoneware of simple design. Individual pieces in porcelain. Geoffrey Eastop's murals can be seen at the children's play area outside Maudsley Hospital, London, and at Reading's new Civic Centre – made to the design of John Piper.

DAVID EELES, Shepherd's Well Pottery, Mosterton, Beaminster, Dorset. Tel: Broadwindsor 257
A family business of half a dozen potters making a wide range in earthenware, stoneware, and porcelain; mostly thrown table and domestic ware, and individual pieces. Just over half the output is wholesaled. Retail sales are through the Pot Shops at Mosterton, and 18 Barrack Street, Bridport in

Dorset, and A303 Watergore, nr Ilminster in Somerset. David Eeles is a founder member and present chairman of the Craftsmen Potters Association.

MICHAEL EMMETT, White Cross, nr Offwell, Honiton, Devon Tel: Wilmington 483
Main production is domestic reduced stoneware, terracotta breadcrocks, and individual pieces in saltglaze and porcelain. Freelance designer for industry.

RAYMOND EVERETT, FRSA, 4 Grange Crescent, Crawley Down, Sussex RH10 4JU
Studio potter producing domestic ware and individual pieces, retailed mainly through local art galleries.

RAYMOND FINCH, The Pottery, Winchcombe, Glos. Tel: Cheltenham 602462
Long-established pottery producing wood-fired stoneware mainly for domestic use, wood-ash glazed. Member of Guild of Gloucestershire Craftsmen.

BILL FISHER, The Sloop Craft Market, St Ives, Cornwall
Ceramic sculpture, mainly terracotta figures.

CHRISTOPHER AND ANGELA FISHER, The Taunton Pottery, 87 Outer Circle, Halcon, Taunton, Somerset. Tel: Taunton 82605
Husband and wife craft potters making hand-thrown table and ovenware. Enchanting range of character animals, each one individually hand-modelled and fashioned with a hat or apron or other distinctive apparel. Sales are made, at the moment, through the wholesale trade only.

MAGGIE FISHER AND EV STEVENS, The Sloop Craft Market, St Ives, Cornwall
Celtic pottery.

SHIRLEY FOOTE, Ganders Ash, Loves Hill, Timsbury, Bath
Ceramic sculptures and domestic ware.

JOHN FORSTER, Blackberry Hill Crafts, Horsley, Glos.
Earthenware pottery.

F. P. FOWLER, 7c Courthouse Street, Hastings, Sussex
Two potters producing oxidized stoneware in a range of table and oven ware. Speciality line is the applying of local town or county crests to goblets, mugs and dishes.

CHRIS GENT, 281 Painswick Road, Gloucester
Pottery pendants.

COLIN GERRARD, Sparrows, Chalford Hill, Stroud, Glos.
Potter. Member Guild of Gloucestershire Craftsmen.

LESLIE GIBBONS, ATD, The Owl Pottery, 108 High Street, Swanage, Dorset
Highly decorated well-made earthenware, hand-thrown and moulded.
Specializing in individual dishes with pictorial motifs and bold graphic
designs. Sales are made in their own shop, adjacent to the pottery, where
their drawings, prints, and small sculptures are also available.

JOAN GODFREY, The Studio at Kiln Cottage, Boase Street, Newlyn, Penzance,
Cornwall TR18 5JE
Studio potter specializing in fused glass decoration on glazed tiles, and tiles
decorated by the majolica techniques in the style of Italian ware. Special
commissions have included tiles with decoration of hand-modelled Egyptian subjects for the National Trust shop in Egyptian House, Penzance.
Member of the British Crafts Centre.

STELLA GOORNEY, The Pottery, The Old Brewery, Newtown, Bradford-on-
Avon, Wilts.
Studio potter making a fairly wide range of domestic oxidized stoneware
with wax resist decoration. Some hand-building also. Commissions undertaken by arrangement. Sales are made through the 'Stone's Throw' craft
shop, adjacent to the pottery, where silk screen prints and crochet designs
by FRANCES SNOW are also available.

MAGGY GRANGER, Camden Lock, Commercial Place, London NW1 8AF
Ceramics and porcelain dolls.

GUILD CRAFTS, The Brewery, Fontmell Magna, nr Shaftesbury, Dorset SP7
OPA. Tel: Fontmell Magna 597
Hand-crafted gifts in pottery with special decorations – which have been
exported to twenty countries. 'Seconds' shop. Visitors welcome at the workshop. Featured on BBC television.

CHARLOTTE HARGREAVES, 22 New Street, Selby, Yorks YO8 OPT. Tel: (home
number) Selby 2536
Original hand-made ceramics: stoneware, porcelain and agate. The work of
Charlotte Hargreaves is highly commended in Yorkshire, her very practical
pottery is used in hotels and coffee shops and retailed in the showroom
(above).

JOHN AND MARGARET HARLOW, Whitnell Pottery, Fiddington, Bridgwater,
Somerset TA5 1JE. Tel: Nether Stowey 663
Husband and wife team producing mainly domestic oxidized stoneware.
Speciality lines are attractive glazes produced from local stones and rocks.
Porcelain and ceramic wall-panels. Commissions undertaken.

MICHAEL HATFIELD, Seckington Pottery Models, Winkleigh, Devon EX19 8EY.
Tel: Winkleigh 478
One-man pottery specializing in miniatures and very detailed models,
among which are mice on cheese wedges, boots from $1\frac{1}{2}$ inches to $4\frac{1}{2}$ inches
with clearly marked stitching, and Devon cider-mugs. Commissions

accepted – recent ones have included making models of Pyrenean Mountain Dogs for the Breed Society of Great Britain.

BARBARA HILL, Phoenix Pottery, 65 Falmouth Road, Truro, Cornwall. Tel: Truro 3408 and 4408
Individual pots and range of porcelain.

ANDREW HOLDEN, The Square, North Tawton, Devon. Tel: North Tawton 513
Craft potter producing a wide range of hand-thrown domestic stoneware pottery and decorative pots in porcelain and stoneware. Member of Crafts-men Potters Association. Sales at own studio shop and others throughout the country.

HOLKHAM POTTERY LTD, Holkham Wells, Norfolk. Tel: Wells 424/5
One of the three leading giftware potteries in the British Isles, Holkham pottery has become renowned as the "distinctive pottery from a stately home". The Ancient House, Holkham, is open for the sale of pottery, gifts and selected seconds all the year round. Details of pottery making demonstrations and special works visits on application. Retail outlets are through high class gift shops throughout the British Isles and many overseas countries.

STEPHEN HUMM, April Cottage, Trumps Green Road, Virginia Water, Surrey
Studio potter producing basically domestic ware. Sales are direct.

ANNE JAMES, Ashley, Gloucester Street, Painswick, Glos. Tel: Painswick 813378
Studio potter whose speciality is delicate porcelain boxes with sculptured landscapes on the lids. Hand-made stoneware mainly for domestic use. Member of Guild of Gloucestershire Craftsmen.

PAT JOHNSON, 182 Stakes Hill Road, Waterlooville, Hants. PO7 7BS
Enamellist whose main output is in large scale enamels for architectural purposes. Recent commissions include a 6-foot cross for a cathedral.

STEPHANIE KALAN, London Road, Newport, Saffron Walden, Essex CB11 3PN. Tel: Saffron Walden 40359
Ceramic artist specializing in glazes, especially reduced red copper, and crystalline glaze.

EILEEN LEWENSTEIN, 11 Western Esplanade, Hove, Sussex BN4 1WE
Sculptural artist potter producing highly individual pieces. Recent commissions include the ceramic screen in the façade of the Convent of Our Lady of Sion, London W11.

ADRIAN LEWIS-EVANS, Stoney Down Pottery, Rushall Lane, Lytchett Matravers, Dorset. Tel: Lytchett Minster 2392
Well established one-man pottery producing wine and water sets, tankards, pitchers, and Oriental design vases with rich glazes. Speciality lines are the

'Dorset Owl' cider-flagon and salt-glaze Bellarmine reproductions.

ROGER IRVING LITTLE, Camelot Pottery, The Old Bakery, Boscastle, Cornwall. Tel: Boscastle 291
  Hand-thrown traditional Cornish earthenware pottery. Traditional slip-wares. Medallion mugs to the trade. Sales direct from studio shop.

JOHN LOMAS, 12 The Green, Jordans, nr Beaconsfield, Bucks. HP9 2SU. Tel: Chalfont St Giles 4556
  Stoneware potter producing mainly tableware.

AVIS AND BERNARD LOSHAK, Esthwaite Pottery, Hawkshead, Ambleside, Cumbria LA22 ONT. Tel: Hawkshead 241
  Husband and wife partnership producing oxidized stoneware. Sales are direct from the pottery.

ROSALIND LOWE, The Shambles, 20 Harmsworth Way, Totteridge, London N20 8JU. Tel: 01-445 3529
  Studio potter. Member of the Dacorum and Chiltern Potters Guild.

DENNIS E. LUCAS, Hastings Pottery, West Hill Villa, Cobourg Place, Hastings, Sussex. Tel: Hastings 2229
  Hand-thrown stoneware and earthenware, pressed dishes, individual sculptural pots and ceramic sculpture. Direct sales.

CHRISTOPHER MAGARSHACK, The Well Walk Pottery, 49 Willow Road, Hampstead, London NW3. Tel: Hampstead 1046
  Earthenware potter specializing in large bowls with traditional slip decoration, individual clay pipes and masks with grotesque heads for fountains.

CLIVE MAGERN, The Bungalow, Elton, Newnham-on-Severn, Glos. Tel: Newnham-on-Severn 397
  Potter. Member of Guild of Gloucestershire Craftsmen.

DEIRDRE MALONE, Hook Pottery, Little Thatch, Hook, Wootton Bassett, Wilts.
  Studio potter making thrown earthenware, mainly individual decorated pots and dishes.

DONALD MARSH, Cranleigh Pottery, High Street, Cranleigh, Surrey GU6 8AS
  Studio potter making pieces mainly to order.

IVAN AND KAY MARTIN, The Cricklade Pottery, Cricklade, Wilts. Tel: Cricklade 436
  A long-established pottery producing hand-made domestic ware in slipware and stoneware. Some salt-glazed ware. Member of the Craftsmen of Gloucestershire.

STEPHEN MILLS, Bath Pottery, 87 Walcot Street, Bath, Avon. Tel: Bath 4992
  Stoneware potter producing hand-thrown domestic ware. Approximately

half the output is for small hotels and restaurants with purpose-designed ware, the rest is retailed mainly direct in own pottery shop.

ANNA MILNER, Old Down House, Horton, Wimborne, Dorset Tel: Witchampton 373
Studio potter making hand-thrown domestic stoneware, and individual items such as chess-sets. Sales are mainly through craft shops and galleries and exhibitions.

CECILIA MILTON, Rock Cottage, Rock Road, Wick, nr Bristol BS15 5TW
Studio potter whose hand-built pots and modelled groups of horses, character figures and sculptured heads are all individual pieces. Commissioned work accepted by arrangement. Sales are direct and through exhibitions.

URSULA MOMMEN, The Pottery, South Heighton, Newhaven. Tel: Newhaven 4408
Potter who works mainly with local clay with wood ash in the stoneware glazes. Some high-fired tin glaze blue and white ware also. Commemorative mugs made to order.

JOSEPHINE MORRISON, Bridgelands, Cowlinge, Newmarket CB8 9HN. Tel: Ousden 387
Studio potter specializing in designs of horses, cocks and phoenixes, greatly interested in Chinese art. Private sales.

IVO MOSLEY, BETTY HOSKINS, MARLENE GRUBERT, Design Brokers Ltd, 90 Lots Road, London SW10
Pottery.

JUNE MULLARKEY, The Windmill Pottery, Chapel Road, Dersingham, Norfolk PE31 6PN. Tel: Dersingham (0485) 40761
Studio potter producing hand-made stoneware and porcelain tableware and individual pieces. Natural glazes of ash and red clays. Sales through own pottery showroom.

JANET MURRAY, The Hall, Kettlebaston, Ipswich, Suffolk. Tel: Bildeston 740357
Potter specializing in ash-glazed stoneware traditional and functional pots for kitchen and garden. Individual orders fulfilled by arrangement.

PAMELA NASH AND ERNEST COLLYER, Railway Station House, Winchelsea, Sussex. Tel: Winchelsea 569
Husband and wife team specializing in magnetic panels and pottery sculpture. Panels have been commissioned from these two ceramic artists by Oxford University; Portland House, London; Coventry Museum; and Mormon University in Salt Lake City, USA.

BRYAN AND JULIA NEWMAN, The Pottery, Aller, Langport, Somerset. Tel: Langport 250244

Husband and wife potters producing a wide range of stoneware: from ceramic sculpture and wall-panels to domestic pottery. One of Bryan Newman's
more unusual commissions was for a stoneware doorstep for The Roland
Browse and Delbanco Gallery, Cork Street, London. Sales are direct from
the pottery showroom.

JOAN NIGHTINGALE, Lacey Close, North Wootton, Shepton Mallet, Somerset.
Tel: Pilton 440
Ceramic artist specializing in terracotta nativity figures, glazed portraits of
children and animals. Small, part-glazed oil jar-shaped vases called 'primrose jars'.

JO PARR, Redcliffe Pottery, 13 Guinea Street, Redcliffe, Bristol 1
Studio potter producing individual pieces in oxidized stoneware, porcelain
and earthenware mainly to customers' orders. Sales are direct from the
studio shop.

C. P. PEACEY, Pennine Pottery, 16a Holmes Street, Heanor, Derbyshire Tel:
Langley Mill 60178
Studio potter producing hand-thrown earthenware and stoneware like Blue
Daisy and Lotus, two domestic lines which have their origins in four-
teenth-century England. Individual pieces to special commission such as
the commemorative pottery of the local (dissolved) Priory of Beauvale.
Sales: direct retail and to the trade from the Pottery.

CLIVE PEARSON, Welcombe Pottery, Welcombe, Bideford, North Devon. Tel:
Morwenstow 305
A one-man pottery concentrating on oven-to-table ware in stoneware. Indi-
vidual pieces include oil-lamps and lamp-bases.

RICHARD AND EMMA PHILPS, Sparrows Hall Pottery, Brentor, Tavistock, Devon
PL19 ONF. Tel: Mary Tavy 507
Husband and wife potters producing hand-made stoneware and traditional
slipware with the principal emphasis on useful domestic ware. Ceramic-
topped coffee and dining-tables in oak or beech also made by hand. Widely
exhibited. Among their more unusual commissions have been 125 Wee
Willy Winky candlesticks for masonic wives, and a 10-pint jug decorated
with clay pipe motifs.

DOUGLAS PHILLIPS, Ridge Pottery, nr Wambrook, Chard, Somerset. Tel: South
Chard 463
One-man pottery producing hand-made domestic stoneware using local
clay.

PILLING POTTERY (Jim and Vi Cross), School Lane, Pilling, nr Preston, Lancs.
Tel: Pilling 307
Craftsmen in ceramics. High quality hand-thrown stoneware pottery –
wholesale and retail. Manufacturers of potters' wheels, kilns and equipment. Private tuition on the premises by arrangement. Large retail craft

shop, office and works at The Pottery, Taylors Lane, Pilling (near the wind-mill).

THOMAS PLOWMAN, Stalham Pottery, High Street, Stalham, Norfolk. Tel: Stal-ham 614
Established and widely exhibited studio potter who, with his wife, produces a comprehensive range of domestic pottery and individually designed one-off pieces, including porcelain. Special orders and commissions undertaken by agreement. Sales direct through retail shop attached to the pottery.

PRINKNASH ABBEY POTTERY, Cranham, nr Painswick, Glos. Tel: Painswick 812239
The range comprises some fifty different lines, mainly produced by modern techniques but finished by hand. Some individual pieces are thrown. View-ing gallery of the pottery open to the visitors. Sales are direct from the pot-tery showroom and shop and retailed throughout the country.

QUANTOCK DESIGN LTD, Chapel Cottages, West Bagborough, Taunton, Somer-set TA4 3EF. Tel: Bishops Lydeard 429
A small firm of ten people making hand-built and hand-pressed stoneware pottery to meet the demands of some 150 retail outlets. Occasional com-missions undertaken, one of the most unusual being for a fountain with five bowls and a dolphin's head.

QUEEN ELIZABETH'S FOUNDATION FOR THE DISABLED, Dorincourt, Oaklawn Road, Leatherhead, Surrey KT22 0BT. Tel: (Workshop) Oxshott 2599
A residential sheltered workshop where disabled artists, trained on site, design, paint, glaze and fire ceramic tiles.
Standard sizes: 6 inches × 6 inches and $4\frac{1}{2}$ inches × $4\frac{1}{2}$ inches. Sales to the home market, particularly the building trade, and available for export. A catalogue and price list on application to the Industries Manager.

JEAN RANDALL-COOK, LSIA, DIPDES, Well House Pottery, Gretton, nr Chelten-ham, Glos. Tel: Winchcombe 602206
Craft potter and industrial designer producing a wide range of hand-thrown mainly domestic ware. Speciality line is Egyptian-style turquoise paste beads.

BILL AND VICKI READ, Clayculters Studio, Sheep Street, Winslow, Buckingham, Bucks. Tel: Winslow 2663
Husband and wife studio potters producing mainly to commission dinner and tea services, ikebana pots, bonsai pots, plaques, and pieces for theatrical productions.

ARTHUR ROBERTS, 29 Warner Avenue, Pogmoor, Barnsley, Yorkshire S75 2EG. Tel: Barnsley 5166
Coiled pots and wheel-thrown stoneware and earthenware. Special lines are a ceramic bull and pebble pots. Full member of British Crafts Centre, and Guild of Yorkshire Craftsmen.

ROBIN POTTERY AND CRAFT CENTRE (A. and E. Robinson), Spring Acre Farm, Thorpe-in-Balne, Doncaster, South Yorks. DN6 ODZ. Tel: (0302) 882565-882444
  Hand-thrown pottery in extensive range. Visitors are welcome and allowed to try their hand at throwing pots.

D. RUSKIN, 17 Maygrove, Great Yarmouth, Norfolk
  Potter producing lamps, vases, ornaments and animal portraiture; also stone-carving. Member of Great Yarmouth Guild of Artists and Craftsmen.

PETER SAYSELL, FRSA, Forest of Dean Pottery, Bream, Lydney, Glos. GL15 6JS. Tel: Whitecroft 414
  Three-man pottery producing earthenware and reduced stoneware; a proportion of local clay and local ash glazes are used. Press moulded platters and sculptural ceramics. One of Peter Saysell's ceramic murals can be seen on the gable end of Gloucester's Shire Hall.

LES SHARPE, The Pottery, Hinton St George, Somerset. Tel: Crewkerne 3630
  One-man pottery producing kitchen, oven and table ware.

JOHN SLADE, 69 Hinton Avenue, Cambridge CB1 4AR
  Studio potter producing a complete range of domestic ware.

KEITH AND MARIA SMITH, The Sloop Craft Market, St Ives, Cornwall
  Studio ceramics – tiles and jewellery.

MARJORIE SMITH, 66 Prestbury Road, Cheltenham, Glos. GL52 2DA. Tel: Cheltenham 52782
  Ceramic sculptress whose work is sought after by collectors from all over the world. Individually modelled small figure sculptures and character owls. Ceramic 3-D tiles in original designs and brilliant colours. Commissions undertaken by arrangement. Member of the Craftsmen of Gloucestershire.

JONATHAN AND DOROTHY SNELL, Wetheriggs Pottery, Clifton Dykes, nr Penrith, Cumbria
  The only beehive pottery in the UK. The designs, some 180 years old, are still in use.

M. STOREY, 213 Palgrave Road, Great Yarmouth, Norfolk
  Pottery and stonecarving. Member of Great Yarmouth Guild of Artists and Craftsmen.

SURREY CERAMIC CO. LTD, Kingwood Pottery, School Road, Grayshott, Hindhead, Surrey GU26 6LR. Tel: Hindhead 4404
  Essentially a small commercial pottery where part of the goods produced are hand-made.

JANICE TCHALENKO, 30 Therapia Road, London SE22. Tel: 01–693 1624

One-woman pottery workshop producing table and oven ware. Tutor at London art schools.

QUEENIE THOMPSON, 4 Crafton Park, Yeovil, Somerset. Tel: Yeovil 22462
Ceramic sculptress who also produces domestic ware.

THREE POTTERS (Alysoun, Caroline and John), Camden Lock, Commercial Place, London NW1 8AF
Stoneware for domestic and garden use. Individually designed pieces.

TINGEWICK POTTERY LTD, Tingewick House, Tingewick, Buckingham. Tel: Finmere 250
Earthenware lamp-bases to match customers' requirements.

ROBERT TINNYUNT, Westward Pottery, 96 Exeter Road, Kingsteignton, Newton Abbot, Devon. Tel: Newton Abbot 61011
Small studio pottery producing hand-thrown stoneware. Commissions for special designs undertaken.

TREMAEN POTTERY LTD (Peter Ellery), Newlyn Slip, Penzance, Cornwall. Tel: Penzance 4364
Stoneware and earthenware lamp-bases with matching hessian shades – large pots based on natural form of weathered stones on the Cornish beaches. Supplies shops throughout the country. Commissions include ceramic panels.

MICHAEL TRUSCOTT, Sancreed House, Sancreed, Penzance, Cornwall. Tel: St Buryan 450
Michael Truscott, a former pupil of Bernard Leach, produces hand-thrown stoneware and also makes slabware and coiled pots, sometimes combining these techniques to produce interesting shapes. His work is in the permanent collection of the Bristol City Museum and Art Gallery and the Schools Art Service of the Bristol Education Authority. A member of the Newlyn Society of Artists and the World Craft Council.

UPTON POTTERY, 17 High Street, Upton-upon-Severn, Worcs.
Studio potters, Lavender Groves, NDD, ROI, and Mark Beard, working in high-fired earthenware in full colour. Each piece is entirely hand-made and unique insofar as the decoration and calligraphy is a technique invented by Lavender Groves. Commissions have included many commemorative pieces. Personal shoppers only (no mail orders) on Saturdays only: 10 a.m.–1 p.m. and 2.30–5.30 p.m.

ROGER VEAL, Tolcarne Pottery Studio Carnsew Gallery, 42–3 Penpol Terrace, Hayle, Cornwall TR27 4BQ. Tel: (0736 75) 2226
Small pottery producing slip-cast, hand-thrown individual pieces, and ceramic panels, designed by Roger Veal whose work has been exhibited widely in Britain, New York, Munich and Hamburg.

JOSIAH WEDGWOOD AND SONS LTD, Barlaston, Stoke-on-Trent ST12 9ES. Tel: 078–139 2141

The name Wedgwood is synonymous with pottery. Founded in 1759, the firm has achieved a dominant position at home and overseas. Some of the most famous and long-established manufacturers in the British ceramic industry have been absorbed into the Wedgwood Group. Those which operate within the following divisions: Wedgwood, Coalport, Crown Staffordshire (fine bone china), Wedgwood, William Adams, Mason's Ironstone (earthenware), and Wedgwood Jasper (jewellery), use the traditional hand-skills. The Wedgwood division is the largest in the group and despite using the latest scientific and technical aids, there is still a remarkable amount of hand-craftsmanship involved. Many techniques, especially in the production of Jasper ware, have remained unchanged since the eighteenth century. Retailed through leading shops throughout the world, a catalogue of tableware patterns will be supplied on application to the Stoke-on-Trent offices. The London showrooms are at 158 Regent Street W1R 6QY (closed on Saturdays). Parties for visits to the factory at Barlaston by arrangement.

ROBIN WELCH POTTERY (Robin Welch) Stradbroke, Suffolk. Tel: Stradbroke 416

A wide range of domestic stoneware is produced by Robin Welch with the aid of a couple of assistants using industrial processes although large pieces are still thrown. Regularly exhibited at the Design Centre.

ROBERT WILKINS, Greenways, Butterow, Stroud, Glos. Tel: Stroud 3536

Potter. Member of Guild of Gloucestershire Craftsmen.

WITHERSDALE TILES, Withersdale Cross, Harleston, Norfolk. Tel: Fressingfield 377

A small workshop producing hand-decorated ceramic tiles. Sales are to the wholesale trade which supplies something like 200 shops. Special commissions sometimes undertaken for tiling swimming pools or murals.

MARY WONDRAUSCH, Wharf Pottery, 55 St John's Street, Farncombe, Godalming, Surrey GU7 3EH. Tel: Godalming 4097

Commemorative pieces.

ANDREW WOOD, South Street, Uley, Glos.

Individual earthenware pottery.

MICHAEL WOOD, Gullivers Farm, East Orchard, Shaftesbury, Dorset. Tel: Fontmell Magna 313

Speciality line of hand-painted and fired enamel mugs. Sold under the name of 'Mikkimugs'. Special designs can be printed to order.

16

Musical Instruments

When I first started to make guitars I copied other makers, it is the best way to learn, but all the sounds, no matter what kind of bracing I put inside, were characteristically my own. It's the same with my bowed instruments. I've made Stradivarius model violins, Amati and Stainer models, but the characteristic sound of them all is absolutely mine. If you understand what a sound-board has to do, and the principles are always the same, then you begin to control wood; I say 'begin' because you can never control wood, everyone's hand feels it differently. If you pick up a piece of wood and you have the feeling of how to work it, that is the one thing you can't teach.

David Rubio

This is a craft which is fraught with complexities, of which the plans and specifications and measurements are but part; there is also an intimate relationship between maker and material.

As Alec McCurdy says, "one cannot give brief details of one's exact range or speciality. Could an artist of a picture?" A film of his work, from the felling of the tree to the moment when it is played as a cello, has been made, financed by CAC. Like the famous violin-makers of Cremona, Alec McCurdy selects his timber as a standing tree from the high-altitude European forests. Here the colder climate restricts the growth-rate of the tree, resulting in the close, straight grain necessary for cello-making. His training as a furniture-maker under Edward Barnsley serves him in good stead as he splits the spruce log down the grain in traditional manner.

Alec McCurdy's methods of craftsmanship are of the old school, and the shape of his instruments is traditional, but they are indubitably unique and in his own style. He believes that slavish copying of old masters is neither the way to creative craftsmanship, nor a means of solving the many problems involved. His maxim is to study the past, then create. Experimenting with transmission of sound through the different thicknesses of the front and back plates, his research into acoustics, in which he was helped by a mathematician and a physicist, has resulted in improvements to both the power and tonal qualities of his cellos. This degree of scholarship is vital in making an instrument where shaving off a sliver too much results in a difference to the performance of the strings.

A unique service of researching into, making, supplying and advising on authentic strings for renaissance instruments is carried out by a small consortium of musician-craftsmen. The result of their researches is often unique until it gets copied by other people, who make use of their published reports. Northern Renaissance Instruments, acknowledging that their strength lies in the combination of the various skills of the group, co-operate with both professionals and beginners on projects involving instrument design.

The reappearance of gut strings is welcomed by people like Charles Ford, who reproduces baroque guitars and lutes. He selects the pine as a standing tree and seasons it himself. The resonant pine is used for the sound-board, with figured sycamore used on the back for aesthetic reasons. Charles Ford uses no man-made materials at all, an elephant tusk acquired through the efforts of a friend provides the ivory for the nuts.

Lutes have to be made by hand and it takes something like 130 hours to make one. Research is a time-consuming business in any craft, but at least in this field there is a remarkable wealth of material available in the way of drawings, engravings and old manuscripts in the museums. Towards the end of the baroque period the decorative appeal of an instrument started to outweigh its musical qualities. But musicians require both now. Charles Ford carves the rose on his lutes with a surgeon's scalpel and uses a good many watchmaker's tools. Although he does not employ an apprentice he does teach guitar-making at adult education classes. Like other woodcraft skills, it is the tedious tasks, the attention to detail, like the constant sharpening of a plane-blade or the angle of the plane to a figured wood, which make that sum total: a craftsman.

The upsurge of interest in early music has resulted in the publication of *Early Music* in 1973, covering all aspects of the subject. Comprehensive in content, universal in appeal, it includes an international register of players and makers of early instruments.

Violin-making, in particular, is becoming increasingly more popular among amateurs, so that the number of entries in the various competitions concerned with this craft have now been restricted. But interest is one thing, overcoming the conservatism of musicians – which has led them to believe that only old instruments are worth buying – is another. They will not contemplate using the factory-made violin and view any new instrument with suspicion. The present situation indicates a big demand for viols of all sizes, an instrument which had declined in popularity until a few years ago. Like the sixteenth-century craftsmen, today's makers usually produce both violins and viols – but they have the added challenge of competing with the craftsmanship of the eighteenth-century greats, such as Antonio Stradivari and Guiseppe Guarneri del Gesu.

It is extraordinary that while a string instrument excites all sorts of academic interest, very little has been said about the bows with which to play them. J. H. Clark, whose speciality is to produce bows that are historically authentic, says:

> The research required is multilingual and very scattered – a few original bows and thousands of remarks and pictures. No one in their right senses would ever make the craft commercially viable if they undertook the research; however, it is historically invalid if they don't, and players of early music have been more or less conned.

The old violins are convertible, but the old bows are not (though viols are a different story), they are of far wider variety and involve several lost crafts. Reviving ancient skills present no problem to resolute craftsmen but obtaining supplies of raw materials does. Snakewood, one of the most important, is virtually unobtainable, and when small amounts do appear they command an astronomical price, and an 80 per cent wastage makes this effectively much higher.

It was once thought that the violin bow prior to the time of Tourte (c. 1780) was a clumsy implement, unworthy of the violins of Stainer, Amati and Stradivari, with which it must have been used. It is only by painstaking research and continual experiment by both makers and players that the truth can be established.

A number of societies cater for specialist musical interests and various federations promote the interests of industry, but it is only recently that a trade association was formed to promote the interests of professional musical-instrument-makers. Advisory services include business management, suppliers of tools and equipment, and the joint purchase of materials – this, in particular, must be welcomed by those craftsmen who find relatively small quantities so difficult to obtain. The association was founded on the instigation of individual craftsmen, and spearheaded by Dr Carl Dolmetsch.

The Dolmetsch International is something of a phenomenon in the recorder world. Rivalling hand-made models, the plastic recorder, with its lightweight, durable qualities, has the added advantage of electronically controlled tone, pitch and intonation. Its advent is analogous to the situation which would exist in the violin world if Stradivarius were alive today and designing violins for mass-production.

The modern renaissance of the recorder, sometimes referred to as the English flute, is due to Arnold Dolmetsch introducing it as a serious musical instrument in his concerts at the turn of the century. The antique recorder which he played was lost one day by his small son at Waterloo Station, but Arnold Dolmetsch's serious study of the recorder's authentic system of fingering was invaluable when he, accepting the loss as a challenge, added recorders to the long list of instruments whose making he had pioneered since the 1880s. Early in 1919, the large-scale renaissance which was to spread across the world started from the Haselmere workshops where the modern Dolmetsch recorders are still made.

The recorder's first peak of popularity was in the fifteenth century when it became standardized, and it is this original authentic English fingering system which is recognized by musicians of all nations. Dr Carl Dolmetsch personally checks and plays each of the recorders which are still hand-made in wood. Until 1945 all Dolmetsch recorders were made by craftsmen from exotic hardwoods and ivory; but the influx of factory-produced cheaper recorders forced new production methods on the firm – now it is the moulded plastic recorder which has sold in its millions that takes the name of Dolmetsch across the world. And yet the range of instruments which Arnold Dolmetsch Ltd produces is wider than that of any other maker. Arnold Dolmetsch, the founder, came from a family of organ- and piano-makers and made his first harpsichord in 1896 at the suggestion of William Morris. The firm, under the direction of his son, Dr Carl Dolmetsch, comprises about forty-five people, including directors and apprentices; much of its success is due to the fact that most of those who make the instruments are also performers and scholars, aware not only of the mechanics of manufacturing the instruments but also of the artistic purpose for which they are intended. Concerts and summer schools are also held by the Dolmetsch Foundation.

Invariably, the often posed question of what is English music is answered by considering the music of the Elizabethan period. The composers of music for the virginals produced the most original work in keyboard music, the earliest dating from the beginning of the sixteenth century.

The premier keyboard instruments in the period from their introduction during the fourteenth and fifteenth centuries until late in the eighteenth century were the harpsichord and clavichord, and it is the increasing interest in early music but, more noticeably, the desire to play it on instruments for which it was written, which has led to one of the musical phenomena of recent years. Because of this renewed interest in early music, the music section of the Victoria and Albert Museum installed a system enabling recordings of rare models to be heard. But the demand for rare instruments has also revived the ancient skills of the instrument-maker who has to meet the new market. Until about twenty-five years ago the large number of antique harpsichords and spinets surviving in England practically satisfied the limited demand.

The virginal, spinet and harpsichord are basically of the same parentage. When the key is depressed it lifts a jack which carries the plectrum and escapement, and the string is then plucked. Originally of crow quill, now too difficult to get, the plectrum is often made of hard plastic or leather.

Currently, one of the most popular early keyboard instruments is the clavichord. Its intimacy is well suited for modern-day closely-knit communities, and anyone who has wondered how Handel managed to practise at night in the attic against the wishes of his father, and escape notice, has probably never been acquainted with the soft, almost secret, tones which carry no more than a few feet.

Harpsichords, on the other hand, can be used for concerts and audiences without losing any of their sensitivity. Commissioned by the wealthy and hired by the poor, they are much in demand today, but the enlarged market has been offset by the fact that there is a marked increase in the number of people making them, including some firms working on a factory scale. This does present the single craftsman with problems, partly because one-man businesses are inherently uneconomic when in direct competition with much larger units. The belief that craft products will command a high price merely because they are hand-made is often contradicted by the widespread feeling among purchasers that factory products are superior because they are efficiently made by machinery to a high standard of accuracy.

If a harpsichord is machine-made like a piano then it is not acceptable to the players, who are mostly purists. Made by hand in the traditional manner even at a low rate per hour, which would not give the craftsman a living wage, still makes the finished piece very expensive. Such high prices are prohibitive to the student and amateur of modest means, so it is with these in mind that George Braithwaite is designing a small two rank organ, and developing a kind of hybrid 'Claviorganum' – a portable harpsichord with two manuals, one of which will play the strings and the other one or two ranks of small organ pipes, taking advantage for the sake of compactness of modern electrical methods for admitting wind to the pipes.

One maker suggested that the working unit in the field of musical-instrument-making should be on a guild system, comprising specialists in the individual aspects – one for research, design and direction; a good cabinet-maker, a case-painter and decorator, and an artist for the sound-boards and so on. And this, of course, is the type of teamwork upon which many firms exist. But craftsmen are individuals, and as such have differing views. Whereas one will be quite happy to be a specialist within a team, another will not, feeling that specialization smacks of mass-production methods: "of course a screwer-up of nuts becomes a specialist screwer-up of nuts if that is all he does all day every day", says one craftsman, conceding the title of musical-instrument-maker only to him who makes the whole thing from start to finish himself. And there are a number who still do; at most taking on a partner or promising apprentice, though only the larger firms lend themselves to formal apprenticeship schemes. It is interesting to note that most of the exceptionally gifted choose to go it alone, making their own mistakes on their own account. They generally make fewer errors than their pioneering predecessors due to the generally increased interest in, education of, and respect for the classical originals.

The London College of Furniture has a musical instrument technology department; there are full-time courses in harpsichord making, and study of fretted instruments as well as the well-established piano-tuning and repair courses. Schemes such as CAC introduced, whereby they award financial help to a craftsman who trains an apprentice, are practical, putting the student in a working situation. Whereas colleges usually have money available, with little space and a degree of unavoidable distraction; the private workshop often has neither money nor space, but the opportunity for apprentices to utilize its facilities to the best advantage with total involvement. In the same way, the restorer is in a unique position of being able to analyse in a detailed, practical way the assembly of an early instrument by having to dismantle it in the course of restoration.

Not every harpsichordist is aware of how much craftsmanship is involved in building him an instrument in which all the essential qualities are united. The appreciative and thoughtful will accord the instrument-makers credit on a programme or record-sleeve, and will invite interest by using their models for public concerts, allowing the audience to look closely at the instrument during the interval. This type of advertisement is valuable to the small craftsman because general exhibitions are, owing to their specialist nature, of very limited value. The really important exhibitions for the makers are held abroad – at Cremona in Italy and Poznam in Poland.

Appreciation for each other's talents is essential in musical-instrument-making. And, conversely, some craftsmen will only make for musicians. David Laws, who teaches harpsichord-making at the London College of Furniture was, quite understandably, more than a little peeved at having undertaken all the necessary hard work and intricate research to make a copy of the Rizzio's guitar for the film *Mary, Queen of Scots*, only to be told "no, of course it hasn't got to make a noise" – *after* he had made it! Nevertheless, he accepts that even serious musicians may request the odd thing from time to time, and has therefore acquiesced to the unusual and made a keyboard for a cello, designed a bowed psaltery, and made a solid electric mountain dulcimer and such incongruous combinations. Dave Laws is profoundly practical; on the premise that the makers of the past must have been influenced by what was available, he does not agree that the raw materials problem is insurmountable; why, he argues, pay an enormous sum for spruce for soundboards when red cedar, relatively easier to get, will do as well if worked in the proper fashion.

It is rare for a harpsichord-maker to be a musician, but Nicholas Keen is both. A pupil of Ralph Kirkpatrick, Nicholas read Philosophy at York, and Music at Cambridge and Yale. A professional musician, he says he could not afford to buy an instrument initially; but coming from a practical background he had the necessary manual dexterity to become a craftsman and is able to apply an academic intensity to his study of the pieces. He had found the distinctive thing about old instruments was the regional influence, which developed from different composers. His rooms are hung around with timbers; harpsichords and spinets in various stages stand elegantly awaiting fluted legs or fine art decoration or a whittling away of strings which have stretched.

The instrument which evolved from the harpsichord is the pianoforte, in its modern form quite removed from its precursor so as to render it unsuited to the performance of harpsichord music. Small, newly-designed pianos are a remarkable achievement of modern instrument-making. Compact, for the smaller twentieth-century home, new pianos are built with regard to the stresses imposed upon them by central heating and advanced methods of construction are used, in which traditional craftsmanship is combined with modern technology. Pianos, unlike furniture, have to support an internal tension of many tons all their life: cheaply constructed pre-war models collapse in hundreds every year due to our changed level of domestic heating.

English pianos are in the minority of the craftsman-built keyboard instruments as far as output is concerned and meet fierce competition from overseas. Japan's output is the world's largest, and Yamaha produce 10,000 pianos a month. The British craftsman's skills are mainly sought for reconditioning the world-famous models so zealously purchased by music-lovers who appreciate instruments built during the Golden Age. The Worshipful Company of Musicians awards the Evelyn Broadwood Scholarship to apprentices of pianoforte-makers.

The heyday of the harp-makers was around 1820–1840, when the harp enjoyed a popularity comparable with that of the guitar today. By 1840 the Erard firm alone had reached its 5,000 serial numbers and the fact that Queen Victoria had harp lessons made it a fashionable instrument. Interest waned in the first half of this century, however, and the old stock of instruments dwindled. It may be that Wilfred Smith has encouraged the renaissance of the harp by reconditioning some 500 instruments over the past twenty years.

There are several makers of small Irish-type harps, but Wilfred Smith is the only maker of pedal-harps in England. To meet the demand and keep down the cost, modern methods of production have been incorporated into the traditional one, but the making of a concert harp is an extremely complicated affair, every single piece of the mechanism has to be hand-made to exact measurements. Each harp uses some ninety-four spindles so it is obvious that a lathe set up to produce 5,000 spindles is the type of automation which can be used effectively, releasing the craftsmen to work on the more intricate pieces which need extensive skilled work done by hand.

Wilfred Smith's design alone required over a year's work on the drawing board before the prototype was made. So the reorganization and equipping of his workshop to a high standard of efficiency did not happen suddenly.

In the heart of Surrey a staff of twelve work to Wilfred Smith's exacting standards – each harp is individually built and designed to last a lifetime. Whilst it embodies all the traditional features, many refinements have been introduced in his concert harp, in particular the curved sound-board and the method of adjusting the pedals quite simply with the tuning-key – a similar device to the one which Stumpf used over a hundred years ago, but not adopted by other craftsmen as it is difficult to make. The difficulty has not decreased but Wilfred Smith considers its complexity justified by the life-long freedom from pedal troubles which it provides.

Tuning a harp is not easy: in fact it is said that the art has totally confounded some harpists. The evanescent nature of harp music may contribute to this phenomenon: the note which does not last long enough to decide whether it is in tune does not last long enough to decide whether it is not! Wilfred Smith is able to ease the uncertain path by making available a 'magic box' which emits every note to tempered intonation at any pitch. The accuracy of the tempered intonation is a mathematical conception, extremely difficult to match by methods used on a harp. Nevertheless, there are modern harps which do give a very close approximation to the accuracy required, the same could not be said of many older harps, about which one celebrated maker is reputed to have boasted that his harps gave not twelve notes to the octave, but no less than twenty-one. Alas, says Wilfred Smith, how right he was!

The fascinating Aeolian harp, the wind-harp of ancient times, whose unpredictable and strangely haunting sounds depend on the breeze passing over the strings and exciting the harmonic series of overtones, is, by comparison, of almost primitive design and is among the vast range of instruments made by Robert Morley & Co.

For over 350 years the name of Morley has been associated with music in England. Thomas Morley was a celebrated musician in Elizabethan times and is remembered for his three part canzonets which inaugurated the English Madrigal School. J. George Morley, a harp-maker of Kensington, established a musical-instrument workshop in 1816 which has developed into the famous Morley Galleries with the most comprehensive range of keyboard instruments in London, the majority of which are made by their own craftsmen.

John Nicholson specializes in designing and constructing small pipe-organs with mechanical key action. Although made specifically for use in the performance of early music, his instruments are not copies or reconstructions of surviving old pieces or from particular historical sources. All are original designs and are produced using modern techniques and materials ensuring reliability in all conditions. The traditional craftwork and hand-skills are taught in the workshop. All his pipe-organs are made according to classical principles; the pipes specially made in English oak, pine, spruce or 75 per cent tin. Whereas most other organ-builders tend to rebuild old organs or assemble new ones from components bought through supply houses, John Nicholson's workshop produces all the pipes, keys, chests, casework and action components. He has reason to be proud of the fact that his work is so much in demand that 80 per cent of his instruments are exported to early music groups and college and university music departments abroad. Most other early stringed and woodwind instruments are also made under his direction. Pan-pipes, as well as pipe-organs; figured wood psalteries of light construction; and rebecs, the bodies and necks of which are carved from the solid wood; all exact different types of skills from the workshop's small group of craftsmen. A diversity of materials are used, including cow horns, one of which acts as a reed cap and mouthpiece in the fruitwood-bodied pibcorns – an English horn-pipe with a single cane reed, similar to a bagpipe drone.

It may at first be assumed that it must be a borderline influence which resulted in Northumbrian small-pipes, but bagpipes in various forms were played all over Europe in medieval times. The characteristics of the Northumbrian pipes are: the stopped chanter, which enables a staccato style of playing and gives them the unique bubbling sound for which they are famous; drones which play a harmonizing chord of a fifth; and the fact that they are dry-reeded (bellows-blown). These combined features distinguish them from other forms of bagpipes. This is a strictly local mode of music, however, whereas the ubiquitous 'Scottish bagpipe' is made and played in various parts of the world.

A number of Northumbrian pipers make sets for their own use; there are excellent adult evening-class programmes catering for this old craft and most of the makers live in the county of Northumberland and around Tyneside.

D. G. Burleigh is the only professional full-time craftsman specializing in Northumbrian pipes. He makes both the original small-pipe, the plain chanter or 'primitive' set, and basic sets where extensions can be made to the range of the chanter. All sets are made in the expensive and rather scarce African blackwood, chosen for having the finest tonal qualities of any known wood and used exclusively by makers of woodwind instruments for over 150 years. The craft skills are diverse: turning of the wood and ivory; metalworking in the making of the ferrules and decoration as well as the complicated key work for the chanter; bellows-making; and hand-stitching olive oil-dressed leather for the pipe-bag. The craftsman also has to be handy with needle and thread to make the bag cover of velvet, shepherd's plaid or tartan; and must have a musical ear, of course, to tune the chanter.

Musicians exploring the techniques of music through the physical contours of an instrument, although possessing the necessary craft skills to make a practical instrument, have rather a different temperament than the ordinary craftsman. To put his essay on speed of sound in bent tubes into practice, Giles Brindley plans to make a bass clarinet, bassoon, and perturbation-toned trumpet to test their acoustical results, but these would probably be prototypes which could be offered to commercial makers, with Mr Brindley in a consultative capacity.

Such a combination has proved immensely successful at The Horn Centre. Richard Merewether, a professional horn-player, had been experimenting for over a decade with several descant-horns from abroad before he approached Robert Paxman and his team, who were already accomplished in re-modelling instruments for Dennis Brain, using some – for that time – unorthodox ideas on instrument-design. The present range of Paxman RM horns results from close collaboration between the skilled craftsmen and the talented designer, producing such a significant advance in the development of the horn that there is now scarcely a country in which the leading performers are not using, or waiting for, Paxman instruments.

Individual players have a predilection for one alloy or another, and the occasional order for instruments partly made of sterling silver does create some hazards for the craftsmen more familiar with the techniques used for the usual brass, gold-brass and nickel-silver.

One aspect of instrument-making to which few craftsmen paid enough attention was that of the valve – which evolved around 1830. Discerning players are critically appreciative of what is now termed the Merewether valve-system, one of the implemented theories contributed by Paxman's designer. Other links between their musical qualities and practical usage have resulted in a great number of exclusive models of their high quality French horns; Paxmans being the only maker in the world of this particular instrument.

England can also claim another notable wind instrument maker at least 70 per cent of whose total output is for the international market. Christopher Monk is the only full-time professional maker in the world, during this century at least, to produce the unique and fascinating lysardene, mute cornetts, cornettinos, cornettos and serpents of wood, leather and metal. John Evelyn wrote in 1662 ". . . the cornet which gave life to the organ, that instrument quite left off in which the English were so skilfull".

SOCIETY

EARLY MUSICAL INSTRUMENT MAKERS, c/o Arnold Dolmetsch Ltd, King's Road, Haselmere, Surrey. Tel: 0428 51432

A recently formed association to promote interest in early musical-instrument-making. Full membership is restricted to professional makers; associate membership is open to those who are interested in maintaining the association's aims.

MUSICAL-INSTRUMENT-MAKERS

GEORGE BRAITHWAITE, Heath Farm House, 15 Station Road, Alresford, Colchester, Essex. Tel: Wivenhoe 2805

Quality hand-made keyboard instruments: Georgian harpsichords, chamber organs and reproductions of seventeenth- and eighteenth-century keyboard instruments. Speciality production of a chamber harpsichord designed to give at low cost an instrument capable of producing strong tone and fulfilling the requirements of all continuo as well as solo work in the periods before Scarlatti. Constructed in the English Rigid Style, it is extremely robust, easily transportable and will keep in tune for long periods in differing temperature conditions. Among the letters testifying to the model's qualities, are those from a BBC musician and Gordonstoun School. Other instruments produced to order are full-size concert models with three choirs of strings based on a Schudi Original of 1789, spinets with five octaves G–G, clavichords and virginals.

Mr Braithwaite is currently engaged in designing a small two-rank organ to suit the needs and modest means of the student and amateur, and a compact 'Claviorganum' – a fairly small and portable harpsichord with two manuals, one of which will play the strings and the other one or two ranks of small organ pipes. Restoration of small organs.

GILES BRINDLEY, 102 Ferndene Road, London, SE24 0AA. Tel: 01–274 2598

Consultant on musical instruments. Very limited number of wind instruments produced, mainly as prototypes for commercial manufacturers, as this musician is basically involved with improving the design. Author of several acoustical papers.

SIMON CHADWICK, 2 Meadow End, Meadow Lane, Dudbridge, Stroud, Glos.

Lute-maker. Member of Guild of Gloucestershire Craftsmen.

J. H. CLARK, M.PHIL., 7 Farriers Close, Droitwich, Worcs. WR9 2ET

Atelier for historic stringed instrument bows.

RICHARD CLAYSON AND ANDREW GARRETT, Lyminge, Folkestone, Kent. Tel: Lyminge 862132

Early keyboard-instrument-makers. Restorations undertaken.

R. P. DAVIES, Hollygate, Levens, nr Kendal, Westmorland. Tel: Sedgwick 482

Keyboard instruments constructed by traditional methods. Harpsichords, based upon the original versions of Rucker, Taskin, Hemsch and the late seventeenth-century Italian models; virginals and clavichords. All instruments finished in the style of their antique models, but owing to the individual construction of each instrument, the client's own preference in the finish can be incorporated. Likewise, stand designs may be interchanged with most models. Commissions welcomed for facsimiles of particular instruments.

ARNOLD DOLMETSCH LTD, King's Road, Haselmere, Surrey GU27 2QJ. Tel: 51432/3

Internationally famous firm, with the longest unbroken tradition of manufacture of any other maker in this field, pioneered by the distinguished concert performer, scholar and craftsman, Arnold Dolmetsch, in the 1880s.

A team of craftsmen trained in the company's own workshops, most of whom are themselves instrumentalists and music scholars, is backed by a continuous programme of research to provide a complete range of instruments: harpsichords (two-manual, single manual and triangular), spinets (large and small), clavichords, virginals, viols, lutes, rebecs, violins, bows, harps, pipes, tabors, tambourins, psalteries and recorders. Restorations are also undertaken. The Dolmetsch moulded plastic recorder is used by millions of school children and has done much to popularize that instrument's value and potential. Hand-made wooden instruments are checked individually under the personal direction of Dr Carl Dolmetsch, the founder's son and present Managing Director.

A. J. DUNHILL, 2 Norfolk Road, Barking, Essex. Tel: 432–4974

Early keyboard instruments, mainly clavichords and virginals produced. Open to commissions.

BERNARD ELLIS, The Coach House, Dilwyn, Herefordshire. Tel: Weobley 583

Early music and traditional stringed instruments.

Hurdy-gurdy (generally known as a barrel-organ): baroque instrument with a chromatic range of two octaves, two chanterelles and four bourdons, ribs, tangent housing and carved scroll in rosewood, boxwood wheel and tuning pegs, spruce front, mahogany or plane tree back, barber's pole edging on body; total length 24 inches, inlaid lid, wheelguard and tailpiece; gut strings.

Lutes: eight-course and ten-course based on a Venetian lute-table made by Pietro Railich. Twenty-three ribs in lacewood, traditional rose, tied frets, ebony or rosewood frets; very light construction, nylon strings.

Rebecs: soprano, tenor, bass. All sizes have a piriform body and neck made of a single piece of home-grown timber. Split-level soundboard, the raised upper portion is a continuation of the finger-board, lateral pegs in boxwood, spruce front and gut strings.

Viola da Gamba: modelled on an anonymous sixteenth-century bass viol in the maker's possession. Traditional floral motif and geometric purfling pattern inlaid in Balkan spruce front; pierced scroll; Bosnian maple bridge; gut strings.

Appalachian dulcimers, with various decorations to order; autoharps, beggars' fiddles, fiedels (medieval five-stringed instrument) and hammer dulcimers (beaters supplied) – the range is currently extending to include crwths and minstrel harps.

CHARLES FORD, Salutation Cottage, The Gibb, Castle Combe, Wilts. Tel: Castle Combe 782688
Renaissance and baroque lutes. Baroque, flamenco and modern classical guitars.

ROBERT GOBLE AND SON LTD, Greatstones, Kiln Lane, Headington, Oxford. Tel: Oxford 61685
A firm of designer-craftsmen with over half a century of experience in making harpsichords, spinets and clavichords. An impressive number of most distinguished harpsichordists, universities and orchestras comprises the list of purchasers. The casework of the instruments is usually of finely figured walnut – special requests are, however, met with for other woods, inlays or painted decorations.

GRANT, DEGENS AND BRADBEER LTD, Organ Works, Campbell Square, Northampton. Tel: Northampton 32504
Organ-builders: entirely new tracker action, classical revival, *werkprinzip* organs. Restoration to original condition of worthy instruments.

HISTORICAL INSTRUMENTS OF MUSICK (Graham Lyndon Jones and Barbara Stanley), 20 Queen Street, St Albans, Herts. AL3 4PJ; (John Hanchet) 57 Ward Avenue, Grays, Essex RM17 5RN
A small consortium of three craftsmen, specializing in reproduction early woodwind instruments. Hand-made to individual requirements, based on careful research on originals in the major European collections, the instruments are made in authentic woods. Flutes, shawms, racketts, cornamuse, crumhorns, curtals, mute cornetts, kortholts, gemshorns, tabors, drums and nakers are included in the current range, but the makers' research is wider than the confines of this list and they will happily discuss commissions for other woodwind instruments. Mr Jones and Miss Stanley of St Albans tend to specialize in curtals, flutes and gemshorns; Mr Hanchet of Grays specializes in shawms and crumhorns, and enjoys a challenge for "awkward" jobs and the one-off commission.

DAVID W. HOLDEN, Moor Edge, Mankinholes, Todmorden, Lancs. Tel: Todmorden 070–681 2916
Maker of violins, violas, cellos; bass, tenor and treble viols; bows rehaired. Speciality line: the full range of viols based on the designs produced by Ernst Busch in 1650.

LEWIS JONES, High House, Kingsmoor Road, Great Parndon, Harlow, Essex
Harpsichords and virginals based on sixteenth- and seventeenth-century Italian originals. Reconstructions of medieval and early Renaissance stringed instruments, including rebecs, fiddles, bowed lyres, hurdy-gurdies, early viols, psalteries, harps, mandoras, citterns, vitzuelas, lutes and other plucked instruments. Some percussion and woodwind instruments of the

same period.

NICHOLAS KEEN, 6 Eastfield Crescent, York YO1 5JB. Tel: (0904) 51873
Classical harpsichords: Italian, English, French and Flemish styles. Connoisseur versions include eighteenth-century English types, Flemish and English virginals. Fretted clavichords, Italian Bentside spinets, Italian virginals, French folding harpsichord. Positive organs, stopped 4 feet TC-f (30) ideal for renaissance music, especially Buxheimer *orgel buch*; house-organs. Kits, with full instructions for self-assembly, also available.

DAVE LAW, 162 Clewer Hill Road, Windsor, Berks. Tel: Windsor 64555
Designer-craftsman of keyboard and fretted instruments to specification based on early instrument construction. Tutor of harpsichord-making at the Musical Instrument Technology Department, London College of Furniture-Making.

S. G. LOWE, 1 Cedar Road, Hale, Altrincham, Cheshire WA15 9HZ
Maker of violins and viols of all sizes, treble, tenor, bass (Viola da Gamba) and double bass (Violine). Repairwork on some fine old instruments of the seventeenth and eighteenth centuries has included violins by Nicolo Amati and P. A. Testore.

ALEC MCCURDY, Woodland Leaves, Cold Ash, nr Newbury, Berks. Tel: Thatcham 63258
Hand-made cellos and furniture.

CHRISTOPHER MONK, Stock Farm House, Churt, Farnham, Surrey GU10 2LS. Tel: 042–873 (Hindhead) 5991
Internationally noted maker of cornetts and serpents.

ROBERT MORLEY & CO. LTD, 4 Belmont Hill, Lewisham, London SE13. Tel: 01–852 6151
Morley Galleries stock what must be the most comprehensive range of keyboard instruments in London, where expert advice, backed by the experience of instrument-making since Regency times, is given on selection of new instruments or the restoration of an antique model. Clavichords, virginals, spinets, harpsichords, fortepianos, Aeolian wind-harps and Clarsach or Celtic harps made by craftsmen on the premises.

JOHN NICHOLSON, Bream House, Hungershall Park, Royal Tunbridge Wells, Kent TN4 8NE. Tel: Tunbridge Wells 37694
Specialist designer-maker of pipe organs and early music instruments. Standard pipe-organs, casework finished in figured English oak, with special attention given to customer's tonal requirements include portative 2 feet, table-organ 3 feet, folding regal, regal positive and chamber-continuo positive. Early stringed and woodwind instruments include panpipes, psalteries, rebecs, rubebes and pibcorns. All parts of the organ are specially made in the workshop including the pipes, keys, bellows, chests, casework and action components. Please note: visitors *must* confirm an appointment

before calling to see the workshop.

NORTHERN RENAISSANCE INSTRUMENTS, 18 Moorfield Road, Manchester M20 8UY. Tel: 061–445 0525
A small specialist group who research, design, construct and play pre-classical stringed musical instruments. Current catalogue lists lutes, citterns, orpharions, bandoras and Renaissance rebecs, bows, cases and strings for their own instruments. Unique specialist services include strings consultancy with specific ones made to order and detailed research.

JOHN PAUL, Parkway, Waldron, Heathfield, Sussex. Tel: Heathfield 2525
Established one-man business: harpsichords and clavichords made, restoration service for early keyboard instruments.

PAXMAN MUSICAL INSTRUMENTS LTD, The Horn Centre, Covent Garden, 116 Long Acre, WC2 – London showroom and offices. The workshops and export department are at Pattenden Lane, Marden, Kent. Tel: Marden 623
Designer-craftsmen of high-quality French horns, the only makers of this particular instrument in this country – and indeed the world – in view of the great number of unique models evolved by them. The horns are individually built by craftsmen to meet the needs of the virtuoso performer. The range, notable for its ease of response and full, rich tone with exceptional clarity and definition in the high register, has resulted from close collaboration between Robert Paxman and his assistants with hornplayer-designer Richard Merewether.

RONALD PRENTICE, Ash Priors Mill, Bishops Lydeard, Taunton, Somerset TA4 3NQ. Tel: Bishops Lydeard 734
Viols made by Ronald Prentice are known all over the world. His speciality is making reproductions of medieval and baroque instruments. A whole range of modern stringed instruments is also made, a number of which are used in the exacting conditions of internationally renowned symphony orchestras. Specialized restoration work has included complete renovation of the earliest known dulcimer in the world made in 1602 in Brescia, Italy. Exhibiting member of The Somerset Guild of Craftsmen.

TOM ROBBINS, Willesborough Windmill, Ashford, Kent.
Craftsman specializing in making positive organs and portatives. Restoration work carried out on eighteenth- and nineteenth-century chamber organs.

COLIN ROSS, 5 Denebank, Monkseaton, Whitley Bay. Tel: Whitley Bay 26585
Northumbrian small-pipes.

WILFRED SMITH, 15 Castelnau, Barnes, London SW13 9RP. Tel: 01–748 6991
Workshop of a dozen craftsmen specializing in making harps. Irish harps, virginals and clavichords also made, special stringed instruments to client's own specifications undertaken; such a commission has included an 18-string lyre. Repairs and accessories. Reconditioned Grecian and Gothic

harps, carefully overhauled and guaranteed, available. Harps – Clarsach, Grecian, Gothic and Concert – available for hire. *First Tutor for the Concert Harp and Clarsach* by Wilfred Smith, contains all relevant information on stringing, maintenance and playing the instruments.

MICHAEL THOMAS, Camden Lock, Commercial Place, London NW1 8AF
Harpsichord-maker.

R. J. WATERSON, 61 Oxhey Avenue, Oxhey, Watford, Herts. WD1 4HB
Craftsman whose range to date includes hurdy-gurdies, guitars, cornettos, celtic harps and reproduction of early woodwind instruments.

STEPHEN WESSEL, Ferryway, Rodley, Westbury-on-Severn, Glos. Tel: Westbury-on-Severn 469
Harpsichord- and virginals-maker. Associate Member Guild of Gloucestershire Craftsmen.

TREVOR WYE, 4 Abbots Barton Walk, Canterbury, Kent. Tel: 0227 66748
Professor of music whose investigations have led to making flutes and experimental headpieces for flutes from precious metals, mostly silver.

D. G. BURLEIGH, 29 Newgate Street, Morpeth, Northumberland. Tel: Morpeth 3367
Northumbrian small-pipes, plain and basic sets, individual modifications incorporated as required, after consultation.

17

Toys and Dolls, Games, Models and Puppets

TOY-MAKING

Fashions in toys are going full circle; a decade ago it was goofy gingham gimmickry that sold; currently it is naturalistic animals which are in demand, popularized perhaps by World Wildlife Conservation Year. And giving animals human characteristics is the key to the appeal of a couple of Britain's most successful toy-makers' products.

Margaret Brown's home is full of mice – adorable little creatures, full of character and personality. Whole families of woodland animals are bred out of Mrs Brown's imagination and reared under her creative fingers. Some ten thousand a year find their way from her Cotswold cottage to many parts of the world, with no sales promotion other than inclusion in the Design Centre index. Mrs Brown holds both the Design Centre, with its index and exhibition schemes, and The British Toy-makers' Guild, in high esteem, attributing the greater proportion of her success to them.

The toy-making is a true cottage industry with Old Bell Cottage the headquarters to which the dozen or so outworkers go every week for a whole day so that the standard of work is carefully supervised. It is Margaret Brown's personal touch to each toy that gives it individuality: it is she who stitches on Mother Mouse's maternal expression, the winsome look on the finger-puppets, and the benevolent beam of Grampy Goose.

A quite different family, the Littles, emerge from the Lakeland canal-side workshop of Robin and Nell Dale. Robin's creative talents were extended to the full whilst working on the Adventure Playground at Notting Hill, to be joined by Nell who had been a needlewoman in a West End theatre costumiers. Their work with the all-age range of children on the timber-, mud-, nail- and box-littered quarter-acre site called for much improvisation of materials, thus following a long tradition, for archaeological sites have revealed evidence that the first toys were made from bones, sticks, horns and tool handles. A splendid example of how the wooden doll, in particular, has been shaped from improvised materials is in the Museum of Childhood in Edinburgh – a doll made from an old shoe with the face appearing on the flat of the heel.

The Dales extended their researches into costume and dolls on their return home to Westmorland, an area with a long tradition of wood-turnery, initially for the cotton and woollen industry in the shape of bobbins and shuttles, perns and spinning-wheels. They bought a lathe and turned beechwood into the dolls for which they are now universally famous.

It was their intention to make all types of toys, but they are currently working almost exclusively on wooden dolls which, being made as individuals, named and signed as such, are collected by both adults and children and sold in many countries. The range is unique – the Little Family, complete with Granny Garnett in lavender gown, and Jemima the maid discreet in grey and white. A naval and military set has been joined by a regional collection including John Peel, Gipsy Meg and the priest, Father Brown. Their peg-dolls embody the original ideas of the true peg-wooden dolls, so called because the joints were held in place with wooden dowels.

Probably the simplest form of wooden doll to evolve in any number came from the forest areas of Germany, Tyrol and Finland, and were initially a stump or peg of wood in one piece, turned and painted. Dorothy Thornton of Warwick makes peg-dolls from a 'dolly-peg' base: endowing each with individual features, and putting on the intricate trimmings and accessories makes this another labour intensive project. Her business, she says, is still in its infancy, but this is due more to capacity of output than retailing problems: again, it is a matter of keeping the supply up to demand.

In the fifteenth and sixteenth centuries dolls became more like models of humans as the demand for realism gathered momentum: hair of tow or string or human locks was added; gesso was put on the heads and limbs to look like skin. Tinted wax was used later. Limbs were made flexible by means of mortice and tenon joints, wire and string. Rag arms have been dated back to the 1680s.

England's most illustrious wooden dolls were saved from exportation in 1974 by the Victoria and Albert Museum. Resisting the application for an export licence to Switzerland, the museum raised the £16,000 to buy back from a collector the pair of William and Mary dolls – reported as being the finest and earliest fully dressed English dolls known to exist.

By 1710 kid was being used; being more flexible and durable it was softer for children to handle. Antique dolls command high prices and it is one field where contemporary craftsmen are often exploited by unscrupulous dealers. Myrtle Smith makes such exquisite dolls in the traditional manner, using kid for the bodies and wax or china for the heads and shoulders, with real hair (donated by girls who have favoured shorter styles) painstakingly rooted into the wax, that disreputable buyers have been known to fake age-spots on their lovely costumes and pass them off as antiques to avid collectors. Mrs Smith now dates and signs each one in an attempt to thwart the unscrupulous dealers for there are still plenty of genuine customers who are proud to collect them, acknowledging the craft of the present-day doll-maker.

There is a store of original and unique designs being worked upon by the enterprising toymakers and most welcome the challenge of a special commission, which can range from copying an inadvertently chewed up favourite toy hippo to making up a doll to a child's own drawing. Diana Ralston did, in fact, do just that, but found it was impracticable: a child's design can present insuperable problems when it comes to finding the right materials; and the desires of children are notoriously changeable. More often it is a copy of a commercially successful toy or a television character which is asked for and this involves the toymaker in the intricacies of copyright laws.

Operating under a formal licence agreement with Margaret Hutchings, toy-designer and author of *The Book of the Teddy Bear*, Desmond Payne and his wife have established a cottage industry in which, operating under the name of Douneway Marketing, they make that perennial favourite, the teddy-bear. There is no question of them being made other than by hand in limited numbers. In this case, the designer laid down acceptable standards of quality – criteria to which the makers faithfully adhere.

Creative studies in toy-making, leading to City and Guilds examinations, are held at the London College of Furniture, which runs the only course of its kind in England for a Higher Diploma in the design and manufacture of play equipment.

The British Toy-Manufacturers' Association was formed in 1944 to bring to the notice of the government the importance of toy-making as a British industry and perpetuates this principle by mounting group ventures at leading trade fairs.

Nuremburg, the traditional toy-making centre of Europe, still holds an international toy fair each year and Britain also has an annual international toy fair held in Brighton, at which the British Toy-makers' Guild exhibits.

The British Toy-makers' Guild was founded in 1955 by the late Leslie Daiken; broadcaster, author and founder of the Toy Museum. Together with Miss Yootha Rose, now president of the guild, and a group of talented craftsmen, he presented the first exhibition of 'Living Toy-makers in Britain'. In a market swamped in the 'fifties by shoddy, mass-produced toys the guild created the vanguard of a whole new movement by promoting good quality hand-made work for children. There are now over a hundred members. All perpetuate the original aims by maintenance of high standards both in original design and production. Its services to the craftsman are through its marketing and distribution methods, advice on production, and exhibiting channels. The guild's seal of approval is awarded by its selection committee and entries are judged on design, construction, durability, suitability of purpose, and safety.

Newly-imposed legislation on safety, which became law on 1st April 1975, was welcomed by craftsmen of integrity who, whilst practising themselves according to the British Standard Code of the British Toy-Manufacturers' since 1961, had helplessly watched the flooding of the market by cut-price inferior foreign toys, some of which were literally lethal. Even the most innocuous-looking materials can be dangerous; such as acrylic fibres which give off toxic fumes when they smoulder; the result of a child sleeping in a room where a teddy-bear was left on a heater tells its own tragic tale. The new Toys (Safety) Regulations (1974) are concerned with paint toxicity, fabric flammability, electricity and general safety. The responsibility for safety of consumer goods is vested in the Department of Prices and Consumer Protection (p. 379).

Although toy soldiers have been waging war according to the whims of their owners since at least Roman times, there are few being made by craftsmen in comparison with other types of toys. I have only traced one who makes Victorian-type lead soldiers. Mass-production has really ousted the hand-made armies of yesteryear. The pride of every boy's toy box (we are told that Winston Churchill had no less than 1500 lead soldiers ranged for battle on his playroom table) the lead soldier became standardized in the 1840s by the scale set by Nuremberg. This made for tidy troop lines as it was now possible to make the toys from moulds.

Sheila Newington melts down old lead on a stove in her garden shed and pours it into original cast-iron moulds. The semi-flat models are filed and their uniforms painted on: riflemen, standard-bearers and mounted trumpeters then emerge as individuals out of the uniformity of the moulds. Mrs Newington makes an almost apologetic comparison of her toy soldiers with their modern mass-produced plastic counterparts: "rather crude" they may appear to her, and confined in range to the limitations of the old moulds, but they embody a simple charm which captures the essence of their original intent. To cater for the collectors of model soldiers there is a society which fosters research into all aspects of the toys, formed in 1935. Its collection, open to the public, is kept at Dodington House in Gloucestershire.

The powerful pressure of industrialized production took its toll of the toy-making craft along with others. Since the late nineteenth century the traditional values have been choked by commercialism. A mass-produced novelty is a contradiction in terms. Dolls, in particular, became wonders in celluloid capable of extraordinary feats such as talking and drinking. Compared with the quality toy made on the Continent, toy-making was a sadly neglected craft in England until recently. The Design Council has now played a major role in getting recognition of the status of the craft, and mounts a toy exhibition at the

Design Centre at Christmas.

Despite that seal of standard, some types of toys are unhappily placed in the crafts field. Toy-makers Keith and Maggie Barnes have experienced certain marketing problems because of this: their attractive hand-built wooden pull-along toys are generally regarded as above the range of the average High Street toyshops, yet not 'irregular' or 'kinky' enough for the craft label, being somewhat incongruous in a display of jewellery and arty pottery. But the makers' unique ten-week guarantee against breakage should fulfil a real need for this type of durable toy in the nursery-schools and play-groups for which it was originally designed.

To meet the special needs of handicapped children, the Toy Libraries Association, formed as a charity in 1972, maintains links at national level with therapists, psychologists, toy-designers and makers. The stimulus a child derives from his playthings is naturally more limited if the child is handicapped, be it mentally or physically; to help overcome these limitations the centres are lending the best, sometimes specially adapted toys for the purpose. There are currently about 200 toy libraries in operation, some of which do commission work from local craftsmen.

Good quality wood is undoubtedly a sound choice of material and takes on many shapes in an extensive range of games. Peter and Dinah Stocken have devised unique three-dimensional jigsaws which they cut by hand into such intricate complexity that they are true puzzles which exact the skill of both maker and player; they challenge their own ingenuity and craftsmanship by inviting commissions for special shapes or pictures.

A commission which Caroline Ford was forced to decline was for a half million of her hand-cut jigsaws for a special offer – obviously the individuality was to have been the selling point, but hardly compatible with the size of the order! Customers do sometimes come up with good ideas, though. Tim Green was commissioned to make the African game of Bau – it is now one of his regular lines and exclusive to Crowdy's craftshop.

The most ubiquitous game must be chess. It is claimed to be the most popular game in the world; sets have been designed for playing under all kinds of conditions – from the beach to a horse-drawn carriage; and now it is played by telephone, post, and even computer. For over 3,500 years craftsmen have been using all manner of materials to make sets in a variety of designs. Today's craftsmen are no exception: Jacquie Baker fashions hers from straw; Peter Brown shapes his from clay; and Anthony Archer turns and carves his from wood.

'Poor man's chess' is one of the oldest board games in the world, its origins enmeshed in the pagan history of pre-Christian times. Gaining immense popularity during the Elizabethan reign, this game is the "nine men's morris" referred to in Shakespeare's *A Midsummer Night's Dream*, and would have been lost, together with other Elizabethan games, but for the dedicated interest of Christine Bolton, whose researches resulted in Stratford Games Ltd. Under the keen eye of 'Perce' Davies, "a veritable Snug the Joiner", who had worked for some time as a carpenter with the Shakespeare Birthplace Trust, a small team of craftsmen produce in wood the games from the plays within a hundred yards of where the poet was born.

There are two distinct markets for dolls: cuddly and comforting, fanciful or functional playthings for children; and miniatures of human beings, costumed in cultural or historical detail for the pleasure of grown-ups, with the doll's house the doyen's delight. It was, in fact, the prerogative of the adults to play around with the baby-houses – a fortunate fact perhaps for their preservation.

Originating in the Continental courts, the vogue for baby-houses reached England by the mid-seventeenth century: one of the earliest surviving houses, constructed in this country in about 1710, is the Heslington Hall baby-house. The designer is thought to have been Sir John Vanbrugh who married into the Yarburgh family, from whom York Museum acquired it.

Interest in the miniature field has increased over the past few years; in America it exploded into one of the most popular new hobbies last year. But the Americans are very well-organized as far as collectors' clubs and conventions are concerned, especially in the field of dolls' houses.

In comparison there are very few groups in Britain: the Doll's House Society is limited in membership and not open to applications, but its magazine, *International Doll's House News,* is available on subscription. Having a world-wide circulation it is an ideal vehicle through which the doll's house craftsmen can advertise their very special forte. The society comprises a small group concerned with the preservation of old houses, and encourage the improvement of contemporary dolls' houses because therein lies a record of domestic history; a point which might be useful for those craftsmen who have only considered producing period houses. A glance at the successful American markets may serve as some guide. Acknowledged as compulsive collectors of antiques, Americans, nevertheless, do not omit the six-storey New Jersey hotel, the doll-sized skyscraper and the folding garden-tent from their collections.

Doll's house doll-makers seem to have no problems with markets; Elsie Fox is well-known to members of the Doll's House Club for her Victorian-style wax and china dolls, but the ultimate in miniatures must be the minikins and tiny teddies for the doll's house nursery – it is not surprising that hers has to be a one-woman concern, the making of a $1\frac{1}{2}$ inch miniature does not attract many assistants, therefore her output is bound to be minimal.

Minutiques, the specialist collectors' shop, has a fascinating range of both materials and craft-made miniatures. Carol and Jeff Jackman say they are always looking for new items to add to their lines which conform to their very high quality standard, and report that some stock items are now in such demand that often the requested quantity cannot be fully supplied owing to individual makers reaching their capacity limits.

If anything, the contemporary craftsman's skill has been extended somewhat from that of his predecessor, for often the 'toys' – a term which generally implied small knick-knacks – which furnished the baby-house around the 1650s were much about the same size, so that there were marked disparities in perspective: a chair, candlestick and model cook might be of similar dimensions. Georgian silver 'toys' were not specifically designed for baby-houses, but the 'smallworking', as that branch of silver-smithing was known, obviously found its way into the model houses. The cult for baby-houses as playthings of adults dwindled as the nineteenth century dawned; Victorian children took over their ancestors' dolls' dwellings, so although still attractive, they lost much of their former opulence. An important microcosm of social and domestic history is captured in these models and interest, revived by the opening of Queen Mary's doll's house at Windsor Castle, is once more resulting in the demand for crafts in miniature.

MODELS AND MINIATURES

It seems that the joy is often magnified by a work of art in miniature.

C. E. Stuart King

Closely related to the miniatures which are indicative of an age and also educative, are apprentice pieces, combining all the intricacies of the full-size article, and proof of the trainee's skill by which a master would assess his apprentice's ability to become a craftsman in his own right. Travellers' samples served for advertising, but were usually of more robust construction, being subjected to the rigours of packhorse travel; the real thing, particularly in the case of furniture, being too cumbersome to carry around. The basic material in which models are made, certainly in the United Kingdom, is still wood, and most model-makers are highly skilled woodworkers: Stuart King's training included veneering and marquetry; George Upfold is an articled cabinet-maker; Eric Homewood is a carriage-builder, and Ray Brown may also be working on such diverse woodcrafts as framing a print or repairing a glider wing.

The professional industrial model-maker appeared at the turn of the century and his work is much in demand today as firms look for more and more display models for sales promotion. Models can be photographed in preparation for publicity campaigns, packaging can also be designed well ahead of the production commencing. Design teams use models not only for selling their ideas to a commercial company, but also for actual functional testing. This is a very wide-ranging field, where the model-making is parallel with the designing, and, although a specialist craft of its own, some model-makers find themselves called upon to do plumbing design within their project. Conversely, working models are sometimes constructed of an industrial design which is already in operation so that the causes of certain results can be seen through a Gulliver's eye. Fully working models are of paramount importance and of explicit intricacy: Ray Brown's model of Brunel's *Great Western*, built to a scale of 1 to 100, had 192 separate hand-cut pieces in each of the paddle wheels alone.

It was probably the seventeenth-century shipwrights of the Royal Dockyards who first built accurately to scale – the complexities of a ship's draught being the more easily demonstrated by a model than the designer's diagrams. A sound grounding in mathematics is obviously essential, for all models are now built accurately to scale; an aptitude for drawing, modelling, sculpture, painting, woodwork and metalwork, as well as an artistic flair, are essential to successful model-makers. Particularly in architectural modelling, whether it be for environmental planning or the exquisite models of period houses, post-mills, farm-wagons, or for industrial archaeology such as Bruce Coombes makes, there is a high degree of artistry involved.

Many large companies have their own model-making departments but there is still extensive scope for the freelance craftsman, whose orders almost always come by way of personal recommendation, either as an individual or part of a team.

In general terms, the craft can be summed up as the initial ability to convert someone else's two-dimensional idea into a three-dimensional object, from either complex drawings or mere sketches. A specific course in model-making is part of the three-dimensional Design Course offered at Medway College of Art in Rochester.

There is no official model-makers' guild as such, although many are members of craftsmen's guilds, and a recently formed Society of Architectural Illustrators embraces the work of model-makers along with that of perspective artists and painters, as being related to buildings. The magazine *Scale Models* also keeps a register of model-makers.

PUPPETS

Our basic aim is the advancement of the art of puppetry, in goodwill without distinction of race, politics or religion.

Union Internationale de la Marionette

Between the doll and the model is the puppet, which has fascinated the world's children throughout the ages. The art of puppetry is a sophisticated blend of ancient artistry and masterful manipulation. Its history and intricacy are beyond the scope of this book, confined as it is to the craftwork involved in each field; suffice it to say that as an art form it is both realistic and ritualistic. The unique combination of art and craft and drama in puppetry has stimulated many famous creative artists.

The potential of puppetry in the widest educative sense is being explored, and utilized to great effect, in spheres as diversified as professional companies, television programmes, universities and pre-school play-groups. The specialist field of psychotherapy and physiotherapy have added new dimensions to the value of puppetry, which is already a flourishing and expanding market.

To support rather than duplicate existing services provided by the three British puppetry organizations, the Puppet Centre Trust was formed in 1974 to administer the Puppet Centre. Those interested in the craft of puppetry welcome this focal point, housed in the Battersea Town Hall Community Arts Centre, and can avail themselves of the facilities which include pottery, photographic studio and arts and crafts rooms. Some 1,000 titles on puppetry and allied subjects are contained in the reference library; advice, lectures, demonstrations, public performances and workshop sessions are available.

Some measure of the increased interest in puppetry can be gauged by the fact that the trust, which is not a membership organization, has a mailing list of 500 for its *Friends of the Trust*, the newsletter of the centre and the puppet world. The trust shares its headquarters with the Educational Puppetry Association, a registered charity, which was formed in 1943 with the object of creating a focal point for all puppetry activities concerned with education in the broadest sense.

A model theatre guild was formed over fifty years ago which subsequently absorbed puppetry, and interest has grown ever since, the membership of the British Puppet and Model Theatre Guild is now world-wide.

Both the guild and the Educational Puppetry Association, which has a membership of some 359, have representatives on the international council, *Union Internationale de la Marionette*, which has a world membership of approximately 5,000. The British Centre has almost 150 members at present: these numbers exclude associate members, who are the individuals belonging to Puppet Theatres, and other groups holding group membership. The British Centre was established in 1957 as the Joint International Committee, and became an official centre in 1963. The Union is a member of ITI of UNESCO and aims at being a means of aesthetic and moral education, whilst safeguarding its members' interests as puppeteers. It is not normally concerned with toy and souvenir puppets offered for sale in retail shops.

The majority of puppeteers are artist-craftsmen in their own right, making their own puppets, props and stages, with a number who specialize in making puppets for others to use; but most have been, or still are, puppeteers. Even so, the Crafts Advisory Committee gave the Puppet Centre Trust a grant to commission a range of craftsman-made demonstration puppets which are housed at the Puppet Centre. Individual craftsmen, like Vicki Rutter, earn orders from health authorities for glove-puppets to use in schools for teaching dental care and hygiene. Famous clowns have also commissioned marionettes of themselves.

ASSOCIATIONS (Toys)

BRITISH MODEL SOLDIERS SOCIETY, Hon. Sec: John Ruddle, 22 Priory Garden, Hampton, Middx. Tel: 01–979 7137
> Membership open to those interested in modelling, painting, animating and collecting model soldiers. Meetings, demonstrations, competitions, trading-stalls and auctions; quarterly magazine.

BRITISH TOYMANUFACTURERS' ASSOCIATION, Regent House, Kingsway, London WC2. Tel: 01–242 9158
> Promotes selected trade fairs, including the British International Toy Fair. Publishes a monthly journal.

BRITISH TOY-MANUFACTURERS' ASSOCIATION, Regent House, Kingsway, London WC2. Tel: 01–242 9158
> Membership is open to professional toy-makers, designers and retailers. Semi-professional enthusiasts are also welcomed, but this is not a guild for the hobbyist. Marketing guidance, and display facilities in public exhibition halls and stores for members' toys which have received awards.

TOY LIBRARIES ASSOCIATION, Sunley House, 10 Gunthorpe Street, London E1 7RW. Tel: 01–247 1386/7
> Membership is open to any person or organization concerned with providing handicapped children with the right kind of play material. Through conferences, newsletters, courses and its publications, the association passes on guidance to individual toy libraries. The aim is to have toy libraries eventually throughout Britain and abroad so potential organizers for this wholly non-commercial project are welcomed.

Publication
International Doll's House News, 56 Lincoln Wood, Haywards Heath, Sussex RH16 1LH
> Quarterly magazine, published by the Doll's House Society, available on subscription.

ASSOCIATIONS (Puppetry)

THE BRITISH PUPPET AND MODEL THEATRE GUILD, Hon. Sec: Gordon Shapley, 18 Maple Road, Yeading, nr Hayes, Middx.
  Founded in 1925 with the aims of advocating the use of puppets and model theatres, raising the standards and forming a means of communication between its members, the Guild holds regular meetings, a week-end puppet school, an annual exhibition, and maintains an extensive library and archives. A newsletter and magazine are also published. Membership open to all interested in the guild's aims.

EDUCATIONAL PUPPETRY ASSOCIATION, The Registrar, The Puppet Place, Battersea Town Hall, Lavender Hill, London SW11 5TJ. Tel: 01–223 5356
  By seminars, practical workshop courses, classroom demonstrations, lectures, performances, festivals and exhibitions, the EPA stimulates exploration of the full potential of puppetry, encouraging the exchange of ideas, providing information and advice on all its aspects, and assisting in experimental projects as diverse as play-groups and adult rehabilitation. Membership, open to all who are interested in the educational and cultural value of puppetry, offers a comprehensive advisory service, a regular newsletter and magazine, specialist library facilities, practical courses and workshop facilities at the Puppet Place.

PUPPET CENTRE TRUST (address as Educational Puppetry Association)
  This is not a membership organization, but a subscription (currently 50p a year) is necessary for inclusion on the mailing-list – free to members of EPA. The aims of the centre for encouragement of interest in puppetry as a serious performing art, creative experiment, and assistance to any company or individual working for the improvement of puppetry in Britain, is mainly financed by local authorities, CAC, EPA, and private donations, and implemented by a great deal of voluntary help. Reference library and advisory services are free and open to all. Evening and week-end courses, and workshop sessions at nominal charges.

UNION INTERNATIONALE DE LA MARIONETTE (British Centre), Hon. Sec: T. E. Howard, 5 Greystoke Gardens, Enfield, Middx. Tel: 01–363 5254
  A world-wide association aiming at preserving the living traditions of puppet theatre by promoting contacts between puppeteers of different countries. Founded in 1929, UNIMA now has centres or representatives in more than fifty countries. Activities range from conferences, festivals, exhibitions, tours, lecture courses and schools, to scholarships for young puppeteers. Publications include a members' magazine, and lists of centres and events. Membership is open to anyone interested in the art of puppetry: on a professional, educational or amateur level. Further details on receipt of a stamped and addressed envelope.

TOYS AND GAMES

Note: BTG indicates membership of The British Toymakers' Guild;
     * denotes award membership.

JOYCE ABBATT (Mrs) BTG, 1 Parish Ghyll Road, Ilkley, Yorkshire LS29 9NG
Hobby-horse, blackboard, stacking toys.

*JOHN ADAMS TOYS LTD, BTG, The Lodge, Crazies Hill, Wargrave, Berks.
Wooden educational toys (retail, mail order, export).

*ADMIRAL TOYS, (Mrs Nina Murray) BTG, 2 The Walled Garden, Ledbury,
Hereford HR8 1PJ
Animal soft toys (direct, retail).

D. D. AGARWALLA BTG; MAXSPEED DISPLAY PRINTERS LTD, 112 Mill Road,
Cambridge
Wooden toys and jigsaws, building blocks, hand-cut and hand-assembled,
screen-printed or hand-painted (retail).

JEAN ALEXANDER (HONORARY MEMBER BTG), Cleveland Square, London W2

APRIL COTTAGE HANDWORK, Diana Ralston, 52 The Ridge Way, Sanderstead,
Surrey. Tel: 01–657 5333
Finely detailed dolls including historical characters and lavender dolls.
Wood paintings. Pen and ink drawings of private houses and well-known
historical buildings within the Surrey area.

A. R. ARCHER, 36 High Street, Ixworth, Bury St Edmunds, Suffolk. Tel:
Pakenham 30186
Designer and maker of chess-sets: pieces, boards, and boxes. Each set is
unique in that Mr Archer makes no copies. All are made of hardwoods
from all over the world.

JOYCE ARNOLD (Mrs) BTG, 75 Fairview Road, Penn, Wolverhampton, Staffs.
Animal soft toys (direct, retail).

JAQUIE BAKER, Weaver's Dream, Barton St David, Somerton, Somerset. Tel:
Baltonsborough 584
Straw chess-sets including marquetry boards.

*LIONEL AND ANN BARNARD BTG, 8 Queen's Park Terrace, Brighton.
Period doll's houses, shops, rooms, furniture and accessories (direct, retail
and export).

KEITH AND MAGGIE BARNES, Barton House, Ashill, Ilminster, Somerset. Tel:
Hatch Beauchamp 469
Husband and wife team whose originally designed and hand-built wooden
toys, approved by the Design Council, have represented quality craftwork
in the field of trucks and pull-alongs.

E. L. BATE (Miss) BTG, Nucleus, Berks Hill, Chorley Wood, Herts.
Hobby-horses and soft toys.

JEAN BAXTER BTG, 4 Weyside, Thames Street, Weybridge, Surrey.
Soft toys (direct).

*ANGELA BENDYSHE (Mrs) BTG, The Home Farm, Broomford Manor, Jacob-
stowe, Okehampton, Devon
Soft toys (retail).

JOAN BEVAN, Bracken Fields, Bisley, Stroud, Glos.
Soft toys.

*MAUREEN BIRD (Mrs) BTG, Cherry Hinton, Rectory Road, Deal, Kent.
Soft toys, animals, glove-puppets, pop-up toys.

SUE BLAKE, Millstones, Bozenham Mill Lane, Grafton Regis, Towcester,
Northants. Tel: Yardley Gobion 542211
Soft toys including character animals, i.e. 'Sherlock Holmes owls'. Mrs
Blake enjoys meeting challenging commissions and has made mauve hippos
to match furnishings.

ELIZABETH BOOTH AND JOHN PATEY BTG, 9 Templemere, Oatlands Drive,
Weybridge, Surrey
Play-structures in wood.

*ALTHEA BRAITHWAITE (Mrs) BTG, Dinosaur, Beechcroft, Over, Cambridge
CB4 5NE
Althea Books (retail, direct mail, National Trust).

*ELEANOR BRICKDALE (Mrs) BTG, Mousehole, Widford, Ware, Herts SG12
8SE
Miniature dressed mice (retail, export).

*MARGARET BROWN (Mrs) BTG, Old Bell Cottage, Bisley, Stroud, Glos. GL6
7AB
Finger-puppet families with houses. Miniature dressed mice and animals
(retail).

PAULA CHALK (Mrs) BTG, 14 Wareham Road, Owermoigne, near Dorchester, Dorset
Soft toys. Stick- and glove-puppets (direct and retail).

*CHILDHOOD (JILL BENNET AND SUSAN ERLAND) BTG, 4 Ruvigny Gardens,
Putney SW15 1JR
Period doll's-house dolls to order (retail, export).

*DR CHRISTOPHER COLE BTG, Longbarn Enterprises, Duckmore Lane, Tring,
Herts.

Wooden doll's houses (direct, retail, export).

*CHLOE COOPER (Mrs) BTG, Meadow Cottage, 25 Ireton Grove, Attenborough, Nottingham
'Lob-Lolly' clowns, doll's clothes.

TOM COPPARD BTG, 44 Ockleys Mead, Godstone, Surrey.
Nursery furniture (direct, retail).

*M. E. CRANFIELD (Miss) A.R.C.A. BTG, 40 Leopold Road, Wimbledon, London SW19
Crannie Toys. Dressed soft toy animals (retail). Models of historical personalities (direct). Teacher and toy-designer.

THOMAS CROOKS BTG, 269 Stenson Road, Derby DE3 7HG
Wooden vehicles, pull-alongs, doll's houses, garages, cut-outs.

CROWDYS WOOD PRODUCTS LTD, The Old Bakery, Clanfield, Oxon OX8 2SP. Tel: Clanfield 216
Hand-made traditional games in wood: whip and top, cup and ball, chess, solitaire and the African game of Bau, unique in this country in this particular design. Wooden toys include pull-alongs, trucks and rocking-horses.

ROBIN AND NELL DALE TOYS, Bank House Farm, Holme Mills, Holme, via Carnforth, Lancs. Tel: Burton (in Kendal) 646
Robin and Nell Dale are trained artists and craftsmen whose hand-made wooden dolls are distinctly English and original. The peg-doll range is a set of turned beechwood characters, finished in bright enamels, completely individual, named and signed as such. There are complete families, naval and military sets and a regional collection of English wooden dolls. Dressed dolls, including a boy doll, have newly designed wooden bodies, glass eyes, real hair (as available), and offer a choice of costumes. The 'topsy-turvy' is two dolls in one. The range includes an inexpensive 'cut and colour' dressing-doll printed on fine card and an impressive period doll's house of four storeys with an attic studio. In addition to the production of dolls, specific 'characters' are made to commission.

*MARY DEAN (Mrs) BTG, 1 Bottisham Hall, Bottisham Park, Cambridge CB5 9ED
Small mascot dolls, finger-puppets (retail).

DEDE, Sloop Craft Market, St Ives, Cornwall
Soft toys in felt, etc.

CHRISTINE DIGHT (Mrs) BTG, 100A Bromley Road, Beckenham, Kent
Soft toys (direct, retail).

D. C. DODDS (Mrs), Lookout Garden Flat, 3 Marine Hill, Clevedon, Avon BS21 7PW

Dolls and soft toys to commission, working to client's own design or photo-graph and own materials where required. Wedding-dresses and other needlework. Illustrated talks by arrangement.

DOUNEWAY MARKETING (Mr and Mrs Payne) The Old Post Office, High Easter, Chelmsford, Essex CM1 4QW. Tel: Good Easter 302
A small cottage industry making traditional teddy-bears, individually and by hand. Fully jointed, the bears are made to the designs of Margaret Hut-chings, author of *The Book of the Teddy Bear*, under a formal licence agree-ment entered into with her, and comply with the British Standard Safety Code. This covers the cleanliness of the filling, security of fastenings and fire-resistance of the fabric. Each bear receives individual treatment in as-sembly so no two are exactly alike; and because capacity of output is governed by availability of women craftsmen with the necessary skill and integrity to maintain the high standard of quality that the Paynes and Mrs Hutchings insist upon, they are somewhat of a limited edition. Selected by Design Council.

GWEN AND PETER EDWARDS, Cober Valley Puppet Theatre, Cobblestones, Coverick Bridges, Helston, Cornwall TR13 OLY. Tel: Helston 4341
Portable marionette theatre includes glove-, rod- and shadow-puppets.

*FABRA, CHRISTOPHER LAWRENCE BTG, 1 New North Place, London EC2 4JA
Sewing-kits, wooden kits, soft dolls (retail, export).

CAROLINE FORD, 5 Ingram Row, Horncastle, Lincs. Tel: Horncastle 065–82
A husband and wife team specializing in hand-made wooden jigsaw puzzles, toys, games, transport and marionettes. Export to at least eighteen countries.

ELSIE FOX (Mrs), Barrets Meadow, Harrietsham, Maidstone, Kent.
Doll's-house dolls hand-made in wax and china (clay) in period costume, miniature teddy-bears and golliwogs for doll's-house nurseries.

FRIDAY TOYS, J. H. HUNT (Mrs) BTG, The Crooked Stile, St Mary's Road, Fil-longley, Coventry CV7 8EY
Rag-dolls, animals, hobby-horses (retail, export).

*RON FULLER BTG, Willow Cottage, Laxfield, Woodbridge, Suffolk.
Sandbox acrobat, boat-kit, wooden planes, longboats (retail).

LONDON COLLEGE OF FURNITURE BTG, THE LIBRARIAN, 41–71 Commercial Road, London E11LA
Department of Furnishing and Interior Design (Head: John Weiss). Higher Diploma in Play Equipment (Design and manufacture) Course Tutor: Roger Limbrick. Creative Studies in Toy-making. Course Tutor: Roger Limbrick.

*MARGARET GLOVER BTG, 42 Hartham Road, Isleworth, Middx.
Wax dolls in *pierotti* and *montanari* style (direct, export). 1974 Charles Bolton Selection Cup Winner.

*JOHN AND CAROLINE GOULD BTG, Farningham, Dartford, Kent.
Toy-designer. Toy repairs and renovations (John Gould is an honorary member of BTG)

MAGGY GRANGER, First Yard, Camden Lock, Commercial Place, London NW1 8AF
Porcelain dolls.

*ILSE GRAY AND MARION FIDDIMORE BTG, 12 Princess Road, London NW1
Dolls, soft toys, glove-puppets (retail). *Making Dolls* a studio handbook by Ilse Gray (Studio Vista).

MARY GRIESE, Througham Court Cottage, Camp, Stroud, Glos.
Rag-dolls, embroidery, patchwork.

*HOLLY GRIFFIN BTG, Lilliput Emporium, 6 Smith Street, Dartmouth, Devon
Puppets (direct, retail). Retailer of toys and puppets.

JUDITH GUNN, HONORARY MEMBER BTG, Avenue Gardens, Teddington, Middx.

DAVID HAIG-THOMAS BTG, 52 Rammey House, Longcroft Drive, Waltham Cross, Herts.
Cartoon objects, pictures and books.

ANNA HALLETT BTG, Pippa toys, 83 Elm Tree Road, Sutton Coldfield, Warks.
Rag-dolls and mobiles (retail).

DOROTHY HANDLEY SMITH (Mrs), The Hollies, Bell Lane, Bedmond, Abbots Langley, Herts. WD5 0QS. Tel: Kings Langley 62818
Victorian-style rag-dolls with embroidered faces and wool hair. Character dolls (period costume from fifteenth century to 1900), to order, also dolls and miniature oil-paintings for doll's houses, to scale and to commission.

*CLIFFORD HEAP HONORARY MEMBER BTG, 702 High Road, Buckhurst Hill, Essex. IG9 5HY
Clifford Heap's miniature theatres.

*CHRISTINA HODD (Mrs) BTG, 9 Sylvan Close, Selsdon, Surrey CR2 8DS
National costume puppets, soft toys (direct, retail, export).

ANNE HOFFMAN, Harwood House, Greenham Common, Newbury, Berks.
Designer and maker of soft toys, from miniature to super-size. Commissions accepted, and have included a 24-inch high Highland cow, a life-

size cat with specific markings, replicas of pets, a mural collage appliquéd with St Francis of Assisi and his animals and birds. Occasional garments, such as kaftans, cloaks, hostess skirts and aprons, to order.

OLIVER AND VALERIE HOLT BTG, The Treasure House, 544 Chorley Old Road, Bolton, Lancs.
Toy-retailer.

*RITA HUMPHREYS (Mrs) BTG, Bentfield Hall Cottage, 11 Cambridge Road, Stansted Mountfitchet, Essex
Peg-dolls in nursery-rhyme and period costume. Winner of 1973 Charles Bolton Selection Cup.

J. L. JOHNSTON (Mrs) 8 Chapelmere Close, Sandbach, Cheshire
Glove-puppets – fur-fabric animals or birds, also hassocks for children. Retail outlet: "Hassocks", Mrs Joan Leadley, Marston Trussell, Market Harborough, Leics.

NESSA KEARNEY BTG, 21 Bathgate Road, London SW19
Hand-painted wooden toys (retail).

REIC KEGGANS BTG, 221 Litchfield Road, Fouroaks, Sutton Coldfield
Wooden toys painted and screen-printed. Toy soldiers 1 to 20 scale.

W. J. KELLY BTG, 104 Gregson Lane, Hoghton, Preston, PR5 0LD
Wooden doll's houses, cots, garages (retail, export).

KERMESSEE (IVAN FOSTER AND JUDI KEIGHTLEY), Second Yard, Camden Lock, Commercial Place, London NW1 8AF
Toys designed and retailed at the above.

KINGSWAY COMMUNITY WORKSHOP, Keveral Farm, St Martin by Looe, Cornwall
Children's wooden puzzles.

*JEFF C. KINNA BTG, Tall Tree Toys, Station Road, Staplehurst, Tonbridge, Kent
Playschool and activity toys in wood. Toy-retailer; "The Hobby Horse" Cranbrook, Kent

RITA KIPLING (Mrs) BTG, 47 Nightingale Road, Rickmansworth, Herts. WD/2DA
Rag-dolls.

A. J. LAIN, Grove House, Redham, Saxmundham, Suffolk 1P17 2AS. Tel: Rendham 567
Craftsman in wood, specializing in play-equipment: climbing-frames, monkey-runs, screens, slides, work benches, book stores and sandboxes. Toys include mobile cranes, brick sets with storage-boxes, carts.

MARGARET LANE (Mrs) BTG, 6 Altwood, Harpenden, Herts. AL5 5RU
    Soft toys (retail).

*DAPHNE LEE BTG, Dilly Toys 115 North Lane, East Preston, Sussex
    Miniature dressed animals, miniature tree-house, swings and see-saws.
    Peg-dolls with maypole. Horse-head rattle and purse (retail, direct).
    Broadcaster.

*ELIZABETH LEETHAM (Mrs) BTG, 6 Burn Bridge Oval, Burnbridge, Harro-
gate, Yorkshire HG3 1LR
    Miniature dressed mice. Miniature soft toy hedgehogs. Dressed soft toy
    cats and teddy-bears.

CHERYL LEIGH BTG, Leigh Gallery (HERMIONE HARPER AND PHILLIPA LEIGH),
19 Kings Parade, Cambridge
    Toy-retailer.

ROY AND PAULINE LILL, Sloop Craft Market, St Ives, Cornwall
    Dolls.

JOAN LITTLEWORTH, East Farm, Belchford, Horncastle, Lincs. LN9 62N
    Designs and makes soft toys.

BRENDA LOWES BTG, The Toy Shop, 5 Museum Street, Colchester, Essex
CO1 1TN
    Retailer.

MARGOT TOYS (Mrs Margaret Smith), Shady Grove, Beccles Road, Holton St
Peter, Halesworth, Suffolk IP19 8NQ
    A husband and wife team making exclusively designed soft toys. Unusual
    fabrics are incorporated to give individuality to a regal-looking stag,
    clowns, and a quite special hobby-horse, to mention just a few of the
    regular range produced.

*DOREEN MASTERSON BTG, 107 Calbourne Road, London SW12
    Teacher of toy-making and design.

*MARION MILLETT BTG, Whim Wham Toys. 8 Greenhill Place, Edinburgh 10
    Activating wooden toys (direct). Author of books on toy-making.

JEAN MITCHELL, Pedlars Pack, Molland Cross, South Molton, North Devon
    Fairy-type toys – glove-puppets, special commissions include life-like toy
    puffins for Lundy Island, has also exported to Europe.

*ROSEMARY MORAN (Mrs) BTG, 30 Mickleton Road, Olton, Solihull, Warks.
    Twenty-inch teddy-bears (retail, direct).

GORMLA MORONEY BTG, The House of Henrietta, 34 Surbiton Road, Kingston, Surrey
Retailer, manufacturer, importer, distributor.

D. AND A. MYERS BTG, c/o Margery Daw, 13 High Street, Pinner Village, Middx.
Toy-retailers.

SHEILA NEWINGTON (Mrs), Barnshill Cottage, Rolvenden Layne, nr Cranbrook, Kent. Tel: Rolvenden 469
Victorian-style lead soldiers: two basic sets of eight figures, 25, 8 inches high, painted with accurate uniforms.

ADA NORRIS (Mrs) BTG, 18 Ael-y-Bryn Road, Fforestfach, Swansea, Glamorganshire SA5 8JA
Soft dolls, animals (direct, retail).

*JIM O'BRIEN BTG, 22 Lees Road, Mossley, Lancs.
Doll's houses, table skittles (direct).

*PAMELA PEAKE (Mrs) BTG, Spring Cottage, Ightam, Sevenoaks, Kent
Large soft toys (direct, retail).

*PEGASUS TOYS BTG, Springfield House, Second Avenue, Weston Road, Crewe, Cheshire
Hand-made rocking-horses (retail, export).

THE PLAYGROUP EQUIPMENT AND APPARATUS CO. BTG, (N. E. S. HALL), 9 Scotch Horn Close, Nailsea, Bristol
Doll's houses, garages, farms, play-group equipment (retail, direct, export).

PLAYPUPPETS, SUSAN AND DAVID MEEK BTG, Chestnut House, The Green, Old Buckenham, Norfolk
Glove-puppets and plays. Play-puppets set one, Little Red Riding Hood, Jack and the Beanstalk (retail, export).

M. PLUMB (Mrs) BTG, Whitegate, Feathers Lane, off Bridge Street, Chester
Soft toys (direct, retail).

QUAYSIDE ANTIQUE RESTORERS, First Yard, Camden Lock, Commercial Place, London NW1 8AF
Toys, rocking-horses restored.

PUZZLEPLEX (PETER AND DINAH STOCKEN), Whitley Bridge, nr Goole, North Humberside DN14 0LE. Tel: Whitley Bridge (097 766) 738
Three-dimensional jigsaws, each cut by hand to make completely unique intricate puzzles which are in themselves beautiful constructions in attractively grained woods. As well as traditional jigsaws, which can be executed

from customers' own photographs and can incorporate shapes of letters to spell out a name or a message as the puzzle is put together, there are shapes from the simple round to the complex filigree in basic English hardwoods or exotic precious woods, packed in presentation boxes. Puzzles in rare wood, such as ebony, and filigree puzzles come in a velvet-lined presentation case with brass catches, hinges and a plaque inscribed with the name of the owner and the date of cutting. Catalogues of designs and prices on request. Commissions undertaken for special designs.

CHRISTINE ROGERS, 14 Haresfield, Stratton, Cirencester, Glos.
Peg-dolls.

EARL OF RONALDSHAY BTG, The Pooh Shop, 12 The Square, Winchester, Hants.
Toy-retailer.

RORY TOYS BTG (WILLIAM AND HAZEL MORRISON), Manor Farm House, Turweston, Brackley, Northants.
Large wooden play vehicles (retail).

*YOOTHA ROSE, Guild President, HONORARY MEMBER BTG, Clermont Terrace, Brighton, Sussex
Hand-carved wooden activating toys. Collage, painted and appliquéd pictures. Broadcaster. Trustee – The Toy Museum, Rottingdean, Sussex. Curator – Penshurst Place Museum, Tonbridge, Kent.

*K. RUSSELL (Mr and Mrs) BTG, 'Farthings', Meadow Close, Bembridge, Isle of Wight PO35 5YJ
Dressed rag-dolls (direct, retail).

*RUTTER PUPPETS (MRS VICKI RUTTER) 27 Lodge Avenue, Cosham, Portsmouth, Hants. PO6 2JR. Tel: Cosham 78259
Designer and maker of marionettes and glove-puppets. Author of book on puppetry. Regular exhibiting member of the British Puppet and Model Theatre Guild, UNIMA and BTG. Commissions accepted for special 'characters' and purpose (direct, retail).

B. SADLER BTG, 51 Breach Road, Heanor, Derbyshire
Soft toys (direct, retail).

VERA SMALL BTG, 6 Shepherds Bush Road, London W6
Soft toys, dressing up toys (retail). Toy-retailer.

MARGARET SMITH BTG, Margot Toys, Shady Grove, Beccles Road, Holton St Peter, Halesworth, Suffolk 1P19 8NQ
Soft toys in unusual fabrics (direct, retail, export).

MYRTLE SMITH (Mrs), 4 Bromley Road, Parsons Heath, Colchester, Essex. Tel: Colchester 5846

Wax dolls, hand-made in the traditional way from kid and real hair; also china dolls, dressed in hand-stitched clothes which are meticulously correct in historical detail. Each doll is signed and dated.

SAM SMITH (HONORARY MEMBER BTG), Kingswear, Dartmouth, Devon
Humorous wood sculptures by this artist, designer, writer, humorist.

*JOHN SPILLER BTG, Oak Lodge, Lavant Road, Chichester, Sussex PO19 4RG
Miniature model period furniture to order.

*PEGGY STENNING (Mrs) BTG, 2 Steeplechase, Hundon, Sudbury, Suffolk
Soft toys in fur-fabric (direct, retail).

STRATFORD GAMES LTD, Merelles House, Henley Street, Stratford-upon-Avon, Warwickshire. Tel: Stratford-upon-Avon 66416
Craftsmen-made games in wood, from Shakespeare's plays: 'Nine Men's Morris', 'Fox and Geese', 'Loggats', 'Troll-my-Dames', 'Quoits', 'Shove-Groat'. Other period games such as 'knuckle bones', whip and spinning-tops, also produced. Intensive research has resulted in authentic detail in these games some of which date back to the medieval era. Exports to at least fourteen countries. On exhibition at Craft Council and Design Centre.

JANET TAPP (Mrs) BTG, Scearn Bank Farm, Limpsfield, Chart, nr Oxted, Surrey
Soft toy student.

*CHRISTINE TAYLOR BTG, 56 Croft Down Road, London NW5
Bird and animal felt glove-puppets (direct, retail, export).

JOSHUA TAYLOR LTD BTG, Sidney Street and Bridge Street, Cambridge
Toy-retailer.

*THINGUMMIES LTD, PETER AND GILLIAN GREENHILL (Chairman and Secretary) BTG, 32/34 Ridgway, Wimbledon Village, London SW19 4QW
Jack-in-the-box, doll's-house dolls, miniature dressed animals. Toy-retailers.

*ALINE THOMPSON BTG, Stag House, Newington, nr Warborough, Oxon.
Seven-inch dressed mascot dolls. Man and lady, Oxford Doctorships (retail, direct).

D. THORNTON (Mrs), 4 Castle Close, Warwick CV34 4DB. Tel: Warwick 43891 (after 4 p.m.)
Peg-dolls: each individually made within a wide range of characters which includes a bridal group and Victorian soldiers in dress uniform. Commissions undertaken for speciality dolls. Member White Rose Dollmakers' Circle.

R. F. TOPLEY BTG, 8 Homefield Rise, Orpington, Kent BR6 0RU
Garages, farms, doll's houses, forts in wood (direct).

*PATRICIA WARREN (Mrs) BTG, 25 Great Wheatley Road, Rayleigh, Essex
SS6 7AW
Large soft toy animals (direct, retail).

CAROLINE WATT AND MICHAEL WATT BTG, 31 Maids Causeway, Cambridge
Period doll's houses, shops and market-stalls, fully stocked and decorated,
gypsy caravans, dolls, and period toys. Toy-kits (retail, direct, export).

*WATT'S (Mrs) VIVARIUM LYN WATKINS AND VIVIENNE DAVIDSON BTG, 18 Uni-
versity Mansions, Lower Richmond Road, SW15
Giant soft toys (retail, export).

*GEOFFREY AND MARGARET WEST BTG, 24 Old Farleigh Road, South Croydon,
Surrey
Period dolls, houses of wood and fibreglass (retail, direct).

*HELEN WHATELY BTG, 13 High Street, Marlow, Bucks.
Thirteen-inch dressed period biscuit dolls (direct, retail).

WOOLCRAFT, Mount Street, Cromer, Norfolk. Tel: Cromer 2514
Retail outlet for locally hand-made dolls and soft toys. An appealing range
from minute felt characters in national costume to beautifully detailed
Cromer fishermen dolls, reasonably priced.

*IAN AND CYNTHIA WRIGHT BTG, 14 Wilton Grove, Wimbledon SW19
Toy design. Movable cut-out and animated models.

MODEL-MAKERS

SANDRA ANSON, Dromore, Livonia Road, Sidmouth, Devon Tel: Sidmouth
3709
Miniature period furniture in mahogany from sketches or actual pieces,
scale 1 inch to 1 foot. Commissions only.

JOHN BENFORD, Guinea Truckle, 8 King William Road, Kempston, Bedford
MK42 7AT
Models of horse-drawn carriages of the eighteenth and nineteenth centuries.
Each model made in explicit detail: the tiny windows are glazed, seats are
upholstered in leather, intricate mechanism enables each part to move in se-
quence. Featured on television. Private sales only.

RITA BLAKE, Cherry Orchard Cottage, Selsted, Sittingbourne, Kent
Beatrix Potter type animal figures. Commissions accepted.

ROBERT · HOLLAND-MARTIN

1872 ~ 1944

whose foresight preserved these precincts

JOHN WOOD
BORN 3 MARCH 1908
KILLED IN
BULLCLIFFE
WOOD PIT 7
CHURCHWARDEN HERE NOVEMBER 1964
FOR EIGHTEEN YEARS

Bryant Fedden's engraving skills are used on such diverse media
as glass and stone

Brother Thomas, chief designer and founder of the famous
Prinknash Abbey Pottery, still does most of the hand-painting

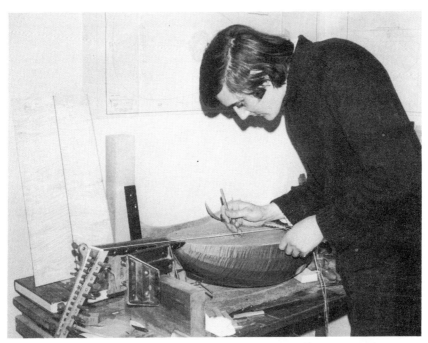

Charles Ford uses a surgeon's scalpel to carve the rose on his lute

Nicholas Keen playing a harpsichord which he designed: shown also are his clavichord and positivorgan

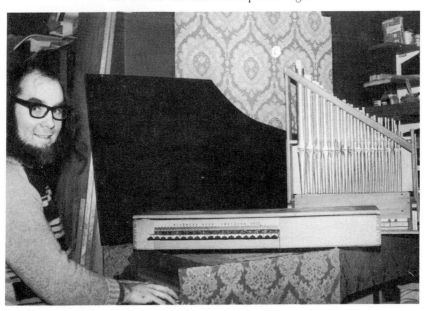

Nell Dale paints a 'topsy-turvy' doll turned by her partner
Robin

Miniature antique chairs made by C. E. Stuart King

Scale model of Brougham made by carriage-builder Eric
A. Homewood

Feathers take the form of floral art for a bridal bouquet

Net-making at Bridport Gundry Ltd

John Makepeace brings a new dimension to furniture design and is the most influential of any modern designer-craftsman in wood

Decorating a table-top with feathers at Pettit's Rural Industries

RÁY BROWN, 6b Victoria Road, Cirencester, Glos. GL7 1EN. Tel: Cirencester 3524 and 4489

Model-maker specializing in architectural and engineering types for environmental planning and industry. Craft woodworker with a wide range of skills working to commission.

BRUCE COOMBES, Prospect Cottage, Lamyatt, Shepton Mallet, Somerset. Tel: Bruton 3415

Specialist in model period houses mainly to commission for the serious collector. Working models of post-mills, wagons, etc., made to order. Models made to scale and in fine detail of private properties. Doll's houses, dioramic wall-cabinets, Regency and Victorian play models, miniature furniture and domestic metalware, as well as models for museums, educational loan services and for commercial promotions of export and business houses.

RUTH COOK, Westend Cottage, Elmstree Farm, Tetbury, Glos.
Miniatures in wood.

JOHN DALL (Llad Engineering), 19 Middlegates, St Agnes, Cornwall. Tel: St Agnes 2872

Well-known in the South West as a model-maker, John Dall's Tamar Bridge and other models can be seen in "Cornwall in Miniature", St Agnes's Model Village. In his small workshop on the site of the old Wheal Kitty tin mine on the cliffs overlooking the Atlantic, this versatile engineer covers a wide range of specialist work (*see also* Iron p. 236).

DAVID AND JOAN DE BETHEL, Stocks House, Udimore, Rye. Tel: 0424 882 330

Unique models of cats in papier mâché – collectors' pieces which are, for the most part, numbered and recorded, sold exclusively in England by the hatters, Herbert Johnson of New Bond Street.

JO DE BONO, Design Brokers Ltd.
Collectors' pieces: military miniatures in pewter.

HARRY FREEMAN, 78 Ayre Road, Erdington, Birmingham 24

Model boats to scale, motor-controlled, ranging from those of the time of Queen Elizabeth II to aircraft carriers.

JOHN GILMAN, 49 Abbotswood Road, Brockworth, Gloucester
Ship model-maker. Associate Member Guild of Gloucestershire Craftsmen.

ERIC A. HOMEWOOD, Mill Farm House, Arlington, Barnstaple, Devon EX31 4LN. Tel: Shirwell 306

Carriage miniatures; these collectors' pieces are hand-produced to scale, exact replicas of the collection of carriages exhibited at Arlington Court, a National Trust estate. Approximately 17 inches long by 9 inches high, the models are finished in the stable colours of the original carriage, lined and varnished by hand. Carriagework: each piece cast separately and assembled with miniature nuts and screws. All appropriate parts are fully movable; caps and wheels are removable – spanner provided. Coachwork: hand-moulded with doors, windows, folding hoods, etc. fully operational. Brass door-handles and coachlamps. Upholstered in morocco leather skives, buttoned and trimmed with hand-made laces, blinds of silk, seude-leather lining cloth, with selected hide fittings, each of these exquisite and quite unique models is presented in a glass case with removable top. Enquiries invited for commissions for specific carriages (see also carriage-maker p. 107).

C. E. STUART KING, Primrose Cottage, 17 Parish Piece, Holmer Green, High Wycombe, Bucks. Tel: Holmer Green 2027
Antique chairs in miniature, mainly Windsor, using traditional timbers, to 1 to 4 scale. Currently extending the range to include tables with marquetry inlay. Each piece is entirely hand-made by Stuart King in his workshop at the bottom of the garden in the traditional High Wycombe manner. The pieces are exact replicas of dated English furniture, the result of intensive research into their history and the old craftsmen's methods. All orders personally dealt with direct. Pieces made only to order and executed in strict rotation, each is signed and numbered. Stuart King also lectures and demonstrates the chair-bodger's craft using the pole lathe and will exhibit his private collection of woodworking tools and models.

MINUTIQUES, 82b Trafalgar Street, Brighton BN1 4EB Tel: Brighton 681862
Hand-made miniatures by craftsmen from all over England, with whom the proprietors work on finished design. Many exclusive items, such as the hand-blown glassware, within which range are such intricately executed individually made pieces as a fluted edge fruit bowl on stem $\frac{7}{8}$ inch high and a Christmas punch-bowl on stem with six glasses hooked on rim, with ladle, $\frac{3}{4}$ inch high 1 inch diameter; hand-made brass and copperware, and collectors' doll-cabinets and rooms. Suppliers of materials for miniature making. Doll's hospital.

DENNIS C. RANDALL, Collier Cottage, New Road, Northchurch, Berkhamsted, Herts. Tel: Berkhamsted 4070
Miniature antique furniture to scale using old wood and veneers. Restoration of antique furniture, conservation of oil paintings, sea and landscape artist.

SHIPS IN MINIATURE LTD, Stockton-on-Forest, York YO3 9UT. Tel: (0904) 768643
Ships in bottles. Retailed throughout the country, expanding export market.

G. F. UPFORD, Coles Farmhouse, Chichester Road, Selsey, Sussex. Tel: Selsey 3161
Miniature furniture. Member of the Guild of Sussex Craftsmen.

18

Flora, Fauna, Feathers and Food

FLOWERS

> I make pictures from local flowers, dried in a dark cupboard, scrounge rose petals for an old *pot-pourri* recipe, and make pillows from the herbs I grow in the garden.
>
> *Joan Smyth*
> *Fleur de Lis Crafts*

The English garden seems to have evolved sometime in the early thirteenth century; although herbs had been grown by monks for medicinal purposes throughout the ages. The Elizabethans developed the idea of a formal garden, and extended the range and purpose of herbs and flowers for use in their toilet, in their cooking and to combat plagues and pests.

Drying flowers has been practised throughout the ages, with the purpose of powdering the petals; the Duke of Bolton's cook recorded a receipt for drying roses in the early eighteenth century, but the notion of preserving flowers in their natural form as decoration from which pictures were composed was a Victorian pastime, to be revived as a creative craft in the past few years. As an art form the designs range from simple gift cards to exquisitely executed floral collages and the ability to preserve special sprays such as bridal bouquets.

The use of flowers goes back to the ancient Egyptians, the most lavish users of perfume in all history, to the days when Mark Antony waded knee-deep in rose petals to pay homage to Cleopatra, but it was the Greeks who recorded the lore of flora, and the Romans who adopted the customs and carried them to their great Empire outposts.

From the Romans came our most fragrant flower, the lovely lavender which has perfumed the still-rooms over the centuries. Whole flower-heads were tossed into the Roman communal baths and the delicately perfumed flower derived its name from that association, *lavre*, meaning to wash.

English lavender is cultivated on a commercial scale by only one firm now. Between the coast and open farmland in north-west Norfolk fields of the deep blue florets roll across ninety acres, and since 1964 these have been harvested in a similar way to a cornfield. The beauty of the crop does not render it immune to the usual horticultural hazards. Geographically the enterprise is well sited; the light soil, high alkalinity, and moderately low rainfall is well suited to lavender, but a really wet

June can ruin the harvest.

At the distillery the flowers are forked into copper stills and packed down by a man trampling on them. About a quarter of a ton of lavender heads is distilled at a time and produces between one and two pints of raw oil which then has to mature before being blended to a secret formula dating back to the time of George IV. Sachets of dried flowers are made up by a school for the mentally handicapped at King's Lynn and sold in East Anglia. The distinctive Norfolk lavender oils (for there are some half a dozen different strains of lavender grown by the company, each with its own character) perfume the Norfolk Lavender Company's own products which range from bath oils, soaps and powders to the delicate English lavender water, enjoyed by French and English women alike.

It is believed that the original perfumes were contained in smoke, from whence the name originated, and the ancient Egyptians made fragrant burnt offerings to their gods before Christianity came to their land.

The Bible is full of references to crafts; the ingredients for holy perfume are given in detail to Moses in the Book of Exodus and it could be that from the Scriptures came the monasteries' first recipes. The Benedictine monks of Prinknash Abbey in the Cotswolds have developed their incense-making into a successful commercial enterprise, with lavender as one of the essential oils. Their ingredients are not regarded as secret, but the formula certainly is.

Charcoal from the Forest of Dean is also supplied by the monks, and is an important factor for the incense must burn white. Prinknash incense is exported to many countries, and is burned at the Cave of Bethlehem every Christmastide; it was also the choice of Pope Paul when the Basilica of Mount Cassino was consecrated at its restoration; and was chosen again by Pope John, when he was Patriarch of Venice, for use in the consecration of the underground Basilica at Lourdes. The incense is retailed through a London stockist.

Flowers are emulated in almost every type of material and the increased popularity of Victoriana has given rise to much reproduction work in the crafts field.

Making pictures from shells is a Georgian art, which reached the peak of its fashion in Victorian times, whereas feathercraft is a relatively new craft, in which Pettitts Rural Industries have become nationally famous for their feather bouquets and flowers.

Started as a hobby by V. C. Pettitt, the feathercraft now engages some thirty workers, some of whom work at home. A competition was organized in 1940 between the game and poultry department and the office staff. Within a fortnight quite recognizable flowers and foliage were produced and competitions have been held ever since. The unique feathercraft of Pettitts is not confined to floral fancies, models are built of feathers of the Norfolk windmill, pianos and buildings, and they are also used to decorate tables; one commission was for a special pony's head to be reproduced in feathers.

TAXIDERMY

It is popularly believed that the Victorians were the originators of taxidermy, but while it is true that it reached its zenith in that era – the humblest home had at least a stuffed squirrel under a glass dome – the art of preservation of skin and tissue is known to have been practised by the ancient Egyptians. Another misapprehension is that only favoured pets, like Queen Anne's parrot – which is still in existence – game trophies or the fantastic fish that never got away, are preserved; hardly enough to keep the craft alive. On the contrary, however, there is now a big demand for natural history exhibits.

The secrets of taxidermy techniques were always jealously guarded, shrouding the whole craft in mystery, but the large Yorkshire firm of World of Nature has opened its workshops to the public recently as a tourist scheme. School-leavers are accepted on a two-year training scheme; other taxidermists offer similar training when possible, but there is no official apprenticeship. I am told there is no more mystery attached to this craft than there is to any other; obviously if one is interested in learning the trade then it helps if basic physiology is understood, there is a great deal of manual skill involved, and a sense of artistry is required in mounting the article; but with no more than a dozen firms in the whole of England, the opportunities are somewhat limited. For the same reason there is no guild of taxidermists.

Taxidermists normally only mount specimens on request: The World of Nature is one of the few who mount animals and birds first and then offer them for sale, the firm undertakes all the taxidermy for Tussaud's International. Films, television, museums and education are the taxidermists' markets today, with advertising agencies becoming increasingly aware of the potential. Not so easily found is the taxidermist who will, or can, do repairs and restoration. A. Sheppy of Bristol, whose workshop is full of off-white red squirrels and blackbirds as brown as cocoa, is one of only a couple who undertake restoration of antiques.

Antiques of the future are now being made by our contemporary craftsmen: Audrey Taunton of Cumbria employs taxidermy techniques to produce her unique bird pictures and has found no other artist doing equivalent work although she has exhibited widely at home and abroad. The Victorians used the minimum of feathers for their pictures, but Mrs Taunton uses almost all the feathers from the birds which are sent to her from breeders, aviaries and zoos. It is, however, the ordinary British birds which are most difficult to find. Only birds found dead in the countryside are used, Mrs Taunton is emphatic on the point that no bird shall be killed for the purpose.

CHEESE-MAKING

> Not all Britain is a bustling, choked jumble . . . a peaceful life may still be found in the green, plentiful countryside where, alongside combine-harvester and purring tractor, cattle graze . . . and where, in the age-old skills of cheese-making, handed down from father to son, a traditional craft is still very much alive.
>
> *Milk Marketing Board*

Curds and whey first became separated, so legend has it, completely by accident: an Arab carrying a supply of milk in a young cow's stomach – the traditional way in days of yore – found that after several hours of rough riding the milk had curdled into a soft substance. From that 'accident' developed the art of cheese-making which still incorporates that essential ingredient – rennet, prepared from the fourth stomach of the calf.

Featuring in the diet of the ancient civilizations, cheese was accorded an honourable status under the protection of Aristaeus, son of Apollo. From the Greeks came the French and Italian names for cheese, derived from *formos*, the wicker basket in which the cheese was drained. The Anglo-Saxon *cese* or *cyse*, which has come down to us as cheese, stems from the Roman name for the cheese-draining basket. But the craft of cheese-making was established in Britain long before the Romans came, and the Celtic cheese-makers were actually praised by the gourmet invaders. It has never lost all of its mystical connotations, however, for we still roll a mammoth cheese down the grassy gradient of Cooper's Hill every Whitsuntide in accordance with ancient rites; but have relegated to the records those "quaint customs of the rustics", the habit of carrying through the streets flower-decked Double Gloucesters to roll down the hill before eating.

Impressive rounds of cheese, completely unrelated to commercial viability, graced the market-stalls throughout the country and issued forth from the farmhouses until the mid-nineteenth century. The art of making mammoth cheeses is not dead, just dormant, for the largest cheese the world has ever known – a magnificent 15.44 tons of cheddar – was hauled to New York World's Fair in 1964. The name *cheddar* has become so synonymous with cheese that one finds cheddar cheeses are universal.

The year 1860 stands out in the English cheese-makers' calendar as a disaster. Disease struck the farms and thousands of dairy cows were killed off, leaving precious little milk for cheese-making and the English market was soon flooded with American cheddars. With the rise in population, the demand for cheese became a national concern and cheese-makers had to adapt to changing conditions. The first cheese factory opened in 1870 and others soon followed – it was the beginning of a new era in which food would be produced for the masses rather than just the local community.

A century later advertising agents are reaching for rural adjectives in the vain hope that by seasoning the descriptions of factory-processed foods some form of osmosis will take place and they actually acquire the flavour of country-fresh, farmhouse, summer harvests; but they remain totally unrelated, of course, to the texture or taste of the genuine thing.

Farmhouse cheese-making has never completely died out in England; there were still 1,500 people engaged in making cheese in the traditional way when the Second World War broke out, but their labours were soon channelled into more urgent service. It was about twenty years before regional individuality returned to cheese.

There are now three English farmhouse cheeses; that is, cheese traditionally made on a farm from dairy herds producing the highest quality milk, generally owned by the farmer making the cheese, under a special contract with the Milk Marketing Board. Cheese-making takes place from 6 a.m. to 3 p.m. without a break, seven days a week, for eleven months of the year, including Christmas Day.

The current figures show 28 farms in the Somerset area producing Farmhouse Cheddar (sometimes called West Country Farmhouse), using some 28 million gallons of milk each year to produce 11,500 tons of cheese. Only six farms now make Farmhouse Lancashire; very little of this distinctive cheese finds its way south.

Farmhouse Cheshire, probably the oldest of our English cheeses – recorded in the *Domesday Book* and praised by Dr Samuel Johnson – is made on 21 farms in Cheshire and Shropshire. One produces 140 of the prized Blue Cheshires a week. Not all Cheshire cheese becomes blue: why it does so remains a mystery. Matured in a cellar in Whitchurch, Cheshire, it is kept for a minimum of three months.

The quality of the cheese depends on the milk (Friesian and pure bred Ayrshire cattle are mainly milked for farmhouse cheeses), the soil and the weather. In fact, the individuality of cheese can be similarly compared with the variety in types of wine produced from different grapes.

Farmhouse English Cheese, accounting for nearly 10 per cent of the total cheese production of the United Kingdom, is clearly labelled as such and is retailed through some of the large chain stores and the specialist grocery shop.

The English Country Cheese Council was set up in 1955 as a division of the National Dairy Centre, and offers a comprehensive service to grocers, including lectures, films and display material to promote the nine famous English cheeses. The Milk Marketing Board issues information on the qualities of Farmhouse English Cheese, and instructions on that other traditional skill, that of cutting the $10\frac{1}{2}$ lb of the cheese which statistics say each of us eats in a year.

STILTON CHEESE-MAKING

Of the magnificent nine English cheeses, Stilton is acknowledged indisputable King. Running like royal blood through its veins, the blue mould of a penicillin strain grows naturally inside the ivory-coloured cheese, giving Blue Stilton a unique marbled effect. The piquant flavour and creamy texture have drawn praises from the pens of poets: Edward Bunyard went so far as to cite Stilton, along with Shakespeare, as one of our great British institutions.

Stilton is certainly the *pièce de résistance* of the craft of English cheese-making, but sadly enough there seems to be no one person to whom the accolade can be accorded for this culinary coup. The technique and recipe were close family secrets of the makers for generations. It acquired its name through being sold at Stilton, although history records no evidence of the cheese ever being made there. It was first called Lady Beaumont's cheese because this particular variety was made by her ladyship's housekeeper, who, in turn, taught her daughter the essential skills. The daughter, having married Farmer Paulet of Wymondham, near Melton Mowbray, was well accustomed to the long arduous days spent in the diary, but put them to good use by turning the farm milk into the blue-veined cheese with its crusty coat, and found a ready market for it at the Bell Inn at Stilton, which was run by her sister and brother-in-law.

The cheese was then served under the name of English Parmesan. Its fame soon spread and travellers came to the staging post of Stilton specially to buy it. It was well-established by the time Defoe toured the country in 1727, for he records having "passed through Stilton, a town famous for cheese"; the cheese had by that time acquired the name of the place where it was sold, a name since protected by copyright. The Certification Trade-Mark was registered in 1969, and is being registered outside England also, restricting the use of the name *Stilton* to cheese made in only three English counties: Leicestershire, Nottinghamshire, and Derbyshire, in accordance with the specifications of the Stilton Cheese-Makers' Association, and in dairies authorized by them.

The Association was formed in 1936 with an initial membership of 23, with the objects of protecting the rights and privileges of the Stilton cheese-making industry, and promoting research in connection with its manufacture, marketing and storing. Improvements on Mrs Paulet's methods had been implemented by Edwardian farmers whose wives were unwilling to wear themselves out in the protracted chore of cheese-making, which involved working in damp and dark dairies from 4 a.m. until dusk, constantly at odds with the vagaries of temperature and humidity, in order to produce a cheese that took eighteen months to mature. Societies were formed through whose channels Stilton cheese-making was taken out of the farmhouse and into centrally-sited dairies. One member reputedly pledging even his bed at the bank to raise money for his share.

Despite scientific advances which regulate and control temperature and humidity, Stilton cheese-making methods can never be mechanized; an immense measure of experience, skill and handwork is essential when producing a connoisseur's cheese. From the time the milk is run into the giant tubs until it leaves the dairy as a fully matured Blue Stilton, there is some three months' attention paid to it. White Stilton, popular in the northern counties, is ready for sale after about seven to fourteen days. Seventeen gallons of full cream milk is needed to make one 14–15 lb. Stilton cheese. The only additives are "a starter" (a pure culture produce lactic acid); rennet to form the curd; and salt. The curd is cut, drained, broken up, mixed, drained again on calico and placed into hoops; the surface is then deftly rubbed up with knives to seal it and make a base for the coat, and bandaged. The curd becomes cheese and the crusty coat starts to form. The cheese is turned every day and oxygenized by being pricked with stainless-steel needles to germinate the mould spores. Each cheese receives some 300 to 350 punctures. The 'investment' involved is likened to that of a wine cellar, for a dairy stores something like 50,000 gallons of its milk on the racks in this way. Maturity is judged by boring the cheese with a cheese-iron to test for ripeness, texture and flavour.

One of the depravations of war-time was the cessation of Stilton cheese-making, for the rigid controls prohibited the production of cheeses other than the hard-pressed and long-keeping varieties. Some dairies were able to adapt to the regulations, but many others were made redundant and for some years after the war, when some dairies were authorized by the Ministry of Food to continue making Stilton cheese there was much discussion over this distinction until all rights were restored to these redundant dairies. Throughout those difficult years, the association pursued their original intent, that of protecting the industry, and fulfilled these aims to their limited ability. By 1947 Stilton-making was resumed on an allocated ration, even so the association saw to it that the redundant dairies' customers received their share. A year later it had achieved a 4 per cent increase in milk allocation and extra was made available to produce blue cheese for the dollar areas and so help the great export drive.

There are now seven dairies engaged in making over half a million

Stiltons each year for sale throughout the United Kingdom, exporting to America, Canada and parts of Europe. Despite the fact that marketing is done directly through the wholesalers, meaning that the cheese-makers are never in direct contact with their consumers, the pride in making is such that the association publish explicit instructions on how to serve, store and complement this cheese, so prized by gourmets all over the world; so now there should never be anyone who will scoop bits out of the middle, then ruin the rest by pouring port over it in an attempt to keep it moist. The Melton Mowbray way is "cut high, cut low, cut level" – and they should know for this is true Stilton country.

There are still isolated farm shops which cater mainly for local customers, owing to the many varying conditions upon which cheese-making on these farms is dependent it would be impossible to trace them all. These cheeses, when chanced upon, prove to be truly individual and indigenous to the locality. And if anyone finds the elusive true Blue Vinny, whose disappearance has been blamed on public health officers and the absence of harness rooms, they should keep it secret and cultivate a life-long friendship with that particular cheese-maker! It would seem that Blue Vinny now belongs to the vanished world of Hardy. 'Dorset Knobs', rusk-like round biscuits which he enjoyed with his local cheese are, however, still made by the Moores family bakery at a rate of some 25,000 a day in much the same way as they were 150 years ago. Each biscuit is individually moulded by hand and has three separate bakings lasting a total of four hours. The whole process takes at least eight hours, starting with the making of the dough at 6 a.m.

Up in Brontë country hand-baked biscuits made according to home recipes were an immediate success when S. Barraclough and his wife started to produce them in 1959. The biscuits have never been advertised and sales are solely on their own merit but even so keeping production up to demand is the Barracloughs' biggest problem. The nature of the product makes this a labour intensive concern and some ninety-three people are now engaged in this company, whose turnover has increased twentyfold. The biscuits are retailed throughout the country.

Home-made foods always find ready customers: specialist and farm shops carry regular lines, and W.I. stalls are often found at town markets; even the local jumbles have at least a cake-stand; but the essence of Old England must surely be on the sweet-stalls such as T. Strutt's in Walthamstow High Street. For over a century four generations of the Strutt family have been pulling toffee products by hand over a hook, flavouring them, pulling them out again and cutting them into lengths. The cream-based sweets are still stirred in the original copper pans, although Mr Strutt admits to using gas now for cooking, whereas his ancestors used coke furnaces, and says he does not have to shell the coconuts and peanuts any more. And there on the stall are the Nutrock,

Stickjaw, Swiss Cream, Coconut Ice, Coconut Candy, Clove, Lemon Acid, Peppermint and Cough Candy Rocks: childhood caught in a sweet, sticky memory.

FLOWERS

SHEILA BEATTIE, 23 St Lawrence Way, Bricket Wood, St Albans, Herts.
Greetings-cards and small pictures with designs made from pressed flowers and leaves. Each carries a different design.

LADY PAMELA LE BAILLY, Good Monday's Farm, Dauntsey, nr Chippenham, Wilts. SN15 4HL Tel: Bradenstoke 366
Pressed flowers, mainly stationery items: boxed notepaper, notelets, packs of gift-cards with gold tie, matchboxes, jotter-pads and bookmarks.

ROSEMARY SHREAD, 1 Grove Villas, Ryeleaze Road, Stroud, Glos.
Dried flower arrangements including wedding-bouquets.

JOAN SMYTH, Middlesex Cottage, 66 North End, Batheaston, Bath, Avon. Tel: Bath 88574
Pressed flower pictures sold in the craftshop, Fleur de Lis Crafts, at address above.

JOY STRONG, 35 Woodend Lane, Cam, Dursley, Glos. Tel: Dursley 45466
Pressed flowers, pictures, paperweights, cards, etc. Wedding-bouquets dried and framed. Demonstrations by arrangement.

FEATHERCRAFT AND TAXIDERMY

OLIVE HEATON CLARKE, 12 Oaklea Close, Old Roar Road, St Leonards-on-Sea, Sussex. Tel: Hastings 751881
Feather collages of birds with embroidered or natural flower backgrounds on cloth. Individual designs. Widely exhibited, examples of Mrs Clarke's craft have been televised and bought for stately homes.

PETITTS RURAL INDUSTRIES LTD, Reedham, Norfolk NR13 3UA. Tel: Freethorpe 243/4
Mounted birds and animals on hire for all occasions, also mounted specimens for sale. Unique feathercraft articles including flowers and bouquets. Natural history and folk museum and ornamental birds in beautiful surroundings make this a Broadland tourist attraction.

A. SHEPPY & CO., High Street, Congresbury, Bristol, Tel: Yatton 832180
Taxidermists and natural history dealers.

AUDREY TAUNTON, 63 Bellingham Road, Kendal, Cumbria LA9 5JY. Tel: Kendal 22030

Bird pictures created from authentic feathers mounted on silk or other fabric backgrounds and tastefully framed. Having closely studied both ornithology and taxidermy, the artist creates pictures by preserving for posterity the beautiful plumage from birds of the English countryside and exotic foreign breeds. The technique which Mrs Taunton has perfected involves a painstaking process of her own invention resulting in absolutely unique works of art, exclusive to her own one-woman business. Widely exhibited at such events as the Royal Society of Art shows and Game Fairs, and in Paris, Monte Carlo, Cannes, Nice, Deauville and Biarritz. Lists of pictures for sale on request. Special commissions undertaken by arrangement.

WORLD OF NATURE, The Old Mill, Kirkby Fleetham, North Yorkshire. Tel: 060–984 643
Scheduled as the world's most versatile taxidermists, a team of artist-craftsmen work on fauna from all over the world, specializing in educational and display creatures. Thousands of specimens mounted ready for sale. A vast range covers supplies for world-wide waxworks exhibitions, interior decor, models for photographic, film and television studios as well as trophies for private collectors. Display and design consultants. Loan services to schools and museums. Exhibition centre, with special displays of live insects, birds and butterflies, rocks and corals and numerous tableaux open every day. Workshops, where practical taxidermy can be seen in progress, now open to the public from Monday to Friday. Reduced rates for parties.

SHELLS

DOROTHY FODDY (Mrs), 206 Score Lane, Liverpool L16 5EG
Shells: mainly floral designs composed entirely of shells, mounted on velvet and framed as pictures – some compositions containing 1500 separate shells; paperweights of resin with real flowers and shells.

VICTORIA ORIGINALS, 36 Greenway Road, Timperley, Cheshire. Tel: 061–973 4039
Shell pictures using traditional techniques and mounted in hand-made frames. Speciality line is the Victorian posy-type picture. Widely exhibited. Commissions undertaken for special designs.

FOOD

S. MOORES, GOLDENCAP BISCUIT BAKERY, Morcombelake, Bridport, Dorset
'Dorset Knobs' – the traditional biscuit of Hardy country. Dorset Gingers and Easter Cakes also made at the bakery. Visitors are welcomed to see production in progress (Monday to Friday 9–5.30) Dorset preserves and West Country crafts on sale at the Dorset Shop attached to the Bakery.

T. G. STRUTT, Markhouse Road Shop, and market stall in Walthamstow High Street
Traditional hand-made sweets.

YORKSHIRE BISCUITS LTD, Brontë Bakery, Bridgehouse Mills, Haworth,

Keighley, Yorks. Tel: Haworth 43508

Hand-baked biscuits from traditional recipes of home-bakers of the past. Available throughout the country.

THE STILTON CHEESE-MAKERS ASSOCIATION, Sec: G. F. Allaway, Midland Bank Chambers, High Street, Melton Mowbray, Leics. LE13 OTU. Tel: 3606/7 and 4389

General publicity and advice to the trade relating to Stilton Cheese. Membership restricted to Stilton Cheese-makers.

19

Candle-making

The candle-maker follows an old and honoured craft. . . . We still claim to be the industrial successors of the craftsmen who, in 1462, formed the Company of Tallow-chandlers. . . . We are also proud of the fact that "still the candle burns".

Extract of foreword to the
History of Price's Patent Co. Ltd

It would seem that candles have been burning for something like 5,000 years according to various writings, but the earliest surviving specimen may be a fragment dating back to the first century A.D., found at Vaison, near Avignon. The ancient civilizations of Egypt and Rome were accustomed to candlelight, and the dipping method used by the Roman candle-makers is still followed today for special candles.

The chandlers, to give the candle-makers their proper name, became recognized as craftsmen entitled to their own guilds. Those qualified to make wax chandlery (which consisted of "torches, clerges, prikits, and great candles") and those who produced chandlery of tallow had quite separate guilds.

The tallow-chandlers went from house to house collecting fat from the kitchens to make candles to order. They also stocked pots, pans, brooms and packthread. They held control over soaps and oil in the City and exercised their powers of inspecting stock and destroying any of inferior quality. There was some ancient link, referred to in royal records, between candles and sauces, no doubt accounting for the once traditional rivalry between the salters and the tallow-chandlers. The Tallow-Chandlers Company was recorded as a guild in 1462, but chandlers received their first mention as a group in 1300.

The Worshipful Company of Wax Chandlers dates from 1358 and was incorporated in 1483. A powerful body, with authority to regulate the wax trade, their work was chiefly making candles for the Church and seals for the legal professions. Candlewych Street, now called Cannon Street, was originally named after them. The sweeter-smelling bees-wax candles were preferred by those who could afford them, but it was the tallow candles in lanthorns which lit the city streets, supplemented by cressets.

An Act of 1599 stipulated "whereby every Householder from the first of October to the first of March in every year for ever should cause a substantial Lanthorn and a Candle of Eight in the Pound to be hang'd without their Doors". Petitioning the Lord Mayor in 1692 against the setting up of "lamp-lights of any sort in this City, as varying from ancient custom", the tallow-chandlers maintained that the experimental oil-lamps "are merely Novel, and should they be encouraged they will cause many more such Intrudings upon other Arts and Mysteries". Oil-lamps eventually took their place alongside the lanthorns in city streets, while rushlights were still in use late in the eighteenth century in country areas.

Pollution is not such a recent incursion as we might suppose, John Evelyn petitioned Charles II for what he called "Inspissation of the Aer" against the "Chandlers and Butchers because of those horrid stinks, nidorous and unwholesome smells which proceed from the tallow".

Thackeray, in *The Virginians*, condemned the "horrible guttering tallow" and went on to "bless Mr Price and other luciferous benefactors of mankind for banishing the abominable mutton of our youth". In fact, the Mr Price afforded this extreme gratitude never existed, despite many claims of would-be relatives and acquaintances of the founder of the nationally known Price's Patent Candle Company. Price was the surname of an aunt of Benjamin Lancaster who, in partnership with William Wilson, founded the business in 1847. A glance through the company's records would account for the eagerness to be associated with the non-existent Mr Price: these showed the provision of schooling facilities for the young workers some twenty years before education became recognized as essential; as well as pension funds, saving banks, and the building for Price employees, of one of the first model villages in the world – a forerunner of those of Port Sunlight and Bournville which, although a later idea than Bromborough Pool village, have received more publicity. Thus Mr Price, if he had existed, would have been a philanthropist to add proudly to any family tree.

The Tallow-Chandlers' Company is still in existence, but its function as a craft guild virtually ceased with the introduction of paraffin wax and the consequent disappearance of the tallow candle in the 1850s.

The discovery of stearin revolutionized the production of candles. Apart from producing a harder type of candle it was, like tallow candles, edible and nourishing (a fact which many Eddystone lighthouse-keepers made use of when rations ran low) while paraffin wax is not! Captain Scott carried a ton of Price's candles on his expedition to the South Pole: his second in command recollected that he had had occasion to eat some and survived to tell the tale!

An attempt to make candles by using a mould was made by a French nobleman, a contemporary of Joan of Arc, but it was not until stearin and spermaceti were introduced to the craft that mould-making could be developed, owing to the softer and stickier consistency of bees-wax and tallow which made them unsuitable for this method.

The candle-makers at Price's use mainly the mould method to meet the wide market demands, but their bees-wax candles are made in exactly the same way as the monks of old made theirs. It still takes about eight days to make a six-foot altar-candle. The candle-maker pours liquid bees-wax down wicks suspended on a circular frame; layer after layer of wax is poured on, allowing time for cooling and hardening between applications, until a cylinder of translucent whiteness is formed. The candles are then rolled and polished by hand, the hands of the candle-makers becoming enviably soft in the process.

Between the big commercial enterprises such as Price's – which has its own laboratory for testing and research, engineering shops for the construction and maintenance of candle-making machines, a foundry for casting moulds, a case-making plant and a printing department – and the single craftswoman making them by hand in her kitchen using, perhaps, a standard candle-making kit and her own creative ability to produce highly individual candles, are Colin and Philippa Hughes, a husband and wife team who have built up a sizeable business which, in Pip Hughes's own words, developed from a chance meeting of two different craftsmen.

Retailed under the name of Alpenhof Design Ltd, their wide range of candles is produced mainly by the mould method and finished by hand. The designs are often drawn from the fascinating and lovely Forest of Dean where they are sited: gnarled wood of an ancient oak becomes the wizened and cheerful faces of the 'old tree men' candles; and the shimmering colours and light of a sun-lit forest is captured in the Saturn range. They also make personalized candles to commission, an idea which is very popular as a gift and makes a change from the usual diary at Christmas time. The company holds a patent for this method of creating a candle with exceptional speed, accuracy, and detail. In about a month the customer's design is presented in finely detailed artwork on the candle itself.

Candle-makers are traditionally secretive and each has developed his own techniques, but the basic understanding of what constitutes a good candle is essential to all. England makes very fine wick but the wick must be designed to suit the diameter and wax-blends of the candle. If the wick is too big the candle will smoke; if too small the flame will be flooded. In good candles the colour is non-fading and non-migrating, i.e. leaving no stains.

The resurgence of interest in candle-making as a craft has warranted a specialist shop selling everything needed for making them and, more important to the self-employed craftsman, will retail original handmade candles.

Traditionally a craft of the monasteries, candle-making is still one of those carried out at Prinknash Abbey in the Cotswolds.

CANDLE-MAKERS

ALPENHOF DESIGN (Colin and Philippa Hughes), Yew Hedge, Great Doward, Symonds Yat, Herefordshire. Tel: Ross-on-Wye 3697
Decorative candles ranging from the block ACTIS "brilliant light" series, pictorial candles including "birthday candles" with the signs of the zodiac, and "old tree men" candles. Speciality line is to commission (minimum order 500) for souvenirs, hotel menus, county maps or drawings of buildings on extremely fine detailed personalized candles. Saturn multi-ring party candles and wide colour range plain block Actis.

CANDLES SHOP (London) LTD, 89 Parkway, London NW1. Tel: 01-485 3232
Complete candle-making supplies. Retails original hand-made candles.

RITA CLITHEROE (Mrs), Park Bungalow, Hedenham, Bungay, Suffolk
Candles.

JOANNA HARRISON, Salterton Candles, 5 The Dial House, Budleigh Salterton, Devon
Decorative candles, some scented, best quality waxes used for longer-lasting and brighter-burning. Retail outlet – Craft Shop, Chapel Street, Exmouth, where other hand-made crafts are also on sale.

PRINKNASH ABBEY, Cranham, Glos.
Candles retailed through their craft shop.

E. H. THORNE (Beehives) LTD, Beehive works, Wragby, Lincoln LN3 5LA. Tel: Wragby 555
Coloured honeycomb for candle-making in complete kits containing 10 sheets of wax, size 15 inches × 8 inches in 5 colours, 3 yards of wick, 6 novelty bees and instruction book. Packs of 6 candles in various colours. Candlewick available by the metre.

20

The Flint-knapper

It is a paradoxical fact that in an age of space travel and nuclear technology there exists a craft which Stone Age man would instantly recognize. And it is still practised in the same locality. James English still carries out his remarkable trade at Brandon, which appears to have been an important mining and manufacturing area in Neolithic times. Grimes Graves, now a favourite picnic spot, is catacombed with hundreds of circular pits dug by these primitive people. Laced together by tunnels, some 700 or 800 shafts were bored through two strata of walling flint, some 45 feet through the Suffolk chalk to the lowest stratum, consisting of the fine black flint which is floor stone – the premier mineral: softer and easier to work, it also produces the spark essential in gunflints.

Brandon boasted a hundred knappers at the time of the Napoleonic Wars, when they often earned as much as ten sovereigns a week. What immeasurable wealth those wages must have seemed in those far off days to the young men at the time, for they were known to have played pitch-and-toss with gay abandon with the golden coins they received for the flints.

The last master flint-knapper to whom the craft was handed down from his father, Herbert Edwards was sought out by all interested in this most ancient of all crafts. Royalty, tourists, archaeologists and anthropologists came to see him working at his craft. And just as he had learned it from his father, Herbert Edwards inducted his son-in-law into its mysteries.

James English has since carried on the family tradition with respect for its history and with loyal esteem for the man who taught him how to knap flint he trades under his late father-in-law's name. His is not an attempt to satisfy the curious as to the fascination of flint-knapping; being something of a survivor by carrying on a craft which is almost extinct in the civilized world, James English has been televised and featured in the Press, but first and foremost he is a craftsman practising alone – except for some part-time assistance – the oldest industry in the world.

There is still a market in Britain for knapped flints, but it is from the United States that James English has the greatest demand, where an extensive interest in antique muzzle-loading guns has resulted in numerous clubs and societies springing up. Gunflints are knapped in various sizes to make black flints for muskets, carbines, flintlock rifles and pistols.

The old knappers used to boast of the speed at which they could "rattle off" the flints, a dexterity of skill exercised more for pennies than pride when the pay fell to one and sixpence for each thousand flints produced. The trade has diminished and the old knappers are but a memory which was perpetuated by the naming of Rattlers Road, where their sole successor, James English, now lives.

It seems incredible that no one else has endeavoured to learn the craft which must surely be the oldest one of all. So James English will probably be the last flint-knapper in the world.

H. EDWARDS, 61 Rattlers Road, Brandon, Suffolk. Tel: Thetford 810240
  Knapped flint specialists. Gunflints, knapped face-flints. Rounds, squares or rectangles and random knapped flint-face to specification.

21

Craftsmen Working in Various Media

ROBERT AYERS, 53 Ryeworth Road, Charlton Kings, Cheltenham. Glos. Tel:
Cheltenham 57936
    Monumental mason. Member of the Craftsmen of Gloucestershire.

MYRTLE BARTER, Church Cottage, Walkley Hill, Rodborough, Stroud, Glos.
    Printed cards.

BLIND ALLEY (Janet and Gillian), Camden Lock, Commercial Place, London
NW1 8AF. Tel: 01–267 0848
    Individually designed roller-blinds.

T. W. CHAMBERS, High Street, Northleach, Glos. Tel: Northleach 372
    High-class gun and rifle repairs carried out on the premises.

PATRICK CONOLEY, 111 Brooklyn Road, Cheltenham, Glos. Tel: Cheltenham
21252
    Sculptor and modeller. Member Guild of Gloucestershire Craftsmen.

D-H STRING CO. (Edith Langley), Ashmore, nr Salisbury, Wilts. Tel: Fontmell
Magna 491
    A cottage industry started by M. Jebb (West of England Champion Archer
    for seven years), now an annual output of some 15,000 archery bow-strings
    enables this small workshop to meet orders all over the U.K.

T. P. DUNCAN, 29 Reservoir Close, Stroud, Glos.
    Stonemason.

JAMES ESSEX, Roselawn, 82 Gretton Road, Winchcombe, Glos. GL54 5EL.
Tel: Winchcombe 603027
    Upholsterer. Member of the Craftsmen of Gloucestershire. Specializing in
    antique and traditional work, using fabric and leather.

GEOFFREY EVANS, The Grange, Woolstone, nr Cheltenham, Glos. Tel: Bishops
Cleeve 2122
    Print gallery and workshops in Cotswold house of monastic origins. Mount
    (mat) cutting a speciality – all shapes, textures and colours.

VIVIEN GEOFFREY, The Grange, Woolstone, nr Cheltenham, Glos. Tel: Bishops
Cleeve 2122
    Picture-framer. Member of the Craftsmen of Gloucestershire.

GILT STUDIO (Edward and Pauleen Paddon), Camden Lock, London NW1
Sculpture.

STUART HOBBS, Woodmancote, Cirencester, Glos. Tel: North Cerney 212
Craftsman-Tailor. Member Guild of Gloucestershire Craftsmen.

JOHN HOPKINS, 56 Church Street, Tewkesbury, Glos. Tel: Tewkesbury 293170
Stonemason. Member of Guild of Gloucestershire Craftsmen.

IVOR HURSEY, Newhouse Court, Sheldwich, Faversham, Kent. Tel: Faversham
3758
Sculptor who, during twenty-five years as a practising craftsman, has carried out commissions of a varied nature: stone and wood carving, letter-cutting and gilding in architectural and heraldic work.

KEITH JAMESON, 19 Hailes Street, Winchcombe, Glos. Tel: Cheltenham 602549
Sculpture, dealing mainly in commissions for figures and architectural sculpture cast in bronze and fabricated in welded metal or other materials. Member of Guild of Gloucestershire Craftsmen.

JORDAN ART GALLERY, Camden Lock, Commercial Place, London NW1 8AF
Picture-framing.

MARTIN MCDONAGH, Coombe House, High Street, Winchcombe, Cheltenham,
Glos. Tel: Winchcombe 602166
Upholsterer. Member of The Craftsmen of Gloucestershire.

JANET AND TIM MOSCOVITCH, 158 Trinity Street, Huddersfield, Yorks HD1 4DX
Husband and wife team, both Dip.A.D.(Hons), designing and producing hand-made decorative mirrors. A wide range is offered with special emphasis on surface design. Occasional fabric designing.

RODNEY P. NAYLOR, MSD-C, Turnpike House, 208 Devizes Road, Hilperton,
Trowbridge, Wilts. BA14 7QP. Tel: Trowbridge (02214) 4497
Designer who, as a versatile craftsman, works in materials as diverse as rose-wood, lime, greenheart, bronze and silver. Carver, restorer and advisor to the National Trust and the Victoria and Albert Museum, Rodney Naylor's work has been highly acclaimed for its outstanding quality and sensitivity. He will consider commissions, or employment on a sub-contract basis as applicable, for craftwork ranging from chair-caning and upholstery to crisp angular bronzes using casting techniques similar to those used by the ancient Greeks.

MAUREEN PEARSON, 32 Holmbury Court, Tooting SW17 7PA. Tel: 01–767
0800
Designer-craftswoman in the widest possible range of materials – stone, steel (mild and stainless), wood, glass, and plastic sheeting. This is a one-woman business in which Maureen Pearson has designed and made such

diverse pieces as toys and games, steel-framed mirrors, a mahogany lattice-work bed-head, brass boxes and rocking-horses.

PONDBANK HANDPRINTS (Mr and Mrs Freeston), 9 High Street, Blisworth, Northampton. Tel: Blisworth 443
Husband and wife team who hand-print linen tea-towels to customers' designs, or drawings can be prepared to specification. Heat-fixed dye. Minimum order 500. Particularly suitable for festivals or groups.

WALENTY PYTEL, Terrace Hall, Woolhope, Hereford. Tel: Fownhope 373
Sculpture. Member of The Craftsmen of Gloucestershire.

VALERIE ROGERSON, 72 Tanacliffe Road, Whitworth, Rochdale.
Painted miniatures on goose eggs.

NADIN SENFT, Camden Lock, Commercial Place, London NW1 8AF
Sculpture.

PEGGY STANCOMB (Mrs), Ironside House, Sherston, nr Malmesbury, Wilts. SN16 0LQ. Tel: Sherston 309
Free-hand painting on silk or chiffon scarves and first-day stamp covers of national events using a technique of her own invention.

STOLWORTHY (Mrs), 32 Maygrove, Great Yarmouth, Norfolk
Pottery, wood-carving, ships in bottles.

M. D. TRACE, Camden Lock, Commercial Place, London NW1 8AF
Sculpture.

SPECIALIST TOOL-MAKERS

ASHLEY ILES (Edge Tools) LTD, East Kirkby, Spilsby, Lincs. Tel: East Kirkby 372
Hand forged wood-carving tools made by craftsmen in the highest traditional methods. Individual tools, kits for the beginner, and for the professional carver. Tool-chests made to order.

22

The Continuity of Craft Tradition

The balance between art and design in education must be adjusted, and everything possible done to generate in our country an interest amongst young people in concerning themselves with the prospects of industry, which are interrelated with the standard of living that we are going to be able to maintain. . . . Design and what I have termed para-art activity that is based on a whim of iron is sustainable only within the educational system.

Professor Lord Queensberry

Training in craftsmanship was isolated from formal education in the days of the crafts apprentice who became indentured to a masterman as soon as he left school – usually for a period of seven years, after which he served a couple more years as an improver. The term *craftsman* is now connotatively applied to a great number of people, from the most idealistic artist to the machine-minded engineer; so defining a craftsman is bound to excite all kinds of academic argument.

The livery companies have always had a special interest in education. They contribute to, or run, some fifteen schools, and give money for research and higher education. Oxford University acquired from the drapers the new Radcliffe Library and an electrical laboratory, and Goldsmiths College, London, has been training teachers since 1894.

The Dartington Hall Trust, although not exclusively concerned with crafts, is deeply sympathetic to them, and has established a considerable variety of facilities where they may be practised within the broad spectrum of the general arts scene; and the trustees sponsored a concentrated study of country craftsmen in the Devon area a few years ago.

The leading educational trust which is totally committed to fostering and teaching a wide range of traditional crafts and arts, with the main emphasis on crafts, is West Dean College, Sussex, opened in 1971 and endowed by the Edward James Foundation.

An exciting innovation and a change from the usual museum-style displays is the recently-opened Crafts Study Centre at Bath. A permanent and extensive collection of the finest British craftwork presents a representative sample of what is being produced in the twentieth century, where the pieces can be handled and studied alongside reference books and the craftsmen's working papers and sketches. Opened in the spring of 1977, the study centre provides demonstrations and seminars which extend its educational role; close links with the University of

Bath further strengthen and broaden its activity in higher education.

It is, however, the problems of practical education in the general school situation which have exercised the minds of educationalists for a long time. Mr Lynn Miller, awarded the Judd Gold Medal in 1930 for research work in this field, emphasized that it is the birthright of every child to be given the opportunity to use his most important personal tools – his hands. Mr Miller believes that schools could provide basic craft training during the formative years, by allowing the child to actually practise the craft, in accordance with the Chinese proverb: "I hear and I forget; I see and I remember; *I do and I understand*".

The Institute of Craft Education has grown from roots struck in 1891 by the formation of the National Association of Manual Training Teachers – a vigorous body which made deputation to the Department of Education and the House of Commons for professional equality with the academics. As an educational experiment, six training centres had been established in London three years previously and showed remarkable results: craftwork became an integral part of the school curriculum. The institute's policies and guidance over the years have greatly influenced the present high standard of craft education in schools to the benefit of further education and industry.

The differences between design (art), craft (practical skill), and manufacturing (a commercial venture) now become more apparent as craftsmanship rooted in the past traditions has become liberated in art-orientated crafts.

The essential reasons for bridging the gap between the designer, the craftsman and the manufacturer were dealt with in depth by Lord Queensberry, Professor of Ceramics and Glass at the Royal College of Art, in his paper presented recently to the Royal Society of Arts. During the ensuing discussion Lord Queensberry said that the Royal College of Art was currently undertaking research into art education in schools "because this is obviously the crucial thing".

"A great weakness in British education" has been blamed for a general lack of public taste, leading to an apathetic acceptance of inferior quality factory-made goods. Educating children to form their own value judgements has been sadly neglected, so that British schools have not developed a discriminating taste as European schools seem.to have done, according to an article "An eye for a line" (*Daily Telegraph*, 10th January 1976), which claims that this national shortcoming "can be traced to our educational system".

The Schools Council, being a representative body, has, in fact, done a fair amount of curriculum development in the field of craft and has a subject committee on craft, science and technology. The Chairman to the CAST committee disputed the challenge that the philosophies of education and craft often appear to be in conflict, and emphasized the necessity for them to be complementary.

Schools are concerned to maintain and improve the standard of traditional crafts, as well as introducing new skills. They are also alive to the need to equip pupils for the ever-increasing complications of modern civilization. It is the attempt to reconcile these factors which is so frequently misunderstood and misinterpreted.

The Local Education Authority Advisers in their working paper (1972) made an intense academic study of craft education, recognizing the role of the education system as guardian of traditional knowledge, skills and attitudes. A further paper (1974) looked into the widest possible implications and effects of design in craft education.

With probably the highest number of art students *per capita* of any country in the world, the interrelation between education and industry in matters of design is being aired publicly so that educationalists and industrialists are made aware of the situation. How aware students are of craftwork as a profession is another matter: the Careers Research and Advisory Centre had nothing to offer to the suggestion that many young people were either not encouraged by careers officers to seek a craft apprenticeship or had not been able to obtain information on what was available anyway. The National Institute for Careers Education and Counselling had no statistics to prove "a personal impression" that insufficient attention was paid in schools and the careers guidance field to handcrafts, and indeed to self-employment in general. It is too easy to apportion responsibility on any one body – but it augurs well for the future of our craft tradition if it can be taken as vindicative of the place of art-crafts in the cultural, and therefore educational, pattern of present-day society that the government grant for CAC was channelled through the arts branch of the Department of Education and Science. An indication of the priorities is the stress laid on grant-aid for training apprentices or art school graduates in need of workshop experience and the establishment of workshops for new craftsmen.

SOCIETIES

SOCIETY FOR EDUCATION THROUGH ART, Bath Academy of Art, Corsham, Wilts. Tel: Corsham 712571
A professional organization represented on the major councils of art, craft and education, and in contact with universities and colleges throughout the United Kingdom and in over forty countries. Seminars, workshops and exhibitions provide a forum for the expression of views and opinions on art and education. Publications: pamphlets on craft and technical processes and aspects related to art and design education, and journal, Athene. Advisory and information service to teachers and students, with slide loan scheme. Membership; full (with voting powers), associate, corporate, and overseas.

Teachers and artists of all disciplines welcome.

THE INSTITUTE OF CRAFT EDUCATION, Hon. Sec: D. Gibbs, 32 Beachcroft Avenue, Tynemouth, North Shields NE30 3SN. Tel: North Shields 76019
The work of the institute is devoted to the professional needs of all who are interested in educational craftwork, by keeping abreast of all changes in educational policy, conducting investigations and research and reporting on the work of the institute and college which it established in 1923. Vacation courses, employing leading craftsmen on the staff, are held concurrently at St John's College, York, and Goldsmith's College, London – the latter puts emphasis on the educational application of craftwork. Further details from the directors.

STUDY

THE CITY AND GUILDS OF LONDON ART SCHOOL, 124 Kennington Park Road, London SE11 4DJ. Tel: 01–735 2306
The City and Guilds Art School, established in 1879 as an extension of the Lambeth School of Art has, since 1971, operated as an independent Art School with charitable status. The aim of the School is to provide a sound, basic training in Fine Arts and certain crafts for those wishing ultimately to become professional artists and craftsmen.

THE CRAFTS STUDY CENTRE, The Holbourne of Menstrie Museum, University of Bath, Pulteney Street, Bath BA2 4DB
A permanent collection of twentieth-century craftwork by leading crafts-men. Exhibitions, displays and study-groups arranged.

THE KNITTING COUNCIL FOR SCHOOLS, Lecture Service Manager: Andrew Wil-liams, B.Sc., Calshot House, Calshot, Southampton SO4 1UF. Tel: (0703) 981300
Educational lecture service available to schools, with colour slides and the latest fashions in knitting and crochet. Full details of the service and publi-cations from the Lecture Service Manager.

APPENDIX OF OTHER USEFUL ADDRESSES

CHARITY COMMISSIONS, 14 Ryder Street, London SW1. Tel: 01–214 6000
Application form and general information on registering as a charity (leaflet No. RE4)

HISTORIC BUILDING COUNCIL FOR ENGLAND, 25 Saville Row, London W1X 2BT. Tel: 01–734 6010

THE STANDING JOINT COMMITTEE ON NATURAL STONE, Alderman House, 37 Soho Square, London W1

THE NATIONAL TRUST, 42 Queen Anne's Gate, London SW1H 9AS. Tel: 01–930 0211

BRITISH TOURIST AUTHORITY, 239 Old Marylebone Road, London NW1 5QT
Often publishes guild activities – exhibitions, etc., which are open to the public.

MUSEUMS ASSOCIATION, 87 Charlotte Street, London W1P 2BX. Tel: 01–636 4600
Travelling exhibitions through the MA's Area Council. Publications: quarterly journal, monthly bulletin.

DEPARTMENT OF PRICES AND CONSUMER PROTECTION, 1 Victoria Street, London SW1. Tel: 01–215 7877
Department responsible for safety of consumer goods – toy safety regulations, etc.

NATIONAL ASSOCIATION OF DECORATIVE AND FINE ART SOCIETIES (NADFAS), Woodland, Loosley Row, nr Aylesbury, Bucks. Tel: Princes Risborough 4587
An organization which gives active help with the many problems facing museums and historic buildings. Many members are training to do straightforward tasks such as cleaning old books, mending fabrics, cataloguing and learning to act as guides.

THE LOCAL AUTHORITY CONDITIONS OF SERVICE ADVISORY BOARD, 41 Belgrave Square, SW1. Tel: 01–235 9731
The board has details of each local authority who should be contacted in the first instance for vacancies in adult evening-classes where craftwork is taught. Payment can vary, depending on level of instruction and qualifications. Local authorities have their own scales.

SOCIETY OF INDUSTRIAL ARTIST AND DESIGNERS, 12 Carlton House Terrace, London SW1Y 5AH. Tel: 01–930 1911
The chartered professional body representing industrial designers in Britain. Advisory service, record of designers' work and a staff vacancy register. Publications: journal and technical information sheets.

SPACE PROVISION (Artistic, Cultural and Educational) LTD, 125–129 Shaftesbury Avenue, London WC2H 8AD. Tel: 01–836 1745
A non-profit-making company acting as a charity – Arts Service Grants, established in 1968 to provide workspace for professional artists at moderate cost. Advisory service.

ROYAL SOCIETY OF ARTS, 8 John Adam Street, London WC2N 6EZ. Tel: 01–839 2366
Lectures are held regularly on artistic, scientific and technical subjects. It administers the affairs of the Faculty of Royal Designer for Industry and awards bursaries to designers of many craft disciplines.

PUBLICATIONS

Design Courses in Britain, published by the Design Council, 28 Haymarket, London SW1Y 4SU. Tel: 01–839 8000 (currently 50p plus 15p postage)
A directory listing 178 colleges which offer full-time design courses for

foundation, BA (Hons), vocational and post-graduate qualifications. Useful information on applying for grants, etc.

GLC BOOKSHOP, The County Hall, London SE1 7PB

Floodlight – the guide to evening-classes in the ILEA area (published annually in August) available direct.

Courses Leading to the Diploma in Art and Design, and other similar publications on art and design courses, available free from the Art and Design Admissions Registry, 16 Albion Place, Maidstone, Kent. Tel: 0622 673 255

COUNCIL FOR NATIONAL ACADEMIC AWARDS (CNAA), 344–354 Gray's Inn Road, London WC1X 8BP. Tel: 01–278 4411

List of approved courses in Art and Design in Great Britain available on request.

FURTHER EDUCATION ESTABLISHMENTS IN ENGLAND AND WALES OFFERING ARTS AND DESIGN COURSES (List A).

Colleges listed by counties, free list from the Department for Education and Science, Elizabeth House, York Road, London SE1. Tel: 01–928 9222

CRAFT MUSEUMS

Most city and large town museums have something preserved of the local crafts – the following have been included here for their particular interest in various fields of the arts and crafts.

AVON
Holborn of Menstrie Museum, Bath: general

BEDS.
Museum and Art Gallery, Luton: lace

BUCKS.
Museum and Art Gallery, High Wycombe: wood

CHESHIRE
Grosvenor Museum, Chester: musical instruments

CO. DURHAM
Bowes Museum, Barnard Castle: precious metals

DERBY
Crown Derby Works Museum: clay

DEVON
William Cookworthy Museum, Kingsbridge: clay
Finch Foundry, Sticklepath, nr Okehampton: metalwork
Royal Albert Museum, Exeter: lace

HANTS.
Curtis Museum, Alton: wood

HERTS.
St Albans City Museum: general

LANCS.

Haworth Art Gallery, Accrington: glass
Pilkington's Museum, St Helens: glass
Henry Watson Museum, Manchester: musical instruments

LONDON

Bethnal Green Museum, E2: toys and models
British Museum, WC1: general
Fenton House, NW3: musical instruments
Geffrye Museum, E2: general
Goldsmith's Hall, EC2 (by appointment): precious metals
Horniman Museum, SE23: musical instruments
Instrument Museum, Royal College of Music, SW7: musical instruments
London Museum, W8: general
Pollocks Toy Museum, W1: toys and models
Victoria and Albert Museum, SW7: contemporary crafts in addition to fine
and applied arts

NORTHAMPTON

Museum and Gallery: leather

OXON.

Ashmolean Museum, Oxford: general
Carlisle Collection, Grey's Court, nr Henley: toys and models

STAFFS.

Brierley Hill Museum, Brierley Hill: glass
Gladstone Pottery Museum, Longton, Stoke-on-Trent: working pottery
museum.
Stoke-on-Trent Art Gallery and Museum: clay
Cheddleton Flint Mill, nr Leek: clay
Walsall Museum of Leathercraft: leather

SUSSEX

Weald and Downland open air Museum, Singleton, nr Chichester
A collection of historic buildings that have been threatened with demolition. The museum's main purpose is rescuing good examples of verna-
cular architecture spanning the centuries from the Middle Ages to the
early nineteenth century. Woodland crafts are demonstrated and serious
students are able to practise their skills under reconstructed medieval (or
earlier) conditions. Ancient crafts and industries of the South-East are on
display. Free car-parks and picnic areas on this lovely 35-acre site on the
West Dean Estate. Open daily – except Mondays – May to September.

WARKS.

Birmingham City Museum and Art Gallery: wood

WORCS.

Avoncroft Museum of Buildings, Stoke Prior, Bromsgrove: Tel: Bromsgrove
31886
Open-air museum where interesting old buildings have been restored and
rebuilt, including a windmill and chain and nail-making workshops.
Council House Museum, Stourbridge: glass

YORK
   Art Gallery: clay
   Castle Museum: various
   Bankfield Museum and Art Gallery Halifax: fabrics

General Index

Index of Craftwork

Index of Craftsmen
(by counties)